Praise for *The Origins of Poverty and Wealth*

"This book is destined to become a one-of-a-kind classic that will rank in its impact with Alexis de Tocqueville's *Democracy in America*, penned almost two centuries ago. It is indispensable today for understanding how various economies are actually performing. Rainer Zitelmann, tireless apostle of economic freedom whose numerous books and articles are published throughout the world, provides on-the-ground insights for over a score of countries about the state of their economies and the policies each is pursuing. He shares the often-surprising findings from in-depth surveys he commissioned to gauge people's attitudes in various nations towards subjects like capitalism and the rich. He has talked to countless people in all walks of life. A true tour de force!"

Steve Forbes

"Dr Rainer Zitelmann takes us on an engrossing and engaging world tour to uncover the sources of wealth and poverty. The importance of freedom, particularly economic freedom, is highlighted as the essential ingredient of prosperity, and illustrated through dozens of illuminating examples. This is a powerful book, highly readable, and highly important."

Madsen Pirie, President of the Adam Smith Institute, London

"In this new book, Dr. Rainer Zitelmann takes us on a world economic freedom tour. Beginning with a comprehensive survey of citizen views on economic freedom, Zitelmann reviews the nation's history and then, as an economic tourist, enriches both the content of the survey and the summary of history with onsite observations. The conclusion in 30 countries around the world is that the level of economic freedom is the primary determinate of prosperity and wealth."

Phil Gramm, Economist and former U.S. Senator

"With characteristic energy and acumen, Rainer Zitelmann presents us with a whirlwind of observations about dozens of countries and the extent to which their institutions and attitudes are conducive to future prosperity. The book also provides a wonderful snapshot of the freedom movement of the early 2020s: the people and civil society institutions that actively work to shape a better appreciation of individual rights and the magic of the market order when government is confined to its proper lane. I'm hopeful Zitelmann's writings will inspire more readers to carry the torch in ever more countries!"

Brad Lips, CEO of Atlas Network - the world's largest association of classical liberal think tanks

"The times they are a'changing, as increasingly liberty-oriented younger generations across the globe reject the welfare statist politics of the past – and shift away from the philosophical underpinnings of sacrifice and envy. As the world's leading authority on researching the levels of envy across populations, generations and time, Dr. Rainer Zitelmann is uniquely positioned to capture this shift in values and perspectives, as he takes the reader along on his "Liberty Road Trip," in which he traveled to 30 countries over the course of a year, combining the academic rigor of his survey technique with a journalistic approach to understanding the actual individuals – their aspirations, attitudes, challenges, and outlooks. It's tour-de-force that will give readers the data-driven optimism to feel grateful to be living in such extraordinary times."

Jennifer Grossmann, CEO Atlas Society

"*The Origins of Poverty and Wealth* by Rainer Zitelmann is a delight to read, engrossing and entertaining throughout. Rainer is a keen observer of all that he experiences along this journey, citing relevant background data, yet efficient and accurate in conveying meaning relevant to global poverty and wealth. I'm thoroughly impressed that he has such an easy to read style that I couldn't put the book down. What's more, he introduces you to so many fine people along the way that one feels an impulse to travel in his footsteps to meet them."

Ken Schoolland, Professor of Economics and author of The Adventures of Jonathan Gullible: A Free Market Odyssey, published in 53 languages.

"Through firsthand observations, groundbreaking surveys, and thought-provoking conversations with everyone from billionaires to grassroots activists, Zitelmann reveals the undeniable connection between economic freedom and human prosperity. With the rigor of a historian, the curiosity of a world traveler, and the passion of a freedom advocate, Zitelmann offers invaluable insights and a powerful case for liberty as the foundation of progress. This book is not just an exploration of global socio-economic conditions – it's a rallying cry for a worldwide recognition of capitalism's transformative potential."

Wolf von Laer, CEO, Students For Liberty

"The best thing is to make your own journey to 30 countries and to study the history and economy of these countries, to talk to politicians, entrepreneurs and ordinary people. If you don't have the time or money for that, read this book and discover the world – together with a historian and sociologist who values freedom and entrepreneurship. What's more, there is no better book if you want to get to know the libertarian and classical liberal world movement."

John Mackey, Founder Whole Foods Market

"Rainer Zitelmann's *The Origins of Poverty and Wealth* is a masterful exploration of global economies, blending rigorous analysis with engaging storytelling. With keen insights, vivid anecdotes, and a hopeful lens, he highlights the shift in values among liberty-oriented younger generations and the enduring power of free markets. Inspiring and thought-provoking, it's a must-read for understanding wealth and freedom today."

Grover Norquist, President of Americans for Tax Reform, a taxpayer advocacy group he founded in 1985 at President Reagan's request

"Dr. Zitelmann's economic tour of some 30 countries reminds me of Lee Yuan Yew's tour of many nations after he became Prime Minister of Singapore in 1965. Before he left he was sympathetic toward socialism, but on his visits, he discovered that the countries that were growing were all followers of free-market capitalism. Being a practical man, he decided to adopt a pro-market approach to governing Singapore. And the rest is history. No doubt anyone reading Dr. Zitelmann's tours will come to the same conclusion! Well done!"

Mark Skousen, America's Economist, Chapman University

"A curious mix of travelogue, recent economic history, political economy, quantitative opinion polling, and qualitative expert accounts. Zitelmann certainly knows how to find the right people in the right places. The challenges classical liberals face differ hugely from place to place, which is why the focus of liberty activists is often purely domestic. But as this book also makes clear, there nonetheless is such a thing as a 'global liberty movement.' Maybe we should act like it more often, rather than pursue a vision of 'classical liberalism in one country.'"

Kristian Niemietz, Editorial Director and Head of Political Economy, Institute for Economic Affairs, London

THE ORIGINS OF POVERTY AND WEALTH

MY WORLD TOUR AND INSIGHTS FROM THE GLOBAL LIBERTARIAN MOVEMENT

THE ORIGINS OF POVERTY AND WEALTH

MY WORLD TOUR AND INSIGHTS FROM THE
GLOBAL LIBERTARIAN MOVEMENT

RAINER ZITELMANN

© Dr Rainer Zitelmann 2025

This edition first published in 2025 by Management Books 2000 Ltd
36 Western Road
Oxford OX1 4LG
United Kingdom
Tel 0044 (0) 1865 600738
Email: info@mb2000.com
Web: www.mb2000.com

This English language Edition with arrangements by Maria Pinto-Peuckmann, Literary Agency, World Copyright Promotion, Kaufering, Germany and Co-Agent Martha Halford-Fumagalli, Martha Halford PR.

British Library Cataloguing in Publication Data is available
ISBN: 9781852527952

Contents

Foreword

Many people dream of traveling the world. I went on a round-the-world trip that took me to Asia, the United States and Latin America from April 2022 to December 2023, as well as to 18 European countries. In total, I traveled over 160,000 miles by plane, a nightmare for any climate activist. But I did it for a good cause, and without any feelings of "flight shame."

I visited countries that I was already more or less familiar with, but also some that I had never been to before – such as Argentina, Colombia, Chile, Nepal, and Mongolia. I also spent time in countries that I had previously only traveled to on vacation, such as Vietnam. When I'm on vacation, however, I like to lie lazily in the sun and read. I don't really get to know the country. On my round-the-world trip, I visited many countries several times during this year and a half: on numerous trips to the United States, I took in New York, Washington DC, Boston, Miami, Las Vegas, West Palm Beach, and Memphis. I also traveled to Chile, Argentina, Paraguay, Poland, Albania and Georgia several times.

I call the journey "Liberty Road Trip" or "Liberty Journey." What does a round-the-world to 30 countries have to do with liberty? I visited these 30 countries in 2022 and 2023 to learn more about the state of economic freedom in each country. Political freedom and economic freedom are both equally important, but the focus for me was on economic freedom because I believe that economic freedom in a country is the most important prerequisite in the fight against poverty. That's why I campaign for economic freedom around the world. I do this with my books, articles, interviews and lectures.

As a result, I have met incredible people in so many countries around the world who are committed to freedom and capitalism. They often call themselves "libertarians" or "classical liberals," which is by no means a closed world view, but more a specific mindset. As different as the people who belong to the libertarian movement are, they have one thing in common: a high regard for freedom. So in this book you will also get to know the global libertarian movement and some of its protagonists. I describe this movement, about which most readers probably know little, from a perspective of critical sympathy: I myself am a historian and sociologist who sympathizes with some of the libertarians' ideas, but does not want to subordinate myself to any dogma. I've had enough of that since I was a Maoist in my youth.

At the beginning of each year, I set myself goals for the next twelve months. I have found that goal-setting, as I describe in my book, *Dare to Be Different*, works. My goal, which I wrote down on New Year's Eve 2021/22, was: "My book, *In Defence of Capitalism*, will be published in 20 languages." I planned to travel to all 20 countries. But after just six months, I had already signed license agreements in 20 countries, so I raised the target to 30. That's a lot, because until then none of my books had been published in more than a dozen languages.

I promised every publisher that I would commission a survey to find out what people in their country think of economic freedom. I also promised the publishers and libertarian think tanks that I would personally visit these 30 countries.

I knew that the entire endeavor would cost me roughly 1.5 million US dollars, because surveys conducted by renowned opinion research institutes are expensive. For the opinion polls on the image of capitalism (35 countries) and the image of the rich (13 countries) alone, I paid 700,000 US dollars. In most countries, the surveys were conducted by Ipsos MORI.

These surveys were very important for this book. They gave me a first impression of attitudes toward the market economy and capitalism in each country.

Both personal conversations and observations on the one hand and empirical research on the other are important. I was often able to understand the results of the polls better once I had traveled to a country and talked to the people there. Conversely, I was able to better classify my impressions from the conversations when I used the data collected in the surveys.

The fact that I was able to travel to all these countries also has to do with a type of freedom: financial freedom. Until I was 40 years old, I had no money at all. I had a decent income, but I spent it all. I was mainly interested in politics, and I often held opinions that were not politically correct. As a freedom-loving person, I always wanted to say what I thought, and that led to my gathering many people around me who appreciated this. But it also repeatedly led to problems – even existential money anguish!

When I was 39 years old, on a walk in Berlin, a friend of mine who is a politician said to me: "If we really want to get away with being who we are and saying what we think, mavericks like you and me need to earn a lot of money." He was not – like so many professional politicians – dependent on his salary as a politician. As a brilliant lawyer, he earned more than enough to make him financially independent. And, as a result of the security this gave him, it was much easier for him to express independent opinions and swim against the prevailing political current. Those words from Peter Gauweiler, that's the politician's name, triggered an almost Damascene experience in me. Immediately after our conversation, I decided to become rich. That may sound strange, but that's exactly how it happened. I would become a millionaire – and I did, in just a few years.

Today I am financially free, which means that I no longer have to work for money. Whether I work, what work I do, where I work, how I work, when I work and who I work with is nobody's business but mine. Without this financial freedom, it would not have been possible for me to commission all those expensive surveys and finance the trips to all those countries.

Incidentally, one of the freedoms I enjoy is that I have several girlfriends and not just one. I've been with them for many years and of course they all know about each other. Some of them have accompanied me on my travels. So please don't be surprised if you find the names of several girlfriends mentioned throughout this book.

So, why did I want to travel to so many countries? Initially out of curiosity and because I had the idea of writing a book on the subject. But there was more, namely a mission. After I sold my company in 2016 and finished my second doctorate, I set myself a new, really big goal: I wanted to conquer the world.

I only played two games with passion as a teenager: *Monopoly* (in which you collect real estate, as you know) and *Risk*. The latter is about conquering the world, occupying one country after another. And it is precisely this game that I am continuing in real life today: by "conquering the world." Of course, I don't mean that I want to become another Alexander the Great. My goals are much more modest – and yet very ambitious. As a thinker and an author, I want to spread my messages worldwide and win people over to the ideals of freedom and capitalism.

My geographical focus changed at the age of 60. Everyone has a geographical sphere for their thoughts and actions. When I was young, I had a girlfriend whose life revolved around the village of Messel, Germany, with its 3,000 inhabitants, where we lived at the time. She sometimes traveled, but the frame of reference for her thoughts and actions always remained Messel. Some of my acquaintances in the real estate industry have the city of Berlin as their frame of reference: they are primarily interested in what is happening in this city and follow the regional media closely. My primary frame of reference in the years leading up to 2017 was always Germany. My company was active throughout Germany and I was constantly on the road in Germany – Berlin, Frankfurt, Hamburg, Munich, Cologne, and Düsseldorf.

For most people, their geographical focus is on their own country. This is understandable, but also somewhat narrow-minded. I always notice this when I offer articles to media in Germany. Anything about Germany is readily accepted. An article about Argentina? "Too far away for our readers." I don't even need to ask about Albania or Mongolia.

My focus today is the whole world. I travel around the globe because I am curious about other people and other countries. And because I want to spread my messages and help popularize the idea of freedom all around the world. My travels are different from those of most people: I'm not particularly interested in "sights" that attract camera-wielding tourists. If I want to, I can look them up on the internet.

No, I am interested in people. I learn more about a country when I meet people who tell me something about it: economists and politicians, for example, or people who campaign for freedom in their countries. I was interviewed by journalists in all of the countries I visited, but I always took the opportunity to switch roles and ask the journalists about the politics and economy in their country before or after each interview. I also like to meet "normal" people, young people who barely have any money, but also entrepreneurs who have become multi-billionaires. I have met hundreds of interesting people and learned a lot in the process. You can read about what I have learned in this book.

I was unable to go to some countries that I would have liked to visit. Many of my books have also been published in Russia, where I have a number of friends. I have many ties with the country, and I was even a member of the Russian Orthodox Church for several decades until I left because the church strongly supported Putin's war. I didn't want to travel to Russia during the war, because saying nothing about the war there would have been a mistake, and if I had said something about the war, it would have been too dangerous for me. But I met many Ukrainians and Russians, especially in Poland and Georgia. I will also report on these meetings.

I visited many cities in China in 2018 and 2019 and had already booked a trip for October 2023. At short notice, however, my Chinese publisher informed me that, contrary to expectations, officials had not yet granted permission for me to give a series of lectures on my book, *The Rich in Public Opinion*. Too bad, as I had been looking forward to the trip to China. I also wanted to travel to Nigeria, where my book, *In Defence of Capitalism,* had been published. But I didn't want to be vaccinated against yellow fever, so I couldn't get a visa for Nigeria and had to give my talk online. I hope to be able to visit Russia, Ukraine, China and other countries in the next few years.

Before I traveled to a country, I researched its history, because I am a historian and therefore know that the key to understanding a country lies in its history. My travels would not have been as informative without the surveys I conducted in the countries before I started traveling and without studying the history of these countries. This book is not just a travel book, it is also a history book – as you might expect from a historian. Perhaps you will become curious to learn more about these countries – and read more books about them or travel there yourself.

Rainer Zitelmann
January 2025

April 2022
Zurich, Switzerland

My "Liberty Road Trip" begins in Switzerland on April 12, 2022. According to the "World Happiness Report 2023," Switzerland is one of the ten happiest countries in the world.[1] And it is a wealthy country: the average wealth of an adult in Switzerland in 2022 was 685,000 US dollars. In Germany it is only 256,000 US dollars and in the United States it is 551,000 US dollars.[2] Of course, this average figure also has something to do with the high density of millionaires. Of the 8.7 million adults in Switzerland, one in eight (1.1 million) is a millionaire. In Germany, which is almost ten times the size of Switzerland in terms of population, there were "only" 2.6 million millionaires in 2022. This means that around one in 32 Germans is a millionaire.[3]

I was invited by the Liberal Institute to give a lecture at the University of Zurich. Switzerland is a good starting point for my Liberty Road Trip, as it ranks second out of 176 countries in the *Index of Economic Freedom*, just 0.1 points behind the leader Singapore.[4] The country has top scores in the categories "Property Rights," "Judicial Effectiveness," "Fiscal Health," and "Government Integrity." The overall result would be even better if the state did not spend too much money and there was less state regulation in the labor market.

---

1 Helliwell, et al., "2023 World Happiness Report," Sustainable Development Solutions Network, https://happiness-report.s3.amazonaws.com/2023/WHR+23.pdf, 34.

2 Ritter, "Die Schweizer sind dreimal so reich wie die Deutschen," *Frankfurter Allgemeine Zeitung*, last updated August 15, 2023, https://www.faz.net/aktuell/finanzen/die-schweiz-hat-die-reichsten-menschen-der-welt-globales-vermoegen-19104655.html#

3 Ritter, "Die Schweizer sind dreimal so reich wie die Deutschen," *Frankfurter Allgemeine Zeitung*, last updated August 15, 2023, https://www.faz.net/aktuell/finanzen/die-schweiz-hat-die-reichsten-menschen-der-welt-globales-vermoegen-19104655.html#

4 Heritage Foundation, *2023 Index of Economic Freedom*, https://www.heritage.org/index/, 34–35.

Nonetheless, Switzerland is the most capitalist country in the world. And a great place to live. One of my girlfriends, Jenna, has lived in the country for many years. She doesn't want to go back to Germany under any circumstances. We were a couple 14 years ago. She was 25 years old at the time and now heads the communications department of one of the world's most renowned luxury brands in Zurich. I invite Jenna – together with Isabelle, who is accompanying me on my trip to Zurich – to dinner at an Asian restaurant. The three of us are big fans of Asian cuisine. Why does she love living in Switzerland so much? One of the reasons is that she earns almost three times as much here as her colleagues in Germany and pays even less tax. She receives around 10,000 francs a month here. "Of course, the cost of living is also higher, but it's not three times as high. And the taxes are much lower."

High cost of living? This was confirmed to me by another friend we had dinner with the night before. She is a medical assistant, comes from Syria and used to live in Berlin. She says that she earns 5,800 francs – but she also pays 1,400 francs for a tiny, twenty-square-meter apartment.

Before I start my presentation in Zurich, Olivier Kessler, Director of the Liberal Institute, gives a short opening statement in which he explains why Switzerland is not a capitalist country, but a semi-socialist one. He refers to the numerous regulations and restrictions that contradict the spirit of a market economy. Capitalism, he argues, is a system in which the only task of the state is to protect private property. There should be, he asserts, unlimited freedom of contract in unrestricted markets. In view of widespread state interventions, he closes, this is not the case in Switzerland. His conclusion: "We do not live under capitalism in Switzerland."

I concur with almost all of his points of criticism. But pure capitalism does not exist in any country in the world, and Switzerland is more capitalist than almost all other countries. I don't primarily judge a country against an ideal, but against other countries.

The audience of about 100 consisted of staunch pro-capitalists. One even came in the "I Love Capitalism" T-shirt that I sometimes wear at lectures (not this time). After the lecture, a Swiss economist, Hans Rentsch, comes up to me and hands me a book: *Wie viel Markt verträgt die Schweiz?* (English, literally: *How much free market can Switzerland handle?*).[5] It is a skeptical book, as it shows that in recent decades Swiss politicians have very rarely initiated nation-wide market reforms of their own volition.[6]

Rentsch is also skeptical about Switzerland's oft-praised system of "direct democracy." Switzerland is very popular with supporters of direct democracy because citizens vote directly on a whole host of issues. The Swiss often prove to be clever in this respect, but Rentsch also cites a lot of examples of his fellow countrymen voting against more market economy and in favor of more state restrictions on freedom, whether in relation to the liberalization of the electricity market or the healthcare system.[7]

According to Rentsch, if Switzerland is economically successful compared to other countries, it is not because of direct democracy, but in spite of it. "The fundamentally pro-government and market-skeptical attitude of the population has political consequences ... In hardly any other comparable country is the electricity network as dominated by state actors with multiple interests as in this country with its cantons and municipalities holding local and regional monopolies. In hardly any other comparable country do the state railroads have such a dominant market position as the SBB in Switzerland ... In the Swiss healthcare system, too, the market and competition have largely been eliminated by state regulation."[8]

At the same time, he sees the competition between the individual municipalities and cantons in Switzerland as a positive thing, which has brought about a lot of good. Many people I know are supporters of "direct democracy." They want the people themselves to decide. I have always been skeptical about this, although I have to admit that the decisions of elected parliamentarians are no better than those of the people. But Germans are not the same as the Swiss. In 2021, 56 percent of Berliners voted in favor of expropriating large real estate companies. Socialism is back. In Germany too.

5 Rentsch, *Wie viel Markt verträgt die Schweiz?*
6 Rentsch, *Wie viel Markt verträgt die Schweiz?*, 12.
7 Rentsch, *Wie viel Markt verträgt die Schweiz?*, 44 et seq.
8 Rentsch, *Wie viel Markt verträgt die Schweiz?*, 21.

Isabelle is instantly impressed by Switzerland, especially as everything here is very clean and you feel safe, even when you walk the streets at night. People are much better dressed than in Berlin. The day after my lecture, we drive to Zug. The city is only a 40-minute drive from Zurich. I don't like train journeys that much, so I hire a chauffeur in an S-Class Mercedes. The outward journey costs 240 francs. We are driven back by the chauffeur of the man we are visiting. It's Hans-Peter Wild, who, like so many billionaires from Germany, lives in Switzerland.

Zug is particularly popular because it is considered a veritable tax haven. Renowned and innovative companies have their headquarters or major facilities here, including the multinational food conglomerate, Nestlé, companies in the biotech and retail sectors, as well as many start-ups working on new technologies in Switzerland's "Crypto Valley." The top tax rate in the canton of Zug averages around 23 percent – a dream come true for taxpayers in many other countries such as Germany.

Hans-Peter Wild is the owner of Capri-Sun, one of the world's leading non-alcoholic drink brands. "Help yourself," his assistant prompts us, indicating a cooler box containing chilled Capri-Sun in a wide variety of flavors. I help myself and am reminded of my childhood, when I often drank Capri-Sun. Today, the characteristic Capri-Sun pouch is produced in 24 countries and sold in more than 100. But in every country, Wild explains, different tastes prevail and the trick is to adapt the product to cater to local tastes.

Wild asks me if I have come with a request. I assume he is often visited by people who want something from him. According to *Forbes*, he is worth 3.5 billion US dollars. No, I don't have a request. I'm just happy to see him again and have a chat. And Isabelle, who is a keen horse-rider, is delighted to meet someone who was a keen equestrian himself when he was younger. Wild is now 80 years old and has just written his autobiography. I was the first to read it because I was asked to write the foreword. I was particularly fascinated by the fact that he has traveled all over the world because his company is global. I'm a little frustrated at the moment that, for example, my partners in South America, who should be organizing a trip to Argentina and Chile next month, have so far been slow and unreliable. We both agree: even if it's difficult for punctual people like us, we can't change the world. "You have to develop a very thick skin," advises Wild. There is a huge globe in his office – a man like Wild, even though he lives in a small town with 30,000 inhabitants, thinks globally.

"From the very beginning, it has always been my goal to establish Capri-Sun and WILD Flavors as global players. You have to set yourself goals and not lose sight of them, despite some imponderables along the way," says Wild, referring to the second global company he built up, the flavor manufacturer WILD Flavors, Inc. His father calculated that if everyone in Germany at the time drank just one Capri-Sun a year, his company would sell 60 million pouches. His employees thought such high numbers were unrealistic, but they were too small for the younger Wild. He wanted to sell several billion Capri-Suns globally every year – and he achieved his goal, which most people would have dismissed as "unrealistic" or even "impossible."

What does Switzerland's economic future look like? I commissioned a survey in Switzerland in 2021 for my book, *In Defence of Capitalism*. The survey found that people in Switzerland, even though it is so widely regarded as a model capitalist country, are just as skeptical about capitalism as people in Germany. The statements that capitalism leads to growing inequality and to monopolies, that it promotes selfishness and greed, that the rich set the political agenda, and that people are enticed to buy products they don't need were the most popular among Swiss respondents. The survey revealed that only 21 percent of Swiss respondents said that capitalism means economic freedom, and only 21 percent said that capitalism leads to prosperity.

We formulated some of the questions without using the word "capitalism" because it has a bad connotation for many people. Approval of capitalism increased in Switzerland (as in many other countries) when the word "capitalism" was omitted. But even then, the attitude of Swiss respondents was not positive, it was neutral – that is, agreement with pro- and anti-free market statements was fairly evenly balanced.

The example of Switzerland proves that there is not necessarily a correlation between the objective level of economic freedom (as measured by the *Index of Economic Freedom*) and popular opinion (as determined by Ipsos MORI in the survey).

But what does it mean for the future if people in a country such as Switzerland are skeptical about capitalism? The results of future referendums could be even more anti-free market than has previously been the case. I had already predicted this immediately after the Ipsos MORI survey, and unfortunately this pessimistic forecast was confirmed soon afterwards: In March 2024, 58 percent of Swiss voters backed a trade union proposal calling on the state to pay pensioners an additional 13th monthly pension payment. The referendum was supported by left-wing parties. This begs the question: will Switzerland retain its leading position in economic freedom rankings for many years to come?

April 2022
Tbilisi, Georgia

I travel to Georgia at the end of April. The small country (3.7 million inhabitants), which used to be part of the Soviet Union, is located on the Black Sea in western Asia, but is proudly referred to by its inhabitants as "the balcony of Europe." Neighboring countries are Turkey, Azerbaijan and Russia. Russian-backed forces attacked the country in 2008. Since then, around 20 percent of the country's territory has been occupied by Russia.

I have been invited by the Free Market Roadshow, an event organized by the Austrian Economic Center. The Free Market Roadshow brings together speakers from all over the world to spread the ideas of freedom and market economy – especially, but by no means exclusively, in Eastern Europe.

I had never been to Georgia before, but I had been in contact with Professor Gia Jandieri, the founder and vice president of a libertarian think tank in Georgia called the New Economic School. I am curious to meet him in person. I am staying at the Radisson Hotel with my girlfriend Alica, and Gia picks us up in the morning and shows us around the city. What strikes me at first glance: the large number of old and fascinating buildings, most of them from the nineteenth century. Gia shows us the panorama of Tbilisi. And amidst all the beautiful buildings in the old town, one ugly building stands out: "It dates back to the Soviet era," remarks Gia.

You can tell from Tbilisi that neither the First nor the Second World War was fought on Georgian territory. The buildings have been preserved, but with around 300,000 dead soldiers, Georgia paid a high blood toll in the Second World War. Gia believes that the Soviet dictator Joseph Stalin – although he himself was born in Georgia – did not want his compatriots to enjoy preferential treatment. If anything, he did the opposite and cast them into the fire.

Some of the beautiful old buildings are in a very good condition because they were renovated after the fall of communism. But there are also many in a poor condition. I tell Gia that this was the same in East Germany after the end of socialism and that extensive modernization of the old buildings was facilitated via tax incentives. Gia shakes his head: "In a country like Germany, where you pay taxes at a rate of 40 or even almost 50 percent, such tax-saving models worked, but here people only pay 20 percent, so there isn't such a big incentive to reduce taxes – such incentive models wouldn't work." Most apartments are privately owned and were privatized after the end of socialism. There are no restrictions under landlord and tenant law, which means rents can be negotiated freely.

I ask Gia how he became a staunch supporter of the market economy. He was born in 1961, grew up in the Soviet Union and was critical of the system in his youth. He worked in the Ministry of Wholesale Trade in Georgia and saw every day that the planned economy system did not work and that corruption dominated the entire economy. In 1988, he read *The Road to Serfdom* by Friedrich August von Hayek. The writings of Hayek and Ludwig von Mises have influenced him to this day. In 2001, Gia founded the New Economic School together with other pro-market economists, drafted a model for radical tax reform and wrote the "25 Principles for Economic Prosperity of Georgia," an economic program for presidential candidate Mikheil Saakashvili. The former Minister of Justice was elected President in January 2004. He advocated a market economy and sought to deprive the old, established elites of power.

The years after 2004 were also the time when Gia was able to make the biggest impact. He was a member of a team that prepared a major tax reform. "I was and remain convinced of this approach, which led to the simplification of the tax system and the reduction of taxes," says Gia. "Together with other deregulatory measures, the reform triggered enormous economic growth in my country."

It was a good time for Georgia. Once again, the principles of the supporters of capitalism proved to be true in practice: lower taxes lead to higher growth and, as a result, even higher tax revenues for the state.

"Kakha Bendukidze played an important role in the reforms and I am proud to call him my friend," says Gia. Bendukidze was a well-known entrepreneur in Russia (one of the leaders of the Union of Russian Industrialists and Entrepreneurs), then left Russia, invested worldwide, but worked in the Georgian reform government from 2004 to 2008 and continued to advise it until 2013. In 2014, he came to Ukraine to offer the same reforms (his famous speech to the Ukrainian government was entitled: "You don't guess in what a shit you live"). A short time later, he died in a London hotel after undergoing heart surgery in Switzerland. Bendukidze was very popular in libertarian circles and also backed them to a massive extent financially, founding a free-market-oriented Free University in Tbilisi.

After the free-market reforms between 2004 and 2007 and two years of double-digit growth, the International Monetary Fund (IMF) office in Tbilisi was closed in May 2008 because "Georgia no longer needed it." The country was better off without help. The IMF office was only reopened after the Russian intervention in September 2008, as the international community wanted to demonstrate its solidarity with Georgia.

And how does Gia see the situation today? He is skeptical. The country is ruled by Bidzina Ivanishvili, who was officially only prime minister from 2012 to 2013, but is still running things in practice. Ivanishvili made billions in Russia, returned to Georgia in 2003, later took French citizenship and now lives in a residence above Tbilisi, which was valued at 50 million US dollars in 2012.

What are the biggest challenges Georgia now faces, I ask Gia. Firstly, of course, the ongoing Russian threat to the country. But he also sees the consistent free-market approach, which he considers to be the best for the country, as being threatened by EU bureaucracy. In negotiations with the EU, Georgia was constantly confronted with proposals for new state regulations that would restrict labor market freedoms, for example, and are associated with high costs and unnecessary red tape.

Gia believes in the power of entrepreneurship. People often assume that intellectuals are morally superior, says Gia. But he believes that entrepreneurs in particular live by the experience that they have repeatedly gained in their professional lives, namely that honesty pays off more in the long run than unethical behavior: because dishonesty damages the entrepreneur's reputation.

"Bad ideas attract bad people," is something he learned during the communist era. I will never forget this sentence. Communism, according to Gia, was such a bad idea and attracted people like the Georgian, Stalin, who was a criminal. Gia shows us the site of the prison where Stalin was held for bank robbery. The Georgian, Joseph Dzhugashvili, the birth name of the future Soviet dictator, was responsible for planning a crime that was committed on June 26, 1907. Dzhugashvili and an entourage of twenty or so men and women ambushed a cash transport belonging to the Russian state bank. The transport consisted of two armored cars drawn by horses.

While the money was in the first car – accompanied by two bank officials and two guards – the second car contained a group of police officers and soldiers. Stalin and his accomplices pelted the small convoy with powerful grenades; many of the accompanying personnel and their horses were killed or mutilated. Almost simultaneously, a series of attacks were launched against the Cossacks and policemen patrolling the surrounding streets. The information about the number of deaths varies between five and 40. Stalin was imprisoned as a result. Gia shows us where the prison once stood. The Soviet dictator had torn it down and the site is now home to a parking lot.

Gia supports the Libertarian Party in Georgia, which is small but, in his opinion, has the best ideas for the country. He is looking for an alternative to both the socialism under which he grew up and the European welfare state. On the surface, the welfare state appears to be working, but in the long term it will fail. Gia argues for an economic system as described by Hayek and von Mises. Georgia, says Gia, needs additional tax cuts, deregulation and currency reform. The euro is not ideal, but he advocates pegging the currency to the dollar or the euro, even if he would still prefer to have various competing private currencies, as Hayek favored.

Before I travel to a country, I study its economy and history and make some notes. Here are some facts: after the collapse of the Soviet Union, many former Soviet Bloc countries had a hard time. But Georgia had a particularly difficult time. Having only become independent in 1918, it was occupied by the Red Army in 1921 and incorporated into the Soviet Union. Seventy years later, it gained independence for the second time. Georgia had two challenges to overcome. The first was a challenge it shared with all former socialist states, namely the need to replace the socialist state economy with a market economy.

The second was that Georgia was highly dependent on Russia and all of the country's foreign trade flowed towards Russia. And: "Already from the beginning of its independence from the Soviet Union, Georgia experienced the harshest possible aggressive pressure from the political authorities of the Russian Federation," for example in the energy sector.[9] In addition, there was Russian military aggression from day one, which culminated in the attack on Georgia in 2008.

While I am in Georgia, Russia launches its war against Ukraine. I see flags flying everywhere, expressing solidarity with Ukraine. Paata Shehelidze, president of the New Economic School, believes that the threat of renewed Russian aggression against the country (20 percent of Georgia is effectively occupied by Russia) is unsettling potential investors from abroad. And, of course, this uncertainty has increased as a result of the war in Ukraine. The enemy is already in the country – as in Ukraine, Russia has installed parts of Georgia as supposedly independent territories.

The threat from Russia was not the only problem for Georgia after the fall of the Soviet Union. The situation was made more difficult by the fact that there was a complete lack of political stability. One new government succeeded another, but it was not the normal alternation between opposition and government seen in most established democracies. After each election, the losing side accused the new government of electoral fraud, and the new government regularly took legal action against its political opponents.

9 Jandieri, "Brief Economic History of Georgia," 3.

The ruling party did everything in its power to make it impossible for the opposition to one day come to government.[10]

The 1990s were characterized by political chaos and economic decline. Corruption and organized crime reigned everywhere. No entrepreneurship could thrive in this environment: "The fulfillment of the tax obligations was simply impossible, especially for small and medium businesses. The starting of a business was a heroic idea, and any entrepreneur could become a criminal simply for making mistakes in accounting and paying taxes. This became a useful tool for discrediting and oppressing of business making the economy very weak," explains Gia.[11]

In November 2003, President Eduard Shevardnadze (the former Soviet Foreign Minister) was forced to resign, in what was later referred to as the "Rose Revolution." Thirteen years after Georgia gained its political independence, Mikheil Saakashvili launched a program of market economy reforms. The number of tax types was reduced from 22 to seven (now there are six) and personal income tax fell from 39 to 20 percent. Extensive privatizations began and measures were introduced to curb corruption.

Corruption is a big problem in many countries. Georgia adopted a very radical approach, which paid off. Gia reports that all of the country's 35,000 police officers were dismissed in one fell swoop and around 15,000 better paid new officers were hired. During the transition phase, crime didn't increase because the worst bandits had been the police officers themselves. There is hardly any organized crime in Georgia today because the state operates a zero-tolerance policy.

However, at least as important for the fight against corruption was the fact that reforms eliminated swathes of unnecessary rules and regulations. An important lesson for other countries, too: the fewer regulations a government imposes, the fewer opportunities there are for corruption. In 2004, Georgia was ranked 133rd in Transparency International's Corruption Perception

---

10 Zedania, 115.
11 Jandieri, "Brief Economic History of Georgia," 16.

Index; in 2022 it had climbed to 41st out of 180.[12] In comparison, Russia is now ranked 137th.[13]

Deregulation and tax reform had a very positive impact: "The results of the reforms were visible soon – with increased GDP, incomes, deposits, the number of cars and so on which illustrated the improvement very well. Therefore, the conclusion of this story can be such: decisive steps, liberalization plus taking responsibilities for internal problems are the best policy solutions for any type of crisis, even and moreover for poorer nations in a transitional crisis."[14]

The example of Georgia shows that tax cuts and a simplified tax system often lead to higher tax receipts – something we have seen time and time again in other countries, but socialists will never understand. The 2005 tax reform, implemented after the Rose Revolution, had these effects, according to Gia: "All types of taxes (except customs tax – whose effective rate is close to zero) increased the related state revenues: Value Added Tax revenues increased by more than seven times, personal income tax revenues increased by more than eight times, and profit tax revenues increased by ten times."[15]

The economic situation improved significantly. Gross domestic product doubled in the first four years and tripled in the first eight years after the reforms were introduced – despite the effects of the financial crisis of 2008/2009.[16] This was a result of the tax reform, but also further deregulation and liberalization in other areas of the economy.

In the period from 1997 to 2020, Georgia's score in the *Index of Economic Freedom* rose more than that of almost any other country in the world and even placed the country in twelfth place in the rankings in 2020. However, Georgia has slipped back since then and was ranked 35th in 2023.[17]

---

12 Transparency International, "Our Work in Georgia," https://www.transparency.org/en/countries/georgia.

13 Transparency International, "Our Work in Russia," https://www.transparency.org/en/countries/russia.

14 Jandieri, "Brief Economic History of Georgia," 30.

15 Jandieri, "Tax Reforms in Georgia," 7.

16 Jandieri, "Tax Reforms in Georgia," 7.

17 Heritage Foundation, *2023 Index of Economic Freedom.* https://www.heritage.org/index/.

In 2011, the Economic Liberty Act was passed and it came into force in January 2014. The Act was a collection of constitutional amendments and a special law restricting government spending (both at central and local government levels) to a maximum of 60 percent of gross domestic product and limiting the deficit to 3 percent. The law also stipulated that there had to be a referendum before every tax increase or the introduction of a new tax.

In 2016, the Georgian Dream party, which came to power in 2012, formed a commission to draft a new constitution. The fact that many Georgians did not want their new constitution to be modeled on the European welfare state, but rather preferred a more market-based model, was also made clear by the adoption of a so-called "organic law," which prohibits the introduction of new taxes or tax increases and, in particular, of a progressive tax system. This means that setting different tax rates depending on income, as is practiced in most countries, is prohibited. The law also stipulates that tax legislation may only be amended if the changes are confirmed by a referendum. However, only the government can initiate such a referendum, and – particularly important – no referendum can address the question of progressive taxation.[18]

But instead of further expanding these laws protecting citizens from the state, the government has taken the opposite approach in recent years and lifted the restrictions. Gia criticizes the free trade agreement with the EU, which led to the reintroduction of a lot of unnecessary government regulations.

Georgia, like many other countries, proves that freedom, including economic freedom, must be fought for again and again. There is always a danger that political shifts will lead to reforms being reversed, as has happened in some cases in Georgia. For example, from 2027, the sensible regulations in the constitution according to which new taxes or tax increases may not be introduced without a referendum, are to be abolished.

I remain friends with Gia to this day. I invited him to Berlin for my 65th birthday, he translated my book, *The Power of Capitalism*, into Georgian, and he gave a lecture on the book at the university.

---

18 Natsvlishvili, 122–123.

Tirana, Albania

At the beginning of May 2022, I visit Albania, having been invited by the Free Market Roadshow. We drive about an hour from the airport to the hotel in Tirana. I am immediately impressed by the beautiful landscape and mountains. The houses on the side of the road are fanciful and varied. "I don't think there are 25,000 building regulations here like there are in Germany," I tell Isabelle, who has traveled with me to Tirana.

Bjorna Hoxhallari from Students for Liberty, who I meet later, confirms that many of the houses were built without planning permission, but while there are too many regulations in Germany (25,000!), there are too few here. During the earthquake in Albania in September 2019, many houses were destroyed because they were built with substandard materials and were not professionally constructed. What is noticeable is that there are water tanks on every house. I can't work out why because they are not big enough to satisfy people's water needs. Bjorna explains to me that local water and electricity supplies are frequently interrupted and, when this happens, people draw water from the tanks on the houses.

We arrive at the Xheko Imperial Hotel in the center of Tirana, which is considered one of the finest addresses in the city. In other European countries it would be considered a mid-range hotel. I was in Tbilisi the week before and my impressions of Tirana compare unfavorably. While there were numerous beautiful old buildings from the 19th century in Tbilisi, these are a rare exception in Tirana. The most beautiful buildings are a few government buildings. The city center is dominated by ugly buildings from the communist era or those that were built afterwards and are typically no nicer. Many are also in very poor condition and it feels like the best solution would be to tear them down.

How safe is life in Albania? A friend sends me a WhatsApp message before I leave: "Don't let yourself be robbed in the rogue state of Albania." My girlfriend and I prefer to leave our expensive watches, a Rolex and a Cartier, in the hotel safe. Bjrona says our worries are unfounded, the streets here are very safe.

I meet Adri Nurellari, an impressive individual who shaped the libertarian movement in Albania. He was an advisor to the Democratic Party in Albania and now advises the Democratic Party in Kosovo. Adri studied economics in London for four years. On the subject of security and crime, he says: Yes, there is a high level of crime in the drug sector. But precisely because criminals can earn huge amounts of money from growing and selling drugs, petty crime is not worth it. "Why steal a few hundred euros from a tourist when you can make millions from illegal drugs?"

At dinner I ask Bjorna how people make a living here. "Do you really not know that?" she asks me and laughs. "On the cultivation and sale of marijuana." She criticizes the Albanian president, who has turned Albania into a "narco-state." Of course, there are no official figures, but the country is now referred to as the "Colombia of Europe."[19] Estimates suggest that between a third and a half of Albania's gross national product comes from drug trafficking. In any case, several billion euros are generated from drug trafficking every year.

According to the 2022 World Drug Report from the United Nations Office on Drugs and Crime (UNODC), Albania is the seventh largest cannabis producer in the world. The report examines the state of drug cultivation worldwide, ranking the countries where drug cultivation is most widespread and those where it is rarely practiced. Out of 154 countries, Albania ranked seventh after Morocco, Afghanistan, Spain, the Netherlands, Pakistan and Lebanon.

Albania ranked first in the Southeast Europe region, indicating that it cultivates a significant amount of cannabis that is either exported or consumed domestically. Albania was followed by Turkey, Romania and Bulgaria. One of the main heroin trafficking routes also runs through the

---

19 Kote, https://albaniandailynews.com/news/smi-accuses-pm-of-creating-colombia-of-europe-after-zdf-s-report-1-1 .

country, starting in Pakistan and leading to Western Europe via Syria, Turkey, Greece and Albania.

A report by the European Monitoring Center for Drugs and Drug Addiction (EMCDDA) found that since 2017, Albanian criminal groups have not only become larger but also more sophisticated, working in the import and distribution of cocaine from Latin America to Europe.[20] There is another problem linked to the drug issue: the high level of corruption in Albania. Albania was recently ranked 101 out of 180 countries in Transparency International's Corruption Perception Index.[21]

The topics we talk about are mostly unpleasant, but the restaurant Bjorna recommends is fantastic. Albania is famous for its particularly good food and, even as vegetarians, Isabelle and I are not disappointed. For the equivalent of 45 euros we had a great dinner for three. And the next day Adri takes us to another restaurant, also with great food. I invite eight people, there are several courses, the bill is the equivalent of 110 euros.

Despite all the poverty in the country, living conditions have improved significantly compared to the socialist era. Bjorna reports that her grandparents used to live with the family in an 80 square meter apartment – which was home to as many as twenty people. It's hard to imagine, but I remember reading that it was not uncommon for four to ten people to live in small, 50 square meter apartments.[22]

Albania was the poorest country in Europe back then. "Anyone who flew over the region in an airplane at that time saw Yugoslavia illuminated beneath them. In stark contrast, the 200 kilometers between Yugoslavia and the Greek border was little more than a dark spot. That was Albania."[23]

There were only 1,265 cars in the whole country, none of them privately owned. As recently as the early 1990s, there was not a single traffic light

---

20 Witzel, https://www.euractiv.de/section/eu-aussenpolitik/news/albanien-ist-weltweit-siebtgroesster-cannabisproduzent/.
21 Transparency International, "Our Work in Albania," https://www.transparency.org/en/countries/albania.
22 Tschinderele, 126.
23 Tschinderele, 126.

anywhere in Albania. Today, Tirana is overcrowded with cars the city was clearly not built for. Similar to Manhattan, drivers are almost permanently stuck in traffic. From time to time we see a strikingly expensive luxury car, a Ferrari, for example – "those are the drug barons," says Bjorna.

On my exploratory stroll through Tirana, I pass several bunkers. Enver Hoxha was paranoid and lived in constant fear that Albania could be attacked by capitalist countries. So he ordered the construction of 200,000 bunkers all over the country, many of which are still preserved to this day. Bjorna tells me that acquaintances of hers have even integrated a bunker into their restaurant. At the airport, I meet a young man who is studying law and has started to invest in real estate. He shows me a photo of a former bunker with a tasteful interior. He tells me it is his dream to convert a bunker like that into a vacation home and rent it out.

However, most of the bunkers are not like the bunkers found in other countries. There is often only room for two or three people in a typical Albanian bunker. I ask Bjorna if she would take a photo of me in one of these small bunkers, but that fails because of the terrible smell: apparently some people have used the bunker as a toilet, so I prefer to have a photo taken outside the bunker. A somewhat larger bunker has been preserved as a Bunker Museum. The exhibition is impressive. It reveals the full scale of the communist terror in Enver Hoxha's state.

The picture the museum paints is the exact opposite of the image I had of Albania when I was younger. As a teenager, I was a Maoist. I had formed a "Red Cell" at my school when I was 13 and published a newspaper called *The Red Banner*. We rejected both the capitalist countries and the Soviet Union or East Germany (the GDR), which, in our view, had betrayed socialism. True socialism, in our opinion, existed in only two countries, Mao's China and Albania. Just as we got our "information" about China from the *Peking Rundschau*, which I received every week from Beijing, we "learned" about Albania from *Radio Tirana*.

I can still remember lying in bed at 11 o'clock at night listening to *Radio Tirana*. The broadcast began with the communist battle song, the *Internationale*:

"Here is Tirana, here is Tirana. With a broadcast in German." This was followed by a series of broadcasts such as "The Marxist-Leninist World Movement is Growing and Getting Stronger."

So, in truth, we knew nothing at all about Albania, we merely projected our socialist utopian longings onto the country where Enver Hoxha ruled from 1946 to 1985. Some of my comrades volunteered to go to Albania during semester breaks to help build socialism and worked there without pay.

What we also did not know – and neither did the Albanians – was that Enver Hoxha and the leading communists were living a far more luxurious life, totally isolated from the rest of the country. From the end of 1960 until his death in April 1985, Hoxha did not leave his country; indeed, he almost never left the so-called *Blloku* (block), a centrally located district in Tirana that was only as large as 21 soccer fields. I ask Bjorna if we can see this isolated district in which Enver Hoxha and the party elite lived. "We're right in the heart of it here, this is the block," she says. Somehow I imagined it differently.

Hoxha lived here from 1944 until his death, sharing the Block with the members and candidates of the Central Committee of the Party of Labor of Albania and their families. "The Block inhabitants received special treatment: they all had waiting and housekeeping staff, special shops where they bought their groceries and Western clothes, government villas and holiday homes across the country, and a host of other privileges," writes Blendi Fevziu in his biography of Enver Hoxha. [24] It was a small, tight-knit community, isolated from its own people – marriages mostly took place within the Block's insulated community.[25] Hoxha spent time completely immersed in his ideologies – he wrote a total of 68 books, more than most writers ever manage.[26] I remember translating one of his shorter works from English into German when I was 14 years old. It seems absurd that the leader of a state should isolate himself and produce book after book about the superiority of socialism – in the poorest country in Europe.

---

24 Fevziu, 164.
25 Fevziu, 163.
26 Fevziu, 241

Of course, I wanted to see the house Enver Hoxha had lived in. It is very large, but less spectacular than I expected. Across the street, there is now an American investment bank. I think to myself that Enver Hoxha would be turning in his grave if he knew that. Unfortunately, the house was being renovated at the time of my visit, so I wasn't able to see it from the inside.

Bjorna is 25 years old and studied political science. She speaks perfect English and, in addition to working as an English teacher, works in a sushi restaurant that she owns with her mother and uncle. 75 percent of young people in Tirana speak English, says Bjorna. She read the books of Adam Smith, Milton Friedman and Ayn Rand, and they shaped her thinking. For Albania, she would particularly like to see less bureaucracy, lower taxes and more legal certainty for investors.

During the socialist era, in addition to the statues of Enver Hoxha, there were also statues of Stalin because Albania worshiped the Soviet dictator even after he had fallen from grace in the Soviet Union.

People were locked up. Anyone who tried to leave the country illegally was, in the best-case scenario, sent to prison or to one of the labor camps for many years, or shot. Almost 1,000 people did not survive their attempt to leave the country.[27]

The country had completely isolated itself from the outside world, a fact illustrated by the following incident: Mother Teresa, who became famous all around the world for her work with the poor, homeless, sick and dying and is revered as a saint in the Catholic Church, desperately wanted to visit her dying mother, who lived in Albania. Heads of state used all available diplomatic channels to help make Mother Teresa's wish come true, but were unsuccessful. Her mother died alone in Albania in 1981, without being able to see her daughter one last time. It was not until 1990, five years after Hoxha's death, that Mother Teresa was able to travel to the country and visit her mother's grave.[28]

In February 1991, 100,000 demonstrators in Tirana's central square,

27 Tschinderele, 178.
28 Fevziu, 178.

Skanderberg Square, toppled the large statue of Enver Hoxha, the fences came down and the labor camps opened.

The situation did not initially improve after the end of communism. Chaos broke out in the 1990s. The reason: people who had lived in abject poverty under socialism now wanted to get rich, and get rich fast. But they didn't understand how building wealth works under capitalism. Instead, hundreds of thousands fell for a dubious pyramid scheme in which they were promised profits of up to 50 percent. The scheme ended like all Ponzi schemes do, but in this case three out of four families in Albania were victims and 1.2 billion US dollars, more than half of the gross national product at the time, was suddenly gone.[29] Bjorna remembers that her family also lost a lot of money – they still have the worthless certificates from the pyramid scheme.

After people realized they had been cheated, what became known locally as the "Lottery Uprising" broke out and the country descended into chaos. A British journalist reported: "Young men high on raki and marijuana drove around in stolen cars at high speed and unleashed automatic weapon rounds like they were Steven Seagal or Chuck Norris."[30]

Many Albanians are fans of America today. Albania is considered the most pro-American country in Europe. We see the Albanian flag everywhere we go; Albanians have a strong sense of national pride. However, we often also see the U.S. flag – and that of the European Union. Albanians hope, eventually, to be part of the European Union. The country has made progress in economic freedom, gaining 16 points in the Index of Economic Freedom since 1995. Even so, it still only ranks 49th out of 176 countries in the index.[31]

The 2023 Index offers the following assessment: "The foundations of economic freedom in Albania are undermined by weak rule of law. The country's relatively low property rights score is largely a result of political interference in the judiciary that is exacerbated by persistent corruption.

---

29 Tschinderele, 113.
30 Quoted in Tschinderele, 114.
31 Heritage Foundation, *2023 Index of Economic Freedom*, https://www.heritage.org/index/country/albania.

Expansionary government spending has led to budget deficits in recent years."[32]

When I ask Adri what went wrong in the transition from socialism to democracy and a market economy, he replies: "There has been no change in elite circles. Essentially, they have remained the same. There were maybe a dozen families who had power at the time of Enver Hoxha and they still have it today." As a result, there is no serious interest in dealing with the past and the crimes of the Hoxha dictatorship. It speaks volumes that perhaps just 20 percent of the entrepreneurs and landowners expropriated by the communists got their property back and received ridiculously meager compensation amounting to ten million dollars.

After the end of socialism, many Albanians left the country. In relation to the size of the population, no other European country has seen more people emigrate since the end of socialism. Over the past 30 years, Albania has lost about 30 percent of its population. Only 2.8 million people still live in the country. And it is often the best and most talented young Albanians who have emigrated. Many have settled in Greece or Italy. In Italy alone, Adri explains, there are now 350,000 Albanians owning 40,000 businesses. They generate 7 percent of Italy's GDP. Today, there are more Albanians living outside the country than in it.

One major source of income for people in Albania, especially those in rural areas, is therefore money sent home by Albanians living in other European countries. In most cases, they transfer money every month to support their families. In Albania, people earn an average of around 350 euros a month. Here, says Adri, talented young entrepreneurs see no opportunities because many areas of the economy are monopolized. And anyone who doesn't have excellent political connections has next to no chance.

In addition, laws and rules are constantly changing, which leads to uncertainty among investors. The laws protecting private property have been revised 16 times since the end of communism alone, and tax laws are

---

32 Heritage Foundation, *2023 Index of Economic Freedom*, https://www.heritage.org/index/country/albania.

constantly changing. This deters foreign investors and banks. Some of them – such as Deutsche Bank and Société Générale – have already left the country. In the International Property Rights Index 2021, which measures the security of property rights in a country, Albania only comes 98th out of 129.

In every country I visit, I meet important people with whom I stay in touch afterwards. One of them is Adri Nurellari. I met him again on June 7, 2022 at a conference in Stockholm to which my friend Anders Ydstedt invited me. During the conference, Adri won first prize in a Dragons' Den competition for his institute's plans to spread libertarian ideas among young people in Albania. Since I think his thoughts deserve emulation, here is his idea that he submitted to the Albanian Liberal Institute (ALI), entitled "Promoting liberalism in Albanian universities":

"The Albanian Liberal Institute would like to organize a tour of 10 seminars in the 10 main public and private universities in 7 different towns of Albania. Inspired by the successful model and experience of the 'Free Market Road Show' this project will aim at popularizing free-market-oriented literature and at identifying and recruiting like-minded youngsters. In addition, ALI proposes to gather a compilation of 20 free-market-oriented books translated into Albanian and make them available to the students and faculty of 10 private and public universities in Albania.

The targeted audience of the project will be students and university instructors in Albania as well as local stakeholders, journalists and civil society activists during the ceremonies in the university libraries of the different towns. The students and lecturers make up a vital segment of the Albanian society because they are highly qualified, hence more apt to understand the meanings of the liberal works, are very attentive to political ideas and debates, are in general very active and engaged in the public sphere and will most probably be the future decision-makers and leaders. Moreover they are also the main opinion-makers, multipliers and disseminators and as such are able to shape the overall public opinion and perceptions with regard to the values of the liberal thought...

Each one of the seminars will consist of a conceptual presentation of ideals such as individual rights, entrepreneurship and liberty promoted by the books of the list and a second presentation that will discuss the main authors and works. The first presentation will highlight the importance of classical liberal for the development of a country and a society. Whereas the second presentation will serve to provide the audience with a better understanding of the history of the liberal movement, the main authors and the most important works. Furthermore, the students will also be informed about the activities of the European Students for Liberty network and will be encouraged to start a local chapter."

I think it's a great idea. Which is why I donated 200 copies of the Albanian edition of my book, *In Defence of Capitalism,* to support the project.

May 2022
Warsaw, Poland

At the end of 2021, Brad Lips, the CEO of the Atlas Network (the world's largest association of classical liberal think tanks) invites me to the "Europe Liberty Forum 2022" in Kiev as a speaker. Then on February 24, 2022, Putin invades Ukraine and the event moves to Warsaw. I am traveling the evening before, Wednesday May 11, 2022. The congress is well attended, with around 200 representatives of libertarian think tanks from all over Europe. Even though it's my first time, I feel like I'm meeting a lot of people I know.

There's a group dinner on Thursday evening, and I'm really lucky. To my left is my girlfriend Alica and to my right is Maryan Zablotskyy, a member of the Ukrainian Parliament and of the ruling party of Volodymyr Zelensky, the President of Ukraine. He introduces himself to me and tells me that he was previously a member of the Ukraine Economic Freedom Foundation, a libertarian think tank founded in 2015. Today he is not only my neighbor at the table, but also a guest speaker at the dinner.

He tells me about the tremendous anger, even the hatred, that he had when he learned on February 24th that Putin had actually invaded Ukraine. His wife and child are safe in western Ukraine (if one can speak of safety), and his thoughts today are primarily focused on the future. We talk about economics. According to Zablotskyy, the income tax in Ukraine was recently reduced to 2 percent and numerous regulations and customs duties were abolished.

It is extraordinary for a country to cut taxes and abolish regulations in a time of war. Normally, war is when taxes are massively increased and government influence is expanded. In 1942, the Victory Act was passed in the U.S., raising the top tax rate to 88 percent, a level that rose to 94 percent in 1944 thanks to various tax surcharges. In Great Britain the top tax rate rose as high as 98 percent in the 1940s, and in Germany it climbed to 64.99 percent in 1941. Of course, Ukraine can afford to pursue such a policy because it receives massive support from the U.S. and other democratic countries. "We believe that we are stronger when we are economically freer," said Zablotskyy. The most important goal is to make the economic reforms, which were only decided as temporary measures, permanent after the war.

No-one from Ukraine at the congress is thinking about how the war might end, but discussions focus exclusively on the question of the opportunities that could arise after a victory. I met Nataliya Melnyk personally in the morning at the breakfast buffet. The young woman greets me: "Hello Rainer, nice to meet you." I didn't recognize her (I'm always very embarrassed at events like this because I have a really bad memory for faces). We had two Zoom conversations and otherwise corresponded by email. That was in January, before the war broke out. Nataliya is the representative of the Bendukidze Free Market Center in Kyiv, Ukraine's main libertarian think tank, founded in 2015. We have breakfast together and she says it is wrong to claim the reconstruction of Ukraine as a goal. "It cannot be about restoring the conditions of the pre-war period, but rather about creating something new." She speaks of a "window of opportunity" and refers to the findings of the Heritage Foundation's *Index of Economic Freedom*, according to which Ukraine is the least economically free of 45 countries in the European region. Before the war began, Ukraine ranked only 127th in the global rankings, behind countries such as India and Nicaragua. The Heritage Foundation sees the greatest deficits in property rights, the rule of law and labor market regulation.

Later in the event, I am introduced to Roman Waschuk, who was Canada's ambassador to Kiev from 2014 to 2019 and is now the Business Ombudsman for Ukraine. He doesn't believe that the findings about economically unfree Ukraine should be accepted at face value, arguing that Ukraine is not as economically unfree as described in the index and other statistics. "Such rankings only evaluate official statistics, which do not reflect Ukraine's enormous shadow economy." Many people in the West were surprised that

Ukraine's army was far better than they thought. And the same, says Waschuk, also applies to the country's economy.

Tax loopholes are used extensively, particularly in the IT sector, which, according to Nataliya, includes at least 250,000 specialists. The top tax rate in Ukraine used to be 20 percent, but there is a regulation whereby "individual entrepreneurs" only pay 5 percent. Actually, according to Waschuk, this tax was intended for completely different cases, perhaps for a woman who sells her products in the marketplace, but entrepreneurs such as IT specialists took advantage of it.

Everyone agrees that reforms are urgently needed because many regulations and laws in Ukraine date back to the 1970s, from the Soviet era. Tom Palmer, Executive Vice President for International Programs of the Atlas Network, hails Ludwig Erhard as a role model for the future Ukraine. Today, there are loud and frequent calls for a Marshall Plan for Ukraine. Palmer believes that a Marshall Plan will not help Ukraine and only market economy reforms based on Erhard's model can do that.

Undoubtedly, Palmer is right. Setting the right economic policy course through Erhard's market economy concept was clearly more important for the subsequent Federal Republic of Germany's "economic miracle" than the so-called Marshall Plan. This plan, named after the then American Secretary of State George C. Marshall, envisaged aid for the needy and partly starving population of Europe after the war. The program was worth 13 billion US dollars. But although the British received more than twice as much money from the plan as the Germans, Great Britain didn't develop anywhere near as strongly: while the British were ruled by socialists, Erhard introduced the market economy in the three western zones of what would later become West Germany, having already forged the concept for its introduction in wartime.

The libertarian think tanks in Ukraine have better political connections than think tanks in most Western countries. Alexander Danilyuk, co-founder of the Free Markets Center, was Finance Minister in Ukraine from 2016 to 2018, and MP Zablotskyy even says that a majority of parliamentarians in Ukraine adhere to libertarian ideas. However, the libertarian Atlas Network

45

also helps Ukraine in a very practical way. Atlas has raised millions of dollars to support Ukraine.

Germans and Americans who are part of the network not only collect money, but also bring medicine, night vision devices, drones and protective vests to Ukraine. I find out about this from Andreas Jürgens, an unconventional guy in shorts (most of the other participants wear suits, even I didn't dare come in my usual jeans).

Even before the event, Frederik Cyrus Roeder, whom I had met in Washington D.C. at a Students for Liberty conference, had written to me. Roeder and Jürgens went to Ukraine a few days after the war broke out and have been helping to supply urgently needed goods to Ukraine ever since. Jürgens shows me an article in *The Spokesman Review* entitled "In Ukraine, an informal web of libertarians becomes a resistance network."[33]

The libertarians' program for Ukraine is clear. "When we talk about the 'new Ukraine,' we mean three things above all," says Nataliya. "The fight against corruption, the establishment of a constitutional state, and economic freedom." Maybe it sounds a bit pathetic, says Nataliya, but "freedom is our religion." At the Atlas event, people keep saying: "Next year in Kiev." At that time, most people could not imagine that the war would last so long.

33 Francovich, https://www.spokesman.com/stories/2022/apr/03/in-ukraine-an-informal-web-of-libertarians-becomes/.

May 2022: Santiago de Chile, Chile

On May 17, 2022, I begin my journey to Latin America. My plans include lectures on the Spanish edition of my book, *The Power of Capitalism,* and meetings with representatives of think tanks, entrepreneurs, and politicians in Chile, Argentina, Paraguay, and Uruguay, as well as a speech at a large libertarian congress in Brazil. It takes 25 hours from my apartment in Berlin to get to the hotel in Santiago de Chile. I fly over São Paulo and at the airport I meet a young lawyer who was born in Chile but lives in Hamburg. He specializes in tax law and tells me that the new left-wing government in Chile under Gabriel Boric is planning to introduce a wealth tax. Initially only for people with private assets of at least ten million US dollars and only 0.3 percent. But we agree: this is the left-wing trick, you start with a high asset threshold and moderate tax rate, but once the tax has been introduced, the cap will soon be lowered and the tax rates increased.

I am picked up at the airport in Santiago by Joanna Gabriela Guerra. She will be my interpreter for the next 16 days and has organized everything. She is Mexican and also lives in her home country, but works for a libertarian think tank in Argentina. I made the right choice. The 30-year-old is incredibly ambitious and has already achieved a lot in her life. She studied law and philosophy and received her doctorate. It is important to me that an interpreter not only speaks English well, but also understands the content.

Maureen Halpern, who works for the libertarian think tank *Instituto Libertad y Desarrollo*, picks us up in the afternoon. She warns us not to take any expensive things with us because we might get robbed. Joanna is advised to leave her handbag at the hotel. At lunchtime, Joanna goes out with a friend, when they return to the hotel a homeless woman tries to steal her bag. She says that this has never happened to her in Mexico. She tries to defend herself and throws her handbag onto the terrace of a restaurant. When the restaurant's visitors see what is happening, they call security, who call the police.

Maureen takes us on a tour of downtown Santiago de Chile, which has changed in just a few months since the socialists came to power. There are barriers everywhere because there are violent demonstrations by left-wing anarchists every Friday. We visit the Presidential Palace, in front of which stands a large statue of Salvador Allende. Although he ruined the country economically during his three years in power, he is still a symbol of the left in Chile. Maureen reports that on March 11, 2022, when Boric took office, he went to the statue of Allende and kissed it before his inaugural speech. A clear signal to his supporters about his political intentions.

In the second round of voting, Boric adopted a moderate tenor in order to strengthen his appeal beyond his traditional political base and attract centrist voters. What I didn't know was that in Chile identity politics is also determining the direction of the left-wing movement. Not only does the Chilean flag fly in front of the presidential palace, it is accompanied by the rainbow flag – not just on special days, but every day, all year round.

The next day, I have a meeting with the *Cámara Chileno-Alemana de Comercio e Industria*. The business representatives present are worried that what Allende started could be repeated in Chile. One says: "We have lost the battle of ideas." Younger people in particular, who have not personally experienced the progress that Chile has made over the past few decades, are increasingly leaning towards the left.

A few hours later I meet with representatives of LOLA (Ladies of Liberty Alliance), an organization of libertarian-minded women. Founded in 2009, the organization now exists in 30 countries. I'm curious to find out what topics interest politicians and libertarian activists. Everything revolves around the discussion about the new constitution. What bothers you most about it? A politician explains to me that the bundle of 499 paragraphs is not a real constitution at all, but rather a collection of left-wing declarations originating from within the "woke" movement.

However, the women also say that the left-wing candidate Gabriel Boric won against José Antonio Kast not least because the right-wing candidate was against abortion and against LGBTQ rights. Surveys showed that women in particular opposed Kast and voted for Boric, ultimately swaying the election in his favor. Apparently, opinions on this also differ among libertarian women, because some think that protecting the family is very important, while for others LGBTQ issues are the priority.

In the evening I am invited to a lecture at *Insituto Libertad y Desarrollo*. The institute resides in the most beautiful building I have ever seen occupied by a think tank, with state-of-the-art technical facilities. The lecture is well attended and will also be broadcast online. And the question is on everyone's minds here too: What can be done to prevent an extreme left-wing shift in Chile? The fact that a majority of Chileans today hold anti-capitalist views was confirmed by the survey I commissioned Ipsos MORI to conduct on the image of capitalism in the county, which took place two months before the elections. The survey confirmed that a majority of Chileans are hostile toward free-market economics and capitalism. The participants in my presentations agree – yes, the survey's findings reflect the opinions they encounter on a daily basis.

On the third day, I meet Axel Kaiser, the most prominent advocate of libertarian ideas in all of Latin America. Everyone knows him in Chile. His full name is Axel Kaiser Barents-von Hohenhagen. The 40-year-old welcomes us to the office of the *Fundación para el Progreso*, which he founded in 2012 and which has become the most influential think tank among the younger generation. Kaiser is particularly successful on social media such as YouTube and often reaches more than a million young Chileans with his posts. He also holds the Friedrich Hayek Chair at one of Chile's most highly renowned universities, the Adolfo Ibáñez University in Santiago de Chile.

His thinking is primarily influenced by Hayek, Ludwig von Mises, Karl Popper and Milton Friedman. Kaiser writes books about economics, but is also, above all, a PR man and understands the art of self-marketing. He is not afraid to polarize – on the contrary, he knows how important provocation is if you want to attract attention. He says: "We have to learn to appeal to emotions that connect to values that are at the heart of classical liberalism.

49

The main fight is not about numbers but about feelings and values. Without an epic grounded on a moral case for freedom the cause is lost."

So, what has happened in Chile? It was long considered a model capitalist country in Latin America. In the *Human Development Index 2022*, it took the top spot among all Latin American countries. And in the Heritage Foundation's *2022 Index of Economic Freedom*, it came in at number 20, ahead of the U.S. and Great Britain (it is still at number 22 in the 2023 index). In 2020, the proportion of Chileans living in extreme poverty was 1.7 percent,[34] compared with 59.6 percent of households in socialist Venezuela.[35] Measured not in terms of households, but in terms of the population, 77 percent of Venezuelans were in extreme poverty in 2021.[36]

Despite the success story of capitalism in Chile, most Chileans, especially the younger generation, are now critical of capitalism. My conversation with Kaiser is also primarily about plans for a new constitution, a major topic that has been occupying people all over Chile in recent months. According to Kaiser, the draft of the new constitution is an expression of deep mistrust in the market and an almost boundless faith in the state. It is the longest constitution in the world, but instead of following the example of the world's best constitutions, such as the German Basic Law, Kaiser says a lot has been copied from Venezuela and Bolivia.

A big problem is that property rights will be undermined. Previously, when the state expropriated companies, it was obliged to pay them the full market price in cash. According to the draft of the new constitution, the state would in future only be required to pay an unspecified "fair price" and not in cash. In addition, there are guarantees for all sorts of "social rights," such as the right to work. This is reminiscent of the constitution of the socialist GDR,

---

34 Statista Research Department, "Extreme poverty rate in Chile," https://www.statista.com/statistics/1401306/extreme-poverty-rate-chile/.

35 See Statista Research Department, "Percentage of households in poverty and extreme poverty in Venezuela," https://www.statista.com/statistics/1235189/household-poverty-rate-venezuela/.

36 See Statista Research Department, "Percentage of population living in extreme poverty in Venezuela in 2021," https://www.statista.com/statistics/1243742/extreme-poverty-rate-venezuela-state/.

where Article 24 stated: "Every citizen of the German Democratic Republic has the right to work."

The proposed constitution stresses the rights of indigenous peoples, which may sound good at first. However, Kaiser criticizes the fact that this would put an end to the uniform application of the law in Chile. There would be, so to speak, autonomous zones where Chilean law would only be applied to a limited extent. Even today, the Chilean government can only assert itself in certain regions by declaring a state of emergency because anarchy and violence prevail in many southern territories. Even the new President Gabriel Boric, who had sharply criticized the use of state of emergency legislation in the run-up to the elections, is now adopting the same strategy because the violence is still escalating. The violent perpetrators are left-wing extremist groups, but they are closely linked to organized criminals, particularly the drug trade.

I ask Kaiser whether Boric could be considered a moderate within the left-wing alliance, as some believe. Compared to the communists, who are becoming increasingly influential despite their modest share of the vote, Boric is of course a moderate, says Kaiser. On the other hand, he is undoubtedly a staunch socialist. The people I speak to in Chile have the impression that Boric and his government are holding back until the vote on the constitution, after which they could take radical action.

Andrea, one of my friends in Berlin comes from Chile and is definitely not left-wing. Nevertheless, she voted for Boric because she saw the opposing candidate, José Antonio Kast, as extremely right-wing. Kaiser thinks that Kast is a national conservative and is therefore to the right of him, the self-identified libertarian. "But on the other hand, the left-wing media exaggerated it, portraying him as an inveterate Nazi. His opponents leveled unfair allegations against him, for example by pointing out that his father was a member of the NSDAP." It is clear that many Chileans voted along the same lines as Andrea – not for Boric, but against Kast.

The mistrust of Boric is understandable. When Hugo Chávez stood for election in Venezuela, he also declared that he was not, under any circumstances, planning to nationalize companies and even described

51

himself as a free-market-oriented social democrat and the "Tony Blair of the Caribbean." In fact, his policies became increasingly radical until they ended in dictatorship and chaos. The anxious question that some are asking is whether Chile will become another Venezuela.

"I still have faith in the common sense of the Chilean people and that it won't come to that," says Kaiser. "But either way, difficult and bitter years lie ahead. What worries me most is the increasing violence in the country. I think it is unlikely that we will see a return to the successful market economy policy, which, by the way, also gained support among socialists in recent decades – albeit with some reservations. Why are the socialists making nationalization easier with the new constitution if they haven't already been drawing up those kinds of plans? The introduction of the wealth tax will also deter investors."

Our conversation lasts longer than planned; we sit together for three hours. Kaiser spontaneously invites me to another dinner meeting the next evening. After giving another lecture to the members of the *Insituto Libertad y Desarrollo* in the afternoon, I meet Kaiser in a vegetarian restaurant on the eve of my onward journey to Argentina. He has brought his pretty girlfriend who is 15 years younger than him. Kaiser is rather pessimistic about developments in Latin America. Was capitalist Chile an exception? In Latin America there are too many people who want to be successful primarily at the expense of others, rather than as a result of their own efforts and work ethic. Of course it is impossible to generalize, but the problems lie deeper than "just" in the economic system. Kaiser is considering moving to Spain or Portugal – nowadays you can be based in any country in the world, and his focus is on social media anyway.

I am very happy with my trip to Chile. I have met so many incredible people, free-thinking people who are fighting against the rising tide of socialism. And my visit attracted media attention: the leading business newspaper *Diario Financiero* published a full-page interview with me and the daily *La Segunda* even printed three complete pages of extracts from my book, *The Power of Capitalism*.

May 2022
Buenos Aires, Corrientes, and San Miguel de Tucumán, Argentina

I set off for Argentina on May 21, 2022. First of all, a long and uncomfortable layover at the airport in Chile, because no seat had been booked in business class for the interpreter Joanna and I can't take a second person into the lounge. When I arrive at the airport in Buenos Aires, the contrast with Chile is immediate – it looks run-down, it no longer feels like Europe. We arrive at the Hilton Hotel, but Joanna has only booked one room by mistake and the hotel is fully booked. We book the Sheraton instead, but it's not so easy to get a cab. They order one for us at the Hilton and explain why it takes 40 minutes – in the very heart of downtown Buenos Aires. The cab that picks us up is so small that we have to stow some of our luggage in the passenger seat and on the back seat, and it's probably the oldest and most run-down car I've ever been in – but the driver is pleasant, which I suppose is the most important thing. I already noticed in Chile that Joanna doesn't order normal cabs or hail them from the street, she always uses ride-hailing services (similar to Uber). Why doesn't she just take a normal cab? "I do it automatically because I know from Mexico that normal cabs aren't always safe." On the way, we see "for hire" signs on every store. Not a good sign for the economic situation of a country.

Argentina holds a sad record. No country in the world has declined so dramatically in the last 100 years as Argentina. In the early twentieth century, the average per capita income of the population was among the highest in the world. The expression "riche comme un argentin" – rich as an Argentinean – was commonly heard at the time.[37]

In the late nineteenth and early twentieth centuries, Argentina's per

---

37 Rieckenberg, 110.

capita income exceeded that of Italy, Japan or France. As Axel Kaiser writes: "In 1895, it even achieved the highest per-capita income worldwide, according to some estimates. Moreover, Argentina's 6 percent annual GDP growth for the 43 years preceding World War I is the largest in recorded history. Argentina's impressive economic performance was not based on the export of raw materials alone: between 1900 and 1914, the country's industrial production tripled, reaching a level of industrial growth similar to that of Germany and Japan. All of this was accompanied by unprecedented social progress. In 1869, between 12 and 15 percent of Argentina's economically active population belonged to the middle class; by 1914, this number had reached 40 percent. At the same time, illiteracy was reduced to less than half of the population."[38]

However, this success story was followed by a hundred years of unprecedented decline. The ratio between real GDP per capita in 2018 and that in 1913 shows that Argentina's ratio has barely risen and is the lowest of all countries for which data are available for both years.[39] Argentina's dramatic economic descent is closely associated with one name: Colonel Juan Domingo Perón, who was born in 1895 in the small town of Lobos in the province of Buenos Aires. In the military government that ruled Argentina at the time, he served as head of the State Secretariat for Labor and Social Affairs. He forged a name for himself as Minister of War and was appointed Vice President of the country in July 1944. Perón gained renown for his "social" policies, which greatly expanded the influence of the state. He was elected president in February 1945 and his first term lasted until 1955.

His political agenda: big government. Argentina's telephone company was nationalized, its railways, its energy supply, its private radio. Between 1946 and 1949 alone, government spending tripled. The number of public-sector employees rose from 243,000 in 1943 to 540,000 in 1955. Many new jobs were created in government agencies and in the civil service to provide for

---

38 Kaiser, "The Roar of the Argentinian Lion," https://www.discoursemagazine.com/p/the-roar-of-the-argentinian-lion.
39 Mitchell, https://freedomandprosperity.org/2019/blog/big-government/argentina-and-the-grim-consequences-of-democratic-socialism/.

the supporters of Perón's Workers' Party.[40] His economic policy was typically socialist: although railway passenger and freight volumes stagnated, the number of employees increased by more than 50 percent between 1945 and 1955. The Perónist trade unions became the most powerful organizations in Argentina alongside the military. Perón's wife, Eva Duarte, was worshipped like a heroine, dispensing money on social welfare hand over fist. She died at the age of 32, but went on to become a global icon thanks to Andrew Lloyd Webber's musical and the global hit "Don't Cry for me Argentina."

Military dictatorships and Perónist governments replaced each other, and Argentina sank further and further into debt. In 1973, Perón came to power for a third time, and again his agenda consisted of redistribution and strong state regulation. From 1976 to 1983, Argentina was ruled by the military, who brutally persecuted all members of the opposition. Some were even drugged and thrown out of planes into the sea. Economically, Argentina's history is a story of inflation, hyperinflation, state bankruptcies and impoverishment. Since its independence in 1816, the country has declared bankruptcy seven times, most recently in 2001.

A tragic story for such a proud country that was once one of the richest in the world. So, how did all this come to happen and what is the current economic situation in Argentina?

On May 22, I meet Professor Iván Carrino. We want to have dinner together, but in order to talk in peace, I rent a room in the hotel so that we can talk to each other undisturbed. I like Iván straight away. The 36-year-old studied business and graduated with a MSc. in Austrian Economics in Madrid and then went on to obtain a second degree in Applied Economics at the Universidad del CEMA in Buenos Aires. Today he is Professor of History of Economic Theory at the Universidad de Buenos Aires and is about to take up a post as Associate Researcher at Universidad del Desarrollo in Chile. He also runs a consultancy firm.

In his youth he was particularly influenced by Ayn Rand; today it is Hayek and von Mises that he most admires. He is frequently invited to appear

---

40 Rieckenberg, 148–149.

on television programs to discuss the current economic situation and has published several books and hundreds of newspaper articles.

Carrino points out that Argentina's turn for the worse began even before Perón, with roots stretching all the way back to the 1930s. Trade was increasingly regulated and Argentina relied more and more on protectionism – industrialization through import substitution was the watchword. "Protectionism was one of the main sources of our country's economic decline," says Professor Carrino.

In the 1990s, as in many countries at the time, the government of Carlos Menem introduced free-market reforms. However, the incredibly high national debt and constant debt crises repeatedly undid everything. At 90 percent of GDP, Argentina's national debt is lower than that of some countries that are not experiencing so many difficulties (Italy, Japan), but due to frequent payment problems and state bankruptcies, investors have no confidence in the Argentinian state – which means that Argentina has to pay very high interest rates when it takes on new national debt.

Savers not only suffer from soaring inflation, they also have no confidence in the state. In 2002, banks paid pesos (which had just lost most of their value) to savers with dollar accounts. Anyone who had saved 1,000 dollars received 1,000 pesos – equivalent to a paltry 250 US dollars. No wonder billions are flowing abroad. And no wonder Argentinians say they prefer to put their money under their mattresses rather than in the bank.

When I ask Professor Carrino which three reforms would be most important for Argentina today, he says: "A hard money plan against inflation; zero deficit policy achieved by spending cuts; opening of the economy, both locally (deregulation) and internationally (reduction of trade barriers)."

On the same day, I speak to Eduardo Marty, who has been fighting against the tide of popular opinion and advocating capitalism in Latin America for decades. He says that Juan Bautista Alberdi and Faustino Domingo Sarmiento developed a great constitution for Argentina in 1852/53, which was significantly influenced by the philosophy of the U.S. constitution. The major problem, however, is that people in Latin America traditionally follow the wrong ideals. Pope Francis, who comes from Argentina and preaches anti-capitalism, is typical. There is a deep tradition in South America of condemning trade and holding the government, the army and the church in high esteem. Sacrificing oneself for the state or the army, glorifying poverty and condemning wealth are all cultural traits that are particularly pronounced in Latin America.

In 1991, Marty founded "Junior Achievement Argentina," an organization designed to teach entrepreneurship to young people. By 2018, it had reached one million young people, who were taught how to start a business. Today, he runs *Fundación para la Responsabilidad Intelectual*, which offers digital courses on economics and philosophy from a libertarian perspective. I arrange to meet him again in Buenos Aires in November 2023 and he invites me to a book launch.

I then meet Fausto Spotorno, Chief Economist at *Centro de Estudios Económicos* of the consultancy firm OJF. He shows me an impressive statistic, according to which Argentina has almost constantly experienced double-digit inflation rates since 1945 – with the exception of the 1990s, when Carlos Menem pegged the currency to the dollar, thereby eliminating inflation for a decade but negatively impacting exports as Argentine goods were no longer competitive.

I come to understand the true meaning of inflation when I pay for the hotel. I don't want to pay with my Visa card – that's something only people who don't have a clue would seriously consider: when you pay with a credit card, you pay the official exchange rate from the peso to the dollar or euro. However, you can get twice as many pesos for a dollar on the open market. This is known as the Blue Dollar, Dollar Blue or unofficial dollar and refers to the parallel exchange rate of the dollar in Argentina, which is the cost of buying and selling a physical dollar bill on the market.

The authorities tolerate the existence of so-called "*cuevos*" (literally, caves), where you can go to exchange dollars or euros into local currency. On the street you are frequently approached by people known as "*arbolitos*" (Spanish for little trees), who show you the way to one of the many *cuevos*.

Officially, these are pawn shops or places where you can buy and sell jewelry or gold, but in fact they are clandestine Blue Dollar trading houses.

Argentines use these *cuevos* to exchange pesos for dollars in the hope of getting even more pesos for their dollars a few weeks or months later. In a country with such rampant inflation, money has lost its function as a store of value and only serves as a means of payment. However, this is not always easy. You can't always get large denomination bills in the *cuevos*. Only about a fifth of the 250,000 pesos that Joanna and I have to pay for four days at the Sheraton in Buenos Aires are in thousands. The rest comes in small banknotes. At the hotel, it takes more than two hours to pay. I ask why they don't use their bill counting machine. I realize it's because they first have to check the authenticity of every single banknote with a special pen and then count the money by hand. Once they are finished with the lengthy process of counting the bills by hand, they eventually run the money through the bill counter. I don't have the patience for all of this and am exasperated after 15 minutes. I'm glad Joanna keeps an eye on them throughout.

I meet a local politician in Buenos Aires, Marina Kienast. She believes the country's problems are largely the result of over-mighty trade unions. As a politician, she is responsible for education and bemoans the fact that teacher training courses are essentially determined by the trade unions, which means they are extremely left-wing. Trotskyists, she explains, are particularly strong, and one of the unions is completely dominated by them.

She is upset by the fact that the state constantly promises "free" services. She introduced a bill to prohibit the state from describing services as "free." The text is short: "If the terms 'free,' 'free of charge,' 'gratis,' or similar are used in official announcements, advertising, election campaigns, cultural events or lectures that refer to goods and services provided by the state, it must be made clear that the expenditure to provide them is financed by taxpayers' money. This clarification must be made in the same medium in which the original claim was made. Anyone who does not comply with these provisions may be reported for violating their responsibilities as a public official."

Of course, her proposed bill didn't get a majority, but I liked the idea. When I published it on my X account (formerly Twitter) my post got almost 2,000 likes in a matter of just a few hours. Every conversation I have in Argentina switches to Javier Milei at some point, and this one is no exception. Although Marina Kienast belongs to a different party, she confirms that he has succeeded in winning the support of lots of young voters, especially those who used to be on the left.

My next interview takes me to Congress for a meeting with the MP Ricardo Hipólito López Murphy. I visit him in the parliamentary building. It looks beautiful from the outside. But in the adjoining building, where the MPs sit, everything is dilapidated. The MPs' rooms are extremely small, everything is worn out and shambolic, and the toilets smell worse than many train station restrooms. The 70-year-old López Murphy is sitting in one of these tiny rooms. An economist by profession, he served as Minister of Defense and of the Economy during Fernando De La Rúa's presidency. Since 2021, he has been chairman of the Republicanos Unidos party, which he founded in 2020 and which is part of the JTC Juntos por el Cambio (Cambiemos) alliance. He was also Chairman of the Liberal Network for Latin America, an association of institutions promoting classic liberal ideas. Today, he is chairman of the think tank Republican Civic Foundation.

What would López Murphy do if he were in charge in Argentina? Above all, he would fight protectionism and dismantle the country's extensive rules and regulations (for example, in the labor market). Today, companies with 200 or more employees are forced to sell some of their products at prices set by the state. This is a major problem that Murphy and others are addressing. In addition, due to high tax rates, the informal economy, i.e. illicit employment, is quite large, he says. According to López Murphy, it is estimated that more people work illicitly than in official employment relationships.

A major problem, López Murphy continues, is the lack of trust in the country among domestic and foreign investors. For example, Argentina has the second largest gas reserves in the world, but is forced to import gas. Why? Because no foreign company is interested in investing in a country that has repeatedly seized assets from oil and gas companies in the past. Another example of a lack of trust: it is said that probably no other country outside the United States has so many dollar bills – buried in gardens or hidden elsewhere. No-one trusts the banks. People only use banks because they need them to process payments – nobody in Argentina leaves their money with banks. López Murphy thinks things will have to get worse before they get better. An opinion I often hear these days. Nevertheless, he is optimistic because free market ideas are stronger in various parties than ever before in Argentina.

López Murphy is considered one of the figureheads of the libertarian movement in Argentina, another high-profile libertarian is José Luis Espert. The 60-year-old looks much younger, and I only believe his age when he shows me his ID card. He is also an economist and holds libertarian views. He has been a member of parliament in the province of Buenos Aires for the Avanza Libertad coalition since 2021. "We need a capitalist revolution," he tells me. And he is optimistic. "Libertarian ideas are exploding in Argentina," says Espert. What would he change if he could? First of all, he mentions the issue of "freedom of trade." He also believes that several corrupt trade union leaders should be put in prison to deter others. Milei and he were initially in the same party, but later fell out.

While I rest in my hotel, Joanna explores the city: "On Sunday, I went to Puerto Madero, a neighborhood near the banks of the Rio de la Plata, and one of the hippest barrios in Buenos Aires. There are good restaurants full of happy families spending time together, that was a highlight for me; the fact that people go out to have a great time together made me think about two things: first, we are Latino, so family and spending time with our loved ones is important. But secondly, we don't think so much about the future. Puerto Madero is very expensive compared to the country's economy, and staying there gives me the feeling that for Argentines, the moment, the now, is all that matters."

Joanna continues to tell me about her explorations in the city: "When I was walking on Avenida 9 de Julio, the biggest street in Buenos Aires, I saw the famous obelisk and really felt like I was in Buenos Aires. Later, I walked down Avenida Corrientes and had the best pizza in Buenos Aires, the oven has been in operation for over 100 years, about 50 people were waiting for a table. A few blocks further on I went to Broadway, there's a street full of theaters, young and old people go there – that made my heart beat faster, because I think that people who get involved in any kind of culture are one step closer to freedom."

On May 24, we fly to Corrientes – the province is named after its capital, which is home to 400,000 people. In a large country like Argentina, with such a diverse range of cities, it is not enough only to visit the capital. The city of Corrientes reminds me of the south of France and is home to palm trees and one of the largest rivers in the world. In fact, it is so large, it looks more like a sea. It's easy to imagine going on vacation here, especially as the city is considered safe – compared to other cities in Argentina.

Alberto Médina Mendez from the libertarian think tank *Club de la Libertad* picks us up from the airport. In his opinion, we will only be successful if we can convince people from other parties of the benefits of free-market ideas. Like Eduardo Tassano, the mayor of the city, who he introduces to me. Tassano is a urologist and practiced until just four years ago. In 2017, he was elected mayor for the first time. He won 45 percent the vote. In 2021 he stood for re-election and increased his share of the vote to 71 percent. You can tell that libertarian ideas are on the upswing when Tassano, who sees himself more as a social democrat, is asked what he would change in Argentina, first mentioning deregulation of the labor market and then tax cuts. Locally, his priorities include tourism and promoting IT companies and green environmental technology.

I then visit the *Camara de Diputados* (Chamber of Deputies) and meet President Pedro Cassani. "Even a few years ago, it was difficult to call yourself a libertarian, You were considered an outsider. The debate has changed. Today, everything revolves around the question of more market or more state," he says.

Pedro Braillard Poccard, the deputy governor of Corrientes, explains to me what is going wrong in Argentina. The Paraná River, one of the longest rivers in the world at almost 2,500 miles, flows right through the city: "You see a lot of boats on the river, but none are flying the Argentine flag. Many fly the flag of Paraguay. It's because of the excessive labor market regulations in Argentina." After we have spoken for a while, Poccard takes me to parliament, where, surprisingly, only children are sitting today. Tomorrow is National Day and the children are being shown around the Chamber of Deputies. I'm supposed to say a few words about why I'm here, but I'm afraid these young children won't be able to understand. So, I do a few push-ups on the floor, show off my biceps and tell the children that they should exercise every day. My impromptu performance even makes it into the local newspaper.

On May 27, I fly to San Miguel de Tucumán, the capital of the Tucumán province in the northwest of Argentina. The wider metropolitan area is home to around 800,000 inhabitants. My first impression is terrifying. Crumbling buildings everywhere I look, flaking plaster, signs saying "for rent" or "for sale." In a word: poverty. It looks like a very poor developing country. At first, I think maybe the buildings on the way from the airport to the hotel are not typical, but later I see that it looks like this almost everywhere, even downtown. In keeping with everything else I see, the "best" hotel in town, a Hilton, is far below the quality you would normally associate with the chain's other hotels.

I have been invited to Tucumán by the libertarian think tank *Fundación Federalismo y Libertad*, which was founded in the city in 2012. It is supported by around 50 entrepreneurs, all of whom have realized that they need to get involved in politics. The think tank has attracted some attention with investigative research into provincial government spending. *Fundación Federalismo y Libertad*, or *FyL* for short, is committed to an open society, a stable republican system and the strengthening of the private sector. *FyL* has a training division, two research centers and an event program that offers activities in various cities across Argentina. In recent years, *FyL* has expanded its programs and is now even active in the U.S.

I am invited to dinner at the villa of a successful entrepreneur. Miguel

Mitre became rich with buses and mines and now promotes the think tank. His villa is in a gated community with security guards and access restrictions. Naturally, the hosts are a little surprised that I don't want to eat meat, but they have prepared delicious vegetarian dishes and offer me milk, my favorite drink.

While I am here, I meet close confidantes from Javier Milei's inner circle. Before going on to study economics, Milei used to play as a goalkeeper for the Chacarita Juniors soccer club. He later served as a chief economist at private financial consulting firms and as a government advisor. In 2021, Milei was elected to represent the city of Buenos Aires in the *Cámara de Diputados de la Nación Argentina* as the *La Libertad Avanza* party scored 17 percent of the vote. Milei's greatest supporters, his aides tell me, are predominantly young, poor and male. Desperate, needy people are more likely to support socialists and call for bigger government – or line up behind right-wing extremists. Poor people who are in favor of more capitalism, like here? I think that's great.

Milei attracted a lot of attention by launching a lottery: anyone who registers via social media can win Milei's final monthly salary as a congressman. That's 350,000 pesos, equivalent to about 1,800 US dollars in May 2022. Considering the average income in Argentina is around 60,000 pesos, it is an attractive sum. In the three months since he announced he was raffling off his last pay check, two million Argentines signed up for the lottery, with which Milei hopes to prove: "I didn't go into politics for the money." Anyone who enters the lottery is asked to give their email address and telephone number. My first thought is that this is a very cheap way for Milei to get hold of data for campaign advertising. Milei's supporters, however, assure me that they will only use the data for the lottery. Either way, it's a very effective marketing idea.

I was impressed by the work this think tank is doing, and especially by the courses on entrepreneurship it offers young people. While I'm in Tucumán, I give a lecture to an audience of around 70, most of whom are probably in their early 20s. The big problem: for decades, many Argentines have become used to getting everything from the government – ideally for free. I ask a young man in the front row if he has a girlfriend. No, he doesn't, he says, but he'd like one. I ask him, "And who do you think will bring you this pretty girlfriend? The government? The state?" He laughs, "Of course not." I follow up by asking, "Who is responsible for getting you a girlfriend?" "I am," he says. And I say: "It's not just like that with your girlfriend, it's like that with all important things in life. The state won't give them to you, you have to take care of them yourself."

I encourage my young audience by telling them that they have already taken the first major step toward taking control of their lives by coming to my lecture today and enrolling in the think tank's courses. And, I think to myself, it's all the more impressive that they've managed to do both of those things in this city – a city that I'm honestly glad to be leaving.

Before I leave, I have lunch with Juan Pablo Bustos Thames, a successful lawyer and investor, who also drives us to the airport. I tell him that over the last few days I have encountered so much optimism from supporters of the libertarian movement, all of whom believe that their moment will soon come. I would like to share their optimism, but I am skeptical: "Even if Milei wins the elections next year, will Argentines have the patience for his reforms to work? After all, he'll need much more than just six weeks or six months to fix what has been going wrong in Argentina for 70 or 80 years." Bustos Thames' answer is clear: they won't have that patience. Nor did they have it in the four years 2015 to 2019, when the reformer Mauricio Macri ruled. "Argentinians have no patience with non-Peronist governments."

I was perhaps most impressed by a meeting I had with three young women in Buenos Aires at the end of May. They belong to LOLA, *Ladies for Libertad*. Valentina is 21 years old but looks younger. She speaks fluent English (although she has never lived in an English-speaking country) and comes across as very confident. She is from the city of Mendoza and started her own recycling company at the age of 13, which she officially founded at the age of 18. In the company's early days, she had a tough time: "Robbers came to my company every day to take things from me. I called the police and the criminals were put in jail for a few hours and then released. The police wouldn't protect me. And with such high taxation, the state takes away almost everything I earn." And she certainly doesn't like the mentality of so many of her compatriots, who would rather live off the state than work themselves. "It's so difficult to find employees," she complains.

That's how she gravitated to the libertarians. At 17, she joined Students for Liberty. At 19, she founded her own libertarian group, which quickly grew to 25 members, many of whom came because they did not agree with the government's Covid policies: "We had a seven-month lockdown – you were only allowed to leave the house for three hours on certain days to go shopping." Opposing these measures raised the profile of her group.

The group meets in apartments or restaurants and compares, for example, Marx's Communist Manifesto with Hayek's *Path to Serfdom*. It is a women's group and its members describe themselves as "libertarian feminists," in contrast to traditional feminists, who are mostly Marxist. Their hero is Javier Milei.

Adriana is 27 years old. She fled Venezuela because she was sentenced to prison after protesting against the socialist regime. She studied law in Venezuela, but works as an IT programmer in Buenos Aires. She became political when her sister and brother-in-law were jailed for their part in the protests. Her parents fled to Peru to escape the economic catastrophe in Venezuela and Adriana now lives in Buenos Aires, where she is also involved in LOLA. I realize that in the same way as it is considered cool for young people to be green in many Western countries, here it is cool to be a libertarian.

Of course, the political scientist, politician and author Christian Moreno, who knows Milei very well, tells me that some people see him as a messiah and hope he will solve all their problems without really understanding the content of his ideas. "That's why we have to work above all on spreading the ideas."

At a lecture I give to leading political and business figures in the exclusive Jockey Club in Buenos Aires, which was founded as long ago as 1882, I meet Lars-André Richter from the German Friedrich Naumann Foundation, who invited me. Richter's partner is López Murphy. For Richter, Argentina's main problem is its bloated public service sector, which is full of employees collecting a monthly salary but not doing any work. Juan Manuel Agüero worked for the Naumann Foundation in Argentina for ten years and is now a political advisor. He mentions the name of Patricia Bullrich, who was Minister of Security under Macri and is leader of the Pro party. She had the courage to take consistent action against the so-called "Piqueteros," the extremist groups that block the roads to draw attention to their poor economic conditions. The politicians before her mostly pursued a policy of appeasement towards these groups, but she took a clear stance against the blockades and also deployed the police. This earned Bullrich, who was part of the left-wing extremist Montonero movement in her youth, a lot of sympathy from the population. Later, in October 2023, she was scheduled to run against Milei in the presidential election and then supported him in the runoff.

May 2022
Asunción, Paraguay

On May 25, we travel from the Argentine city of Corrientes to Paraguay with Alberto, a representative of a libertarian think tank. On the way we see idyllic landscapes and a lot of cattle (which, as a vegetarian, I of course feel a little sorry for because they are all intended for consumption). There are complications at the border because the border officials claim that an Egyptian wanted by the police has the same first and last name as me.

Endless columns of trucks want to go in the opposite direction, towards Argentina. The border is extremely dirty and neglected – just like you see in films about third world countries. In Asunción, the capital of Paraguay, we spend an age stuck in a traffic jam. The roads are in a miserable condition, there are potholes everywhere. This is because the companies that build the roads are the same companies that have fixed contracts with the ministry to repair them. The more often they are broken, the more the companies earn – and presumably the officials in the ministries too.

The buses are hopelessly outdated and just as hopelessly overcrowded. I learn that there is a "bus mafia" that has secured lucrative contracts with state guarantees. They effectively have a monopoly, buying the oldest, most dilapidated buses from Argentina and raking in huge profits. When the city began negotiating with a foreign company that promised modern buses, the bus mafia threatened a "strike" that would have crippled the entire city for weeks.

We arrive just in time for a lunch hosted by Carsten Pfau, a German entrepreneur who emigrated to Paraguay 25 years ago and who owns 40 companies here, including Agri Terra. He is one of the largest cattle owners in Paraguay and runs the largest greenhouse complex for fruit and vegetable cultivation in the country.

At lunch I meet an economist who was formerly Minister of the Economy in Paraguay. An intelligent man who studied in the United States. I ask him what three things he would change in Paraguay. Among other things, he thinks that taxes should be reduced. I'm always in favor of tax cuts, but I don't quite understand the demand in a country with a top tax rate of 10 percent. He says that in reality the tax burden is 30 percent because you have to pay around 20 percent for various services. He would therefore be in favor of reducing taxes to 1 (!) percent.

Paraguay is a great place for entrepreneurs, as Carsten Pfau's story confirms. He is one of the most respected people in the country and has invited the most important politicians and business leaders to my lecture this afternoon. The most beautiful woman in the group is Pfau's wife, a former Miss Paraguay. She now organizes beauty competitions herself, but has also taken over the management of her husband's companies. The second most beautiful woman I immediately notice in the audience is the mayor's wife.

I ask Pfau what he finds particularly positive and negative about Paraguay. The low taxes are positive. The official tax rate for corporate profits is 10 percent; if the profits are distributed as dividends, an additional 7 percent is added. There are also quite generous write-offs, so that the tax burden at the end of the day is pleasingly low.

The light-touch regulation of business activities is also positive: "Whatever is not expressly prohibited is generally permitted," says Pfau. "Refreshing compared to Germany, where it's more of the opposite."

The country offers huge potential. "You can still make (excessive) profits with businesses that only allow small margins in other countries. Typically for developing countries, it's still possible to achieve very high returns here. According to the UN report, there is an average return on investment of 22 percent in Paraguay." Pfau is planning to build the biggest hotel in the city and have it operated by a renowned chain, but also wants to sell condominiums on the upper floors – with optional hotel services.

Despite all the opportunities, there is a lot of room for improvement in the country. Large sections of the population work informally. It is difficult to say just how widespread this is, but it is quite likely that between half and three quarters of the population work in the shadow economy. "This sometimes makes it more difficult for legally compliant companies to operate," says Pfau. There are also major deficits in state agencies. "The authorities and the police work very slowly and often completely inefficiently," explains Pfau. "The Paraguayan Land Registry is an example. The office is hopelessly overburdened: it sometimes takes two or three years until a property is re-parceled, simple changes can take several months to a year."

It is a paradox: on the one hand, government in Paraguay is weak because it fails to provide basic services and, when it does provide them, they are provided poorly. On the other hand, it is bloated when you consider that around 300,000 civil servants are supported by only 600,000 net taxpayers – and this in a country with 7.5 million inhabitants. At least that's what the former economics minister explained to me over lunch.

You can't rely on the police. An entrepreneur like Pfau has hired five security guards, which costs him about 2,000 US dollars a month. In front of his house we see a security guard with a gun, and our car is constantly followed by another car occupied by Pfau's mobile security team.

Despite these shortcomings, Paraguay is a country that offers massive opportunities. This is also what I am told by the people I meet in more highly developed, more European-looking Uruguay, which I visit the next day. They admire the recovery that Paraguay has made. The country doesn't offer the same quality of life as Uruguay, they say, but it does offer far greater opportunities for entrepreneurs.

I only have a single day in Paraguay this time around, but I promise to come back to get to know the country better. I have a full program: after lunch, I give a talk about my book to leading business and political figures, followed immediately by a recording of a talk show on one of Pfau's television channels. Then I have to sleep for an hour (in the very good Sheraton Hotel, by the way) before I get ready to appear on the country's most popular talk show at 10:30 p.m. I only have three hours of sleep that night because Uruguay is on the agenda the next morning.

May 2022
Montevideo, Uruguay

On the drive from the airport to the hotel, I experience a different world than the one I have seen over the last few days. Cleanly-cut lawns everywhere and well-kept houses that look like they would be perfectly at home in any German city. The contrast to Argentina and Paraguay could hardly be bigger, I feel like I'm back in Europe. In Uruguay, even before I arrive, the libertarian think tank CED (*Centro de Estudios para el Desarrollo*) has arranged an interview with the country's leading daily newspaper, *El País*, and another interview has also been arranged, this time on television.

My main message in both interviews is this: Uruguay is already the second most economically free country in Latin America. According to the 2022 Index of Economic Freedom, Uruguay is only 4.4 points behind Chile, which is currently the most economically free country in Latin America. In the interviews, I predict that Chile will continue to slip down the index (in fact, Chile was only 0.9 points ahead of Uruguay in the 2023 index). Unfortunately, Chile has strayed from the capitalist path with the election of the socialist Gabriel Boric. Uruguay should seize this opportunity and position itself as the economically freest country in Latin America, thereby strengthening its appeal to investors. This requires further free-market reforms, i.e. tax cuts, privatization and deregulation. It is good that the current government is striving for a free trade agreement with the U.S. and China; that is also a step forward.

Uruguay already has some very good news to share. According to Transparency International, Uruguay is perceived as the least corrupt country in Latin America. Scoring 71 out of 100 points, it even ranks ahead of the U.S. and Chile, which are both tied on 67 points. For comparison, socialist Venezuela is perceived as the most corrupt country in the region on just 15 points. Uruguay is also in a very good 15th place in the *Economist's* Democracy Index (2020), ahead of Chile (17th). This confirms Uruguay as the most democratic country in Latin America.

Since March 1, 2020, the country's president has been Luis Alberto Lacalle Pou, the son of former president Luis Alberto Lacalle Herrera. Luis Lacalle Pou is a member of the *Partido Nacional* and the representatives of the libertarian think tank in Uruguay who invited me to lunch describe him as libertarian – although he has been forced to make some compromises because he is in a coalition with a "right-wing" party whose economic policies could be more accurately described as socialist. Luis Lacalle Pou wanted to privatize oil and gas companies, but failed due to resistance from his coalition partner.

At lunch I meet a number of people, including the economist Isabelle Chaquiriand, Dean of the *Facultad de Ciencias Empresariales en Universidad Católica del Uruguay*, and Agustín Iturralde, Director of the libertarian think tank *Centro de Estudios para el Desarrollo*. They have high hopes of the libertarian president and see a tremendous need for reform. They believe that heightened levels of protectionism hinder economic development and are particularly damaging for Uruguay. The main problem, according to the people I speak to, is that the dominant mentality in Uruguay is distinctly social-democratic in nature. Gas, oil, water and electricity are in state hands, termination of employment rules are too strong, and the unions have too much influence.

If Uruguay continues to strengthen its commitment to a market economy, it could attract entrepreneurs and wealthy people from other Latin American countries who value the additional security the country offers. One of the richest Argentines, Marcos Eduardo Galperín, whose fortune is estimated at 6.6 billion US dollars, has recently moved to Uruguay. He earned his wealth with the company he founded, MercadoLibre S.A. ("free market"), a multinational corporation modeled on eBay and Amazon.

June 2022
São Paulo, Brazil

On June 1, 2022, I fly from Buenos Aires to São Paulo. After the frequently uncomfortable planes in Latin America, a first-class seat on a Swiss Air plane feels good. The head of the think tank *Instituto Liberal*, Lucas Berlanza, picks me up from the airport. A young man, 28 years old, nearly always wearing sunglasses. We already knew each other from Zoom calls and he put me in touch with the publisher who released my book, *The Power of Capitalism*, in Brazil. He has also written several books himself, including one that highlights the differences between various libertarian thinkers such as Hayek, Friedman, Ayn Rand, and more. I ask him how he got involved in the libertarian movement:

"I would say that I have always been averse to leftist ideas, even when I was in school, mainly due to my spiritual convictions, which preceded my political convictions. However, my most consistent theoretical engagement with the tradition originating from classical liberalism occurred through the Internet, between the end of the 2000s and the beginning of the 2010s. I belong to a generation that congregated in virtual communities in Brazil to explore alternative literature to the prevailing left-wing ideologies in academia, journalism, and government. In 2014, while still a journalism student, I attempted to publish an article about Carlos Lacerda, an anti-communist Brazilian politician inspired by German Christian democracy and the so-called 'social market economy.' The article was rejected without justification, despite it being Lacerda's centenary, while works on North American comic books, for example, were accepted. I managed to publish it at the *Instituto Liberal*, the oldest organization in Brazil with the mission of promoting the agenda of freedom, founded in 1983."

Lucas continued to write articles for to the institute's website, becoming a member of staff in 2015 and its president in 2018. I ask him for his take on developments in Brazil. It is not easy for libertarians, he explains, because opinions of Jair Bolsonaro (he was still president at the time, but lost to his left-wing opponent Lula in October 2022) tend to vary widely. Some people see him as a sociopath and a dangerous politician, others take a less negative view. Lucas has a differentiated view. Most libertarians in Brazil viewed the then Economics Minister Paulo Guedes, who has a clear free-market profile, positively. But has he achieved anything? Lucas says there has been some deregulation, but little or no progress on taxation and privatization. This was also because Guedes did not have a majority in parliament and the other parties blocked his attempted reforms.

When I arrive at the Sheraton Hotel in São Paulo, there are thermoses of warm milk and chamomile tea in my room. This was organized by Joanna, who knows what I like to drink. I have already said goodbye to her and thanked her for everything she has done for me during my time in Latin America. Without her, my trip would not have been anywhere near as great a success.

The Sheraton in São Paulo is also a pleasant surprise. Unlike in some hotels, where you meet hotel employess who start off by explaining in detail exactly why they can't help you, here my small requests are immediately fulfilled: from a multiple port plug adapter and desk lamp, to a plaster and disinfectant because I slightly injured my foot two weeks ago and the wound hasn't completely healed yet.

The next morning it's time to have breakfast alone. At the buffet I see a beautiful American woman with Indian roots. Of course, I sit down with her and breakfast lasts an hour and a half instead of 15 minutes (if I had stayed alone) – she later visits me in Berlin.

A few days before I arrived I had given an interview to the most historic and respected newspaper in Brazil, *O Estãdo de S. Paulo*. José Fucs, the most prominent free-market journalist in Brazil, conducted the interview, which appears in time for my arrival. I point out that Brazil still ranks very poorly in the Heritage Foundation's economic freedom rankings – and the ranking has not really improved in the past five years. Fucs takes a more positive view and says there have been some successful privatizations. I'll be giving many more interviews over the next few days – my book is also generating a lot of interest in Brazil.

The next day I meet 20 representatives of *Rede Liberdade* (the Freedom Network), a loose association of think tanks in Brazil, including *Instituto Liberal, Instituto Mises Brasil, Liderancas Nas Escolas, Instituto de Formação de Líderes, Instituto Millenium,* and *Instituto Liberdade.* I meet Tom Palmer from the Atlas Network again. He estimates that there are around 6,000 active members of libertarian think tanks in Brazil. Why are there so many different organizations? Palmer: "As market economists, we believe in competition. It's a friendly competition, but we are united by the same goal." Rodrigo Marinho from *Mises Brasil* explains to me that this is the difference to the U.S., where libertarian think tanks are deeply divided. Here in Brazil, he explains, they enjoy a friendly, cooperative relationship and work together under the *Rede Liberdade* banner.

The network's big conference is taking place in São Paulo on June 3, 2022, with a line-up of prominent speakers. Among the invitees is the former Argentine President Mauricio Macri (2015 to 2019). I have heard a lot about him, but didn't manage to meet him while I was in Argentina. His lecture is dull – as is that of Michel Temer, the former President of Brazil (2016-2018). When a participant asks Macri what he would do differently today in comparison to the four years of his presidency, he can't think of anything. But how can you do better if you don't learn from the mistakes of the past? Thatcher and Reagan were both re-elected for second terms because they pushed on with even bolder reforms. Macri was voted out after his first term.

I prefer Salim Mattar's introductory words. The entrepreneur, whose net worth is estimated at three to four billion US dollars, is the owner of the largest car rental business in Latin America (and No. 4 in the U.S.). He uses the word "capitalism" at least 20 times in his speech. This is a contrast to the libertarian event in Warsaw, where I never heard the word used even once. To me, this is a sign that many libertarians have allowed themselves to be pushed onto the defensive. They believe that if they use more pleasant-sounding words, such as "liberalism," things will be easier. That would be nice. But unfortunately, it's not the word that bothers most people, but what the word "capitalism" actually means.

What surprised me previously in Chile is confirmed in Brazil: the similarity of the issues we have to deal with both here in Latin America and in Europe and the U.S. One focus of the conference is free speech, which is also seriously under threat in Brazil. Political scientist Fernando Schüler says that people are constantly afraid to express their opinions freely. In Brazil, the threat comes from the Supreme Court, which has repeatedly convicted people for making certain statements, sometimes even sentencing them to several months in prison. The statements in question are indeed more than worthy of criticism, but the danger is that you start by condemning extreme speech and that leads to freedom of speech being increasingly stifled as the boundaries of what you are allowed to say become ever more restrictive. Hélio Beltrão from *Mises Brasil* expressly advocates that even the most absurd opinions should be freely expressed: "Then we can all see who's talking nonsense."

An example of cancel culture that is brought up in the discussion: a scientific study in Brazil has shown that women earn less because they are less confident and too modest about making salary demands. The study triggered a hysterical reaction. Apparently, it was claimed, the authors wanted to blame women themselves for being underpaid. Conclusion: any search for the causes of inequality that does not result in men getting the blame is fanatically rejected, and anyone who tries to take a differentiated view is walking into a minefield.

I also speak at the conference and sign books afterwards. A great success – demand exceeds the number of copies delivered in advance. I say goodbye to Salim Mattar, who invites me to come back and, when I do, says I should visit him at his home. His assistant, who is looking after me during my stay, shows me some photos of his house. I've been in a lot of expensive villas, but never one like this.

Igor Matos, one of Salim Mattar's employees, takes me to the airport. Mattar is not only a successful entrepreneur, but was responsible for the privatization of state-owned companies under the Economy Minister Paulo

Guedes in 2019 and 2020. Igor also works in the *Secretaria Especial de Privatizações.*

He gives me a presentation showing that just a few years ago there were 698 state owned enterprises (SOEs) in Brazil, of which 46 were under direct state control, 164 were subsidiaries, 257 were affiliates (related companies) and 231 were minority holdings. This goes against the principles clearly set out in Article 173 of the Brazilian Federal Constitution, which states: "With the exception of the cases set forth in this Constitution, the direct exploitation of an economic activity by the State shall only be allowed whenever it is necessary to national security or to a relevant collective interest, as defined by law."

From January 2019 to February 2020, a start was made and companies worth about 135 billion Brazilian reals (27.6 billion US dollars) were privatized. A report to the OECD stated: "The federal government is divesting their direct and indirect stakes of SOEs. The divestments between January 2019 and February 2020 reached R$ 134.9 billions, though R$ 29.5 only in the first two months of this year. It includes surplus stakes in state-owned listed companies such as IRB and Banco do Brasil. The big five SOEs as being called BNDES, Petrobras, Eletrobras, Banco do Brasil and Caixa are revising their portfolios assets to focus on their core businesses."

But then the Covid crisis came along and the Brazilian President Jair Bolsonaro pursued catastrophic policies. The fight against the pandemic dominated and privatization stalled.

My visit to Latin America is drawing to an end. I have spent three weeks here, learned a lot and met so many fantastic people. In Argentina, I became acquainted with the strongest libertarian movement in the world. For me personally it was a huge success. Everywhere I went, leading daily newspapers reported on my visit and I gave a lot of television interviews, the highlight of which was the one-hour interview on Argentina's leading television station and the four-page interview in the leading Sunday newspaper *PERFIL*. I have promised to come back as soon as my next book is published in Spanish and Portuguese.

July 2022
Washington DC and Las Vegas, United States

I have never visited any country as often in my life as the United States. The first time was in October 1986, when I was invited by the German Studies Association, a renowned association of American scholars who study German history and politics, to give a lecture on my research on Adolf Hitler. Since I had no money to fly to America, my trip was paid for by the German Foreign Office. Not only was it the first time I flew to America, but it was the first time in my life that I had ever been on a plane. Back then, flying was still very expensive and as a university and doctoral student I had no money. I gave a presentation on the results of my doctoral thesis at a conference in Albuquerque, New Mexico.

Since then, I have been back to the U.S. again and again. I helped a friend who emigrated to the United States 30 years ago sell shares in his real estate company to a German bank. After just a few days of work, I earned a million dollars. In 2012, I bought two apartments in Manhattan (right opposite the Rockefeller Center), partly because I sometimes thought about emigrating to the U.S. myself at some point. I wanted to apply for a Green Card, but didn't because you have to file a U.S. tax return on your worldwide income.

I like Americans and can't stand German and French anti-Americanism. And I don't think much of the constant prophecies predicting the imminent end of the U.S. as the world's most important economic power. Despite all the problems, the number of U.S. companies among the 100 most valuable companies in the world in mid-2022 is 60. In contrast, only 16 come from Europe and not a single one is German.[41]

---

41 Tagesschau, "Deutsche Konzerne nicht mehr in Topliga," 03 July 2022: https://www.tagesschau.de/wirtschaft/kurse/top-firmen-boerse-wert-101.html.

I positively associate the United States with Ronald Reagan. In the intervening years since his presidency, the country has not had a better president, but there have been many bad ones. And for me, the U.S. is still the only country in which anyone can have an unprecedented career, as Arnold Schwarzenegger showed us: he came from a small village in Austria and went from bodybuilder to Hollywood star and governor of California.

However, there are also things I don't like about the U.S., above all the blind belief in rules and regulations and the rampant bureaucracy, which is often even worse than in Europe, and that's saying something. Just try debating with an American whether an obviously nonsensical and inappropriate rule makes sense or not. You have no chance.

When I buy an apartment in Germany, I sign a contract that runs to around 20 pages. When I bought my apartment in Manhattan, the hundreds of pages wouldn't even fit into a thick A4 binder. And the Home Owners' Association rejected my proof of assets from the bank because they were in euros and not dollars – for some Americans, anything that isn't exactly what they are used to in the U.S. must be wrong. I lost count of the number of times I was met with total incomprehension when I explained that I didn't have a social security number.

In July 2022 I fly to the U.S. for the first time since the Covid crisis, to present my first film *Life behind the Berlin Wall* at Freedom Fest in Las Vegas. How did this come about? It was all Bob Chitester's idea. In case you haven't heard the name yet, the *Wall Street Journal* called Bob Chitester "The Man who made Milton Friedman a Star."[42] Even without Chitester, Nobel Prize winner Friedman would also have been one of the most important economists of the twentieth century, but he and his ideas would never have achieved such a massive level of popularity. Chitester produced the world-famous television series *Free to Choose* with Friedman.

In November 2019, he invited me to a multi-day meeting at Milton Friedman's former summer residence *Capitaf* in the mountains of Vermont.

---

42 McGurn, https://www.wsj.com/articles/the-man-who-made-milton-friedman-a-star-11604073953.

At that time, he was already suffering from prostate cancer and knew that he would never recover. But he was full of energy and enthusiasm throughout the three days and we discussed how we could effectively spread the idea of capitalism in the modern world. Two British politicians introduced me to Chitester. He had read my book, *The Power of Capitalism*, and suggested turning it into a series, a *Free to Choose* for today. He died in May 2021, but his successor at the Free to Choose Network, Rob Chatfield, approached me and took up the idea. That is how the film project came about.

In October 2021, a film team from the U.S. traveled to Berlin to visit me. The team included Jim Taylor and his wife Barbara Potter. Two absolute professionals – Jim has been in the film business for four decades. We spent a whole week in Berlin and Leipzig, shooting from 8 a.m. until it got dark. The film is based on the third chapter of my book, *The Power of Capitalism*, which compares socialism and capitalism in East and West Germany. After all, East and West Germany had the same language, the same history and the same culture – just different economic systems. That all makes these two countries (along with North and South Korea) ideal candidates for any comparison of economic systems.

Before I flew to Las Vegas, I stopped in Washington D.C. I had been invited by my friend Andreas Hellmann, who I first met in 2019. I was in the U.S. at the time because I had been invited to be a panelist in a debate on capitalism at a conference held by the world's leading financial industry lobbying organization. I asked my friend Madsen Pirie, president of the Adam Smith Institute in London, who else I should meet while I was in Washington. He said I should definitely meet Grover Norquist, the founder of Americans for Tax Reform. Norquist welcomed me back then and I liked him straight away.

Andreas Hellmann, a German who is responsible for the association's foreign contacts, was there. He wrote me an email that same evening and invited me to dinner. Since then I have counted him as a friend, and in July he invited me to Washington D.C., to talk about the film before the Las Vegas festival.

After my lecture, I have dinner with Hellmann and Grover Norquist. Grover, a year older than me, looks younger than when we last met, has lost his beard and obviously does a lot of exercise. No-one in the U.S. has been as passionate about tax reduction and tax simplification over the last few decades as Grover Norquist. He is the initiator of the Taxpayer Protection Pledge, a written promise by legislators and candidates for office that commits them to oppose tax increases in any and all circumstances. In the run-up to the November 2012 election, the pledge was signed by 95 percent of all Republican members of Congress and by all candidates for the Republican presidential nomination, except one.

In the "Taxpayer Protection Pledge" legislators and candidates for office promise to "oppose any and all efforts to increase the marginal income tax rate for individuals and business; and to oppose any net reduction or elimination of deductions and credits, unless matched dollar for dollar by further reducing tax rates." Norquist's campaign has also been very successful in numerous states across the United States where taxes have been significantly reduced.

The next day, we attend Freedom Fest in Las Vegas. I arrive a day early and stay a day longer because I want to meet my girlfriend Alica there. She is traveling down from New York. I've never been to Las Vegas because I always associate the city with gaming and slot machines, which I don't like. I can't understand how people can feed money into a machine that is programmed to make them lose and still feel joy. Having said that, I didn't see any joy on the faces of the people sitting there at the slot machines. If anything, most of them looked tense and grim.

I don't spend any time in the casinos or arcades, but you can't escape them because they are everywhere, even the lobby of the Hotel Mirage, where I stay with Alica, is full of slot machines. It's not uncommon to see extremely overweight Americans who seem to sit at these machines for hours and watch as the small amount of money they have becomes even smaller.

When I travel alone, I don't need the biggest and best hotel rooms, but when I'm traveling with a girlfriend, I try to get something special. The organizer had booked a room for me, but I upgraded to a large suite at my own expense. I actually wanted the very best category with its own pool, but unfortunately that was already booked.

I like heat. Even when the thermometer hits 95 degrees Fahrenheit, I lie in the blazing sun from morning to evening and feel good. But here, for only the second time in my life (after Dubai), it is too hot even for me. 110 degrees is too hot for my taste. After half an hour in the sun, I have no choice but to move into the shade for a bit – only to lie down in the sun again afterwards. I burn my feet that first day because I stupidly walk around barefoot.

Freedom Fest in Las Vegas is an impressive event with 350 speakers and 2,500 attendees. On the first day of the conference, I happily meet Jim Rogers again. I met him twice a few years ago in Singapore, where the legendary investor now lives. Rogers made a great deal of money very early on as a so-called "contrarian" investor. Contrarians base their investment philosophy on swimming against the tide and pursue a countercyclical strategy. From 1973 to 1980, the value of the Quantum Fund portfolio, which he managed at the time with George Soros, increased by 4,200 percent, while the American S&P index rose by about 47 percent.

In 1980, Rogers decided to "retire" and traveled around the world on his motorcycle. He is in the Guinness Book of Records for traveling through 116 countries on his bike. He then traveled around the globe again, this time through 120 countries by car. I can't recommend his book, *Investment Biker*, highly enough.

Rogers has stuck to his philosophy. At Freedom Fest, he declares that he will continue to trade on the principle of buying panic and selling euphoria. His statement that he is currently betting on the dollar was a bit surprising to me. A few days earlier, the dollar had reached parity against the euro for the first time, so there was no sentiment against the dollar, quite the opposite. The dollar had gained significantly over the previous few months (to my delight, by the way, since more than a third of my portfolio is in US dollars).

At the conference, Jim Rogers explains that while he himself did not consider the dollar to be a safe haven by any means, that is precisely the view held by a majority of investors. This reminded me of the saying of the late

Hungarian-American investor André Kostolany, who died in 1999, and who spoke at a conference on countercyclical investments I attended shortly before his death: "In principle, you can only make money by swimming against the tide, but sometimes you have to play dumb and go with the crowd."

Roger's argument sounds similar: in uncertain times, the dollar gains because investors (wrongly, in his opinion) view the dollar as an anchor of stability. Therefore, he is betting that the dollar will continue to rise strongly. "But at some point there will be a huge dollar bubble, and I hope I'll notice the first signs of its collapse in time. That's when I'll sell the dollar." Rogers is not a fan of the euro, which he sees as an artificial currency that will eventually collapse.

Rogers believes that U.S. equities are highly overvalued, as are government bonds, which are experiencing the biggest bubble in history. In equities, he believes there are more opportunities in emerging markets, which have performed very poorly over the past 10 years. "Maybe there are opportunities in Uzbekistan or Cambodia," Rogers says, but he doesn't want that to be taken as an investment idea, but rather as an example that investors are more likely to find opportunities to buy cheap in markets that no-one else is interested in.

However, the most important advice Rogers gives investors is, "Don't listen to hot tips. Don't buy anything because some guru recommends it. Don't listen to anyone, including me. You need to understand for yourself exactly what you're doing. Which, unfortunately, many investors don't."

Inflation is a big topic everywhere right now, including at this conference. Steve Forbes, the Editor-in-Chief of *Forbes* magazine, which, among other things, publishes the annual list of the richest people in the world, spoke about inflation. The libertarian, who is himself worth around 430 million US dollars, distinguishes between two types of inflation: "Non-Monetary Inflation" and "Monetary Inflation." Non-Monetary Inflation is caused by external events, such as the current Ukraine war or supply chain bottlenecks. The state, he explains, should do nothing about this type of inflation because it disappears when the causes disappear. More serious, he says, is "Monetary Inflation," which is caused by central banks' monetary policies. Forbes is among the harshest critics of the Fed, which was still printing gigantic amounts of money even in 2021, when the economy had long since recovered.

Like many other libertarians, Forbes is a supporter of the gold standard: "The gold-based Bretton Woods monetary system that was created in the closing days of WWII and blown up on August 15, 1971 had worked remarkably well. Unfortunately, our political leaders and most economists back then didn't understand the basics of a gold-based system or how to manage it." In the event of inflation, Forbes explains, politicians and central bankers naturally deny any responsibility and look for scapegoats (e.g. large international oil companies) to blame.

Speakers repeatedly complained about the dominance of anti-capitalist attitudes in the mainstream U.S. media. One outlet that was singled out was *CNN*, which was subjected to repeated criticism. But, from time to time, the media achieves exactly the opposite of what they intended. One speaker tells us about a libertarian children's book, *The Tuttle Twins*, that *CNN* zeroed in on. From a sales graph, it was clear for all to see how sales soared after the negative *CNN* coverage. It's a nice example and shows that no-one should be overly afraid of adverse media coverage because sometimes – as in this example – it can even be very helpful.

On Thursday, July 14, 2022, the time has finally come and my film *Life Behind the Berlin Wall* has its premiere. I'm nervous about whether the film will attract a large enough audience because I've seen some screenings with only a couple dozen people in attendance. Of course, that would have been extremely frustrating, because after all, I came to Las Vegas primarily for the film's premiere. But my tension is unfounded. It is a huge success: the hall is full and the audience is thrilled. There are laughs when the audience hears that people in East Germany had to wait 12 to 17 years to get a Trabi, the iconic (and very basic) German car. The audience's engagement with the film is also reflected in the fact that no-one leaves the hall halfway through and most stay for the question and answer session afterwards, which lasts around 40 minutes. Several people, including the well-known journalist, John Fund, approach me afterwards and promise to do everything they can to publicize this film in the U.S. And before and after the film I am invited to give numerous live interviews with American media from the libertarian scene. When it's all over, I'm relieved and happy. But for me the work is far from over. The Free to Choose Network will show the film in schools up and down America. I, of course, also want it to be distributed worldwide. I therefore immediately contact my friends around the world to have the film's subtitles translated into as many languages as possible and to find ways to distribute the film in other countries (the film now has subtitles in 17 languages and, as of November 2024, has been viewed over 485,000 times).

In the front row at the film screening, I notice a man who, as he later tells me, is 115 cm (about 3 foot 9 inches) tall. I talk to him after the event because I immediately like him and because I am interested in successful people living with disabilities – I wrote the book, *Unbreakable Spirit. Rising Above All Odds,* on this very subject.

His name is Shawn T. Miller and he has a beard longer than Karl Marx's. Otherwise he has nothing in common with Marx. He is a professor of economics and a disciple of the Austrian School, a dedicated supporter of capitalism. He wrote the book, *Personal Economics: Economic Freedom and Work are Conducive to the Development of a Human Person.* Unfortunately, he received rejection after rejection from the publishers he approached and decided to self-publish the book. Among the many subjects it touches on, the book is about disabled people: "I am disabled and have learned some things that most economists don't know." We exchange email addresses and arrange to meet up the next day.

He tells me that he was born with osteogenesis imperfecta, a genetic disorder. Osteogenesis imperfecta means imperfect bone formation. People with this condition have bones that break easily, often from minor trauma or for no apparent reason at all. This happened to him repeatedly in his youth, but later his bones became stronger, although the deformities remained. I ask him how the disease affects life expectancy. "If you make it to my age," says the thinker, who was born in 1972, "you could live to be around 65."

Miller has decided not to take the easy route and adopt a "victim mentality," as so many other people facing adversity do today. No-one should feel like a victim, he agrees, but rather as shapers of their own destinies. I think we can learn a lot from successful people living with disabilities. I've got to know some of them, such as Erik Weihenmayer, who was the first blind person to climb Mount Everest and has conquered all of the Seven Summits, the highest mountains on the seven traditional continents. And Felix Klieser, who was born without arms and is now one of the best horn players in the world.

Miller says to me: "Yes, but my life has not been all success, there have been very difficult times and setbacks." We agree that all successful people have experienced difficulties, setbacks and defeats, but that it is crucial how you respond to them. Do you blame society or other people? Or do you take responsibility for both your successes and your failures? It's an interesting encounter at Freedom Fest, for which I was happy to skip a lecture that I had been hoping to attend.

Beyond inflation, Freedom Fest focused on the topics that move libertarians: growing government intervention in people's lives and the economy, political correctness and Cancel Culture, criticism of the prevailing energy policy and pleas for nuclear energy. Or the question of whether gold or Bitcoin is the best hedge against inflation. Those who think – like many Europeans – that the United States is the land of unbridled capitalism were disabused of their belief by the fact that for the very first time, government spending in the United States hit 50 percent of GDP.

As a cautionary example, many speakers repeatedly turned to Germany, where ideologically motivated interventions in the energy industry have created huge problems. We don't want to become like Germany – that was the warning in many speeches.

In one respect, however, most of the participants would prefer a system akin to the one in Germany. When asked who likes a two-party system like the one in the U.S., hardly any participants agreed. There was an almost unanimous consensus that America needs more political parties – and it was not only supporters of the Libertarian Party, which was represented in large numbers at the congress, who held this opinion.

The discussion heated up when it came to the topic of "election fraud." Radio host Wayne Allyn Root argued that Joe Biden's victory was made possible by numerous electoral frauds. He received a lot of applause for his claims, while the journalist Isaac Saul, who represented the opposite thesis, was greeted by a chorus of booing. Saul said that, as in every election, there had been electoral fraud, but that it had not had an impact on the outcome of the election. Moreover, numerous judgements from courts up and down America had confirmed that the supporters of the election fraud thesis were wrong.

Apparently, this was not what most of the audience wanted to hear, and Saul was interrupted several times by vehement objections. Finally, moderator John Fund stepped in and explained that if you don't let a speaker whose opinions you don't like finish, you are acting just like the left-wing Cancel Culture supporters you criticize. There was much applause for this statement as well.

Freedom of expression is a frequent topic. The title of one talk was "Make George Orwell Fiction Again." The practices of social media companies, including Facebook and X (formerly Twitter), came in for sharp criticism. One particularly absurd example was a story published by the satirical website *The Babylon Bee*: "CNN Purchases Industrial-Sized Washing Machine To Spin News Before Publication." According to the story: "The custom-made device allows CNN reporters to load just the facts of a given issue, turn a dial to 'spin cycle,' and within five minutes, receive a nearly unrecognizable version of the story that's been spun to fit with the news station's agenda."

Facebook's fact checkers, who clearly have no understanding of satire, determined that no such washing machine exists in reality. In this and similar cases, posts were deleted or social media accounts shut down. However, in the case of *CNN* and the washing machine, even Facebook had to admit that it was wrong.

Freedom Fest culminates on July 16, 2022, with a grand evening banquet, a lecture by the well-known libertarian and U.S. Senator Rand Paul and, my personal highlight, the presentation of awards for the best films screened at the Anthem Film Festival. My film *Life Behind the Berlin Wall* wins the "Audience Choice Award for Short Films." In my acceptance speech, I express my gratitude to the late Free to Choose founder Bob Chitester, whose idea it was to turn my book, *The Power of Capitalism,* into a movie.

July 2022
Gogolin, Poland

I have had a very long and very personal connection to Poland because Monika, the woman I was with the longest, was born there – and came to Germany when she was one year old. Anyone who has ever been to Russia, Ukraine or Poland knows that they have a much higher proportion of beautiful women than Germany or the U.S., and my girlfriend Monika was one of the most beautiful. It was with her that I visited Poland for the first time, on a trip to Krakow.

I remember the first time I became more intensively involved with Poland, its economy and the real estate market. That was 2002, when the real estate subsidiary of Deutsche Bank (it was called DB Real Estate at the time) launched the first closed-end real estate fund in Poland. The fund owned a shopping center managed by the German market leader for shopping centers, ECE, in Lodz, Poland's fourth largest city. The fund had an investment volume of just under 100 million euros.

At the time, DB Real Estate was a client of Dr.ZitelmannPB.GmbH, my PR consulting firm. They asked us to explain to German investors why it made sense to invest in Poland. That was not an easy task, especially as there were so many prejudices about Poland at the time. At one sales event an investor asked, "Do Poles even shop there, or do they just steal things?" I didn't find that funny, but that's an example of the stereotypes and prejudices we had to deal with back then. As an acquaintance of mine who was very successful in raising money for real estate projects worldwide once told me, "prejudices cost money."

We had a somewhat easier time of it back in 2006 when we did PR for another client, the Hamburg-based HGA Capital (a subsidiary of HSH Nordbank), for a fund that also invested in a shopping center managed by ECE, this time in Gdansk.

And today, 20 years after I first had to explain to investors why it was worth investing in Poland, how does it look? So much has happened in the meantime! Poland is now one of the most economically successful countries in Europe, with consistently high growth rates for decades. Under socialism, Poland was one of the poorest countries in Europe. In 1989, a Pole earned the equivalent of just 50 US dollars a month, a tenth of what the average West German was earning, and even after making adjustments to take account of the differences in purchasing power between the two countries, the value of a Polish worker's take home pay was one-third that of a German employee.[43] Poles were poorer than Ukrainians at the time, and GDP per capita was only half that of Czechoslovakia. Inflation in Poland was 260 percent in 1989 and 400 percent in 1990.[44]

In 1910, the average income in Poland was 56 percent of that of a Western European. But by the end of the socialist era, which spanned the years from 1945 to 1990, incomes had fallen dramatically. By 1990, a Pole earned only 31 percent of the average salary in Western Europe.[45]

However, through a consistent program of capitalist reforms, the standard of living in Poland has risen considerably and, by 2016, had reached 57 percent of the level of Western Europeans, whose standard of living had risen considerably after the war. Across all income groups, Poles have benefited from capitalism.

In his excellent 2018 book, *Europe's Growth Champion*, Marcin Piątkowski states: "Yet, 25 years later it is Poland that has become the unrivalled leader of transition and Europe's and the world's growth champion. Since the beginning of post-communist transition in 1989, Poland's economy has grown more than in any other country in Europe. Poland's GDP per capita increased almost two-and-a-half times, beating all other post-communist states as well as the euro-zone."[46]

But not only has the standard of living in Poland improved enormously, so has the environment. Contrary to the claims of anti-capitalists that capitalism

43 Piątkowski, 125
44 Piątkowski, 126.
45 Piątkowski, 129.
46 Piątkowski, 127.

is responsible for environmental degradation and climate change, the example of Poland shows that the opposite is true. Energy intensity, i.e., the ratio of energy consumption to gross domestic product, halved in the years from 1990 to 2011. And the increase in CO_2 emissions in Poland has now decoupled from the increase in gross domestic product. Capitalism is not the problem, it is the solution – both in relation to improving living standards, as well as to protecting the environment and mitigating climate change.

How did Poland manage this and why has Poland been more successful in the transition to capitalism than other former socialist countries? One of the main reasons was that the country's capitalist reforms have been more far-reaching and implemented more quickly. It is not only Poland's economy and institutions that have changed, so have people's thinking and behaviour.

As so often in history, it is important not to underestimate the commitment and influence of certain individuals. First and foremost, there is former Finance Minister Leszek Balcerowicz. A free-market economist, Balcerowicz was Finance Minister in Poland's first democratic government, which was elected in 1989. He was also Chair of the National Bank of Poland (2001–2007) and twice Deputy Prime Minister of Poland (1989–1991 and 1997–2001).

In socialist times he began with ideas that would lead to more market economy and competition within the framework of a socialist system, but he soon realized that no real changes were possible within the narrow corset of a planned economy and that Ludwig von Mises had been right to declare that the effective reform of socialism entails a return to capitalism.[47]

He studied Ludwig Erhard's economic reforms, which had made West Germany so successful after the Second World War, and saw them as a role model for Poland because they were built on the foundation of a "massive liberalization of the economy and radical stabilization via currency reform."[48]

Balcerowicz developed a program of capitalist reforms that was later called "shock therapy." "Based on my previous studies of reforms and my

---

47 Balcerowicz, "Stabilization and Reform," in Åslund / Djankov, 20.
48 Balcerowicz, "Stabilization and Reform," in Åslund / Djankov, 20.

realization of how dramatic the economic situation in Poland was in 1989, I was deeply convinced that only a radical strategy could succeed..."[49]

"The reform program," Marcin Piątkowski writes in his book, "was among the most radical economic reform programs ever implemented in peace time in global history."[50]

It is in the nature of such radical reform programs that the situation initially gets worse, at least temporarily, although the Poles were more than rewarded for their perseverance, as Balcerowicz's program ensured that in 1992 Poland became the first former socialist country to get back on the economic growth track and was the basis of the country's subsequent success. For example, in blue- and white-collar households, stereo radio ownership increased from 22.6 to 40.8 percent between 1989 and 1992 and ownership of color television sets shot up from 50.7 to 91.4 percent. In 1989, less than 5 percent of these households owned a video cassette recorder (VCR); by 1992, more than half did. The proportion of blue- and white-collar workers who had a washing machine, a freezer or a car also increased by at least 10 percent in each case from 1989 to 1992.[51]

According to data from the World Bank, GDP per capita in 1989 was 30.1 percent of the corresponding figure in the U.S. and had risen to 48.4 percent of the U.S. level by 2016.[52] Such gains made themselves felt in people's lives. The income of Poles grew from about 10,300 US dollars in 1990, adjusted for purchasing power, to almost 27,000 US dollars in 2017.[53] Although East Germany received billions in subsidies from West Germany, the income of Poles – in relative terms – improved more than that of East Germans.[54]

Like Margaret Thatcher, Leszek Balcerowicz was a follower of staunchly free-market thinkers such as Friedrich August von Hayek and Ludwig von

---

49 Balcerowicz, "Stabilization and Reform," in Åslund / Djankov, 25.
50 Piątkowski, 167.
51 All data is taken from Balcerowicz, *Socialism, Capitalism, Transformation*, Table 16.3, 334.
52 Gomułka, unnumbered.
53 Piątkowski, 114–115.
54 Piątkowski, 128.

Mises. Poland is an outstanding example of just how successful these ideas, often dismissed as "neoliberal," can be. One can only hope that the people of Poland do not forget the reasons for their economic success.

In recent years I have visited Poland on a fairly regular basis for lectures, as is now the case from July 22–24, 2022, where I am attending a conference in Gogolin, a small Upper Silesian town of 6,000 inhabitants in Krapkowicki County in the Opole Voivodeship. The reason for my trip is a conference to commemorate the life of Milton Friedman, at which I am due to publicize the Polish edition of my book, *The Power of Capitalism*.

I initially wanted to fly, but that proved to be overly complicated and would have taken me eight hours from my apartment in Berlin to the hotel in Gogolin. So, I get a limousine service to take me from Berlin to Gogolin in an S-Class Mercedes. Due to heavy traffic and numerous jams, the outward journey takes seven hours, but the return journey only takes about four hours. The driver takes a few detours because of the traffic jams and I am impressed by the beautiful scenery and the modern houses I see in the villages.

During the conference I hear two talks, one given by a Ukrainian woman and one from a Kenyan woman. The young Ukrainian, who fled her now completely destroyed hometown of Mariupol, calls on the people of her city to talk about their fate, and this later evolves into an online documentary with 350 shocking reports from contemporary witnesses. Her talk includes a series of beautiful pictures of what her city used to look like – and pictures of the terror that destroyed everything. The Kenyan, a member of LOLA (Ladies for Liberty), reports, among other things, on how free deliveries of clothes are destroying her local industry. Another example of why development aid often has the opposite effect of what is intended. The problem in Africa is corrupt governments that cream off a large proportion of development aid for themselves. Her reports remind me of those of Dambisa Felicia Moyo, an African economist who rose to prominence for her excellent book, *Dead Aid*, and whom I met at a conference in Washington.

Unfortunately, the other talks are all in Polish. That isn't a problem for me as about half of the conference participants are sitting outside enjoying the nice weather anyway, so I take the opportunity to find out more about the libertarian scene in Poland. I catch up with Jacek Spendel, the president of Liberty International, who I last spoke to at the Atlas conference in Warsaw in May. Liberty International is a smaller organization than the libertarian Atlas Network, but is particularly relevant in some developing countries.

The biggest and most influential libertarian organization in Poland is the Civic Development Forum (FOR), which is well-connected in business and economic circles, especially thanks to its prominent founder Leszek Balcerowicz. In Gogolin, I meet the organization's former director, Marek Tatała, who has been CEO of the newly founded Economic Freedom Forum in Warsaw since 2021. He tells me about Arkadiusz Muś, the organization's president. According to *Forbes*, Muś is worth 2.8 billion zlotys (equivalent to 700 million US dollars) and ranks 17th on the list of the richest Poles. He founded his company Press-Glas at the beginning of 1991 as a Polish-Swedish joint venture which is now one of the leading companies in Europe in its industry.

Arkadiusz Muś is not at the conference because he is celebrating his 60th birthday. However, he sent me greetings and explained that he would immediately order 460 of my books, one for each member of the Polish parliament, the Sejm. By the way, Jürgen Leibfried, a real estate entrepreneur and a friend of mine, had the same idea when the book was published in Germany and purchased around 700 copies, which he sent to all members of the Bundestag.

There are other libertarian organizations in Poland, such as the Warsaw Enterprise Institute, which works with the Union of Entrepreneurs and Employers in Poland. In the Polish Parliament there are libertarians in some parties, including in the PO (Civic Platform) of Donald Tusk, who was President of the European Council from 2014 to 2019 and Prime Minister of the Republic of Poland from 2007 to 2014, a post he took over again in December 2023. Those present here regard Tusk as a politician who used to be a classic liberal, but no longer is. There are also some libertarians in the right-wing populist party *Konfederacja Wolność i Niepodległość* (Confederation of

Freedom and Independence, short: *Konfederacja*), a heterogeneous political party that unites monarchists, libertarians, Euro-skeptics, nationalists and populists.

Everyone I meet here is highly critical of the PiS party, which ruled in Poland from 2015 to 2023 and combines ideologies from the right and left. PiS has become a party of redistribution, which at the same time pays homage to nationalism and uses slogans against Germans to attract votes. However, says Jacek Spendel, most young Poles are not at all hostile toward Germans because old prejudices have disappeared as a result of increased economic cooperation and open borders. What is interesting about the Polish party system is that there is only one party that describes itself as left-wing, namely *Lewica*, an alliance of socialists and social democrats.

The conference also gives me an opportunity to catch up with Marcin Chmielowski, an excellent networker. He was recommended to me as a PR consultant by my amazing Polish publisher Krzysztof Zuber, but he did much more than that for me: he helped me make contacts all over the world – not just in Eastern Europe, but as far away as Mongolia! Networks are so important in life, but what is crucial is the ability to create and cultivate great networks. I have this ability and I recognize immediately when someone – like Marcin – has it too. We arrange for me to visit Poland again for a week at the beginning of September to meet interesting people, learn more about Poland and at the same time promote my book.

August 2022
Tbilisi, Georgia

I already mentioned Liberty International in the previous chapter. From August 11–15, 2022 I am attending the organization's World Conference in Tbilisi. I have been invited to give a lecture on the topic of "financial freedom." It is not an especially large event, but it is very international with guests and speakers from Georgia, Russia, Poland, Serbia, Romania, Tajikistan, Chile, Venezuela, Colombia, India, Japan, Nepal, South Korea, the U.S., Great Britain, Denmark, Iceland and Germany.

Are libertarians on the left or the right of the political spectrum? If you heard them talk about socialism and capitalism, you might think of them as "right-wing." But at the same time, there are many – not all – libertarians who vehemently advocate open borders and unrestricted immigration.

One of the highest-profile libertarians is the American, Ken Schoolland, an economics professor who lives in Hawaii and whose book, *The Adventures of Jonathan Gullible: A Free Market Odyssey,* has been published in 61 languages. "Embracing the Freedom of Refugees" is the topic of his talk. Why, he asks, is Europe so willing to accept refugees from Ukraine – in contrast to the reaction of many Europeans to the refugees who came in 2015?

Schoolland explains the different reactions by saying that the refugees from Ukraine are more likely to be women and that the culture, religion, and ethnicity of Ukrainians are all closer to many Europeans than those of refugees from Arab states or Africa. In his view, these are explanations, but not justifications for an anti-migration attitude. The belief that many refugees come to Europe to take advantage of the blessings of the welfare state is not an argument against refugees, he explains, because they are not to blame for the welfare state, which Schoolland – like all libertarians – also rejects.

Every entrepreneur, he argued, should have the right to hire whoever they want to hire and who they deem to be the best for a job, regardless of nationality. For example, he rejects laws that prioritize labor market access for Americans over immigrants from Latin America. Nobody should have better chances of getting a job just because they were born in a certain country, he says. I myself only share this opinion to a limited extent. The welfare state that he rejects is a reality and understandably attracts large numbers of immigrants from other countries. The combination of a welfare state and open borders is clearly economically unfeasible. And anyone who is for freedom should also accept it when the majority of people in a country decide that there are upper limits for welcoming migrants – for whatever reasons.

Nevertheless, I learn a few things from Schoolland, for example how he reacts to my criticism: he has the kind of warm manner that I have rarely found in a person who is being criticized. When he smiles and holds out his hand after hearing your criticism, you don't see it as weakness, but as human strength.

Ken Schoolland's wife Li is also one of the most famous speakers on the libertarian scene. She gives a harrowing talk about her life in China from 1958 to 1984. This was the worst time in China, because in 1958 Mao's "Great Leap Forward" began, the greatest socialist experiment in human history, in which around 45 million Chinese people died. In 1966, at the age of eight, Mao's next campaign began, the "Great Proletarian Cultural Revolution," which plunged the country into chaos for ten years.

Schoolchildren and students in particular were mobilized. They rioted in the streets and turned against "filthy rich peasants," "son-of-a-bitch landlords," "bloodsucking capitalists," "neo-bourgeoisie" and "alien class elements,"[55] but often simply against their own teachers or professors, who were accused of capitalist thinking. The first death occurred in a girls' school administered by Beijing Normal University, where the vice-principal was tortured. Students spat in her face, filled her mouth with soil, tied her hands behind her back and then beat her, including with nail-spiked clubs. After several hours of torture, the vice-principal lost consciousness and died.[56]

---

55 Dikötter, *Cultural Revolution*, 62.
56 Dikötter, *Cultural Revolution*, 73.

A school principal in Beijing was ordered to stand in the scorching sun while Red Guards poured boiling hot water over him. A biology teacher was tortured for hours until she died, after which the other teachers were forced to beat her corpse. In elementary schools, where students were no older than thirteen, some teachers were forced to swallow nails and excrement, others had their hair shaved off and were forced to slap each other in the face.[57] Fellow students were also humiliated and sometimes tortured to death because they had "bad family backgrounds" or came from "exploiting families."[58] So much for the reports in Dikötter's book.

Li Schoolland reports that her father, a surgeon, was thrown into prison for making a politically incorrect joke. Her mother, a professor, was publicly humiliated. Women like her suffered having half of their heads shaved, in a hair style called "yin-yang head," so that they could be immediately recognized as members of the "blacks," the name given to the "evil" supporters of capitalism – in contrast to the "reds" who supported Mao. In front of her eyes, her mother was beaten by Mao's fanatical followers. When Li was nine years old, she experienced Red Guards coming into her home and taking everything from her and her family. This was a decisive situation for her, because the thought formed in her: you can rob me of everything, but not my thoughts and feelings.

The Red Guards asked little Li and her eight-year-old brother to report what their mother had said against the communists. The two children refused. Their silence was taken as evidence against the mother: their refusal to denounce their mother, in the eyes of the Red Guards, proved that their mother had told them not to obey the authorities. Other children had even more traumatic experiences: one child was forced to watch as dynamite was tied to his father and he was blown up in public.

At every one of my talks – all over the world – I ask how many people in the audience heard about Mao's "Great Leap Forward," the largest socialist experiment in human history, in which so many died, while they were at school or college. Only very few people, if any, say they ever did.

---

57 Dikötter, *Cultural Revolution*, 75.
58 Dikötter, *Cultural Revolution*, 75.

Another big topic at the conference is a panel discussion on "Is Big Tech a Threat to Freedom?" The debate sees a collision of different opinions. In one camp, there are libertarians who advocate anti-trust policies against monopolies and cartels in order to limit the power of the Googles, Facebooks, Amazons and Apples of the world. In the other camp are economists who note that the seemingly omnipotent "monopolies" of today are by no means as inviolable as they may seem and will lose their power in the same way that companies like Xerox, IBM, Kodak, Nokia, and many others did in the past.

One of the chapters in my book, *In Defence of Capitalism,* is on this specific topic – and offers the following conclusions: first, monopolies do not only have negative sides, but, as the Austrian economist Joseph Schumpeter showed, they often serve an economically useful function, and second, they are eliminated in the medium term by innovations and new companies. The greatest enemy of monopolies is capitalism itself, not government anti-monopoly legislation.

Libertarians are a relatively small group and their influence on political policy, public opinion and the media – despite the large number of libertarian think tanks around the world – is also small. The Swede Per Bylund puts it in a nutshell in his lecture: although we libertarians understand the market better than socialists, socialists are much better and more successful in the market of public opinion. The libertarian message of freedom, he said, is often too abstract and does not reach people. Libertarians talk a lot about entrepreneurship, but fail when it comes to their own ideas. "Who is the customer? What is the product?" – questions that every entrepreneur has to answer in order to be successful. Yet libertarians ask these questions far too rarely. What is the benefit for the public at large? How, in real terms, can "more freedom" improve their lives? "Think of the libertarian movement as a business that provides a valuable product, not as a non-profit or charity," he recommends.

Jan Bertram, a speaker from the German Free Cities Foundation, outlines the concept behind Free Cities and showcases a number of real-world examples. Ideally, Free Cities are cities with their own police forces and prisons, their own laws and their own tax systems, libertarian islands within countries governed by a completely different state constitution. Relations between cities and their citizens should be governed exclusively on the basis of treaties. I will address this concept in more detail in the section on Monaco, later in the book.

Georgia itself also has a libertarian movement, and its own small libertarian party, *Girchi* (More Freedom), which is represented at the conference by the professor of politics Zurab Japaridze. He is popular among young Georgians and hated by many older voters because, for example, he advocates the legalization of drugs and is a vocal supporter of LGBTQ+ rights. He also opposes universal conscription. At a time where 20 percent of the country is occupied by Russia, many people are afraid of another Russian attack in the wake of the war in Ukraine, this has turned many people against him. He points out that he is in favor of strengthening the army and joining NATO, but considers universal conscription to be an unsuitable approach. As a ploy to get around conscription, he has even founded his own "religion" and appointed 70,000 "priests," who are exempt from conscription.

At breakfast I get into conversation with a Georgian called Nika, who has also been a "priest" for a few years: "I have parents to support, so I couldn't afford to go to the military for a year," he explains. Now he is one of the 70,000 "priests." He tells me that Zurab Japaridze's "priest" model now even has competition from the Orthodox Church in Georgia, which also offers young men a similar status to avoid military service. Not all libertarians at the conference are supportive. One Georgian woman sharply attacks Zurab Japaridze, saying that refusing military service objectively benefits only one person: Vladimir Putin.

Zurab Japaridze frequently attracts attention as a result of his unusual marketing methods. During the 2018 presidential elections, Japaridze posted his own election banners on the porn site Pornhub with the slogan: "More sex, more freedom." And when the government banned private landlords from renting out housing to prostitutes, he rented an apartment in an upscale residential and commercial building in protest, demonstratively passing it off as a brothel (though it wasn't actually one) and hanging sex toys in the window. On the street, he distributed free marijuana joints. For many of these stunts, Japaridze has already been jailed several times for several days, which has increased the popularity of the unconventional professor of political ideas among young Georgians.

Whether such libertarian micro-parties can bring about political change seems questionable to me. In the meantime, the small party with the name *Girchi* has split and there are now two minor libertarian parties with the same name (to help voters distinguish between them, Japaridze's party has added "More Freedom" in parentheses after the name).

There is a passionate and heated discussion about the war in Ukraine. Of course, everyone condemns Russia's war of aggression, but the representative of the U.S. Libertarian Party speaks out against supplying Ukraine with weapons. Some sections of the libertarian movement in the U.S. are committed pacifists and/or isolationists. The argument of the representative from the U.S.: throughout American history, war has only ever led to an extreme strengthening of the state.

There is also a representative from Russia's libertarian party, which has seen about a third of its members emigrate, many to Georgia. Others are in prison. Members of the Russian libertarian party are overwhelmingly critical of Putin's war. Most libertarians in Europe are clearly backing Ukraine, as was evident the other day at the European congress of the libertarian Atlas Network in Warsaw. "Our ultimate goal is not peace, but freedom," said a libertarian from Poland. Ultimately, she stated, only Russia benefits from a pacifist stance.

My favorite talk was given by the beautiful daughter of Ken and Li Schoolland, KenLi Schoolland. The title of her session was "Free the World by Freeing Yourself" and her core message was: don't feel like a victim of society and don't wait for society to change, start with yourself. She gave a very impressive account of how she went through a very difficult time as a "digital native" but then found more happiness in life through meditation and other techniques. Every day, she said, she did something she was afraid of or spent ten days in silence. "When we want to reduce the power of the state, we have to strengthen the individual." And, "It is not a good idea to bet all your freedom on political freedom."

This is so important because, unfortunately, libertarians sometimes argue along the same lines as socialists: the inadequacies of the existing society, which many libertarians (rightly!) also criticize, are used as an excuse for their own lack of success, and any improvement is supposedly only possible in a perfect society.

September 2022
Warsaw, Poland

September takes me to Warsaw and Hanoi. Poland and Vietnam have more in common than most people know. These are two countries that suffered terrible wars; from 1939 to 1945 in Poland and from 1955 to 1975 in Vietnam. Millions of people were killed and both countries were devastated. In the immediate aftermaths of these wars, neither had a chance to recover and rebuild economically because of the socialist planned economies that were established. These planned economies led to misery, poverty and skyrocketing inflation. In both countries, the ruling communists first tried to reform their systems from within, but after these attempts failed, the people realized that only the introduction of private property rights and market economy principles would help their countries. In no other countries of comparable size has economic freedom increased as much over the last few decades as in Poland and Vietnam, and in both countries life for ordinary people has improved dramatically.

Because of all these similarities – and because I have very good contacts in both countries – I have decided to write a book called *How Nations Escape Poverty* about these two countries.

In Poland, I am accompanied by Marcin Chmielowski, with whom I have been working very well for several months now. Before I travel to a country, I begin by studying its history so that I can understand it better. That's why I meet Alicja Wancerz-Gluza, co-founder of the Karta Center, a non-governmental historical archive. Alicja was initially active in the *Solidarność* trade union and later – after martial law was declared in Poland – in the anti-communist underground. On January 4, 1982, together with her husband and a small group of friends, she founded the underground newspaper *Karta*. Over time, it evolved from a rough-and-ready newspaper written on a typewriter and then photocopied into a publishing house that distributed illegal newspapers and books.

The Karta Archive now encompasses 5,000 books and brochures, around 35,000 newspapers, 300 posters and 1,000 postcards from the anti-communist underground movement. This includes the largest collection of documents from the *Solidarność* trade union. Alicja proudly shows me the UNESCO document confirming that the collection has been added to the International Register of World Documentary Heritage of the UNESCO Memory of the World program – along with wooden plaques detailing the 21 demands made by workers during the August 1980 strike in Gdańsk shipyard. The Karta Archive also documents 6,000 interviews with contemporary witnesses (including 1,000 interviews with former prisoners of the Soviet Gulags) and around 400,000 photos.

During our conversation, Alicja explains the realities of everyday life in Poland under the socialist planned economy. She shows me the pile of ration cards Polish people needed to buy food and other products until the collapse of the socialist regime in the late 1980s. The first ration cards were for sugar in 1976. Until the end of socialism, more and more of these ration cards were added – for all kinds of products, including meat, fat, butter, detergent, soap, cigarettes, gasoline, and even shoes.

There were also special tokens on the ration cards, and these were numbered. For example, it might suddenly be announced that you could buy school supplies for children or sanitary pads for women using token number 3. In every shop, the sales people would use scissors to cut the small token from the ration cards. To get a ration card with a special token, Poles needed another card, which their employers used to register all the cards they had been issued with each month. It was a disaster if anyone lost one of their ration cards.

"It was a truly special occasion," remembers Alicja , "when I got a special card from the registry office that would allow me to buy white tights for my wedding. I was also given a certificate stating that because we were getting married we were allowed to buy gold wedding rings in a jewelry store. But we didn't have the money for that, and we didn't want rings anyway. So, there were special cards for all occasions, for example, for a funeral you could get a card for black pantyhose."

But just because you had a ration card didn't mean you could go out and buy what you wanted. Often you had to stand in line for hours to get a specific product. People also exchanged their cards if they needed a different product to the one their card allowed. For example, a vodka card (an adult was allowed to buy one bottle per month) could be exchanged for a coffee card.

For children, there were cards for powdered milk and sweets (so-called "chocolate substitutes"). To buy furniture, a washing machine or a television, people had to stand in what were known as "kolejki społeczne" (social lines). In some cases, they had to join the line every day for a month or two, queuing for hours at a time. Family members joined the queue and waited in line and swapped places with other family members every few hours. Often it was the grandfather or grandmother who were chosen to stand in line because they were the most likely to have the time to persevere in line for many days. Every couple of hours, names were called out – and if someone had left the line, they lost their place and the time they had spent in line didn't count.

It was also difficult to get a telephone. Alicja: "In my neighborhood, in 1986, there was only one phone booth for all of the streets and buildings in the new district. It was a public phone, no-one in my neighborhood had a private phone." Her parents moved into their cooperative apartment in 1960 and immediately applied for a telephone line. The phone was eventually connected – 13 years later in 1973. And that only happened so "quickly" because her father was a member of the Polish United Workers Party. The only place you could make international calls was at the post office, where you had to register several hours in advance.

In Poland, only around 14 percent of the population owned a car in 1990, in West Germany the figure was almost 68 percent (in 1989). Poles had to wait several years for a car, without the certainty of actually being able to buy one in the end. Of course, it was possible to buy a used car, but they were sometimes even more expensive than a new car. It was only because Alicja's father was in the party that he received a special voucher for a car, a Fiat

126p. But he had to wait until 1980, when he got the voucher as a reward for becoming First Party Secretary in his factory.

People had to wait for everything, including an apartment. Alicja remembers: "When my future husband was five years old, his parents started paying money into a cooperative, so that 25 years later they would have the right to buy a small apartment. My parents started saving a little later because they had to save for my older sister first." Twenty-five years later, when she was 29 and her husband 30, they were able to pool the entitlements they had acquired over many years of saving and move into a small three-room apartment, which was nevertheless far from debt-free and still had to be paid off.

Over the next few days, I meet so many interesting people in Warsaw, including Marcin Nowacki, vice-president of the employers' association ZPP, and Adam Szłapka, the leader of the *Nowoczesna* party. His party works with Donald Tusk's Civic Platform (PO), the Greens and the *Inicjatywa Polska* party in the *Koalicja Obywatelska*. The descriptors "left-wing" and "right-wing" have taken on a very different meaning in Poland than in other European countries: Szłapka believes that 80 percent of the 130 MPs in *Koalicja Obywatelska* are pro-capitalist, while the then ruling *Prawo i Sprawiedliwość* (PiS, or Law and Justice Party) is a firm believer in centralized state control. PiS is widely regarded as right-wing, but the libertarians I meet in Poland classify the party as socialist because it advocates redistribution, nationalization and bigger government.

These explanations are important to me because in the survey I commissioned in 35 countries (of which Poland was one) on attitudes toward economic freedom and capitalism, we discovered something strange. In almost all of the surveyed countries our findings were very clear: respondents who described themselves as left wingers were critical of market economies and capitalism, while respondents on the right of the political spectrum were pro-capitalist. In Poland, in contrast, most pro-capitalists belonged to the moderate left.

At that time, I remember calling Thomas Petersen from the Allensbach

Institute. He is also my contact to the British opinion research institute Ipsos MORI – and is certainly Germany's preeminent opinion poll expert (at one point he was chairman of the World Association for Public Opinion Research). I told him: "Well, I have significant doubts about the validity of our data from Poland. Overall, they are plausible, but something must have gone wrong with the right-left political orientation assignment, perhaps an error in the coding." Petersen had everything meticulously checked, every piece of data, the translation of the questionnaire, the coding, etc., but there was no doubt, the data were correct.

If I'm honest, I still didn't quite believe the data were correct. Although some friends in Poland told me that this wasn't as implausible as it seemed to me, it only became clearer for me after my conversation with Szłapka from the *Nowoczesna* party: "What applies in Western Europe absolutely does not apply here. In our country, the former communists are more free market than the PiS party, which is regarded as right-wing." He clarified that the PiS combines nationalism with anti-capitalism and has been particularly successful in attracting voters by claiming that privatization of state-owned enterprises is a sellout to foreign capitalists. PiS has put a complete stop or even partially reversed privatizations, some of which had been carried out by the "left." For someone who is familiar with the left being anti-capitalists and the (moderate) right being pro-capitalists, this can be confusing at first. Yes, sometimes you have to travel to the country to properly understand the survey data.

The next day, I meet Tomasz Wróblewski from the Warsaw Enterprise Institute, which promotes the market economy and in particular small and medium-sized enterprises in Poland. He has a very critical view of the EU: in the beginning it made a positive contribution in Poland, but now it has increasingly shifted to advocating state interventionism and restricting economic freedom.

I ask him about his opinion on a subject on which I am undecided. I am expecting to be invited to speak at the Adam Smith Conference in Moscow (which later does not take place, so the question is moot). Should I, a fierce critic of Putin and Russian imperialism, go to Moscow? Even though it would be too dangerous to formulate my position clearly in Moscow? On the other hand, and this was Wróblewski's objection: "If you go to Moscow and remain silent, if you only talk about your topics but say nothing about the war, then that means doing 'business as usual' at a time when Russia is waging a murderous war of aggression." His words convince me, even though my friends in Russia are clearly anti-Putin – they are libertarians who are having more than a hard time themselves. One of them, with whom I had a Zoom call, was in prison for ten days a few months ago. I've always been against any collective guilt theory – these people are not responsible for Putin and the war, quite the opposite.

There are lots of people from Belarus in Poland. In total, Belarusians submitted more than 2,800 asylum applications in Poland between 2020 and April 2022. The approval rate was 79 percent in 2020 and almost 100 percent in 2021 and 2022. Looking at the total number of applications for residence in Poland, as well as temporary work permits, Belarusians have been the second largest migrant group in Poland after Ukrainians since 2019.[59] I meet six entrepreneurs from Belarus who fled after the dictator Lukashenko rigged the presidential election in August 2020 and mass protests broke out. More than 33,000 people were arrested and over 250 injured during the demonstrations.

Alexey was a senior manager for various companies in Minsk, but then joined the protests and led a group of 4,500 opposition activists in the Belarusian capital. It was clear that he too would have been imprisoned if he had not fled. In Poland, he founded an organization that supports the families of political prisoners in Belarus and refugees from the country. With his business acumen and excellent language skills, he has no doubt that he will also be successful in Poland in the future.

Even before the events of 2020, Serg had repeatedly thought about emigrating. The brutal suppression of the mass protests tipped the scales and

---

59 Jaroszewicz, https://www.laender-analysen.de/polen-analysen/294/polen-als-land-der-politischen-immigration-aus-belarus-zwischen-schwieriger-geschichte-technokratischer-einstellung-und-grosser/.

he also moved to Poland. He cannot understand anyone who still wants to live in a country ruled by Lukashenko. Serg was a senior manager in Minsk for 20 years and is now pursuing a project in Warsaw to finance start-up companies. Before he moved to Poland, he spent some time in Denmark: "In Copenhagen, I met a lot of happy people with a smile on their faces. I have also met a lot more cheerful and friendly people in Poland than I ever saw in Belarus, although not as many as in Denmark. In Belarus, you see a lot of sad and bitter people and very little laughter." Incidentally, his subjective impression is largely in line with the World Happiness Index, which happiness researchers compile on the basis of surveys. Denmark ranks second, Poland 48th, and there are no data for Belarus.[60]

Mikhail is a specialist in alarm and security systems. He emigrated from Belarus to Poland in November 2021. He wants to set up his successful company here too and then expand into other European countries, such as Italy. He is optimistic because the Poles, he says, like Belarusians and appreciate their efficiency. Many Polish companies are quite slow, and he hopes speed can be his USP. And demand for security systems is huge everywhere, including in Poland.

Rita is a marketing consultant. She also hopes efficiency will help her make a name for herself in Poland. She set up a small consultancy company with ten employees in Belarus and is now planning to do the same in Poland.

Olga has set up six beauty studios in Warsaw with 40 employees. She came to Poland in May 2021 and manages the company from Warsaw. She founded her first salon here with seven employees. She appreciates that there is much greater legal certainty in Poland. In Belarus, laws that would have required her to obtain a permit for the laser techniques she uses were changed overnight. But because she doesn't have the necessary permit, her business has been under constant threat of closure ever since. It could easily happen if, for example, a state authority or even a single official had something against her.

Vasily is an entrepreneur and has an IT infrastructure company with 25

---

60 Helliwell et al., https://worldhappiness.report/ed/2022/happiness-benevolence-and-trust-during-covid-19-and-beyond/#ranking-of-happiness-2019-2021.

employees in Belarus, which he now manages from Poland: "Since the Covid crisis, employees have been working from home rather than in the office anyway, so it doesn't make much difference to manage the company from Poland or Belarus."

I used to think that many Poles disliked Russians for historical reasons. After all, the Russians – like the Germans – repeatedly invaded and partitioned the country. But today I learned that Poles make a very clear distinction between Russians and Belarusians. Everyone tells me that Belarusians are held in high esteem in Poland. People in both countries feel connected by history, and unlike many other neighbors, Poland has never been at war with Belarus.

On the last day of my stay in Poland, I meet the legendary Leszek Balcerowicz in person for the first time. More than anyone else, this is the man to whom Poland owes its economic success. His reforms put Poland on the road to capitalism. Balcerowicz is ten years older than me, but still just as active. He is the founder and chairman of the Civil Development Forum Foundation (FOR), which is committed to promoting the free-market economy.

At the time, I am writing my book, *How Nations Escape Poverty*, and ask him for critical feedback on the chapter about Poland and to help me with a film I am making about Poland. Tomasz, the film's producer, is also at the meeting to take the first shots. Balcerowicz promises me his full support because he is very worried about the future of his country. Instead of continuing the reforms he initiated, PiS, which has ruled since 2015, is pursuing policies that are, he tells me, more statist than any government since the end of socialism in Poland.

PiS has unleashed a torrent of nationalist slogans, branding Balcerowicz's reforms a sellout to Americans and Germans and painting a highly distorted picture of recent Polish history. The problems in the 1990s were supposedly nothing to do with the communists, who had run the country down, PiS now claims, but were caused by Balcerowicz's reforms. He notes that people in the 1990s understood how important the reforms were and how much their situation improved as a result. Otherwise he would not have won the 1997 elections with his party in Silesia, Poland's most industrialized region.

During our conversation I am struck by something I noticed when I read his books: Balcerowicz is not a typical theoretical economist. He even tells me that a theoretical economist is a contradiction in terms, since economists have to deal with practice. This reminds me a little of Marx's well-known saying that earlier philosophers had only interpreted the world in various ways, but the point is to change it. Balcerowicz changed Poland just as Margaret Thatcher changed Great Britain. For me he is one of the greatest economic reformers of the twentieth century. And since he already wrote the foreword for the Polish edition of my book, *The Power of Capitalism*, I am proud to have finally met him in person.

September 2022
Hanoi, Vietnam

Vietnam played an important role in my youth. Like many young people at the time, I was outraged by the U.S. war in Vietnam. I was a Maoist back then, and of course all my sympathies lay with the National Front for the Liberation of South Vietnam. I wrote articles on the Vietnam War in my school newspaper and sold National Front for the Liberation of South Vietnam pamphlets at my school when I was 14 years old.

Many years later, Vietnam again came to play a significant role in my life, because one of the longest relationships in my life was with a beautiful woman called Trang. She was born in Germany, but her parents came from Hanoi. Trang also showed me Vietnam for the first time, in 2014, and introduced me to her family, which owns the largest wedding planning company in Vietnam and is also involved in real estate.

A few years ago, my book, *Dare to Be Different and Grow Rich,* was published in Vietnam and I started writing and giving interviews to Vietnamese newspapers. In August and September 2022, my two books *The Wealth Elite* and *The Rich in Public Opinion* were also published in Vietnam. There is probably no other country in the world where the pursuit of wealth is as important as it is in Vietnam. I commissioned the opinion research institute Ipsos MORI to conduct a survey of about 1,000 representatively selected people in each of 13 countries to find out more about popular attitudes toward wealth and rich people. One of the questions was: "How important, if at all, is it for you personally to be rich?" The result: in Europe and the U.S., an average of only 28 percent of respondents said it was important for them to be rich. In the four Asian countries, by contrast, an average of 58 percent said it was important for them to be rich. And nowhere did so many people say it was important for them to be rich as in Vietnam, where the figure was 76 percent.

In September 2022, I travel to Vietnam to promote my two books, foster links with Vietnamese scholars and give lectures. The two weeks are inspiring, but also exhausting, because I have three to four appointments every day, each lasting about two hours, sometimes longer. I give lectures at four universities and attend other events, which I really enjoy. But since I put a lot of energy into every lecture, these days are challenging. Most days I am unable to take the afternoon nap that I've been used to in Germany since I was a teenager, and I also have to cope with the time difference (Vietnam is five hours ahead of Germany). I often get up around 4:30 a.m., go to the gym, take care of my email correspondence, work on this book and have breakfast, then sleep for another hour before the appointments start around 9 a.m. After four days my girlfriend Alica comes from New York City. In the evening we tend to book a 90-minute massage and then go out for dinner. While in Germany I rarely go to sleep before midnight, here we are usually in bed around 11 p.m.

Of course, I studied the history of the country intensively before my trip and bought 20 books on the history and economy of Vietnam. Here are a few key facts: Vietnam was ravaged by war from 1946 to 1975. The first Indochina War took place from 1946 to 1954, with the Vietnamese liberation movement Viet Ming fighting against the French colonial power. Shortly after the end of this war, which led to the partition of the country into a pro-communist north and anti-communist south, the next round of military conflict began, in which China and the Soviet Union supported communist North Vietnam and the liberation front in South Vietnam, and the U.S. supported the government of South Vietnam. This Vietnam War, also known as the Second Indochina War, lasted from 1955 to 1975.

In 1965, U.S. President Lyndon B. Johnson ordered an increase in air strikes. The U.S. used the defoliant Agent Orange, a plant killer that destroyed rice fields and poisoned water reservoirs. The chemical weapons used by the U.S. not only struck the communist liberation army, they also hit the civilian population. American napalm bombs also inflicted heavy casualties among the civilian population. The South Vietnamese alone lost 1.5 million people, including 300,000 civilians. The U.S. military suffered 58,200 casualties, plus another 300,000 wounded. Civilian losses in North Vietnam were lower than in the South, but it lost far more soldiers.[61]

"In the North, the war destroyed the main industrial centers and basic infrastructure ... All industrial enterprises were destroyed. As were three of the six largest cities, 12 of 29 provincial capitals, and two thirds of villages. All electricity plants, railway stations, ports, bridges, roads and the entire railway network were also totally destroyed. In the South, two thirds of the villages were also destroyed, large parts of the forest were destroyed and 20 million farmers lost their homes," writes Tam T.T. Nguyễn.[62]

Given the destruction and suffering of the Vietnamese people, it would not be surprising if Vietnam was a hotbed of anti-Americanism. But anti-Americanism is far more pronounced in many other parts of the world. It is something you encounter far more often in Arab countries and Russia, as well as across Europe, than you do in Vietnam.

I never once heard Trang or her family talk badly about Americans, and the same can be said of the other Vietnamese people I speak to. Đinh Minh Tuấn, a scholar from a libertarian think tank I meet in Hanoi, says: "We Vietnamese don't look back to the past, but to the future. Unlike with China, we have no territorial disputes with the U.S. Many Vietnamese people also appreciate that the working conditions in American companies here are often better than in Asian companies that invest in Vietnam. In addition, the people of Vietnam know that the U.S. is our most important export partner." Indeed, in 2020, Vietnam exported as much to the U.S. as it did to China and Japan, its second and third largest export markets, combined.[63]

I also talk to Ngyuen Xuan about the topic. She is the founder of the audio book company Fonos, and I meet her in an unusual way: she knocks

61 Statista Research Department, "Verluste im Vietnamkrieg," https://de.statista.com/statistik/daten/studie/1165881/umfrage/verluste-nach-kriegspartei-im-vietnamkrieg/#:~:text=Im percent20Vietnamkrieg percent20in percent20den percent20Jahren,und percent20weitere percent20300.000 percent20wurden percent20verwundet.
62 Tam T. T. Nguyen, *Vietnam und sein Transformationsweg*, 14.
63 USA: 54.8 billion euros (23.2 percent of the country's total exports) China: 37.0 billion euros (15.7 percent) Japan: 18.2 billion euros (7.7 percent), WeltExporte, https://www.weltexporte.de/exportprodukte-vietnam/.

on my door because she is staying in the same hotel in Hanoi (Metropol) and recognizes me. She actually lives in Saigon. "I was born in 1987, when the war had already been over for twelve years. My parents and grandparents told me about how terrible the war was, but they never had a bad word to say about Americans. On the contrary, they told me, 'You have to learn English, dress like Americans, eat what Americans eat, and above all, learn to think like Americans think. Then you will be successful.'"

Perceptions of China, which has frequently waged war against Vietnam in the past and also has territorial disputes with the country today, are, in contrast, far more critical. In a survey conducted by the PEW Research Center in 2014, 76 percent of Vietnamese respondents said they had a positive view of the U.S. Among better educated Vietnamese, the figure was as high as 89 percent, and among respondents aged between 18 and 29, as many as 89 percent had a positive view of the U.S. Even among those over the age of 50, those who had lived through the war, over 60 percent had a positive view of the U.S.[64] Views of China are quite different. In a 2017 survey also conducted by the PEW Research Center, 64 percent of Vietnamese agreed with the statement: "China's growing economy is a bad thing for our country."[65]

I admire people who succeed in looking more to the future than the past. They are usually far more successful in life than those who constantly focus on the past. And this applies not only to individuals, but also to nations. So many African countries complain about the effects of colonialism and use this as an explanation for all their problems. The Vietnamese could easily enough do the same, but they don't: they look forward.

Of course, this does not mean that they ignore history. I visited an impressive memorial in Hanoi, a former prison first used by the French colonists to incarcerate Vietnamese prisoners and later by the North Vietnamese to hold American soldiers. Today, Hỏa Lò Prison is a museum. At the time, American prisoners of war ironically referred to the prison as the "The Hanoi Hilton,"

---

64 Devlin, https://www.pewresearch.org/fact-tank/2015/04/30/vietnamese-see-u-s-as-key-ally/.

65 Silver, https://www.pewresearch.org/fact-tank/2017/10/16/how-people-in-asia-pacific-view-china/.

and a film about the experiences of American prisoners of war there was made under this name in 1987. The prison's inmates included the later U.S. presidential candidate, John McCain. Today, the exhibition displays photos of his rescue from a lake near Hanoi in 1967 after his fighter plane was shot down. It also documents his visit to the prison museum in 2000.

In 1975, the Vietnamese defeated the Americans, and this already proud country became even prouder, for they had defeated the greatest military superpower in history. But their pride suffered over the next ten years as the introduction of a socialist planned economy had a devastating effect on the south of the country. Vietnam was the poorest country in the region. While other Asian countries that took the capitalist path – South Korea, Hong Kong and Singapore, for example – achieved incredible growth and escaped poverty, most people in Vietnam lived in bitter poverty, even ten years after the war had come to an end.

Forced collectivization of agriculture had been no more successful in Vietnam than it had in China or Russia. In 1980, Vietnam produced only 14 million tons of rice, despite the fact that the country needed 16 million tons to meet its own population's basic needs. During the period of the second five-year plan (1976 to 1980), Vietnam was forced to import eight to nine million tons of rice and other foodstuffs.[66]

Production stagnated, and state-owned industrial production actually declined by 10 percent from 1976 to 1980.[67] Until 1988, only small family businesses were allowed as private enterprises in Vietnam; otherwise, everything was state-owned.

The Vietnamese realized that they were at an impasse. At the Sixth Party Congress in December 1986, the country's leaders adopted a comprehensive package of reforms known as Đổi Mới ("renewal"). As in China under Deng Xiaoping, private property was allowed and the party increasingly focused on the development of a market economy. Đinh Minh Tuấn emphasizes the role played by Võ Văn Kiệt, who had already carried out market economy reforms

---

66 Tam T. T. Nguyen, *Vietnam und sein Transformationsweg*, 17.
67 Tam T. T. Nguyen, *Vietnam und sein Transformationsweg*, 17.

in Hồ Chí Minh City in 1983 before Đổi Mới began. From August 8, 1991 until his resignation on September 25, 1997, Võ Văn Kiệt was Prime Minister of Vietnam. He was one of the driving forces of the Đổi Mới economic reforms, supported privatization and called for the end of special privileges for army and party leaders. Under his aegis, Article 21 was also inserted into the Vietnamese constitution, thereby guaranteeing the protection of private ownership of the means of production against expropriation.

Today, Vietnam has shaken off its past and totally reinvented itself. GDP per capita has increased six-fold since the reforms (in constant dollars), from 577 to 3,373 US dollars.[68] Vietnam is now one of the world's largest rice exporters, after India and only slightly behind Thailand.[69] But Vietnam has long been much more than a country that exports agricultural products and textiles. It has now become a major producer of electronic goods and exported 111 billion US dollars of electronic products in 2020 alone.[70]

"Poverty in Vietnam has gone from being a majority problem to a minority problem,"[71] is the conclusion drawn in an analysis of the transformation of Vietnam. In 1990, with a per capita GDP of 98 US dollars, Vietnam was the poorest country in the world, behind Somalia (130 US dollars) and Sierra Leone (163 US dollars).[72] As late as 1993, 79.7 percent of the Vietnamese population was living in poverty. By 2006, the rate had fallen to 50.6 percent. In 2020, it was only 5 percent.[73]

Rising inequality is not an issue for the Vietnamese, they view it as a sign of greater justice. In this context, there is a very interesting essay by

---

68 The Global Economy, "Vietnam: GDP per capita, constant 2010 dollars," https://www.theglobaleconomy.com/Vietnam/GDP_per_capita_constant_dollars/.

69 Ahrens, https://de.statista.com/statistik/daten/studie/456376/umfrage/exportmenge-von-reis-weltweit/#:~:text=F percentC3 percentBCr percent20das percent20Erntejahr percent202023 percent2F24,rund percent2055 percent2C8 percent20Millionen percent20Tonnen.

70 Trading Economics, https://tradingeconomics.com/vietnam/exports/electrical-electronic-equipment.

71 Tam T. T. Nguyen, *Vietnam und sein Transformationsweg*, 84.

72 Tran, *Rethinking Asian Capitalism*, 3, footnote 1.

73 World Bank Group, *From the Last Mile to the Next Mile*, 28, Table 1.1, https://openknowledge.worldbank.org/handle/10986/37952

the Vietnamese social scientists Nguyễn Trọng Chuẩn, Nguyễn Minh Luan and Le Huu Tang in the book, *Socioeconomic Renovation in Viet Nam*, which addresses the question of inequality in the rural population: "Those households who have good opportunities, better experience, talent for working and trading, and healthy labour, will be richer. Thus, the polarization does not represent inequity but equity: Those who work hard and well earn more, while those who are lazy and work inefficiently and ineffectively will earn less." And the authors make it clear that they oppose proposals for redistribution: "In comparison with the subsidy system, where distribution was egalitarian, the current polarization between the rich and the poor shows the reestablishment of social equity." Inequality, they assert, is not worthy of criticism and the pursuit of wealth should be promoted: "Polarization has itself become an important motivating force behind the recent considerable economic growth."[74]

These Vietnamese sociologists and philosophers conclude that it would be wrong to abandon the course of free-market reforms just because inequality between rich and poor is increasing. You would be hard pressed to find similar statements from sociologists in the U.S. or Europe.

Armed with this information and my initial impressions, I start my second trip to Vietnam, from mid to late September 2022. I decide to return to the Metropol Hotel, whose service I had been impressed by during a previous stay in 2014. An example: at that time I wanted to watch a DVD with my girlfriend Trang in the evening, but the European region coding of my DVD disc did not match the Asian region coding of the room's DVD player. At 10 p.m., the hotel found me a DVD player with European region coding – I don't know where. The next morning the hotel manager visited me personally to apologize for "what happened yesterday." I replied that it is a great hotel and I am happy with everything. His answer: "The problem with the DVD player shouldn't have happened, but I immediately noted that you will always find a European standard DVD player in each of our hotels." This is typical of

---

74 Nguyen Trang Chuan et al., "Social Policy," 158.

the service in many Asian hotels. It is certainly something Europeans and Americans can learn a lesson from.

My first impression of Vietnam's roads: I have to be more careful when crossing. No-one pays any attention to zebra crossings here. If a pedestrian starts to cross the street, no car or moped driver seems to even notice. I ask my interpreter how anyone who is old, can't run fast, or doesn't have the same level of alertness, ever makes it to the other side. "No problem, the young people help them across the street." My impression is that 80 percent of road users travel on motorcycles or mopeds, and according to statistics there are actually a few more.[75] There's even more honking than I've ever heard in Italy.

On the second day of my stay, I speak in front of more than 1,000 people at an event hosted by an online real estate agent. My lecture is about the psychology of the super-rich. The book of my second doctoral thesis, *The Wealth Elite*, has just been published in Vietnam. It has already been successful in South Korea and China. When I ask everyone in the room who wants to become rich, only a few people respond at first, but that's because many older people still don't speak English. After my interpreter translates the question, most people raise their hands.

I have lunch with a group of business people, including the founder of a private equity firm that invests in high-tech companies in Vietnam. I ask him what he thinks of the official commitment to socialism. "Well, some people may still talk about Marxism-Leninism, but in reality everyone here takes a capitalist approach to business." I ask whether Vietnam is experiencing the same kind of reversals you see in China, where after decades of putting more and more faith in the market, the state has started to exert more influence again in recent years? "No, definitely not. We believe in the market economy here, and we are currently even seeing some investors who previously favored China now switch their attention more to Vietnam."

A businessman from Korea who I arrange to meet for lunch at a vegetarian restaurant explains: "Because China has been increasingly regulating private

---

75 Kapur, https://thediplomat.com/2016/05/vietnams-lethal-traffic/.

companies in recent years and making life difficult for them, many are now coming to Vietnam. 'Escape from China' is the watchword."

My conversation with Đinh Minh Tuấn, who founded a small think tank, confirms this: "There is no tendency here to move away from more market and toward more state, as has been the case in China in recent years." The top tax rate in Vietnam is something high earners in Frankfurt or New York can only dream of: income tax peaks at 35 percent, and to pay at that rate you have to earn around 14 times the average income. From the example of Vietnam, it is clear that fighting poverty is not a battle that can be won with taxes on the rich and redistribution, but through strengthening the market economy.

In any case, envying the rich is a foreign concept in Vietnam. Wealth is admired here. Of the 13 countries in which I conducted surveys to analyze attitudes towards the rich, Poland was the only country in which general attitudes were slightly more positive than in Vietnam. The great majority of people in Vietnam hold no grudges against the rich, they want to become rich themselves – as confirmed by the survey cited above.

What's also interesting is that in all of the countries where I conducted the survey, men said it was important to them to become rich more often than women. It was only in Vietnam that significantly more women than men want to become rich: 72 percent of men and 80 percent of women in Vietnam said in the survey that it was important to them to become rich.[76]

During our conversation, Đinh Minh Tuấn highlights the important role played by women in business in Vietnam. According to a survey by Grant Thornton in 2019, 36 percent of executives in Vietnam are women, compared to 19 percent in Thailand. In my home country, Germany, the figure is 29 percent.[77] In a profile of Vietnam, the *Neue Zürcher Zeitung*, the leading Swiss quality broadsheet, wrote: "Unlike women in other Southeast Asian

76 Zitelmann, "Attitudes towards the rich in China, Japan, South Korea, and Vietnam," https://onlinelibrary.wiley.com/doi/10.1111/ecaf.12524.
77 Destatis, https://www.destatis.de/Europa/DE/Thema/Bevoelkerung-Arbeit-Soziales/Arbeitsmarkt/Qualitaet-der-Arbeit/_dimension-1/08_frauen-fuehrungspositionen.html#:~:text=Lettland percent20war percent20mit percent20einem percent20Frauenanteil,mit percent20lediglich percent2021 percent2C3 percent20 percent25

countries, the door to all professions and management levels is wide open for Vietnamese women."[78]

In Hanoi, I give lectures at several universities, including the renowned NEU (National Economics University) and the Foreign Trade University. At the Foreign Trade University, I am invited to a workshop on the motivation to become rich. Scholars at the university have read my publications on the subject, and have also conducted their own research. The motto of the workshop is "Rich people, rich country." It's about how to improve the image of the rich. No university in the U.S. or Europe has yet invited me to a workshop on this topic.

The Foreign Trade University has 20,000 students, two thirds of whom are female. The university has 850 faculty and staff members, and according to the university, the proportion of women working there is even higher than among the student body. And in Vietnam, all of this has been achieved without feminist ideology. Xuan has the following to say: "In Vietnam, it's less about demanding rights for women and more about doing something yourself to succeed as a woman. We don't want to rely on men, we want to rely on ourselves." This is something I had observed from previous visits to China: Asians, who are supposedly "collectivist" from a Western perspective, are much more individualistic in this respect than Europeans and Americans. They don't think you should expect the state to do something for you, they believe you should do it yourself.

Xuan herself is a good example: she started her first company, a chain of sandwich restaurants (similar to Subway), when she was only 23. She now owns 12 eateries in Vietnam and 20 in the South Korean capital, Seoul. Once her restaurant chain was up and running, she started a chain of pharmacies and, three years ago, a publishing house for audio books, which has already published 700 titles.

Today, Vietnam is home to seven billionaires. This wealthy circle is still dominated by men, but there is at last one woman among them: Nguyễn Thi

---

78 Rist / Phnom Penh, https://www.nzz.ch/international/in-vietnam-spielen-frauen-eine-starke-gesellschaftliche-rolle-ld.1605284?reduced=true.

Phương Thảo. In the U.S., in comparison, there is only one woman among the 20 richest individuals, Alice Walton, and she is an heiress.

Nguyễn Thi Phương Thảo was born in 1970 and is among the 1,400 richest people in the world with a fortune of USD 2.8 billion, according to *Forbes* (March 2024).[79] She earned her first million at the age of 21 as a student in Moscow by selling fax machines. In 2011, she founded the low-cost airline VietJet Air. She had a great affinity for marketing from day one. In 2012, her airline hit the headlines with commercials that showed flight attendants in bikinis. Flight attendants could choose whether they preferred to fly in traditional uniforms or bikinis, and most opted for the latter. Nguyễn Thi Phương Thảo says she has no problem with people associating her company with bikini stewardesses: "If that makes people happy, then we are happy." In response to allegations that this turns women into sex symbols, she says: "If a beautiful image helps our customers feel happy, we will always try our best. In this world, there are a lot of beauty contests where the contestants wear bikinis ... The bikini shows beautiful characteristics. Our message at VietJet is we did this for the benefit of beauty and happiness."[80]

In 2017, her Saigon-based company went public and she became a billionaire. In addition, the entrepreneur is active in the banking sector (HD Bank) and has also invested in real estate, including owning three beach resorts.

The pursuit of wealth doesn't have to be about millions or even billions. Many Vietnamese women are also interested in earning money on a small scale. Cosmetic products are often very expensive as a result of customs duties and taxes. I notice this myself when I want to buy sunscreen in a store and have to pay the equivalent of 30 US dollars for a tiny bottle, much more than I would ever have to pay in Germany. My interpreter Huong explains to me that a lot of women in Vietnam order cosmetic products from China or the U.S. and then sell them on the internet.

At first, I thought this all involved the shadow economy and must be

---

79 Forbes.com, https://www.forbes.com/profile/thi-phuong-thao-nguyen/?sh=54de2bf91a22.
80 Chiou, https://www.cnbc.com/2016/05/24/nguyen-thi-phuong-thao-takes-vietjet-from-bikini-flights-to-ipo-in-5-years.html.

illegal but somehow tolerated by the authorities. However, Trân Hửu Đúc, a representative of a private equity fund I speak to on my last day in Vietnam, explains that it is all perfectly legal and that the state charges a flat 7 percent tax on all such sales. The products are largely sold on Facebook, TikTok and Vietnamese eCommerce platforms.

Speaking of eCommerce, online channels are also increasingly reshaping the Vietnamese retail landscape. However, Amazon is not active in Vietnam. There are four major eCommerce platforms, but the first two have now been bought by the Chinese online giants Alibaba and Tencent. The third largest online retailer started by selling books, just as Amazon once did.

Trân Hửu Đúc founded a venture capital fund, VIISA, with a modest investment volume of five million dollars. The fund initially invests very manageable amounts of between 20,000 and 25,000 US dollars, which is a lot in Vietnam. When I spoke to him, he was preparing a second fund, which would have a slightly larger volume of 20 million US dollars.

The importance of entrepreneurship is writ large at Vietnam's universities, including the state-run VNU Vietnam University of Economics & Business. Here, I was invited to give a talk as part of the Business Challenge Session. The competition is jointly organized with a number of partners, including the Friedrich Naumann Foundation from Germany. During the competition, several teams of students develop business ideas over a few months, supported by a team of mentors made up of entrepreneurs and former entrepreneurs. At the end, there are cash prizes for the winners. This is intended to promote entrepreneurial thinking among students.

Is the government getting too involved in the economy? People I talk to, who I don't want to name here, tell me that the state often places certain demands on companies but describes them as "voluntary." But anyone who doesn't meet these demands soon runs into problems, for example with the tax authorities. Another interviewee tells me that one of her friends is very, very wealthy, but has decided against building a large company because he thinks it is better to fly "under the radar." So, he has set up ten medium-sized companies. When I reply that the authorities could easily discover his ruse, she responds: "No, people are very creative: formally he only owns one company, the others belong to other family members or trusted relatives."

One of the biggest problems in Vietnam is corruption. Although things have improved in recent years, bribes are still very popular. One businessman tells me: "The official lists of party and state functionaries' salaries are published in the newspapers, and many only get 500 or 1,000 US dollars a month. Any yet, they often drive expensive Mercedes and lead lavish lifestyles. Of course, one wonders: where does the money come from?"

Another businessman, this time the manager of the Vietnamese branch of a Korean company, complains that the country's IT infrastructure, such as data centers, is still not up to scratch. Startups are still too often founded by the children of rich parents with good connections. Others don't have the money. I object that you need good ideas rather than money, because there is money for good ideas from venture capital and private equity companies. "Yes," he acknowledges, "but that brings us to the next problem. There are people with good ideas, but often their English is not good enough, and that is of course the prerequisite for pitching ideas to financiers, most of whom come from abroad."

Another problem, and one I have previously encountered in China, is that many people in Asia confuse investing with gambling. The motto is often "get rich quick," and all too many try their luck with cryptocurrencies or speculating on the stock market – which probably doesn't lead to quick riches for most people and is more likely to make them poorer.

When I am asked for investment advice during a press conference to launch my book, I reply: "Rather than thinking about where to invest the little money that most Vietnamese people have and then ending up with dubious cryptocurrencies or stock market losses, I have another recommendation: invest everything in learning English. This will help you more than anything else, it is by far the best investment anyone can make. You don't have to be able to speak English perfectly, I can't do that either and I've never had a talent for foreign languages, on the contrary. But I know that anyone can learn English well enough to be able to use it in business."

On the subject of learning languages: Kwon Hyuck Jun from South Korea has lived in Vietnam for 18 years. He came here because he didn't want to join the military in South Korea. There was an opportunity to work overseas for the South Korean government instead of joining the military. Nevertheless, he still had to complete basic army training in South Korea. "Then they told me: So, instead of continuing to serve in the army here – which meant more than two years back then – you can do this job in Vietnam, but you have to speak Vietnamese. You have three months to learn the language. If you can't do it, you'll have to go back to South Korea and join the military."

He didn't like the prospect of that at all. "For three months I did nothing but study Vietnamese, day and night. I only slept a few hours and ate my meals quickly, but I had a good reason: you definitely don't want to go back into the army. No way. After three months I spoke Vietnamese and deleted the word 'impossible' from my vocabulary." I admit that many years ago, I asked Trang to explain to me how to write and speak Vietnamese and gave up after an hour. I just didn't have as strong a reason as the businessman from South Korea.

In Hanoi I meet numerous people from other countries who have been living here for several years, such as the former German ambassador to Vietnam, Christian-Ludwig Weber-Lortsch, who married a Vietnamese woman and has settled here. However, it is no longer so easy to get a residence permit. Because he is married to a Vietnamese woman, he has a permit for three years, which he will then need to renew.

Nowadays, it is often said that the Vietnamese have become stricter about who can take up residency in the country, even if the person has a lot of money. They are worried that too many rich Chinese people might settle here, and they don't want that. And since you can't pass a special law to make it more difficult for Chinese people to obtain a residency permit, you have to make it apply to all foreigners.

My conversations constantly come back to the topic of freedom of expression. Vietnam is a one-party system and there is no freedom of the press as we know it in Western countries. The newspapers are state-owned and they always adhere to the government line. A YouTuber from Saigon who did an interview with me explains: "I used to work for state TV, where there were very strict regulations. I wanted to express myself more freely and launched my own YouTube channel, which now has 250,000 followers. In any case, young people in Vietnam hardly watch TV any more and don't buy the print editions of newspapers, they get their news from YouTube and social media."

A journalist explains to me that normal people can express themselves relatively freely on the internet and social media, including critically about the government. "But if someone is prominent, for example a prominent athlete or entrepreneur, and they are critical of the government, then they quickly get into problems."

Whenever one of my books is published in Vietnam, it first has to pass through the state censorship office. With books like *Dare to be Different* or *The Wealth Elite* this is just a formality and no problem at all. I found a publisher in Vietnam for my book, *The Power of Capitalism*, and they had already finished the translation. We hoped that in Vietnam it would be enough to replace the word "capitalism" with "market economy". But after everything had been prepared, the publisher told me that the censors had not approved the book after all.

A few years ago, I published an article about the development of the economy in Vietnam. The tone of the article was positive, although I also noted a few negative aspects, such as there still being a lot that needed to be done in the fight against corruption and to strengthen the rule of law. In the same article, I praised Vietnam for its market economy reforms. Interestingly, these positive sentences were deleted and my contact in Vietnam said that sometimes newspapers don't want the government to be praised.

Overall, it is fair to say that Vietnam is far from Western standards in terms of freedom of the press and freedom of speech, but is nevertheless freer than China. This is evident from the fact that Google, Facebook, X (formerly Twitter) and similar platforms are blocked in China. Without a VPN you cannot access them. In Vietnam, on the other hand, you have free access to the internet and can read Western media and use all social networks. I had a Facebook page in Vietnam for several years. Facebook is by far the most important medium for communication in Vietnam.

With only two days left in Vietnam, I give a lecture at the German Goethe Institute. There are lively discussions and also critical questions. One member of the audience asks: "But isn't prosperity without freedom also a form of slavery?" Apparently, he wanted to express that economic freedom alone is not enough if it is not accompanied by intellectual and political freedom. I am of the same opinion, but at the same time I resist downplaying the importance of economic freedom (even if it is not accompanied by political freedom). For the millions of Vietnamese who lived in abject poverty 20 or 30 years ago, it makes a major difference that their standard of living has improved significantly as a result of economic reforms.

Last day: dinner with Oliver Massmann, who many people tell me is the best German-speaking lawyer in Vietnam. He is also licensed in Germany and the U.S., but – unlike his colleagues – speaks perfect Vietnamese. He came to Vietnam 25 years ago because he saw a lot of beautiful Asian women at a party in Germany and his friend explained to him that the women came from Vietnam and that everyone there was so beautiful. Well, of course that's not true. But in fact there are more beautiful women here than in the United States. I met one of them at a lecture at NEU University: Linh, 28, studied international law and finance in Boston for several years and graduated with honors. She is the most beautiful and at the same time most intelligent woman I met on my trip around the world. It's a shame there was only time for dinner on my penultimate day in Vietnam.

Back to Massmann. He explains the importance of the free trade agreements and international trade agreements for Vietnam that he has been so instrumental in drafting. A likeable guy who also does bodybuilding, which is another interest we share.

On the journey home I feel bad and under the weather. At first I think it's a cold. When I arrive in Germany, I realize I have picked up Covid for the second time. The timing is ideal: it would have been really annoying if I had gotten sick in the first few days in Vietnam. I am forced to cancel a planned trip to the Mont Pelerin conference in Oslo, but am healthy again in time for my trip to Miami for the Students for Liberty conference. And I am able to use the time to write my part of a book about attitudes to the rich in Chile, which I will be publishing with Axel Kaiser. [In fact, it was published about a year later under the title *El Odio a los Ricos*.]

October 2022
Miami, United States

Two weeks after returning from Vietnam, I have recovered from my second Covid infection and travel to Miami for the Students for Liberty annual conference. I have already spoken at a previous annual meeting of this globally active organization in Washington D.C., in February 2018.

As I enter Miami, I avoid the often-annoying lines because I flew first class – sometimes I fly business class, but since my girlfriend Alica is with me, I chose first class this time. We want to vacation together in Miami after the conference. My last vacation was a long time ago, before the Covid pandemic.

The officials you meet when you enter the United States don't usually tend to be particularly friendly, and that is initially the case this time, too. But things brighten up when the officer asks me how I earned the "Dr." title in my passport. His face lights up when I explain that I am a historian. He is very interested in history and comes from Ukraine. He exchanges a few friendly sentences in Russian with Alica, who speaks five languages, including Russian, because her mother is from Belarus.

I spent some time in Miami a few years ago, but found the concrete hotels on the beach ugly, and this time, again, my first impressions are quite negative. Even before I arrived, I was annoyed at the hotel for not being able to provide a printer for my room despite a hefty price tag of several tens of thousands of dollars for two weeks. There is no question that the service in hotels in Asia is much better than is the case in the United States.

The Students for Liberty event is truly international – around 500 participants from 50 countries come together here in Miami. Unfortunately, I have an extremely poor memory when it comes to faces, which can be a bit embarrassing when people come up to me with greetings like: "Hi, we met in

Tbilisi;" "We met a few months ago in São Paulo;" or "I met you at a lecture in Milan."

The event begins on October 14 with a conversation between Students for Liberty CEO Wolf von Laer and Whole Foods Market founder John Mackey. I had shopped at Whole Foods the day before and picked up my dinner – they have a great selection of vegetables that you'd be hard put to find anywhere else. John Mackey studied philosophy and religion for several semesters and also worked in a vegetarian cooperative. In 1978, he and his girlfriend founded a vegetarian supermarket, SaferWay, which two years later merged with another grocery market to form Whole Foods Market. Mackey reports how, after founding the company, he initially lived on 200 US dollars a month and, since he didn't have an apartment, he lived in the store with his girlfriend. As there was no shower, they had to wash in the sink. But he has very fond memories of those early days; he was in love and founding the company was a great adventure. He didn't need any money for himself. He later became very wealthy, taking the company public on the NASDAQ technology exchange, and in 2017 it was acquired by Amazon for 13.7 billion US dollars. Today, Whole Foods operates more than 500 stores in the United States, Canada and the United Kingdom.

Whole Foods was the first major grocery chain to embrace animal welfare. Mackey was persuaded to make changes by the animal rights activist Lauren Ornelas, who criticized Whole Foods' animal welfare standards for ducks at a shareholder meeting in 2003. Mackey gave Ornelas his email address and they communicated on the topic. He became concerned with the problems of factory farming and decided to switch to a predominantly vegetarian diet that included only eggs from his own chickens. He has been vegan since 2006. He advocates stricter animal welfare standards. A non-meat eater and enthusiastic believer in capitalism – how can I help but like him given I am both of those things myself.

Mackey is an ardent champion of capitalism. "Capitalism is the greatest thing that mankind has ever done," Mackey declares at the event. He even wrote a book called *Conscious Capitalism*. But he sparked a shitstorm when he published an article opposing Obama Care in the *Wall Street Journal* in August 2009. Left-wing groups called for a boycott of his businesses.

Wolf von Laer praises the modest, soft-spoken entrepreneur for his courage in taking a political stand, but Mackey himself says he would never write an article like that again because the damage to his business was too great. A pity. But that's how it is today, and not just in the United States. Political statements from leading business figures are only tolerated if they are critical of capitalism or "woke." Otherwise, there is a risk of a shitstorm and boycotts, like the one against Whole Foods. "Cancel Culture" is the name given to this phenomenon. It is actually the opposite of "culture" and is nothing more than an attack on freedom of expression.

Another of the speakers at the event is Joe Walsh, who represented the state of Illinois in the U.S. House of Representatives from 2011 to 2013 on the Republican ticket but has since left the party. Walsh initially supported Trump, but later became one of his harshest critics within the Republican Party. After Trump's summit with Putin in Helsinki in July 2018, he stated: "I will never support Trump again" and called him "a danger to this country." Walsh recommended using the Twenty-Fifth Amendment to remove Trump from office. Despite everything, however, he says it would be wrong to think the problem lies solely with Trump. Even if the second most popular Republican at the time, Florida Governor Ron DeSantis – who has attracted support from a number of libertarians – were to run, Walsh says it wouldn't make a difference.

Walsh explains that he was one of the first activists in the Tea Party movement that emerged in 2009, but that it was actually two movements: one that advocated a leaner government, lower taxes and less debt, and the other advocating an authoritarian state, ultimately a Christian country, even a theocracy. This second school of thought, which also espouses extreme nationalism, has now become established in the Republican Party. There should be no illusions, warns Walsh, that the average Republican voter has given up on the idea of democracy. In February 2021, he wrote on Twitter (now X): "I left the Republican Party almost exactly one year ago. Someone asked me that day why I left. I said, 'Because the GOP no longer supports democracy. It embraces fascism. It believes in conspiracies. And it's a cult. I don't want to belong to a cult."'

Most libertarians would certainly not put it in such harsh terms, but in one respect Walsh probably speaks for them all: he describes himself as "homeless" in the American two-party system, and that is how so many libertarians see themselves. Walsh criticizes the Democratic Party and Joe Biden just as harshly, saying it is no alternative. He even blames the Democrats for the way the Republican Party has developed. Ultimately, he says, today's Republican party is the revenge of the right against the left.

The libertarians seem to inhabit the space between two political ideologies – by European standards they combine elements of both the left and the right. On the one hand, they are enthusiastic supporters of capitalism and staunchly opposed to socialism, the welfare state and redistribution. On the other, they are, for example, vehemently committed to LGBTQ+ rights and the decriminalization of drugs.

The issue of drug legalization marks a dividing line between conservatives and libertarians, according to a panel discussion on the topic "It's Time to End the Drug War." One participant, who used to be against the legalization of drugs and now supports it for all drugs, explained that the turning point for her was the realization that the question of what she personally likes or dislikes has nothing to do with what should be legal and what should be illegal. The state has lost the war on drugs and legalizing drugs will lead to fewer drug-related deaths and less crime, a stance all of the participants in the discussion agree upon.

Another topic: why are a growing number of Latin American countries slipping into socialism? Daniel Di Martino, a Venezuelan who, like a quarter of his country's population, fled the socialist country and has been living in the U.S. for six years, speaks of an "epidemic of envy" in Latin America. However, he also criticizes conservative governments who, when they were in power, did not seize the opportunity to implement the kind of radical free-market reforms that would have really changed people's lives. He points to Mauricio Macri in Argentina as an example.

However, he believes that the U.S. sanctions against Venezuela, which are often criticized by libertarians, are justified: they have indeed helped to force the government in Venezuela to make corrections, which has improved life for people in Venezuela somewhat. The socialists' claim that the sanctions are to blame for their country's problems is therefore wrong – the opposite is true.

Martha Bueno, whose parents fled Cuba and who, like so many of her compatriots, now lives in Miami, warns young Americans who are in favor of socialism not to be too sure that what happened in Venezuela could not also happen in their country: "Venezuela was a democracy and had one of the highest standards of living in the world. The country also has the largest oil reserves in the world. People thought it would be impossible for a country in such a position to be run into the ground by socialists in just a few years, losing its freedom and prosperity. But that's exactly what happened. And it can also happen here, in our country."

Venezuela should indeed be a warning to us all: in 1970, it was the richest country in Latin America and one of the 20 richest countries in the world. The gross domestic product per capita was higher than that of Spain, Greece or Israel and only 13 percent lower than that of Great Britain.[81] The downturn began in the 1970s with an unusually high degree of state regulation of the labor market, which was steadily subjected to ever tighter regulation from 1974 onward. In hardly any other country in Latin America (or anywhere else in the world, for that matter) was the labor market so heavily regulated. From adding the equivalent of 5.35 months' wages to the cost of employing someone in 1972, non-wage labor costs soared to add the equivalent of 8.98 months' wages in 1992.[82]

But, as the example of Venezuela shows, when the problems keep getting bigger, it does not necessarily mean that people will learn. History is not like a Hollywood film with a guaranteed happy ending. Or, to put it another way: things can always get worse.

---

81 Hausmann / Rodríguez, 1.
82 Bello / Bermúdez, 117.

Many Venezuelans put their faith in the charismatic socialist leader Hugo Chávez as the savior who would deliver their country from corruption, poverty and economic decline. Chávez was elected president in 1998. A year later, the Republic of Venezuela was renamed the Bolivarian Republic of Venezuela (*República Bolivariana de Venezuela*) in honor of Simón Bolívar (1783–1830), who went from being a South American freedom fighter, particularly against the Spanish, to a dictator.

We know how this story ended: Venezuela lost first economic, then political freedom, inflation rose to an absurd 1,000,000 percent, people suffered from hunger, and, to date, 7.5 million Venezuelans (25 percent of the population) have fled the country. The UNHCR concluded: "This is the largest exodus in Latin America's recent history and one of the largest displacement crises in the world (as of February 2023)."[83]

Venezuela's history should be a warning to us all: even prosperous, democratic countries are not immune from losing their prosperity and freedom in a matter of just a few years. Freedom, economic as well as political, cannot be taken for granted; it has to be fought for, over and over again.

The reports from Ukrainian refugees, who speak about their ordeals and terrible experiences, are also harrowing to hear in Miami. However, opinions among libertarians in the U.S. differ on the question of how the U.S. government should react to the Russian invasion. There are two opposing camps. First, there are those, including a representative of the conservative Heritage Foundation, who believe the U.S. should not get involved and it should be up to Europeans to deal with the problem, not Americans. Then there are those who take the opposite position and believe that the history of the twentieth century proves that the U.S. has always been drawn into conflicts when it tries to stay out of them. Several speakers criticize the attitude of Europeans, who have long been free riders in terms of security policy, constantly relying on the U.S. to step in when the going gets tough.

---

83 UNHCR, "Venezuela Humanitarian Crisis," https://www.unrefugees.org/emergencies/venezuela/#:~:text=More percent20than percent207.3 percent20million percent20Venezuelans,(as percent20of percent20February percent202023).

However, there is also a counter-position to this: Europeans can sometimes be more sensible than the Americans, for example when Germany – rightly – warned against invading Iraq.

However, there is almost universal astonishment when it comes to questions of energy policy: Germany, Austria and the Czech Republic, according to one speaker, are having serious problems with their gas supplies, for which they only have themselves to blame. And not only because they have become so dependent on Russian gas and – like Germany – have decided to phase out nuclear power. "It is an absolute mystery to me," says one speaker, "why Germany has banned fracking but has no problems whatsoever importing gas obtained through fracking from the U.S."

The bottom line is that it has been well worth coming to Miami to an event with so many interesting discussions and debates. Wolf von Laer, CEO of Students for Liberty, has succeeded in establishing the organization as the world's largest network for libertarian students. And this annual event, which is not attended by as many students as you would hope – the cost of attending is too high for many students – is not even the most important item on the Students for Liberty program. That honor goes to the thousands of events the organization holds every single year for students all around the world.

November 2022
Lisbon and Porto, Portugal

At the beginning of November 2022, I travel to Portugal. It's been four decades since I was last in this beautiful country. The first thing that strikes me is how many people here speak more than passable English. No comparison with Spain, Italy or France. One reason is probably that – as in Scandinavian countries – almost all of the movies and TV shows are broadcast in English with Portuguese subtitles.

Some people think they can get to know a country by seeing the sights. I, on the other hand, use my time here to meet people. On the first day, I'm in Porto and give lectures there. The next morning, I have to get up at five o'clock and take the express train to Lisbon, where I have appointments with politicians, representatives of a libertarian think tank, and journalists. Of course, I read a lot about the country's history in preparation for the trip.

You might be surprised to hear that Portugal had the longest-standing colonial empire of all European countries. Its colonial history began with the conquest of Ceuta in North Africa in 1415 and ended with the return of its last overseas province, Macau, to China in 1999. Little Portugal was a global empire that even ruled Brazil for more than three centuries – a country that covers an area almost 100 times larger than Portugal. Today, it is only the fact that the people of Brazil speak Portuguese – unlike the rest of Latin America, where Spanish dominates – that reminds us of this.

Portugal is a comparatively young democracy; after the abolition of the monarchy in 1910, the military repeatedly held sway over the country. In May 1926, a coup ended the "First Republic." António de Oliveira Salazar ruled as Prime Minister from 1932 to 1968, backed by the powers of the military. He was a staunch supporter of left-wing Catholic social doctrine. In September 1933, a "National Labor Statute" was introduced, establishing the right to work and a decent wage, fixed working hours and paid annual leave. In 1935, the "Law of Economic Reconstitution" was passed – the state dominated the economy.[84]

The economic outcomes were correspondingly poor: Portugal remained at the bottom of the European league tables in terms of labor productivity, agricultural output, degree of mechanization and fertilizer use. Despite the high rate of employment in the agricultural sector, the food supply was therefore not guaranteed and agricultural imports remained necessary.[85] Industrialization only began in the 1950s and 60s, and the gross domestic product per capita in 1970 was only 934 US dollars (Spain, 1,209 US dollars; Italy, 2,100 US dollars; France, 2,862 US dollars; USA, 5,247 US dollars).[86] Between 1971 and 1973, around 1.4 million people left Portugal to look for work elsewhere[87] – a high proportion of the population, especially when you consider that less than nine million people lived in Portugal at the time.

On April 25, 1974, another military coup took place, led by left-wing generals against the authoritarian state leadership, which became known as the "Carnation Revolution." It was led by the *Movimento das Forcas Armadas* (Armed Forces Movement): "At times, the revolutionary process also seemed to take on a communist orientation, and in the first few years after the fall of the corporatist-dictatorial regime, all the center and right-wing parties also adopted a 'leftist' character with regard to the left-wing 'Armed Forces Movement.'"[88] Even the party initially founded in 1974 under the name *Partido Popular Democrático*, which had a more libertarian-conservative bent, changed its name to *PSD Partido Social Democrata* (Social Democratic Party) in 1976. For a non-Portuguese, this is all rather confusing.

The new constitution of 1976 defined the state's goal as to open up a path towards a socialist society.[89] And the government did not stop at

---

84 Bernecker / Pietschmann, 109.
85 Bernecker / Pietschmann, 117.
86 Wikipedia, " "Liste der Länder nach historischer Entwicklung des Bruttoinlandsprodukts pro Kopf," https://de.wikipedia.org/wiki/Liste_der_L percentC3 percentA4nder_nach_ historischer_Entwicklung_des_Bruttoinlandsprodukts_pro_Kopf.
87 Bernecker / Pietschmann, 118.
88 Bernecker / Pietschmann, 122–133.
89 Bernecker / Pietschmann, 123.

words. From the beginning of 1975, the structure of property relations was partially amended through nationalizations, state administration of companies, land occupations and expropriations of large estates, as well as the takeover of companies under a system of workers' self-administration. In 1975, the Revolutionary Council decided to nationalize the banks, insurance companies, transport, traffic and energy sectors, as well as basic industries. Around 600 companies were expropriated in this way.[90]

As always, Portugal's socialist experiment failed. Things only started to look up in the 1980s and 90s. "Those were good years in Portugal," says Manuel Pinkeiro from the *Mais Liberdade* think tank when I meet him in Porto. As in many other countries, the economic upswing followed a series of market economy reforms. Aníbal Cavaco Silva of the pro-market "social democratic" PSD party governed from 1985 to 1995. He rolled back nationalizations and pursued free-market policies that were very good for the country.

Between 1985 and 1995, the country's economy grew by 3.2 percent annually, inflation decreased from 20 to 4 percent, foreign investment increased tenfold and foreign debt fell.[91] The reference to a "socialist society" was removed from the revised constitution of 1988 and the extreme dominance of the state was reduced somewhat. These policy shifts improved the lives of people in Portugal: in the mid-1980s, the average income in Portugal was only 52.5 percent of the EU average; in 1998 it was 70 percent.[92]

The rise in economic freedom in Portugal since 1995 has been similar to that in neighboring Spain. Both began in 1995 with an *Index of Economic Freedom* score of 62.4 (Portugal) and 62.8 (Spain), which had improved to 70.8 (Portugal) and 68.2 (Spain) by 2022. According to the Heritage Foundation, Portugal has made progress in recent years and has now joined the group of countries that are considered "mostly free" for the first time – primarily thanks to positive ratings for "Property Rights," "Judicial Effectiveness," and "Monetary Freedom." However, Portugal receives very poor marks for

90 Bernecker / Pietschmann, 125.
91 Marques, 651–652.
92 Bernecker / Pietschmann, 127.

"Government Spending," which has amounted to 45 percent of GDP over the past three years. In comparison, the level in Switzerland is only 33 percent.[93] Public debt increased from 51 percent at the end of the 1990s to 127 percent in 2021! The representatives of the libertarian movement that I meet in Porto and Lisbon are surprised that Portugal has improved in the Heritage Foundation's rating in recent years.

Overall, Portugal is not in a bad position – in the *Index of Economic Freedom* it ranked 30th in 2023, ahead of Poland (40th), France (57th), Italy (69th) and Greece (107th).[94] In recent years, the Portuguese economy has developed positively thanks to tourism and a real estate boom, despite being governed by the socialist António Costa since 2015. Portugal is one of the most popular countries in Europe for tourists, who are particularly drawn to the Algarve.

The country's real estate boom is far from healthy – as is always the case when taxes play a major role in real estate investments. Tax advantages have attracted investors, but it is by no means clear if the upturn in the real estate market is at all sustainable. Prices have been rising since mid-2013, as data from the National Statistics Institute (INE) shows. For five consecutive years, property prices have been above the level at which the European Commission considers a market to be at risk of a price bubble, as Eurostat declared in August 2021.[95]

One topic that comes up in many of the conversations I have with the people I meet in Portugal is the state-owned airline TAP. In 2011, the Portuguese government announced it was privatizing the airline as part of the EU's 87 billion euro rescue package, which Portugal needed to access as it had been particularly hard hit by the global financial crisis. After several attempts, privatization failed in December 2012 and was suspended until 2015. In that year, the state sold 61 percent of TAP to a consortium formed by two entrepreneurs for around 350 million euros. However, the state then

93 Heritage Foundation, *2022 Index of Economic Freedom*, 345.
94 Heritage Foundation, *2023 Index of Economic Freedom*, https://www.heritage.org/index/.
95 TPN, https://www.theportugalnews.com/de/nachrichten/2022-01-30/immobilienblase-in-portugal/64874.

bought back shares until it owned 92 percent of TAP.[96] Now the company is to be privatized again ... an absurd back-and-forth. The state has invested a total of 3.2 billion euros in its airline, which is a constant loss maker. Think of what could have been done with all that money! Why does a state even need its own airline? There would certainly be enough private operators to quickly fill the gap if TAP were simply closed down.

It's a similar situation with the largest and most important financial institution in Portugal, *Banco Comercial Português* (BCP), which belongs to the state. Why? Have state-owned banks ever worked better than private ones?

I meet Carlos Guimarães Pinto, who founded the *Mais Liberdade* think tank and is also a member of parliament for the libertarian party *Iniciativa Liberal*, together with the party's chairman João Cotrim de Figueiredo. I am invited to the parliament building in Lisbon, one of the most beautiful houses of parliament I have seen. I ask Carlos, who is presenting my book at a *Mais Liberdade* event in the evening, what he would change in Portugal: "First of all, taxes should be lowered. Even someone earning 30,000 euros a year pays a marginal tax rate of 38 percent; at 50,000 euros it's 45 percent; and at 80,000 euros you pay 48 percent." The libertarian party also believes that the state television station and the state-owned bank should be privatized.

The labor market in Portugal is particularly heavily regulated. Extremely restrictive employment protection regulations require employers to pay substantial severance payments if they want to let employees go. And according to the law, overtime cannot be offset against days on which less work is done; instead, the moment someone works more than eight hours, 300 percent of their salary must be paid for each hour of overtime. Many companies in the private sector do not adhere to this. The minimum wage in Portugal is not particularly high at 822 euros (2021) per month, although it did rise by 72 percent between 2002 and 2019, while gross domestic product only increased by 49 percent in nominal terms.[97]

Another of the *Iniciativa Liberal's* demands is for cannabis to be legalized,

---

96 Haße, https://www.airliners.de/hintergrund-uebernahmekandidat-tap-air-portugal/69772.
97 Jorge, 3.

says Carlos. "Wait a minute," I interject, "I thought drug possession had been legal for two decades?" He explains to me that although the possession of drugs has been decriminalized, which means you won't be punished for possessing certain amounts of cannabis (or even hard drugs such as heroin), trafficking it is illegal. Absurd.

How do the Portuguese, who – as I have shown – have a long statist tradition, feel about the market economy and capitalism today? From May 27 to June 6, 2022, I commissioned the opinion research institute Ipsos MORI to conduct a survey on the image of capitalism in Portugal. First, we asked a few questions to find out what Portuguese people think of the market economy – and we deliberately avoided the word "capitalism." The statement that received the most support in Portugal in this first set of questions (40 percent) was "The state should set the prices for rent and food and should set minimum and maximum wages," while the opinion that "Private businesses alone should decide what products to manufacture and what prices to charge for them ; the state should not be involved in that" elicited the least support (17 percent). When responses to the three statements in favor of the state and the three statements in favor of the market are combined, we seen that 32 percent of respondents agreed with statements in favor of greater state influence and 24 percent supported pro-market statements in favor of a reduced role for the government.

The survey's respondents were also presented with 18 statements on capitalism, ten of which were negative and eight positive. Clearly, agreement with negative statements (averaging 33 percent) outweighed agreement with positive statements (averaging 16 percent). Without exception, the nine most frequently selected statements were all negative. For instance, 43 percent of Portuguese respondents say that "Capitalism leads to growing inequality," which is matched by 43 percent who believe that "Capitalism promotes selfishness and greed"; 42 percent agree that "Capitalism is dominated by the rich; they set the political agenda"; 38 percent claim that "Capitalism leads to monopolies"; 33 percent are of the opinion that "Capitalism entices people to buy products they don't need"; and 30 percent think that "Capitalism is responsible for environmental destruction and climate change." The survey's findings are therefore quite clear: in Portugal, popular opinion is dominated by anti-capitalism.

From the book presentations in Porto and Lisbon, I will remember one woman's statement in particular: "I am in favor of capitalism because I am a woman," she says. "Throughout history, women have always been economically dependent on men. Only capitalism has made it possible for women to stand on their own two feet financially." Actually, that's quite obvious. But sometimes you don't even see the obvious any more.

In Lisbon, I meet Zita Maria de Seabra Roseiro, one of the most important figures in the Portuguese libertarian movement. During the dictatorship, she was a member of the resistance and belonged to the Communist Party. She lived underground for several years and fought against the dictatorship. Zita was a member of the party's Politburo. But even then she was a non-conformist. She was expelled from the Politburo in 1988 as a result of her criticism of the party, then from the Central Committee, and then from the Communist Party itself. She published her autobiography in 1988. She initially joined the center-right "Social Democratic" Party and is now a member of the Libertarian Party and a key instigator of the libertarian think tank *Mais Liberdade*.

Alexandra from *Alétheia Editores*, the publisher of my book, also used to be member of the Communist Party. There we are, three former communists, sitting together over lunch and thinking about how we can make capitalism stronger in Portugal. I ask what role the Communist Party plays in Portugal today and what policies it advocates. Little has changed. Its role model is North Korea. Together with the Green Party, with which they ran a joint list, they won 6.7 percent in 2022.

A year after I visit Portugal, a corruption scandal rocks the country. The investigations under "Operation Influencer" are targeting Costa, the socialist head of government who had been in power since 2015. After more than 40 house searches and five arrests in early November 2023, Costa tenders his resignation. His chief of staff, his most important advisor, and three other people are all arrested.[98] Early elections are subsequently held in Portugal on March 10, 2024, and the conservative Democratic Alliance (AD) of lead candidate Luís Montenegro wins a narrow victory with 29.49 percent of the vote. Pedro Nuno Santos' Socialist Party (PS), which had been in power since late 2015, comes second on 28.66 percent. The right-wing Chega party more than doubles its share of the vote compared to the last election, securing 18 percent.

---

98 Rössler, https://www.faz.net/aktuell/politik/ausland/portugal-mit-politischer-krise-ein-ruecktritt-der-nun-voreilig-wirkt-19368127.html.

November 2022
Prague, the Czech Republic

The last time I was in Prague was almost ten years ago – back then I went to see an international bodybuilding championship where Arnold Schwarzenegger was a special guest. This time I'm coming to Prague to promote my book, *In Defence of Capitalism*.

This is a fascinating city and, at the same time, one I associate with the brutal suppression of the "Prague Spring" in August 1968. I was eleven years old at the time, but already very interested in politics. The politicians Alexander Dubček and Ludvík Svoboda had tried to introduce "socialism with a human face" in what was then Czechoslovakia. The Russians responded with tanks and the suppression of liberalization efforts, as they had done in East Germany in 1953 and Hungary in 1956. Only the collapse of the Soviet Union raised the prospect of freedom for the Czechs and Slovaks. However, unlike in Yugoslavia, the 1992 division of the country into two parts – the Czech Republic and Slovakia – was peaceful.

Entrepreneurship and private companies were eliminated even more radically by the communists in Czechoslovakia than they had been in other socialist countries. As early as 1948, almost all private companies with more than 20 employees were nationalized.[99] Between 1948 and 1953, independent handcraft, commercial production, and small-scale trade were completely nationalized. With this radical intervention in the small-scale private sector, Czechoslovak nationalization policy surpassed that of all other Central and Southeast European states. From 383,000 small businesses with 905,000 employees in 1948, there were only 47,000 small businesses with 50,000 employees in 1956. This number decreased from year to year and, in 1972, only 2,000 self-employed craftsmen were registered in the country.[100]

99 Teichova, *Wirtschaftsgeschichte der Tschechoslowakei 1918 – 1980*, 89.
100 Teichova, *Wirtschaftsgeschichte der Tschechoslowakei 1918 – 1980*, 89.

While there were attempts to modernize the economy during the reform period in the 1960s, the guiding principle of state ownership was never challenged. The reforms were limited to giving companies greater decision-making powers.[101] However, as Alice Teichova writes in her study on the economic history of Czechoslovakia, "in the course of introducing the reforms, the incompatibility of the new economic instruments, which were based on the interaction of plan and market, with the persistent conditions of bureaucratic-centralist planning in the party and state apparatus, were laid bare."[102] Though the economic situation improved somewhat as a result of the reforms,[103] the suppression of the "Prague Spring" in 1968 not only put an end to the political reforms, but also halted the economic reforms.

At the end of 1990, the proportion of private companies in Czechoslovakia was only 1.5 percent – significantly lower than in East Germany (8.5 percent), Hungary (14 percent) and Poland (26 percent).[104] Even more so than in other former socialist countries, the focus after the collapse of socialism was on the privatization of state-owned enterprises. The economist Václav Klaus, born in 1941, who was Minister of Finance from 1989 to 1992 and later Prime Minister and President of the Czech Republic, played an important role in all of this.

Klaus was a staunch follower of Hayek and Mises. He did not believe in the illusions of a "third way" between capitalism and socialism. He later recalled: "Explicitly and very early on we proclaimed that we wanted capitalism. We were not afraid of using that term. We lived in the country of Ota Šik, the main Czechoslovak reformer of the 1960s, who later became one of the main exponents of the ideology of the so-called third way. He returned from Switzerland a few days after the Velvet Revolution. We met with him then and told him 'No' – we were not interested in any kind of third way, we were already a generation ahead."[105]

Of course, the reformers were aware that it was neither possible nor

101 Teichova, *Wirtschaftsgeschichte der Tschechoslowakei 1918 – 1980*, 125.
102 Teichova, *Wirtschaftsgeschichte der Tschechoslowakei 1918 – 1980*, 127.
103 Teichova, *Wirtschaftsgeschichte der Tschechoslowakei 1918 – 1980*, 129.
104 Klaus, "Czechoslovakia and the Czech Republic," 65.
105 Klaus, "Czechoslovakia and the Czech Republic," 56.

desirable to save all state-owned companies – some would go under and make way for young and healthy private companies. Klaus took a pragmatic approach: privatization was not about achieving the maximum purchase price for companies, nor was it about setting up a "perfect" process. Speed was more important than perfection. "We believed it was neither useful nor possible to try to find 'optimal' owners. On the contrary, it was vital to get the privatization done so that the market rather than the state could sort out who the best owners really were."[106]

Like other countries, the Czech Republic experienced a "transformation recession" in the first years of the economic reforms. In the first three years after the end of communism, the Czech economy lost one third of its industrial output, one-fourth of its agriculture, and one fifth of its GDP. This decline in output opened the way to economic recovery and growth in subsequent years.[107] The growth rate for gross domestic product (GDP) returned to positive territory as early as 1993, reaching 2.9 percent in 1992 and 6.2 percent three years later.[108] Inflation, which had initially risen to almost 57 percent following the abolition of price controls in 1991, fell to below 9 percent by 1996.[109] Foreign investment, which had been zero in 1989, rose to over one billion US dollars in 1992 and climbed again to over 2.5 billion US dollars in 1995.[110]

From 1995 to 2022, the Czech Republic gained ground in the *Index of Economic Freedom*, increasing its score from 67.8 to 74.4, although it fell to 71.9 in 2023. In the 2023 ranking, it ranks 21st out of 176, ahead of the UK and the United States.[111] Strong property rights are a positive factor, while excessive government spending and excessive regulation of the labor market have a negative impact – the Czech Republic scores below average in both areas.[112]

---

106 Klaus, "Czechoslovakia and the Czech Republic," 68.
107 Klaus, "Czechoslovakia and the Czech Republic," 62.
108 Klaus, "Czechoslovakia and the Czech Republic," 62, Table 3.1.
109 Klaus, "Czechoslovakia and the Czech Republic," 64, Table 3.2.
110 Klaus, "Czechoslovakia and the Czech Republic," 66, Table 3.4.
111 Heritage Foundation, *2022 Index of Economic Freedom* and *2023 Index of Economic Freedom*.
112 Heritage Foundation, *2022 Index of Economic Freedom*, 167.

GDP per capita in the Czech Republic has almost quadrupled since 1990,[113] and people's standard of living has improved massively, with the gains continuing in recent years. In 2019, the average wage in the Czech Republic was 43 percent of the average income in the European Union. In 2014, it was only 35 percent.[114] Life expectancy has risen from 71.4 to 78.1 years since the end of socialism.[115]

Accordingly, the image of capitalism in the Czech Republic is better than in most other countries. A survey I commissioned in 2021 on the image of the market economy showed that in only two out of 35 countries – Poland and the United States – are attitudes toward the market economy more positive than in the Czech Republic. And even in the sections of the survey that used the word "capitalism," there were only five countries in which popular perceptions of capitalism were better than in the Czech Republic and 29 in which they were worse.

Incidentally, it is interesting to note that the difference between men and women and between people with lower and higher education is greater in the Czech Republic than in other countries. In almost all of the countries in which the survey was conducted, women and the less educated are less pro-capitalist (or more anti-capitalist) than men and the better educated, but in the Czech Republic the difference is particularly large.

In Prague, I meet Vladimír Pikora, a well-known Czech journalist and author. The 45-year-old is a financial market analyst and chief economist at the consultancy Next Finance. I ask him how he interprets the results of my survey. His answer: Václav Klaus "educated" the Czechs to appreciate the benefits of capitalism in the 1990s. Klaus was very influential back then, and his influence extended to the media. Many people trusted his economic policy expertise, Pikora explains. "But that changed later. Perhaps this is because so

---

113 The World Bank, https://data.worldbank.org/indicator/NY.GDP.PCAP. PP.CD?locations=CZ.
114 Kachlíková, https://deutsch.radio.cz/loehne-tschechien-bei-43-prozent-des-eu-durchschnitts-8682554.
115 Statista Research Department, https://de.statista.com/statistik/daten/studie/18645/umfrage/lebenserwartung-in-tschechien/.

many Czechs had exaggerated expectations and thought that in ten years we would be doing as well as the Germans or Austrians."

It would make more sense for Czechs to compare their situation not with Germany, but with other former socialist states. They would soon realize that hardly any other Eastern or Central European country launched such successful reforms or improved the standard of living as much as Poland and the Czech Republic. It is therefore not surprising that – as my survey confirms – approval of capitalism is particularly high in these countries, despite some disappointments.

However, opponents of the reforms in the Czech Republic have denounced every single case of individuals unjustly enriching themselves or things going wrong during privatizations because they opposed the entire reform agenda. And of course, in a process where hundreds of companies are being privatized, there are always going to be a few examples of unlawful enrichment and other negative developments.

From Pikora's point of view, Andrej Babiš, multibillionaire and Prime Minister from 2017 to 2021, is guilty of implementing policies that are bad for the country: "He is the second richest man in the Czech Republic with an estimated fortune of almost four billion US dollars, but he is a left-wing populist. He promised the voters everything, especially the elderly." Pikora accuses the Civic Democratic Party (ODS), which is widely regarded as center-right, of having engaged in a competition to outbid populists: "You can only lose in a competition like that."

I speak in detail with Professor Josef Šíma, the leading free-market economist in the Czech Republic. His room is adorned with pictures of Ludwig von Mises and Murray Rothbard, as well as of the Italian economist Bruno Leoni. He is also critical of Babiš. Basically, Šíma explains, Babiš has no convictions, he is a Machiavellian and populist who is only interested in power for power's own sake. Šíma believes that support for the market economy is strongest in the governing party, ODS, which governs together with Christian Democrats and Pirates. However, the ODS has announced lots of reforms and implemented little, Šíma notes critically.

Šíma invites me to speak to his students at Metropolitan University Prague (MUP), one of the oldest and largest private universities in the Czech Republic. Every year around 1,500 students enroll for their first year of study at MUP and the university currently has a student body of around 3,000. When I ask Šíma which reforms he believes are most urgently needed in the Czech Republic, he replies: school reform. As revealed by the annual PISA tests, students in the Czech Republic are falling further and further behind their international peers and the country's school system performs poorly.

The next day I meet Marek Pyszko, the Czech Republic's Chief Economist, in the beautiful Czernin Palace, the headquarters of the Ministry of Foreign Affairs. He shows me around the historic building, which is one of the most beautiful I have ever seen. However, he thinks that at some point the ministry may have to move to a new building because of the current building's poor energy efficiency.

Pyszko also notes that many entrepreneurs are disappointed that the center-right government led by the ODS announced reforms that it did not implement. He is worried about his country's rapidly increasing debt. The Czech Republic has so far been considered a model in this regard in Europe. In the *2023 Index of Economic Freedom*, the country still managed to get a healthy score in the "Fiscal Health" category (73.5 points). But "Government Spending" is the Czech Republic's worst category with 39.5 points. Pyszko believes this is because the populist Babiš has initiated a change for the worse with ever new social promises and corresponding measures. The center-right government that replaced him in 2021 did nothing to change this in view of the Covid crisis, inflation, and the war against Ukraine that Russia launched soon afterwards.

The Czech Republic's national debt, as reported in March 2023, ballooned to a record of almost 2.9 trillion korunas (120 billion euros) in 2022. Theoretically, every resident of the Czech Republic is around 275,000 korunas (11,730 euros) in debt. Compared to 2021, national debt increased by 429 billion korunas (18.3 billion euros) in 2022.[116]

---

116 Honigmann, https://deutsch.radio.cz/staatsschulden-tschechiens-steigen-auf-rekordwert-von-knapp-drei-billionen-8776405.

Two months after my visit to the Czech Republic, the country elects a new president in the third direct election of the Czech head of state. In the runoff between Petr Pavel and Andrej Babiš in late January, Pavel received 58.3 percent of the vote and was elected president. Unlike Andrej Babiš, Petr Pavel – who was himself a general until 2015 – has always stressed the importance of providing unwavering support to Ukraine. On several occasions he has stated that the West should have reacted much more assertively after Russia's annexation of Crimea and the secession of Donbas. He has also said that, under certain circumstances, he would even agree to deploying NATO soldiers to protect humanitarian corridors in Ukraine and enforce a no-fly zone.[117]

---

117 Bazydło, https://www.mdr.de/nachrichten/welt/osteuropa/politik/petr-pavel-praesident-tschechien-100.html.

December 2022
Sarajevo, Bosnia-Herzegovina

I am invited to Sarajevo at the beginning of December 2022. I've never been to Bosnia-Herzegovina before – and I never visited the former Yugoslavia or any of its successor states either. What are the first thoughts that spring to mind when you think of this city? For me it is the outbreak of the First World War and the "ethnic cleansing" of the Balkan Wars in the 1990s.

It is impossible to understand the causes of this war without briefly looking at the history and disintegration of Yugoslavia. Anyone who has taken even a cursory interest in the twentieth century's first major armed conflict will have heard of the city that is today the capital of Bosnia-Herzegovina. Although the First World War had many causes, one of the key events that led to war is the assassination in Sarajevo on June 28, 1914 of the heir to the throne of Austria-Hungary, Archduke Franz Ferdinand, and his wife Sophie Chotek, Duchess of Hohenberg, by Gavrilo Princip, a member of the Serbian nationalist movement *Mlada Bosna* (Young Bosnia). The Sarajevo attack was used by Austria-Hungary to justify a localized military strike against Serbia.

During my stay in Sarajevo in December 2022, I visit the scene of the crime: the assassin's footprints are marked on the sidewalk, exactly where he shot at the car that was carrying the Duke and Duchess. A museum at the scene provides a constant reminder of what happened all those years ago.

After the First World War, the collapse of Austria-Hungary gave rise to the Yugoslav state, which was constituted in 1918 as the Kingdom of Serbs, Croats and Slovenes (*Kraljevstvo Srba, Hrvata i Slovenaca*, also known as the SHS State for short). The new state united Serbia and Montenegro with areas of the collapsed Habsburg Monarchy – Croatia-Slavonia, Vojvodina, Dalmatia, Carniola and Southern Styria, as well as Bosnia-Herzegovina. But the kingdom only lasted for 23 years.

In 1941, Germany and Italy invaded Yugoslavia. The war lasted twelve days, from April 6 to 17, 1941. Yugoslavia collapsed into a mosaic of annexed, occupied and seemingly independent territories. Just a few months after the attack, Josip Broz, who called himself Tito, declared an uprising and organized the partisans in a fight against the occupiers. The partisans chose the five-pointed red star as their emblem, and on Stalin's birthday they formed the First Proletarian Brigade in Bosnia, which saw itself as the military arm of the Communist Party.[118]

During the Second World War, Yugoslavs not only fought against the Italian and German occupiers, fierce battles and atrocities also took place within Yugoslavia between Serbs, Croats and other groups in the multi-ethnic state.

The charismatic leader Tito became a legend, especially as he managed to liberate Yugoslavia without significant help from the Allies. In the other Eastern European countries – Poland, Bulgaria, Romania, the Czech Republic, etc. – the Soviets installed communist governments. But Yugoslavia was the second country, after the Soviet Union, in which communism came to power on its own – although the Red Army had also played an important role in the liberation of Serbia.

In Tito's People's Liberation Army, 305,000 fighters lost their lives, and of the Communist Party's 12,000 original members, 9,000 lost their lives.[119] On May 15, 1945, Yugoslavia was able to end the occupation. Now, Tito finally became a folk hero.

His tactics were the same as those of communists in many other countries: he promised a "people's democracy" and avoided terms like "dictatorship of the proletariat" and "class struggle," but little by little all non-communists were driven off and Tito and his party seized the reins of power.

After the fierce fighting between ethnic groups during the war, Tito sought to reconcile a host of diverging interests. The new Yugoslavia was therefore to consist of six republics: Slovenia, Croatia, Bosnia-Herzegovina, Serbia, Montenegro and Macedonia.

---

118 Calic, *A History of Yugoslavia*, 134.
119 Calic, *A History of Yugoslavia*, 156.

Economically, too, Tito initially followed the same path taken by other communist countries: companies were nationalized and the leadership decided to introduce the collectivization of agriculture in villages. The results of collectivization were as disastrous as in every other country.

Tito was stubborn and self-confident and did not want to become a pawn in Stalin's machinations, which led to an increasingly serious rift between the two leaders. The Yugoslavs lived in fear that the Soviets would invade, using force to bring them to heel – as the Soviets did in Hungary in 1956. Tito managed a clever balancing act between the West and the Soviet Union, and received significant funding from the West in the process. From 1948 to 1960, between 1.5 and 2.4 billion US dollars flowed into the country.[120] Economically, Yugoslavia also benefited from the fact that over a million "guest workers" who had left the country because they could not find work under socialism or were lured by higher wages in the capitalist West sent part of what they earned back home.[121] And in the 1970s, the Yugoslavs took out billions in foreign loans from capitalist countries, which temporarily led to an artificial boom, but also to massive debt and inflation.[122] In 1982 alone, the country had to raise 1.8 billion US dollars just to service its debt.[123]

Tito's Yugoslavia followed a special path to socialism based on so-called workers' self-management of factories. Some leftists in Europe and the United States still dream of "workers' self-management" today. But, in fact, "workers' self-management" was just a chimera, because, as the historian and political adviser Marie-Janine Calic writes in her book on the history of Yugoslavia: "Real power lay in the hands of a self-aggrandizing political caste of functionaries, factory directors, managers, and experts, who used the workers' collective only as a quasi-democratic guise for technocratic decision-making."[124]

This variant of socialism also led to a bureaucracy that grew like a cancer.

---

120 Calic, *A History of Yugoslavia*, 186.
121 Calic, *A History of Yugoslavia*, 199.
122 Calic, *A History of Yugoslavia*, 241.
123 Calic, *A History of Yugoslavia*, 252.
124 Calic, *A History of Yugoslavia*, 256–257.

By the end of the 1970s, 1.5 million new regulations had been adopted. The administration swelled to eight to eleven times the size of bureaucracies in countries of comparable size, and 94,415 "grassroots democratic entities" were operating across the country in 1980. "The Yugoslav system represented merely a higher form of institutionalized ineffectiveness that placed political opportunism ahead of economic rationality, canceled the rules of a market economy and entrepreneurial professionalism, bloated the size of the bureaucracy, and invited irresponsibility, wastefulness, and abuse of office."[125]

None of this bore any resemblance to the socialist ideal of "equality". Tito ruled like a king and resided in seventeen palaces, villas, and hunting lodges, while his symbols of power included a fleet of state-owned cars and yachts, and he regularly traveled around the country on the "Blue Train."[126] The population, on the other hand, was poor – the annual per-capita income was 1,850 US dollars in 1985, only about a third of that in the GDR.[127]

But the economic problems were not the only problems the country had to deal with. The communists' attempt to force different nationalities and ethnic groups into a unified state also failed, and as soon as the popular hero and figurehead of integration Tito died in 1980, the old animosities resurfaced. With the collapse of the socialist system, hostilities escalated into hatred and barbaric wars. The year 1991 saw the collapse of Yugoslavia.

It is important to know that only 60 percent of Serbs actually lived in the Republic of Serbia; the rest lived elsewhere, mainly in Bosnia and Croatia. Serbian President Slobodan Milošević, first leader of the Communist and later the Socialist Party, sought to establish a "Greater Serbia" by annexing the Serb-dominated areas.

In pursuit of his vision of a Greater Serbian state, Milošević expelled Bosniaks and Croats from the regions of Bosnia and Croatia that he declared to be parts of the new state; many were brutally murdered. The term "ethnic cleansing" emerged as a name for these processes. In 1999, Milošević became

---

125 Calic, *A History of Yugoslavia*, 244.
126 Calic, *A History of Yugoslavia*, 246.
127 Calic, *A History of Yugoslavia*, 254.

the first head of state in history to be charged with genocide while still in office. He died before a verdict could be announced by an international war crimes tribunal in The Hague.

It was by no means only Serbia that committed atrocities. Croats and Bosnians also acted cruelly. But the Serbs' crimes were systematically planned. It is impossible to cover the entire history of the wars, which lasted a decade from 1991 to 2001, here. Suffice it to say that 200,000 people died in the confusing conflict between the various successor states to Yugoslavia.

The city of Sarajevo was under siege for almost four years. The siege began with the capture of the international airport in the suburb of Ilidža by the Yugoslav People's Army on the night of April 4 / early morning of April 5, 1992 and ended on February 29, 1996 after Western governments had intervend. At 1,425 days, it was the longest siege of the twentieth century. The airlift, which provided relief for hundreds of thousands of people trapped inside the city, lasted longer than the Berlin airlift.

The Serb massacre in Srebrenica has gone down in history. UN courts classified it as genocide under the Convention on the Prevention and Punishment of the Crime of Genocide. The massacre lasted several days in July 1995 and took place across a large number of crime scenes near Srebrenica. More than 8,000 Bosniaks were murdered, almost all of them boys and men. Women and girls were systematically raped. In Sarajevo, I visit the museum that commemorates these massacres with shocking photos and films.

At the beginning of the twenty-first century, the former Yugoslavia was broken up into seven successor states: Slovenia, Croatia, Bosnia-Herzegovina, Serbia, Montenegro, Macedonia (now North Macedonia) and Kosovo. Bosnia-Herzegovina and Kosovo were placed under international supervision. But to this day, hatred and conflicts between different ethnic groups and countries continue to flare up.

Given all the fighting, devastation, suffering and economic decline, it is no surprise that so many people in Yugoslavia long for the supposedly good old days, the "perfect" past under Tito, and that he is still revered today. I am looking forward to finding out more about the reasons in Sarajevo.

Professor Damir Bećirovic picks me up from the airport. He speaks German very well, studied medicine in Graz in Austria for three years and then economics. He is a follower of the Austrian School and founded a private university, *Internacionalna poslovno-informaciona akademija* in Tuzla, the third largest city in Bosnia-Herzegovina. He says that Tito is still revered today, especially in Bosnia-Herzegovina, because he stood against nationalism and there was peace in his time. "Many people in the former Yugoslavia are proud of Tito, not because he was a communist, but because he led Yugoslavia to victory over Hitler. He is also something of an icon – someone who is said to have had affairs with film stars and who rubbed shoulders with the world's celebrities and powerful people."

According to Damir, to date only around 25 percent of companies in Bosnia are truly private and independent of the state. Some companies in the IT industry and numerous automotive suppliers in particular are independent. Although the proportion of private companies is significantly higher, many depend totally on government contracts. A lot went wrong with privatization, while true capitalism, Damir explains, has never been given a chance to establish itself. It is high time, he says, for a professional approach to privatizations including, for example, of the state-owned telephone companies.

Professor Faruk Hadžić is the highest-profile economist in Bosnia-Herzegovina. In 2008, he began his professional career in the Directorate for European Integration. In 2010, he moved to the private sector, where he worked as a director of two companies and later as a management consultant for an IT company. He currently works as a freelance macroeconomic analyst and consultant. His research focuses on macroeconomics, economic policy, international economics, data analysis and visualization.

He has invited me to give a lecture at the Sarajevo School of Science and Technology. The foundation of this private university was supported by Margaret Thatcher, after whom the lecture hall is named. 95 percent of students want to become entrepreneurs, while the majority of students in state universities would like to work for the state or state-owned companies.

Hadžić sees excessive taxes as one of his country's biggest problems.

In the *Index of Economic Freedom*, the tax system is awarded almost the highest possible rating because the income tax rate is only 10 percent and the system is not progressive. The index's authors comment: "The top income and corporate tax rates are 10 percent, but various governing entities have different tax policies. The overall tax burden equals 20.1 percent of total domestic income."[128] But the low tax rate is deceptive, according to the economist: "In fact, in addition to the 10 percent, there are also 42 percent of other taxes, for example for the state pension fund. If you add everything up, you end up with a tax burden of 52 percent. And when it comes to consumer goods, there are other special taxes in addition to VAT, so the overall tax burden is very high," Hadžić explains to me. "Our economic system," he says, "is very, very far removed from capitalism; the state interferes everywhere."

That's why he's not surprised that Bosnia-Herzegovina was one of the lowest-scoring performers in the international survey I commissioned from Ipsos MORI on the image of capitalism. Of the 35 countries in which we conducted the survey, Turkey was the only country in which perceptions of capitalism were as negative as in Bosnia-Herzegovina. The survey also showed that it is not just the word "capitalism" that repulses the majority of people here, they support extremely strong state intervention and expect all services to be provided by the state. Even in the sections of the survey that did not use the word "capitalism," a similar picture emerged: only in Russia was the image of the market economy worse than in Bosnia-Herzegovina. Proponents of the market economy clearly still have a lot to do here.

I also meet Danijal Hadžović from the leading daily newspaper *Dnevni Avaz*. We talk for a long time, and two days later the newspaper publishes a large, two-page interview. Danijal Hadžović also founded the libertarian think tank *Liberalni Forum* in 2015. The forum's work is based on two program areas. The first concerns education on the philosophy of libertarianism and libertarian politics. The forum holds educational seminars for young people and business journalists, but also does lobbying work to persuade politicians to implement economic reforms. Hadžović is proud of having initiated a craft

---

128 Heritage Foundation, *2022 Index of Economic Freedom*.

industries law in Bosnia and Herzegovina, which was eventually passed and is now one of the most laissez-faire craft industries laws in Europe.

A little older than *Liberalni Forum* is another libertarian think tank, *Multi*, which was founded in 2011 by Admir Čavalić. He is my first contact in Bosnia-Herzegovina and helped me get my book, *In Defence of Capitalism*, published in the country. Čavalić is the first libertarian member of the Bosnian parliament. The 36-year-old belongs to a small party that has four members of parliament.

As a student of economics, Čavalić began reading the works of Milton Friedman, which motivated him to make a documentary called *Economy*, the first Bosnian documentary to promote libertarian economic ideas in the country. Čavalić gathered distinguished university professors from all over the country and presented a libertarian economic agenda for his country in 60 minutes. He has initiated dozens of events with more than 10,000 participants that promote ideas associated with freedom.

A topic that particularly interests Čavalić is the connection between Islam and the idea of a market economy, and he has written a book on the subject, *Islam i slobodno tržište – Islam and the Free Market*. In the book, he and his co-author Dženan Smajić argue that something akin to a minimal state existed at the time of the Prophet Muhammad: "The tax burden at that time was only 2.5 percent, or 10 percent for non-Muslims. Price controls were forbidden and tax collectors were hated, for religious reasons."

In this context, I also have an interesting meeting with the translator of my book, Resul Mehmedovic. He studied Islamic studies, is very religious and at the same time a staunch supporter of capitalism. He thinks Islam and capitalism go particularly well together. Why? His answer: "Mecca, the birthplace of our Prophet Muhammad, was a market economy at the time. Benedikt Koehler demonstrated this in his book, *Early Islam and the Birth of Capitalism*. For example, believers came to Muhammad and asked him to impose price controls because of rising prices. Muhammad opposed price controls, arguing that the ups and downs of prices were in God's hands."

I am reminded of Professor Martin Rhonheimer, a member of the

Catholic Opus Dei and a staunch supporter of the Austrian School of Economics and ardent supporter of capitalism. He thinks Christianity and capitalism go particularly well together. The great thing about capitalism is that it seems to suit very different religions and worldviews. I would be interested in a dialogue between Benedikt Koehler and Martin Rhonheimer: "Islam, Christianity and Capitalism."

Muslims make up the majority of the population in Bosnia-Herzegovina and, as I learn in many conversations, it is primarily young people – not the old – for whom faith is becoming increasingly important. In view of difficult social conditions, they look for solace in Islam. However, young people are also leaving the country in increasing numbers. Many go to Germany. The total population of Bosnia and Herzegovina has been shrinking or stagnating for 19 years in a row and fell to around 3.23 million in 2022.[129] In addition, Bosnia and Herzegovina's fertility rate is one of the lowest in the world. I have seen this in many Eastern European countries, for example in Albania and Bulgaria, where more and more people are leaving their homelands because of a lack of opportunities.

129 Urmersbach, "Bosnien und Herzegowina," https://de.statista.com/statistik/daten/studie/383927/umfrage/gesamtbevoelkerung-von-bosnien-und-herzegowina/#:~:text=Die percent20Gesamtbev percentC3 percentB6lkerung percent20von percent20Bosnien percent20und,ebenfalls percent203 percent2C2 percent20Millionen percent20prognostiziert.

January 2023
Bratislava, Slovakia

My first journey of 2023 takes me to the Slovakian capital Bratislava in January. Slovakia shares borders with Austria, the Czech Republic, Poland, Ukraine and Hungary, and is home to 5.5 million people. If you are traveling from Germany to Bratislava, it makes sense to fly via Vienna, because from there it only takes 45 minutes by taxi to Bratislava. I meet Peter Gonda at my hotel. I immediately like Peter, who somehow reminds me of John Lennon. He has a very unconventional hairstyle that would be harder to describe than that of the Beatles musician – you immediately recognize him as a likeable non-conformist.

Peter is the head of a think tank that calls itself the "Conservative Institute of M. R. Štefánik," but is quick to emphasize that it is more libertarian than conservative. "The first step on my journey to libertarian economic thought and libertarian ideas was reading the Czech edition of Milton and Rose Friedman's book, *Free to Choose,* in my early twenties," he tells me. He has written and edited several books, including *Eurozone and Alternatives of European Economic Integration* (in Slovak), and organized lectures by renowned foreign speakers as part of the "Conservative Economic Quarterly Lecture Series." The program won the 2009 Templeton Freedom Award in the Ethics and Values category.

Later, I also meet Richard Ďurana, who founded the libertarian think tank *Iness* 18 years ago – I had previously met him in Warsaw. The two represent the most important libertarian think tanks in Slovakia.

Downtown Bratislava – a city of 480,000 inhabitants – is very beautiful, but small. Peter says many of the buildings in the old town were destroyed by the communists. After a lecture in front of about 100 people and an hour of discussion, we go to dinner. Somehow, I meet a group of die-hard heavy metal fans among the libertarians, one of whom has even founded a band with his two sons: "Capitalism and Heavy Metal" is their slogan. Of course I'm asked about my taste in music and I'm a little embarrassed to explain that I've been listening to the same music every night for 20 years, namely Ennio Morricone.

To my surprise, the heavy metal bandleader (a qualified mathematician, by the way) was also at a Morricone concert, and Peter explains to me that the band Metallica even begins their concerts with a Morricone song. I don't really know much about heavy metal; the hardest rock band I listened to when I was young was Grand Funk Railroad, but I was more of a Pink Floyd fan. In any case, all is well. It turns out that Slovak capitalism and heavy metal fans also like Pink Floyd. Peter says: "Pink Floyd is rock music, and rock is the basis of metal." I've learned something again. Everyone is amused when the group of seven men all toast with beer and I raise my glass of milk in cheers.

Peter has organized everything for me very well and filled my days from morning to evening with interviews with TV and daily newspapers. Nevertheless, I do still manage to rest up in the hotel between appointments.

When it comes to the country's politics and economy, socialism ran the country down. Peter says: "While in 1948, GDP per capita in Czechoslovakia was higher than in Austria (at the level of 121 percent), by 1989, it had dropped down to 58 percent, even according to the officially overestimated data."

After the collapse of socialism, unlike in the former Yugoslavia, Czechoslovakia split into the Czech Republic and Slovakia peacefully. On January 1, 1993, the independent Slovak Republic was created. Slovakia had belonged to Austria-Hungary since 1867 and became part of the newly founded Czechoslovakia from 1918 onward.

During the socialist period, the Slovak economy was focused on heavy industry, primarily metallurgy, the defense industry, the energy industry and the chemical industry. The transition to a market economy initially led to massive declines in production because state-owned companies were unable to compete. The separation from the Czech Republic in 1993 also brought disadvantages: Slovakia was less developed than the Czech Republic in many economic sectors.[130]

Mikuláš Dzurinda, Prime Minister from 1998 to 2006, adopted a market economy approach and introduced a flat tax of 19 percent. The World Bank recognized Slovakia's reform policies as world leaders and Steve Forbes described the country as an "investor's paradise." The government focused on privatization. As early as 2002, 88.9 percent of gross domestic product was generated in the private sector; in 2009, that figure had risen to 93 percent. Slovakia's economic growth reached a peak in 2006 at 8.3 percent.[131]

Robert Fico, a member of the Communist Party until 1990 and then head of the left-wing populist *Smer-SD*, won the election in 2006 and served as Prime Minister until 2010 and again from 2012 to 2018 – and became Prime Minister for a third time in October 2023. Fico is an avowed statist.

In the *Index of Economic Freedom*, Slovakia gained around ten points between 1995 and 2008 (from 60.4 to 70). Since then, however, there has been little improvement: after fluctuations, the country's 2023 index score was practically at the same level as in 2008, at 69.[132] In comparison, the Czech Republic started with a score of 67.8 in 1995 and had gained seven points by 2022 (74.4). In 2023 it had 71.9 points.[133]

Above all, the Heritage Foundation praises Slovakia for its

- property rights
- tax burden
- monetary freedom
- fiscal health

...and awards negative ratings for:

- government integrity
- labor freedom
- government spending.

---

130 LPB, https://osteuropa.lpb-bw.de/wirtschaft-slowakei.
131 LPB, https://osteuropa.lpb-bw.de/wirtschaft-slowakei.
132 Heritage Foundation, *2023 Index of Economic Freedom*, 324.
133 Heritage Foundation, *2023 Index of Economic Freedom*, 116.

A comparison of labor market regulations in Slovakia and 40 other OECD countries published in 2020 puts the country in 36th place, meaning that the labor market is only more tightly regulated in four countries (France is at the bottom), and it is freer in 35 countries. The Czech Republic is much higher, in eighth place.[134]

The global economic crisis also triggered an economic downturn in Slovakia in 2009. The economy returned to growth between 2011 and 2013, although it never managed to get back to the high growth rates from before the financial crisis.

Foreign trade with EU countries is regarded as one of the Slovak economy's strengths. The country has a relatively high industrial share of around 35 percent of GDP (compared with: Germany, 27 percent; United States, 18 percent; France, 17 percent). Industry in Slovakia is heavily export-led, with the automobile industry in particular playing an important role. In fact, the automotive industry's share of exports stands at 40 percent. Various European and Asian manufacturers have large production facilities in Slovakia, including around 500 German companies. Nowhere in the world are more cars manufactured per capita than in Slovakia.[135]

My Ipsos MORI survey in Slovakia, which was conducted in July 2022, showed that attitudes towards the market economy and capitalism in Slovakia tend to be negative. Of the 35 countries in which the survey was conducted, Slovakia is in 19th place. So there are 16 countries that are more anti-capitalist and 18 countries in which perceptions of capitalism are more positive (including the Czech Republic in sixth place).

The survey showed that Slovaks who place themselves on the moderate right or far-right of the political spectrum are clearly pro-capitalist. Interestingly, the survey also revealed larger differences between income groups in Slovakia than in other countries. Higher earners in Slovakia have a far more positive attitude towards the market economy.

---

134   Lithuania Free Market Institute, 7.
135   LPB, https://osteuropa.lpb-bw.de/wirtschaft-slowakei.

What is worrying, however, is the widespread nostalgia for socialism. A 2018 survey conducted by the Focus agency in Slovakia found that 55 percent of Slovaks believe that living standards were better under socialism than they are today; 77 percent said there were enough meaningful jobs for everyone; and 59 percent said socialism was an economic success.[136]

I ask Peter, Richard and the other people I meet how they explain the big differences between the Czech Republic and Slovakia. In their opinion, there is simply no entrepreneurial tradition in Slovakia – unlike in the Czech Republic – and a lot of mistakes were made during privatization. As in some other previously socialist countries, privatization often just meant that (former) communists bought and sold each other's companies at ridiculously low prices. Not a good advertisement for the market economy. These problems also existed in the Czech Republic, but not to the same extent.

---

136 Gonda, https://tearingdownmyths.com/socialism-reality-instead-of-myths/.

January 2023
Belgrade, Serbia

Many people in Serbia look back fondly on the time when Josip Broz Tito ruled the country. Not because they long for a return to communism, but because life in socialist Yugoslavia was not as bad as in other socialist countries and because the transition to capitalism and democracy in Serbia – unlike in Poland and the Czech Republic, for example – never really succeeded. And also because, in retrospect, a lot of things look better through rose-tinted spectacles. In the eyes of many Serbs, Tito represents a time when Yugoslavia was great, its president was respected on the international stage, and peace and social security reigned. In Serbia, even more than in other countries, the "privatizations" that followed the collapse of the socialist system meant that the elites took over formerly state-owned companies on the cheap.

There is an obvious "Tito nostalgia" here, a widespread longing for what people think of as "the good old days." Every year on May 7, Tito's birthday, celebrations are held in his birthplace Kumrovec. They attract several thousand visitors from every corner of the former Yugoslavia. Tito's mausoleum, *Kuća cveća* (House of Flowers), in Belgrade is a popular destination for tourists and Tito admirers.

The word "capitalism" has extremely negative connotations in Serbia. Our Ipsos MORI survey showed that Serbs do not have a decidedly anti-market economy attitude, but neither do they have a decidedly pro-market economy attitude. In the section of the survey on opinions of the market economy (which did not use the word "capitalism"), agreement with the positive, pro-free-market and negative, anti-market statements was about the same. This could relate to the fact that the market economy was not fundamentally frowned upon under the Yugoslav version of socialism.

However, when we presented our Serb respondents with 18 statements on "capitalism," opinions were more negative than in almost any other surveyed country. This discrepancy in responses – depending on whether a survey item used the word "capitalism" or not – existed in many countries, but hardly anywhere was it as great as in Serbia.

I suspect that this is somehow connected to a widespread anti-Americanism and critical attitude towards the West in Serbia. "Capitalism" is associated with the United States and the West, and many Serbs, unlike Poles or Albanians, are acutely anti-American and anti-Western. When my driver picks me up from the airport, he makes a point of showing me a building that the Americans destroyed.

The roots of this anti-Americanism are to be found in the late 1990s. Thousands of people died when NATO troops occupied Kosovo and bombed Belgrade between March 24 and June 12, 1999. The military operation, which was essentially led by the United States, was the first war to be fought by NATO both outside the alliance's mutual defense clause, which had until then been considered the basis of any NATO-wide operation, and without an explicit UN mandate. In total, the operation's aircraft dropped 28,018 explosive devices, 83 percent of which were dropped by U.S. aircraft.

In October 2000, the war criminal Slobodan Milošević was overthrown, Vojislav Koštunica became president, and the "Democratic Opposition of Serbia" won early parliamentary elections shortly afterwards. But Serbia did not become a democracy. Aleksandar Vučić has been President of Serbia since 2017. His "Serbian Progressive Party" (SNS) dominates almost every aspect of life in the country. Vučić was last re-elected on December 17, 2023. Anyone who wants a job, an entrepreneur who wants a contract, or a local politician who needs tax revenues for their community, has to come to terms with the party. With its 730,000 members, SNS is the largest party in all of Europe – not relatively, but absolutely. Serbia ranked 101 out of 180 countries in Transparency International's *2022 Corruption Perceptions Index*.

According to the Heritage Foundation, economic freedom has improved in Serbia in recent years, but the country ranks just 34th out of 44 countries in the Europe region and 58th in the world.[137] On the positive side, Serbia has a low tax burden, while the biggest negative point is its overall weak rule of law.

In January 2023, Helik publishers, who published *In Defence of Capitalism* in Serbia, together with the libertarian club *Libek*, invite me to Serbia. I meet Petar Čekerevac and Mihailo Gajic, who tell me that *Libek* was founded in 2008 by students as an alternative to the political left on the one hand and right-wing nationalists on the other. Above all, they criticize the fact that Vučić and his party have brought almost the entire media landscape under their control.

There are still exceptions, such as the television station *N1*, which invites me for an interview about my book. The journalist who interviews me is certainly not a left-wing ideologist, but the questions she asks lead me to believe that she must have had a Marxist education at some point, because she draws on Marxist theories, such as surplus value theory.

The people at *Libek* are trying to spread free-market ideas in the media and political circles – a difficult task given the enforced conformity of the country's media. *Libek* founded the online magazine *TALAS* in 2018, which has now achieved a certain level of influence in Serbia. The magazine's creators provide a daily commentary on political events and their magazine is read by journalists and politicians.

I meet the Trade Minister of Serbia, Tomislav Momirović. He comes from a very wealthy business family and is among the Serbian libertarian movement's key supporters. He is particularly active in the hotel business and owns several hotels in Serbia. He points to the country's economic successes. In recent years, the government has privatized a large number of companies, and only one small bank is still state-owned. Average monthly salaries have risen from 210 euros in 2005 to 418 euros in 2018 and again to 642 euros today. Gross domestic product increased from 37 billion euros in 2016 to 53 billion euros in 2021, while foreign direct investment (FDI) more than doubled between 2016 and 2022, from two billion euros to around 4.5 billion

---

137 Heritage Foundation, *2023 Index of Economic Freedom*, 316–317.

euros. Leading the way are investments from Germany. The next important step is to establish an "Open Balkan" economic zone together with the other countries of the former Yugoslavia (except Croatia and Slovenia, which are members of the EU) and Albania.

Of course, we also talk about the Ukraine war, and here our opinions differ. Momirović says that only Russia and China have supported Serbia in the UN Security Council regarding Kosovo, so Serbia cannot now oppose Russia and has therefore attempted to maintain a "neutral" stance. In addition, he explains, Serbia is 100 percent dependent on Russian gas.

From time to time, the conflict between Serbia and Kosovo continues to flare up, and in the fall of 2023 the Serbs massed troops on the border with Kosovo. My friend Adri, who is politically active in Kosovo, attributes this to Russia and says that Russians and Serbs want to test the West's strength and commitment in the region.

Warsaw and Gdansk, Poland

After the success of my first film *Life Behind the Berlin Wall* in 2022, I decided to produce more films on the subject of socialism/capitalism. I found an excellent partner for this endeavor in Poland: Tomasz Agencki, a skilled filmmaker who studied movie production and film direction and has produced numerous films. One of his films, *Where the Directives Grow*, a critical documentary about the EU Parliament, won an award at the Anthem Film Festival in 2020.

Tomasz is 41 years old and is part of the libertarian movement in Poland. We arrange to meet for six days in January 2023, first in Warsaw, then in Gdańsk, and then back to Warsaw.

Producing a movie is exhausting, especially in winter. This time it's very cold, often wet – and the icy wind makes the temperatures seem even colder. Luckily, I'm wearing long johns. I have also asked for someone with a car to be with me so that I can sit in the warm and practice my lines between takes while Tomasz sets up the next shot.

I am glad to have found such an experienced professional in Tomasz, who above all has a lot of patience, as I have hardly any experience making films myself. I can tell that he is a real perfectionist who leaves nothing to chance and checks everything several times over. I think the amount of material we shoot would easily be enough for a 90-minute film, but we decide to make a short film of around 35 minutes.

This film is based on my book, *How Nations Escape Poverty*, about Poland and Vietnam, for which I also conducted intensive research here in Poland. I have now established a very good network of contacts in Poland and have many people who help me here, especially my publisher Krzysztof Zuber.

In Poland, one major problem we encounter is that the rights to use archive footage are very expensive. Tomasz has a fantastic idea to get around this, namely to film in museums as well as outdoors. We visit the Museum of Life in PRL in Warsaw, the *Europejskie Centrum Solidarnośći*, and SALA BHB, another *Solidarność* museum, in Gdansk. The huge *Europejskie Centrum Solidarnośći*, the European Solidarity Center, is particularly impressive. It consists of a museum about the trade union, its central archive, a multimedia library, and an education center. It is also home to numerous historical sites, such as Plac Solidarnośći and its monument to the fallen shipyard workers, the famous shipyard gate, and the Gdańsk Shipyard Health and Safety Hall, which served as a conference hall for trade union activists. The museum opened on August 31, 2014.

At the end of January 2019, the Polish Minister of Culture and National Heritage, Piotr Gliński, demanded that the museum include elements more closely aligned with PiS's historical policy and hire a deputy director appointed by the ministry. If the museum refused, he threatened, its annual subsidy would be cut from seven to four million złotys. The museum duly refused to meet his demands and the three million złotys that was subsequently cut was raised in a fundraising campaign.

The Gdańsk shipyard is a uniquely historical place because this is where the end of communism began. Poland's entire post-war history is punctuated by repeated strikes and ongoing protests by the country's workers, many of which were brutally suppressed. For example, there were the strikes that started in the Gdańsk shipyard on December 14, 1970. On the night of December 15, the striking workers were surrounded by army units with tanks. When the workers left the plant, the soldiers opened fire on them before marching onto the premises. That same day, strikes also broke out at the Gdynia shipyard. There were fatalities and injuries. In prisons and temporary detention centers, demonstrators were beaten to unconsciousness and seriously injured. Strikes and demonstrations also occurred in many other cities during that week of December 1970, and resulted in the loss of forty-five lives. Of the victims, twelve were under the age of twenty and twenty-four were under the age of thirty. In total, 1,100 people were wounded, the majority of whom were workers. The country was on the brink of civil war.

August 1980 marked the start of a new wave of strikes. Workers at the Lenin Shipyard in Gdansk demanded not only higher wages but also official recognition for a free-trade union. It is remarkable that the working class, which was supposedly the ruling class in the "dictatorship of the proletariat," was the force that repeatedly rebelled against the country's rulers and lent weight to their discontent with strikes and demonstrations. The communist government was finally forced to cave in to the workers' demands and officially recognize the union. Soon, around ten million Poles joined *Solidarność*. At the same time, party members were increasingly deserting the PZPR communist party. By 1981, 350,000 members had left the PZPR, overwhelmingly workers.

The shipyard is adorned with memorial plaques listing the names and ages of the workers who were killed. Some were only fifteen, sixteen or seventeen years old. An ideology conceived by intellectuals, whose goal was a paradise for the workers, was brought down by workers' uprisings.

In Gdańsk that evening, I meet Maria and her husband, who is also called Tomasz. They both belong to the libertarian scene, and Maria is currently translating my book, *Hitler's National Socialism,* into Polish. We talk about perceptions of socialism. In Poland, it is not only the term "communism" but also the word "socialism" that has a negative connotation for the vast majority of people. The system is seen as foreign, imposed on the Poles by the Russians. Nevertheless, in Poland – as in other countries – there is also a kind of nostalgia and glorification of the past, which is particularly driven by the PiS party, who were in government at the time of my visit. But hardly anyone wants socialism back.

I also return to the KARTA Museum and meet Alicja, who tells me all about the Polish ration card system. I learn more and more details that illustrate the absurdity of the system. For example, if you went on vacation for a couple of weeks, you had to hand in your regular food cards at the hotel when you arrived and were then given new ration cards so that you could eat meals in the hotel. If you lost your cards, you had to go on a diet for a few days.

We decide we are going to submit our new film to the Anthem Film Festival, which is part of Freedom Fest in Memphis in July 2023. I hope to win an award again, as I did at Freedom Fest in Las Vegas in 2022. In May, Tomasz receives the news that the film has not been accepted. He is very disappointed and sad. I'm disappointed too, but I say to Tomasz: "Let's think about what we can do to promote the film without Freedom Fest." He comes up with the idea of premiering the film at an event at Aspiro University in Warsaw on June 24.

The event is a great success: 400 students watch the film and Leszek Balcerowicz gives a speech. What he says makes me very proud: "Rainer Zitelmann edukuje na temat Polski tak jak kiedyś edukował na temat Stanów Zjednoczonych Alexis de Tocqueville." ("Rainer Zitelmann educates about Poland the way Alexis de Tocqueville once educated about the United States.") I later find a way to show an abridged version of the film at Freedom Fest in Memphis on July 13, albeit out of competition. And I hope to produce more films with Tomasz in the future.

February 2023
London, United Kingdom

When I arrive in London on February 6, I find out that Madsen Pirie, President of the Adam Smith Institute, and Eamonn Butler – certainly the two best-known champions of the libertarian movement in the UK – want to invite me to dinner at the venerable Carlton Club. The Carlton Club is one of London's most prestigious gentlemen's clubs. Founded in 1832, it has always been a meeting place, especially for members of the Tory party, the nickname by which the Conservative Party is still known today. The Tory's leading lights have included Benjamin Disraeli, Robert Peel, Winston Churchill, Harold Macmillan, and Margaret Thatcher (the "Iron Lady" is the only full female member accepted by the Carlton Club to date).

The only problem is that, as usual, the only clothes I have with me are jeans and a polo shirt. There's no way I'll be allowed into the most venerable club in London in those. Well, most gentlemen's clubs will let you borrow a tie, but what about the jeans? My British PR agent Claire Barry, with whom I have worked for many years, calls the club and offers me some welcome reassurance: the club has plenty of pants, shirts and ties they can lend me. In fact, the club has a walk-in closet the size of a room. So, I change and have no choice but to laugh at my outfit – pants that don't quite fit me properly, a polo shirt, and a tie.

In Berlin, I'm a member of the China Club, the most exclusive private members' club in the city. The really rich people who go there often come in jeans and polo shirts. From their point of view, suits and ties are more commonly associated with insurance agents, bank employees and politicians – which doesn't mean that they (and I too) don't wear suits from time to time.

Madsen Pirie is both a likeable and highly intelligent man. From 1979 to 1992, he was secretary of Mensa International, the organization for people with well above-average IQs. I got to know him a few years ago because he was the first person to review the English edition of my book, *The Power of Capitalism*. I consider this a great honor, especially because this opinion leader, who knew Margaret Thatcher, Friedrich August von Hayek, and a host of other major figures personally, writes in his review: "He has a fascinating chapter on 'Why Intellectuals Don't Like Capitalism,' which does more than revisit Hayek's earlier insights."[138]

When we meet, the now 82-year-old compliments me again: he has just read my book, *How People Become Famous*, and says that I write the way people speak. Others have already told me that my books read as if I had dictated them, but that's not true. I don't think written language should be too different from the spoken word, so I was pleased to receive his compliment.

I ask Madsen if he can give me some background on the founding of the Adam Smith Institute, and he does:

"As the winter of 1976 drew to a close, there was change in the air in both Britain and America. Ronald Reagan was fighting for the Republican nomination he was finally to win three years later. Margaret Thatcher was Conservative leader in Britain. But there was more than this. The United States was gripped by its forthcoming bicentenary, as it prepared to celebrate the passage of 200 years since its first Independence Day.

I wrote one of my newspaper columns on the subject, pointing out that the year 1776 had been a significant year in several ways. It had marked the death of David Hume, the philosopher with whose ideas I had most sympathy. It saw the publication of volume 1 of *The Decline and Fall of the Roman Empire* by Edward Gibbon. In the same year, James Watt had demonstrated in Glasgow what was described as the first modern, efficient steam engine. On July 4, the American colonists had issued their Declaration of Independence. And by no means the least important event of the year was the publication by the Scottish Enlightenment thinker, Adam Smith, of *An Enquiry into the Nature and Causes of the Wealth of Nations*, the book that virtually invented modern economics.

---

138 Pirie, https://www.adamsmith.org/blog/the-power-of-capitalism.

Smith had argued that countries were wealthy not because their rulers had gold and silver stored in vaults, but because of the productive labor of their peoples. He had set out an account of how wealth can be created by the division of labor, and augmented by trade. He had described the activities of investors, entrepreneurs and governments, and concluded that governments usually brought profligacy, rather than efficiency, into economic activity. His attack on subsidies, monopolies, and all the trappings of government intervention seemed to have lessons for the modern world, and especially for Britain.

It was all very well to win theoretical arguments, but nothing seemed to happen afterwards. Governments continued on their wayward courses, while academics devised new follies to set upon the wreckage of the old ones. We wanted to change reality; to have an impact on what actually happened. We wanted to make policy.

Adam Smith might have been one strong influence on our thinking, but there were others. One was James Buchanan, the Nobel Laureate who, with Gordon Tullock, William A. Niskanen and others, developed what came to be known as Public Choice Theory. In essence it took the ideas of economics into the domain of politics and administration. Instead of treating politicians and civil servants as selfless seekers after public good, the theory treated them as if they were ordinary economic participants, out to maximize their advantage, just like other people. It proved a very fertile theory for explaining what would otherwise have been incomprehensible outcomes.

It told us how minority interest groups can hijack the political agenda to have advantages created for themselves. It explained how politicians respond to pressure from vociferous and self-identified groups, but not from a public at large which might be largely unconscious of the way it was affected by policy. Public Choice Theory was basically a critique, but we began to wonder if there could be a creative counterpart to it. Just as Public Choice Theory told us why certain policies were doomed to political failure, however economically sound they might be, could it not be used to create policies which would not be subject to these limitations? Could new free market policies be crafted which flowed with political reality by building in the support of the interest groups which might otherwise derail them?

We started the Adam Smith Institute to develop and explore policies that would enable legislators to assuage the interest groups that might otherwise thwart them. We called this approach 'Micropolitics,' because it was the equivalent of microeconomics, but in the field of public policy rather than economics.

Not surprisingly, many politicians warmed to policies that could achieve their objectives without losing them popularity. In this fashion the Adam Smith Institute began to influence events. That was its aim."

So much for Madsen Pirie's recollections.

My second host at this dinner, Eamonn Butler, was also one of the co-founders of the Adam Smith Institute. He is known for his countless books on libertarianism, which have been translated into many languages worldwide. I last met him at the Atlas Network conference in Warsaw, and he has helped me time and again to expand my network.

I tell them about the results of my survey on the image of capitalism, including in the UK. The background: I commissioned two international surveys, one on the image of the rich (in 13 countries) and one on the image of capitalism (in 35 countries). In most countries where the image of the rich is relatively positive, the image of capitalism is also positive, for example in the United States, Poland, South Korea, and Japan. We found the reverse, i.e. that the rich and the concept of capitalism have a negative image, in Germany and France, among others. There was only one country where I was surprised by our results. The survey on the image of the rich, which I commissioned Ipsos MORI to conduct in the UK from May 24 to June 10, 2018, showed that social envy was lower in the UK than in all other European countries (with the exception of Poland). At 0.37, the Social Envy Coefficient in the UK was even slightly lower than in the U.S. (0.42). And the only countries in which the Rich Sentiment Index, which depicts overall attitudes toward the rich, was more positive than in the UK were Japan, Vietnam, and Poland.

However, the results of the UK survey on the image of capitalism, which

Ipsos MORI conducted from July 30 to August 9, 2021, were very different: in only 13 countries is the image of capitalism worse, while in 21 countries it is better than in the UK. Yes, there were around three years between the two surveys, but it is unlikely that this time lag explains the differences. As mentioned, in most countries the image of the rich and that of capitalism corresponded, and nowhere else is there such a large discrepancy as in the UK.

Neither of my hosts can come up with a convincing explanation for this discrepancy, but they are convinced that the findings are correct: anti-capitalist sentiment is becoming more and more dominant in the UK.

I meet Iain Martin, a Scotsman who publishes the online magazine *Reaction* and writes a weekly column for *The Times*. How does he explain the discrepancy in the polls? He says that the British associate being rich less with "capitalism" than perhaps with the footballer David Beckham or the Queen – and they like them. But in economic terms, it is quite clear that Britain is becoming increasingly anti-capitalist and collectivist.

Kristian Niemietz, Head of Political Economy at the second major libertarian think tank in London, the Institute for Economic Affairs, agrees. Niemietz comes from Germany, but has been living in London for almost twenty years. He wrote the great book, *Socialism: The Failed Idea That Never Dies*, which I recommend to everyone. His findings: wages in the UK have barely risen in ten years, while rents and house prices have skyrocketed. The British attribute this to "capitalism" because, since Thatcher, the UK has seen itself as a particularly capitalist country, especially compared to continental Europe. "The truth is, of course, quite different," says Niemietz. "Rising house prices and rents are not the result of too much capitalism, but of too little. Building laws are extremely restrictive, which is what has caused the housing shortage. But the media's interpretation of the problems here is different. Even the *Financial Times* has become a left-wing newspaper – *The Guardian*, so to speak, for people who are also interested in share prices."

For the first time since Thatcher, major strikes are crippling the country again. Niemietz finds it remarkable that these strikes – unlike in the past – tend to attract quite favorable media coverage, or at least meet with a great deal of sympathy. In contrast, the media response, especially in the *Financial Times*, to the tax cuts proposed by Liz Truss (Prime Minister from September 6 to October 24, 2022) was extremely negative. In short, it is anti-capitalists rather than pro-capitalists who now dominate the public discourse in the UK.

Alongside the Adam Smith Institute, the Institute for Economic Affairs, for which Niemietz works, is the most important libertarian think tank in the UK. Here are some facts about the history of this institute, compiled by Kristian Niemietz:

"In 1949, Friedrich Hayek published a paper 'The Intellectuals And Socialism,' which can be seen, indirectly, as the founding document of what later became the Institute of Economic Affairs (IEA). Hayek's paper was about how and why political ideas spread and become political reality.

Hayek's thesis runs something like this: In a society based on the division of labor, we produce almost nothing that we consume ourselves. Nor do we purchase goods and services directly from their original producers, but from specialized intermediaries. The same applies to political ideas. We do not develop our own political ideas, nor do we obtain them directly from the thinkers who originally designed them, we obtain them from specialized 'idea dealers.' For Hayek, these idea dealers are above all those who are active in the media, the education sector, and the cultural sector.

The ideas that these people make their own are gradually accepted by the vast majority of people. They become what is called the 'zeitgeist.' In this model, politicians are located downstream. Major political upheavals do not take place because a visionary politician comes along and makes his or her mark on society. Instead, politicians act within the zeitgeist that they find, but which they themselves cannot significantly influence.

Anthony Fisher, who later founded the IEA, originally wanted to go into politics himself, but Hayek advised him against it. It was more important to change the zeitgeist. To do this, he said, you had to reach a critical mass of 'idea dealers' and make the free-market economy palatable to them again.

In 1955, Fisher founded the IEA to do precisely this. The IEA, under the leadership of the two economists Arthur Seldon and Ralph Harris, began its work two years later and soon made a name for itself with its high-quality studies. In the intellectual wasteland of the post-war statist consensus, there was now a decidedly libertarian dissenting voice.

The influence of think tanks is difficult to measure, but both opponents and supporters of the Institute agree that the IEA played its part in shaking up the post-war consensus in the 1970s. Opposition leader Thatcher was now also a frequent visitor to Institute events.

In the 1980s and 1990s, much of what the Institute had long advocated was finally put into practice, including the abolition of capital and exchange rate controls and the privatization of state-owned enterprises. This was the period in which the Institute's influence was at its greatest, although unfortunately its influence cannot be repeated in this form today.

The revolution under Thatcher was necessary, but did not go far enough. There are key policy areas that remained virtually untouched by the Thatcher-era reforms, such as the national health service and the extremely restrictive building regulations, to which the country owes its current chronic housing shortage. The state also tends to constantly seek out new areas of activity, for example when it comes to protecting supposedly disadvantaged minorities or regulating private lifestyles in the name of public health.

At the end of the 2000s, the Institute began to drastically increase its media presence through TV and radio interviews. In the mid-2010s, new media were added: an in-house podcast, a YouTube channel and Facebook and Twitter accounts. Guest lectures at schools and universities mean that the 'middleman' is now often bypassed and end consumers are addressed directly.

Hayek himself was never formally employed at the Institute, but he remained associated with the IEA, which was founded at his suggestion, throughout his life. If he could visit it again today, many things would certainly surprise him, but there are also many things he would recognize."

So much for the report from my friend Kristian Niemietz.

And how do things look today? The UK is one of many sad examples of how little people learn from history and how forgetful most people are. Let's take a little look back at recent British history:

In 1966, the Beatles released a track called 'Taxman,' which starts with the lines:

"Let me tell you how it will be
That's one for you, 19 for me ...
Should 5 percent appear too small,
Be thankful I don't take it all."

The song was written as a protest against excessive taxation in the UK, which up until the 1970s was tantamount to the expropriation of high-income individuals, with an income tax rate of 83 percent for those in the highest tax bracket, while capital gains were taxed at up to 98 percent.

The victory of the left-wing Labour Party in the 1945 general elections had led to the implementation of a form of democratic socialism under the then prime minister Clement Attlee, at the core of which was a massive program of nationalization. Once banks, civil aviation, and the mining and telecommunications industries had been nationalized, the railways, shipping canals, road freight transport, power and gas soon followed, as did manufacturing industries including iron and steel. In total, about a fifth of the UK economy was nationalized. In many cases, senior executives stayed in their jobs, although they were now working as civil servants.

The result was the same as it always is whenever a country massively expands the government's role in the economy. The German economist Holger Schmieding, who first visited the UK in the late 1970s as a young man, remembers feeling shocked by the terrible standard of living across the country. "Many households lacked the appliances we had in our kitchen, utilities room and living room at home. Large parts of the country looked picturesquely dilapidated. The antiquated transport system and the abominable quality of many goods and services made matters worse. At the time, the UK was miles away from the standards I was used to from home or those I had been privileged to experience a few years earlier as a high-school student in the U.S. If it hadn't been for the memory of the many British soldiers stationed close to my parents' house near Osnabrück at the time, my first visit to the UK might have made me wonder which country had actually won the war."[139]

The crisis came to a head in the 1970s and, in May 1979, Margaret Thatcher became Prime Minister. One of her first steps towards a more business-friendly economy was to cut marginal tax rates from 33 to 30 percent in the lowest brackets and from 83 to 60 percent in the highest brackets (followed by further cuts to 25 and 40 percent respectively in 1988). She also took steps to reduce bureaucracy by expediting planning permissions for industrial and office developments and simplifying or abolishing a range of planning controls.[140]

No other European politician has ever implemented a pro-market-reform program as uncompromisingly as Thatcher did. During her second term in office, she pushed the privatization of state-owned enterprises. Thatcher saw privatization as "one of the central means of reversing the corrosive and corrupting effects of socialism."[141] Far from putting the people in control, public ownership was simply "ownership by an impersonal legal entity: it amounts to control by politicians and civil servants," she argued. "But through privatisation – particularly the kind of privatisation which leads to the widest possible share ownership by members of the public – the state's power is reduced and the power of the people enhanced."[142]

Productivity increased considerably in privatized businesses. Ten years after privatization, telecommunications prices had fallen by 50 percent, while prices for the products and services of other privatized companies also dropped. Studies have shown improvements in service quality in privatized businesses across the board. Before privatization, it had taken months and sometimes a bribe to get a new telephone line. Over the decade following privatization, the share of service calls completed within eight days rose from 59 percent to 97 percent.[143]

---

139 Schmieding, https://www.welt.de/wirtschaft/article115147486/Vor-Thatcher-war-Grossbritannien-ein-Truemmerhaufen.html.
140 *Thatcher, 43–44.*
141 *Thatcher, 676.*
142 *Thatcher, 676.*
143 *Edwards, 95.*

Although Thatcher confides in her Downing Street memoirs that there "was still much I would have liked to do," her overall assessment of her time in office is a positive one: "Britain under my premiership was the first country to reverse the onward march of socialism. By the time I left office, the state-owned sector of industry had been reduced by some 60 percent. Around one in four of the population owned shares. Over six hundred thousand jobs had passed from the public to the private sector."[144] Her policies had resulted in a rise in profitability and productivity that in due course enabled the creation of 3.32 million jobs between March 1983 and March 1990.[145]

Thanks to the tax revenue generated by these increases in productivity, the UK was able to significantly reduce its public debt. In 1976, the country had been on the brink of sovereign default and had been forced to take out a loan from the International Monetary Fund.[146] In 1978, the deficit stood at 4.4 percent of GDP (compared to 2.4 percent in Germany). A decade later, in 1989, the UK economy generated a surplus of 1.6 percent. Public debt fell from 54.6 percent of GDP in 1980 to 40.1 percent in 1989.[147]

Pre-Thatcher, Britain had been the country with the highest marginal tax rate in Europe (up to 98 percent). By the time she left office, the UK's maximum tax rate of 40 percent was lower than that of any other European country except for tax havens such as Liechtenstein and Monaco. The stuffy socialist culture of envy was replaced by a pro-market and pro-business environment where ambition was richly rewarded, which in turn led to a sharp increase in the number of private businesses and self-employment. From 1.89 million in 1979, the total number of businesses registered in the UK rose to over 3 million by 1989, while the number of people registered as self-employed grew from 1.9 million to 3.5 million during the same period.[148]

If you think back to the UK before Margaret Thatcher and recognize the

---

144 *Thatcher, 687.*
145 *Thatcher, 668.*
146 *Poller, 45.*
147 *Poller, 50.*
148 *Eltis, 26.*

positive impacts of her reforms, you can only rub your eyes in disbelief at the fact that anti-capitalism has come to dominate again today. This confirms my thesis that, after a certain amount of time has passed, people forget the reasons for the prosperity in which they live.

February 2023
Washington DC, and New York City, United States

Before I head back to the United States in mid-February, I read one of the most impressive books on socioeconomic issues in the U.S. that I have read in recent years. In Europe, there is a misplaced belief that the United States is a land of unbridled capitalism and has no welfare state. The opposite is true. Nowadays, the welfare state and redistribution in the U.S. have reached such proportions that it is worth asking whether it still makes sense for middle-class Americans to work at all.

An analysis of incomes in the U.S. has shown that on a per capita basis the average bottom-quintile household (i.e. the bottom 20 percent of income earners) receives over 10 percent more than the average second-quintile household and 3 percent more than the average middle-income household after taxes and transfers.[149]

This is one of the shocking findings of research conducted by Phil Gramm, Robert Ekelund and John Early for their book, *The Myth of American Inequality*. A member of an American middle-class family in which both parents work ends up with no more than a member of a family in which neither works at all.

There are 100 federal programs in the U.S. alone that each distribute more than 100 million US dollars a year, plus countless programs at state and local level.[150] At the same time, there are federal, state and local taxes, resulting in an unmanageable tangle of tax payments on the one hand and transfer payments on the other. The absurd result is that the typical middle-

---

149 Gramm / Ekelund / Early, 32.
150 Gramm / Ekelund / Early, 14.

class household receives almost as much in government transfer payments (17,850 US dollars) as it pays in taxes (19,314 U.S. dollars).[151]

Of course, the bureaucracy that runs all of this swallows up a massive amount of money. Many middle-class Americans sense that there is something wrong with the system, which is largely financed by the top 20 percent of income earners, who have an average household income of 295,904 US dollars but pay taxes of almost 107,000 US dollars.[152] This refutes the popular belief that America's top earners get off lightly when it comes to paying taxes.

No. More than every third dollar earned by these households ends up in the government's coffers. And the top 20 percent of households pay more than 60 percent of all taxes. If you look at federal income taxes alone, the top 20 percent pay 83 percent of the total income tax bill![153]

So, the system fleeces higher earners and discourages the middle class by removing any financial incentive to work. And perhaps the most absurd aspect of all this is that it does nothing to help in the fight against poverty, because since the "War on Poverty" began in the U.S. in the mid-1960s with government programs that have constantly ballooned in size and scope, the poverty rate has remained virtually the same, with slight fluctuations. In the two decades before the "War on Poverty" began, poverty in the U.S. had steadily declined from 32.1 to 14.7 percent.[154]

The only people who benefit from the current system are politicians who first take money from American households and then make election promises to give it back to their own clientele.

But now to my trip. When I arrive in Washington D.C. and unpack my suitcase, I realize that, for the first time on all my travels, I have forgotten the charger for my laptop. I'm traveling with Alica again, who has accompanied me on many of my trips. She helps me find a Best Buy store, where I buy a charger. But I make the mistake of not trying it out first. When I get back to the hotel,

---

151 Gramm / Ekelund / Early, 29.
152 Gramm / Ekelund / Early, 29.
153 Gramm / Ekelund / Early, 26.
154 Gramm / Ekelund / Early, 35.

it turns out that the 180 Watts the charger delivers are not enough. I call my IT specialist in Germany, where it is late at night, and he Googles a store on the way to Dulles International Airport, which is where I have to catch my flight to NYC the next day. They have a single 300-Watt charger in stock. I simply can't do without a laptop, especially as I conduct interviews with journalists via Zoom, Skype and other tools, and write something every day.

In Washington D.C., I have been invited to speak at the Cato Institute about my film *Life Behind the Berlin Wall*. Cato is widely regarded as one of the most influential libertarian think tanks in the United States, if not worldwide. It was founded by Edward H. Crane, Murray Rothbard, and Charles G. Koch in San Francisco in 1977.

I had already heard a lot about Cato, but lady luck had been my friend the first time I came into direct contact with the institute: Students for Liberty, a global association of libertarian students, had invited me to speak at their annual convention in Washington in January 2019. In the cab from the airport to my hotel, I looked out of the window and saw the word "Cato" on the office building directly opposite my hotel. I had already had the idea of working with Cato to publish a book. Now fortune had smiled on me! As soon as I arrived at the hotel, I wrote an email to Cato, briefly introducing myself and explaining that I was a speaker at LibertyCon, the annual convention that was being held at the hotel across the street. I asked for an appointment the next day to present a book project. Cato confirmed an appointment the next morning with the head of its book publishing division, and I pitched my book, *Die Gesellschaft und ihre Reichen*, which was subsequently published by Cato under the title *The Rich in Public Opinion*.

This time – as I mentioned above – my visit primarily concerns my film, which Cato also wants to use in its educational work with students. For many viewers, the realities of life in East Germany under socialism shown in the film are new.

In Washington D.C., I of course also visit my friends from *Americans for Tax Reform* and meet Grover Norquist and Andreas Hellmann. Hellmann is currently building a house outside Washington D.C. He is moving because of the crime rate in the American capital, which he says has become unbearably high. Other people I meet in Washington D.C. also confirm that crime has risen sharply. By comparison, the crime rate in New York City is 9 percent below the national average, whereas the crime rate in Washington D.C. is 87 percent above the national average, with violent crime 147 percent higher (2022). Even during the day, cars are stopped on the street by armed criminals and "carjacked" or the drivers robbed.

It's a bit stressful to be flying off to New York so soon after the movie. Alica, who lived there for a while and is a total New York fan, is really happy when we land. I'm happy for her, albeit with mixed feelings, because I'm afraid she'll move from Berlin to New York for good at some point. I've been to New York a lot myself and have owned two apartments in the city since 2012, right next to Rockefeller Center, which I rent out. However, I haven't been back to the city since the Covid pandemic.

In New York I meet quite a few people, including the well-known American columnist Deroy Murdock, the political commentator and close confidante of Steve Forbes, Elizabeth Ames, and the film producer and journalist Kelly Jane Torrance.

Murdock is a libertarian. He is black and gay – and he hates "woke" identity politics. He says people sometimes confuse him with the well-known author and journalist Jason L. Riley, whose book, *Please Stop Helping Us: How Liberals Make It Harder for Blacks to Succeed*, I read and really enjoyed. People would sometimes come up to him, praising him for a column Riley had written: "Well, we're both black, wear glasses, shave our heads, and hold similar opinions," Murdock says with a laugh. His columns appear in *The New York Post, The Boston Herald, The Washington Times, National Review, The Orange County Register* and many other newspapers and magazines in the United States and abroad. He is also a contributor to *Fox News* and a Senior Fellow at the Atlas Network in Washington D.C., and an Emeritus Media Fellow at the Hoover Institution at Stanford University. He has long been engaged in the libertarian movement and was involved in the Reagan for President campaigns in 1980 and 1984.

But he also criticizes the fact that many libertarians seem to be content in their minority position and prefer to pay homage to "pure doctrine" in small, like-minded groups rather than gain real social influence. Later it will become clear that meeting him has been particularly valuable for me.

Kelly Jane Torrance is an editor at the *New York Post*. She used to be a senior editor at the *Washington Examiner* and deputy editor at *The Weekly Standard*. She also worked at Cato early in her career. Of course, the *New York Post* does not have anywhere near the same kind of intellectual cache as the *Wall Street Journal* or *The New York Times*, but it is very influential and is read by people from all walks of life. It's only intellectuals, she says, who turn up their noses at the *New York Post*. "But intellectuals never understood why workers voted for a billionaire president," says Torrance. I think too many libertarians ignore blue-collar workers and try to appeal to other intellectuals, rather than trying to convince workers of the merits of their ideas. After all, it is workers whose lives have been most improved by capitalism – not by socialism. And it was workers who brought down socialism in Poland.

Elizabeth Ames is a well-known commentator and author. She has collaborated with Steve Forbes on several books, including *Money*. She is co-producer and author of the award-winning TV documentary *In Money We Trust?* "We have the same mission," she greets me. It's always nice to see that there are people like Elizabeth who are supportive and helpful – knowing that there are only a few of us who stand up for a common cause.

Ames is currently working with Steve Forbes on a series for *Free to Choose* featuring portraits of significant and forgotten figures from American history. Forbes is a great defender of capitalism and I am very proud that he wrote such a glowing endorsement for my book, *In Defence of Capitalism*: "One of the most important books in decades defending capitalism. Well researched and well written, it not only makes the case for free markets but also demolishes Thomas Piketty's much publicized tract trashing capitalism. Adam Smith would have been impressed – and proud."

From New York, we head to West Palm Beach, where I enjoy the sun with Alica and can relax a bit. There is only one lecture planned while we are here, for students at Florida Atlantic University. From West Palm Beach, we return to Washington D.C., where the Federal Society has invited me to a live-streamed lecture about my film *Life Behind the Berlin Wall* and I am able to present my book, *In Defence of Capitalism,* at an Americans for Tax Reform event.

Before that, I attend the weekly Wednesday meeting of Americans for Tax Reform, which I have been to several times in the past as a guest from Germany. It is an interesting format: politicians, representatives of think tanks and business people all come together to discuss the latest topics, especially tax policy. Many people are following the meeting online from all over the world – including my friend Gia from the country of Georgia. One guest reports on tax plans in Italy, another on Germany's crazy energy policy. The meeting is chaired by Grover Norquist himself.

I'm staying in Washington's elegant University Club hotel, barely a five-minute walk from the White House. The hotel is furnished in a time-honored fashion, but it's a disappointment. My room is way too cold and stays cold even after someone tries to fix the problem. The water from the shower is no more than a weak trickle. From time to time in the past, I have experienced similar in venerable, well-known hotels, such as the elegant Le Negresco in Nice. They have impressive foyers, but the service cannot be compared to Asian hotels, for example.

While I am in the United States, I conduct several interviews with radio stations every day. I find myself telling the same stories over and over again, often with the same wording and examples. Some authors get bored and think they have to come up with something new. No, I'm sure most radio listeners in the U.S. have never heard of me or my books, and even though I've said it so many times, I know that it's new for them, they're hearing it for the first time. The same applies, of course, to most countries.

March 2023
Athens, Greece

I arrive in Athens on March 10, 2023. I'm due give lectures at the university and speak with local newspapers about the Greek edition of my book, *In Defence of Capitalism*, but none of this is possible due to violent left-wing riots. Sections of the university have been occupied by left-wing extremists. The riots were triggered by an accident on the train tracks between Athens and Thessaloniki two weeks earlier, on February 28. Shortly before midnight, a passenger train and an oncoming freight train collided head-on on the same track. At least 57 people died. Of over 80 injured, 14 people were still being treated in hospital at the time of my visit to Greece. It is the worst train accident in the country's history. A station master has admitted failing to reroute trains and has been remanded in custody and charged. According to media reports, the 59-year-old had only been a station master for 40 days, following three months of training.

Left-wingers blame the accident on capitalism, or more precisely the privatization of Greece's railways, which is absurd. The accident could have happened at any time, even in the past when the railway was state-owned. In addition, the railway network is still state-owned. But capitalism is more despised in Greece than in other countries, and the train accident only galvanized existing anti-capitalist sentiment. Our survey of the image of capitalism in 35 countries shows that there are only four countries in which capitalism has an even worse image than in Greece. And this negativity is not primarily linked with the term "capitalism" itself. Yes, support for capitalism in Greece does increase somewhat when "capitalism" is not used in the question. But even when the survey's questions did not use the word, attitudes toward the market economy in Greece were clearly negative, similar to our findings in France and Spain.

The left-wing violence escalated in the days before my visit, and my publisher Phaedon Kidoniatis of Eurasia Publications told to me the day after my arrival that extremists had beaten the Marxist economist Yanis Varoufakis to the point of hospitalization. Varoufakis served as finance minister in the cabinet of the ultra-left-winger Alexis Tsipras from January to July 2015, but Tsipras's Syriza party was not left-wing enough for him so he founded a pan-European anti-capitalist movement, DiEM25, in February 2016. In parliamentary elections on July 7, 2019, Varoufakis was re-elected to the Greek Parliament with the Greek branch of his movement, the MeRA25 party.

On Twitter (now X), Varoufakis denied reports that his attackers were anarchists or other leftists. Rather, he pointed the finger at hired thugs who accused him of selling Greece out to foreign interests during the 2015 debt crisis when he was finance minister. The evening before, I ask my publisher Phaedon whether he could invite Varoufakis to a controversial discussion about capitalism, and he sends Varoufakis a copy of my book with a personal dedication. But the economist does not answer our invitation to take part in a debate.

My publisher says he has considered postponing my visit completely because of the chaotic situation, but I'm against it. The interviews with the newspapers can still take place and the publisher decides to move the event from the university to a major bookstore in the center of the city.

The opening speech at the book launch is given by Alexander Skouras, the leading figure in the libertarian movement in Greece. Alexander studied marketing at the American College of Greece and political administration at George Washington University. He has held key positions in national election campaigns in Greece and in the Republican Party presidential campaign in the United States. Before becoming president of the Greek libertarian think tank KEFiM, he was deputy director of international relations at the Atlas Network in the U.S. capital, Washington D.C., for six years.

On Sunday, together with my girlfriend Jenna, who has joined me for two days, I watch a demonstration of a few thousand leftists in front of Parliament from the balcony of our room in the Hotel Grande Bretagne. The speeches are repeatedly interrupted by emotional music, and I say to Jenna: "Do you see why the anti-capitalists are better at marketing than we are? We only have the facts, the left has the music and the emotions. Why don't libertarians have any moving, pro-freedom songs?"

Before I travel to Greece, I find out about the country's economy and history. According to the *2023 Index of Economic Freedom*, Greece is doing very badly. The report states: "Greece's economic freedom score is 56.9, making its economy the 107th freest in the 2023 Index … Greece is ranked 42nd out of 44 countries in the Europe region, and its overall score is below the world and regional averages. Bold adjustments are needed in such areas as government spending and labor freedom. The fiscal deficit remains unsustainable with public debt close to 200 percent of GDP. The lack of competitiveness and fading business confidence are serious impediments to economic revival. The rigid labour market discourages productivity gains and dynamic entrepreneurial activity."[155]

Greek politics is confusing – no matter how many years you go back in history, the prime minister is almost always called Mitsotakis, Karamanlis or Papandreou. Sometimes a member of one family wins, sometimes a member of one of the other families. What remains the same is the clientele policy. If a member of one family gains power, their favorites expect to be provided with positions. Already in 2010, Petros Markaris (Athens) wrote an article called "*Griechenland: Wo alles 'sozialistisch' ist*" ("Greece. Where everything is 'socialist'"): "Greece is the last country in Europe where real socialism still exists." Nevertheless, he says there is no difference between right-wing and left-wing politicians. The right established a system of dependency that was "much closer to the centrally controlled Soviet-style power apparatus than to a democratic constitutional state … The state apparatus was where the privileged of this system gathered. Every young woman and every young man dreamed of securing a government job after they graduated … Even being hired as a gardener or cleaning lady was a privilege. Every party member, the heads of government agencies and the entire government, from

155 Heritage Foundation, *2023 Index of Economic Freedom*, 158.

state secretaries to the prime minister, found places for their favorites – 'our children,' as they called them – in the public service, indefinitely and without oversight."[156]

Nothing changed after the social democratic transition of 1981, when Andreas Papandreou, founder of the Panhellenic Socialist Movement, Pasok, became prime minister. 59 percent of Greeks voted for left-wing parties, with Pasok becoming the strongest party with 48.1 percent, and the Communists coming third on 10.9 percent.

Pasok placed its own people in the state apparatus en masse, with the striking argument: "The right has been living off the state for years. Now it's our people's turn."[157] Immediately after taking office, Papandreou began building a party clientele system. The infiltration of the public service took on a whole new dimension; It was based not only on the awarding of posts to one's own supporters, which had long been common practice under earlier governments, but also on a fundamental redefinition of the relationship between state and party, which had much more far-reaching consequence.[158] The lines between party and state became increasingly blurred, and from 1982 to 1988, the number of public sector employees grew by 82,000, accounting for nearly 60 percent of the total employment increase over that six-year period. As the historian Ioannis Zelepos writes: "What made matters worse was that, at the same time, salaries and perks continued to improve, creating supply conditions that were in inverse proportion to the steadily declining performance of the public sector. Finally, the situation was further aggravated by the underlying anti-competitive tendency of economic policy, which was expressed, among other things, in a strong propensity to nationalize ailing companies and definitely had ideological dimensions."[159]

In 2011, I founded a publishing house, *Ambition-Verlag*. One of the first books I published was by Wassilis Aswestopoulos and was called *Griechenland – eine europäische Tragödie* (*Greece – a European tragedy*). Reading the book,

---

156 Markaris, https://www.woz.ch/1021/griechenland/wo-alles-sozialistisch-ist.
157 Markaris, https://www.woz.ch/1021/griechenland/wo-alles-sozialistisch-ist.
158 Zelepos, 215.
159 Zelepos, 217.

it soon becomes clear why it was so attractive to work for the public sector in Greece. As well as being unsackable, civil servants' salaries were generally almost twice as high as those in the private-sector for people with the same qualifications. "They had health insurance with lower deductibles in the event of illness. They enjoyed more vacation, longer maternity leave and were able to retire earlier. Mothers over the age of fifty with at least three children, including underage child, could retire, as could police officers over the age of forty," writes Aswestopoulos. And the Greek pension system guaranteed pensions of up to 80 percent of the final salary.[160]

There were technicians earning five-figure monthly salaries at state transport companies. "Stories circulated of dead people who continued to collect their pensions. Investigations revealed that deceased clergy had pregnancy tests done. Equally curious were medical records proving that the dead and buried in cemeteries had received heart bypasses after their supposed deaths."[161]

The majority of the private sector, writes Aswestopoulos, lived from public contracts.[162] "Anyone who wanted to become something in politics, business or even just simple working life, depended on relationships and connections. If the mentor enriched himself with public money, he could hope for the solidarity of his protégés. Over time, almost impenetrable and almost mafia-like structures emerged almost everywhere."[163]

The Greek government is, on the one hand, far too weak and, at the same time, far too strong. Too weak because government agencies are understaffed – for example, there are not enough tax officials – and too strong because a maze of regulations and bureaucratic rules has developed that is unparalleled in any other country. Wassilis Aswestopoulos reports in his book: "It took the Temes company longer to get a hotel complex in Messenia on the Peloponnese approved than Odysseus needed for his ten-year journey home to Ithaca. The 'Costa Navarino' complex is a 1.2 billion euro investment by shipowner

160 Aswestopoulos, 19–20.
161 Aswestopoulos, 170–171.
162 Aswestopoulos, 65.
163 Aswestopoulos, 64–65.

Vassilis Konstantopoulos. From 1997 to 2009, he collected more than 3,000 signatures from ministers, officials and ordinary employees. Konstantopoulos wasn't launching a petition, he just wanted to get his investment approved. He ended up needing more than twenty ministerial decrees and 600 different permits, issued by 80 planning offices employing 1,200 specialists, for the approval phase alone. The courts had to rule more than sixty times. The Prefecture of Messinia met twenty-five times to discuss the topic of Costa Navarino."[164]

In 2002, Greece introduced the euro, but it later emerged that this should not have been allowed because Greek politicians had falsified statistics to meet the European Union's entry criteria. Since money was suddenly cheap, the debt orgies really took off. Greece hosted the 2004 Olympic Games. The country's application estimated the games would cost 7.7 billion euros. Official documents later put the figure at eleven billion; but estimates range from 20 to 30 billion euros.[165] According to forecasts, the renovation of the Olympic Stadium in Athens was supposed to cost 3.1 million euros, but it actually cost 399 million, a cost overrun of 12,771 percent.[166]

Staggering waste of taxpayers' money, excessive corruption, a state that was both inefficient and meddling everywhere, and ever more extreme levels of debt led to an desperate situation. Greece could only be saved from bankruptcy thanks to several "euro rescue packages" worth 278 billion euros.[167]

Greece had already been bankrupt four times in its history. In principle, it was already bankrupt in 1827, before it was officially founded in 1830. The second bankruptcy occurred in 1843. Further bankruptcies followed in 1893 and 1932 – insolvency is as normal for Greece as inflation is for Argentina.

Countless conferences and billion upon billion in payments meant that Greece remained in the euro zone. You have to ask yourself whether it made any sense to invest all that time and energy. If the then German Chancellor

---

164 Aswestopulos, 23–24.
165 Aswestopulos, 109–110.
166 Aswestopulos, 110.
167 Rose, https://www.tagesschau.de/wirtschaft/weltwirtschaft/rettungspakete-101.html.

Angela Merkel and the other European countries had only spent half as much effort and money on preventing Brexit, i.e. the UK's exit from the EU, that would certainly have made more sense. So the UK is out of the EU and the Greeks are still in the Eurozone. For the British and the Greeks, as well as for the rest of Europe, it might have been better if Greece had left the Eurozone and the UK had stayed in a reformed EU.

I meet a number of journalists and business people in Athens who say that some things have improved a little under the conservative government that has been in office since 2019. Bureaucracy and the regulation of the labor market are still oppressive, but the conditions are no longer as bad as they used to be. But the state is still seen as the big "provider," just like in Argentina. The government's initial response to the train accident was to offer public service jobs as compensation to the survivors and their families. Hardly any other country in the world would have come up with such an idea.

A question that I repeatedly ask business leaders, scholars and the media is about the Greeks' attitude to the state. One of the people I speak to describes it as a "love-hate relationship," and many agree. On the one hand, Greeks love the state and expect a lot from it, but because the state cannot satisfy their expectations, they end up hating it. It is like a child who expects everything from their parents, but is then disappointed when the parents cannot meet such excessive expectations. Several of the people I speak with use this image.

Many Greeks are frustrated that corruption is such an ever-present aspect of their lives. Corruption has two causes: cultural and traditional on the one hand, and too many government regulations on the other. Since cultural traditions are more difficult to change, it is even more important to cut government regulations to the bone.

At least, many people tell me, corruption is no longer as bad as it used to be. Back then, they explain to me, you couldn't visit a doctor without bringing a "stuffed envelope" with you and handing over a pile of cash. That has changed. But in some sectors, such as the construction industry, it is still impossible to navigate the maze of permits and regulations without bribing officials.

The majority of Greeks are disillusioned by the disastrous policies of the left. Three months after I visited Athens, there was another election. Kyriakos Mitsotakis, in office since 2019, was confirmed for another four years. His conservative New Democracy (ND) won an absolute majority. The left-wing Syriza party, which was formed in 2004 as an electoral alliance of communists, Maoists, Trotskyists and other leftists and became by far the strongest party in the 2015 elections with over 36 percent of the vote,[168] received only half as many votes in the 2023 elections (17.8 percent), while the social democratic Pasok party got 11.9 percent.[169]

168 Wikipedia, "Parlamentswahl in Griechenland," https://de.wikipedia.org/wiki/
Parlamentswahl_in_Griechenland_September_2015#:~:text=Die percent20Parlamentswahl
percent20in percent20Griechenland percent20im,Tsipras percent20angef percentC3
percentBChrte percent20linksgerichtete percent20Partei percent20SYRIZA.
169 Geiger, https://www.sueddeutsche.de/politik/griechenland-wahl-mitostakis-wahlsieg-
wahlrecht-1.5968221.

March 2023
Warsaw, Poland

Nowhere does capitalism have a better image than in Poland – as confirmed by the findings of the Ipsos MORI survey I commissioned in 35 countries.[170] This is also reflected in the fact that Poland is home to such a wide variety of pro-capitalist events and initiatives that you would only find in the United States, not elsewhere in Europe. In March 2023, I am speaking at two of these events and am able to gain a first-hand impression of the strength of the Polish libertarian scene and its activities. At the beginning of March, I am invited to speak at an Asbiro University event in Warsaw. This private university was founded in 2006 and offers courses in entrepreneurship, bachelor's degrees in management, sales and marketing, and postgraduate MBA programs in business and real estate. Its unique selling point is that it is the only university in Poland where every lecturer is either an entrepreneur or a CEO.

In contrast to many MBA and business administration courses, which are highly theoretical and teach students a lot about financial mathematics and theories, this university is primarily practice-oriented. There are a number of basic courses for students who still want to become entrepreneurs, but most of the enrolled students have already set up their own companies. The university organizes trips to different countries around the world, where participants can collect new business ideas and build new relationships. During the trips, the students meet local entrepreneurs, lawyers, auditors, and so on. For example, there have been trips to Germany and China. The university explicitly upholds the ideas of the Austrian-American economist Ludwig von Mises and has close links to the libertarian scene in Poland.

The Polish libertarian scene comes together every two years for the "Weekend of Capitalism," where I am giving the introductory lecture to

170 Zitelmann, "Attitudes towards Capitalism," https://onlinelibrary.wiley.com/doi/full/10.1111/ecaf.12591.

several hundred participants at the end of March 2023. I find the title of the event remarkable because even in the libertarian scene, many people avoid the word "capitalism" given its negative connotations in the minds of so many people. I remember another libertarian conference in Warsaw where, apart from me, hardly any speakers even mentioned the word "capitalism."

I think that's wrong. If it was just the word that bothered people and they were otherwise in favor of a free-market economy as long as it is not called "capitalism," that would be worth discussing. But that is not the case. My survey in 35 countries showed that support for capitalism (as expected) increases in most countries when the word "capitalism" is not used in the survey questions. More important, however, is the finding that even when the word is not used, pro-capitalist opinions dominate in only seven out of 35 countries. When the word is used, this figure decreases to six countries. I think avoiding the word "capitalism" shows insecurity and weakness, and so I begin my talk with a request to never change the name of the event.

At the "Weekend of Capitalism," I meet many of the people with whom I worked so closely the year before. Unfortunately, I cannot follow most of the lectures because they are held in Polish.

One of the speakers who does deliver his speech in English is Remigijus Šimašius. He was mayor of the Lithuanian capital, Vilnius, for eight years and is only now leaving office. The 49-year-old was on the board of a libertarian think tank from 2006 to 2008, and also describes himself as a libertarian during his talk. Before being elected mayor of Vilnius in 2015, he was Minister of Justice of Lithuania from 2008 to 2012 and leader of the *Lietuvos Respublikos liberalu sajudis* (LRLS; Libertarian Movement of the Republic of Lithuania) from 2016 to 2017. In 2019, he became mayor of the capital for a second term. He was also considered a possible candidate for the 2019 Lithuania presidential election, but he decided not to run. In June 2019, Šimašius joined with a group of LRLS dissidents to found the new libertarian *Laisves partija* (Freedom Party) and is its deputy leader.

Most people, he begins his lecture, believe that a mayor has to make pragmatic decisions on a daily basis and that ideas or ideological convictions

With *Free to Choose* founder Bob Chitester outside Milton Friedman's summer residence in the mountains of Vermont, USA

Giving a lecture to students at the HSBC Business School in Shenzhen, China

Filming in Berlin for the documentary *Life Behind the Berlin Wall*

With Alica in Tbilisi, Georgia

With Andrea in Tbilisi, Georgia

With the economist Professor Gia Jandieri in Tbilisi

Tbilisi, the capital of Georgia

One of the 200,000 bunkers Enver Hoxha had built in Albania

The »Pyramid of Tirana« was designed as a memorial to the dictator Enver Hoxha by his daughter and is now an IT hub.

Talking with Sali Berisha, former Prime Minister of Albania

Libertarians in Chile

After his election, Chile's President Gabriel Boric kissed this monument to Salvador Allende

With Eduardo Tassano,
Mayor of Corrientes, Argentina

Montevideo, the capital of
Uruguay, looks European.

Sao Paulo, Brazil: With
multi-billionaire Salim Mattar,
founder of Localiza Rent a
Car, Latin America's largest
car rental company

With Alica at Freedom Fest in Las Vegas

With economist Shawn Miller at Freedom Fest in Las Vegas

My film *Life Behind the Berlin Wall* wins the »Audience Choice Award for Short Films« at the Anthem Film Festival, the largest libertarian film festival in the world.

With Marek Tatała, CEO of the Economic Freedom Foundation, and my polish publisher Krzysztof Zuber (Wydawnictwo Freedom Publishing)

In Warsaw with the great reformer Leszek Balcerowicz, who started Poland on the path to a market economy

Lecture to around 1,000 real estate agents in Hanoi

Workshop at the Foreign Trade University in Hanoi: »What motivates people to become wealthy«

Hanoi: In the citadel of Thăng Long, the imperial court of several Vietnamese imperial dynasties

In Miami with Whole Foods founder John Mackey, who campaigns for animal welfare and capitalism

On the beach in Miami

Porto, Portugal, at the launch of my book

In Sarajevo at the scene of the assassination of Prince Ferdinand on June 28, 1914, which triggered the First World War

With my libertarian friends in Bratislava. Everyone drinks beer, I drink my milk.

In Bratislava: The motto of these libertarians »Capitalism and Heavy Metal« – Mario Blaščák and Peter Gonda

Filming with Tomasz Agencki in Gdansk for my documentary *Poland. From Socialism to Prosperity*

In Belgrade with Tomislav Momirović, Serbian entrepreneur and Minister of Internal and Foreign Trade

With Jenna in Athens, the Acropolis in the background

Lecture at »Weekend of Capitalism« in Warsaw

With Steve Forbes and Elizabeth Ames in Manhattan, New York City

With Deroy Murdoch in New York City

Bucharest, Romania, in the »House of the People«, the largest government building in the world after the Pentagon, which Nicolae Ceaușescu had built when his people were living in abject poverty

Bucharest, Romania, with Tudor Smirna, President of the Ludwig von Mises Institute

If you ask for a knife in Korea, don't be surprised if you get a pair of scissors.

In Seoul at the Buddhist Dongguk University, a prestigious private university in South Korea founded in 1906

This photo was published by the daily newspaper in Mongolia – with three books translated into Mongolian

In front of the world's largest equestrian statue (of Genghis Khan), near the Mongolian capital Ulaanbaatar

Puerta del Sol in Madrid with my friend Diego Sánchez de la Cruz, who has translated five of my books into Spanish

Two days after Javier Milei's election victory, at his party's headquarters in Buenos Aires

With Axel Kaiser at the presentation of our book *El Odio a los Ricos* in Santiago de Chile

With my friend Basanta Adhikari on Hanuman Dhoka Durbar Square in Kathmandu

Kathmandu, Nepal: Too much state always leads to abject poverty.

A typical store in Kathmandu, Nepal

The house of former dictator Enver Hoxha in Tirana, Albania

At the end of my trip with Jenna at the New Year's Eve party in Monaco

play little or no role. However, he says, that is a big mistake. Cutting bureaucracy was one of his priorities. He proudly reports that Uber was licensed in Vilnius three weeks after submitting its application. That is a record timeframe, unparalleled in other countries, and the fastest approval in the world. The results of Vilnius's free-market housing policy are also impressive: in eight years, rents in the city have risen by 70 percent, but wages have risen by 100 percent, while in many other cities rents have risen faster than wages over the same period. Relatively speaking, tenants are paying less rent after eight years than they had been before.

In the libertarian scene, as in all political movements, there are pragmatists – such as Šimašius – and fundamentalists, who are more interested in pure doctrine and see pragmatism as a betrayal of principles. One of the participants at my lecture had earlier revealed that he is generally skeptical of politics and politicians. He now critically asks Šimašius how he reconciles being a politician with his libertarian principles, since politics means exerting power over people, which is something libertarians reject. I admit that I am suspicious of such libertarian fundamentalists. They don't really want to make a difference, often feel comfortable in the role of guardians of the holy grail of pure doctrine, and frequently remind me of the dogmatic Marxists I met in my youth.

Perhaps this is one of the main problems with libertarians in many parts of the world: they feel comfortable being seen as outsiders and a minority. Basically, they don't want to change anything because practical politics involves compromises, and compromises don't fit with their utopian thinking.

After my lecture, I am able to exchange a few words with Šimašius. He is outraged that there are people in the libertarian scene in the United States who are not backing Ukraine and that some even go as far as to express sympathy for Putin. How can you be for freedom, he asks, and not take a decisive stand against an enemy of freedom like Putin? There are no such attitudes in Poland, where libertarians are clearly on the side of Ukraine.

April 2023
Washington DC, New York City and Boston, United States

In March and April, I have several interviews a week with American radio stations, sometimes several times a day. These interviews are arranged for me by A. J. Rice's Publius PR agency. Our partnership is a new experience for me, having previously worked with four different public relations agencies in the United States, all of which had the following in common: they promised a lot, cost a lot, and delivered nothing. As I was the owner of one of the leading public relations agencies in Germany, I can judge what makes a good or bad public relations agency. Unfortunately, 95 percent of agencies are bad, and that's probably the case all over the world.

Because of the time difference, these interviews – when I conduct them from Germany – often take place very late, sometimes after midnight. When I once told A. J. Rice that I only wanted to take appointments at 3 a.m. in Germany as an exception, he quickly replied: "The fight for Western civilization doesn't end at midnight." I liked that.

Mostly, though not always, I talk to conservative or right-wing talk show hosts. Previously, I had only seen U.S. talk shows on television, and one of my favorite films, which I have seen dozens of times, is about this kind of American radio format: *Talk Radio* by Oliver Stone.

Conservative talk shows have played a major role in the United States since the Reagan era. Before that, radio stations were subject to the Federal Communications Commission's "Fairness Doctrine," which obliged them to maintain a political balance. However, this was abolished in 1987. While the major newspapers in the U.S. tend to be dominated by left-wing opinions, the situation is different on the radio airwaves. Left-wing radio stations have not been able to attract such large audiences as right-wing stations. In the fifty or so interviews I conduct, I notice two things: first, my interviewers were overwhelmingly "pro-capitalist." Second, this does not prevent them from believing in populist, anti-big-business, conspiracy theories. Some interviewers claim that all of the billionaires in the United States today are left-wingers. I try to explain to them that this only applies to a small minority – people like George Soros, who attract a lot of media coverage, but whose opinions are by no means representative of successful entrepreneurs and investors in the United States. A number of my interviewers clearly subscribe to the widespread conspiracy theory – as do some conservatives and some libertarians – that there is a grand plot to establish a "New World Order" led by Klaus Schwab, the head of the World Economic Forum (WEF). I myself do not believe in conspiracy theories, as they grossly overestimate the role of planning and intention in the course of political and historical events. I don't need conspiracy theories to understand political developments. The power of ideology, the power of stupidity, and the power of conformism are all the explanations I need.

In the United States, bias against the rich and super-rich is not exclusively limited to those on the left of the political spectrum, it extends far into the right-wing camp. No doubt this also applies to some of the talk shows, as I gather from the interviewers' questions. But by no means all of them. Many are simply refreshingly pro-capitalist – the way we Europeans sometimes imagine Americans to be. There are, thankfully, still Americans who believe in capitalism and entrepreneurship and are skeptical of "big government."

Having already been to the United States once in March (and having also visited Poland twice in the same month), I set off for the U.S. again at the beginning of April. The journey gets off to a difficult start: the flight from Frankfurt to Washington is postponed several times, first by two hours, then by three hours and then by five. In the end, it is unclear whether we will be able to fly at all that day. As a precaution, I ask the friendly Lufthansa staff in the Senator Star Alliance Lounge at Frankfurt Airport to put together an alternative plan for me to fly to Washington via Amsterdam the following day so that I can still arrive in time for my lecture. In the end, they say the flight is leaving after all. We board the plane. I put on my pajamas. The announcement for take-off plays over the loudspeakers. Then the captain comes into first class, apologizes, and says that there is another problem. They had forgotten the digital logbook and someone opened the door again to fetch it, which activated the emergency inflatable slides. The plane could not be used for the time being, the captain explained, and everyone had to disembark. So, I put my clothes back on, got off the plane, and spent the night in the airport's Sheraton Hotel with the promise that we would be flying to Washington at 11 a.m. the next day and arriving before 2 p.m. That should give me enough time, because my lecture in Washington is due to start at 5 p.m. Unfortunately, the rescheduled flight is also two hours late, and when we land I have to queue for 90 minutes at immigration. In the end, however, everything works out fine and I'm only 20 minutes late – I call ahead and ask them to screen my film *Life Behind the Berlin Wall* until I arrive.

I used to get quite annoyed by such things but, at some point, I realized that getting angry doesn't achieve anything except souring my mood, and that you have to accept flight delays in the same way you have to accept the weather. I've also been very lucky with my flights over the past twelve months, which have mostly been on time. When you travel so much, you have to expect a few hiccups.

Ralph Benko, who has been posting and sharing my articles for a few years now, also attends my lecture. In 2020, he wrote *The Capitalist Manifesto: The End of Class Warfare, Toward Universal Affluence*. Benko knows the libertarian scene in the U.S. very well, but takes a critical view of it. He tells me that I need someone to support my activities with substantial, long-term funding. It is true that I will not be able to do what I have done in recent years, namely finance all my research and lecture tours privately, in the long run. But, unfortunately, I don't know any entrepreneurs who could provide the funding I need. Perhaps a reader of this book has an idea?

Two weeks after our meeting, Benko publishes a very flattering article about me and my book in *Newsmax*, in which he crowns me "the reigning public intellectual champion of capitalism. He is capitalism's Thomas Piketty. Anti-capitalist Piketty's works are extensively reviewed and on the bestseller lists. Zitelmann's work is rigorously data-driven. Not dogmatic. While the left, shrewdly, never lets the facts stand in the way of a good story, Zitelmann utterly demolishes its arguments. All right (in both senses) thinking people should be enthusiastically promoting him."[171]

On the second day, in New York, I write to John Fund, who I met at Freedom Fest in Las Vegas, and ask him if he has time for a meeting. He is one of the most influential journalists in the libertarian scene in the U.S. and wrote for the *Wall Street Journal* for 26 years. Today, he works for the libertarian-conservative magazine *National Review*, among others. We meet at 5 p.m. and talk for almost five hours. He tells me lots of stories about people who interest me, such as Arnold Schwarzenegger and Donald Trump. I get the impression that he knows pretty much everyone who is anyone in the United States. An impressive person indeed.

In New York, I also meet Mary O'Grady. She has worked at the *Wall Street Journal*, the largest and most influential pro-capitalist newspaper in existence (the *Financial Times* is more critical of capitalism), for 28 years. The key question that concerns not only her, but also me: Why are anti-capitalists so much more successful than we are? She offers the following explanation: "We argue that GDP per capita has risen by x percent, and they tell the heartbreaking story of a family whose children live in poverty." We need to learn to be much more emotional, she says.

She visited Cuba and the terrible plight of the people there had a huge impact on her. That, she suggests, should be made into a movie. People simply don't know anything about it.

At lunchtime, I watch the action on 5th Avenue in front of Trump Tower. I've never seen so many photographers (was it more than 1,000?) in one place as on this day. They are all waiting for Trump, who is expected here on April 3 because he is scheduled to give testimony in court on April 4 – the first

---

171 Benko, https://www.newsmax.com/ralphbenko/capitalism-myths-debunk/2023/04/12/id/1115921/

president in the history of the United States to be prosecuted after his term in office and to have to appear before a judge. There will be many more similar summonses later, but this is the first.

My meeting with Steve Forbes, arranged by Elizabeth Ames, takes place on the same evening. Forbes has been the highest-profile figure in the U.S. libertarian scene for decades. We meet at an Italian restaurant on 54th Street and talk about many people he knows personally, and I'm interested to hear what he thinks about them. Like me, he is not a Trump fan. He says that Trump called him every year when the Forbes ranking of the richest people came out, claiming to be much wealthier than the ranking would have it. But Trump was never able to prove his claims. However, it shows the cultural difference between the U.S. and Germany: in the U.S., Trump inflates his wealth because he believes it could benefit him. In Germany, CDU chairman Friedrich Merz pretends to be much poorer than he is because he believes that it will hurt him if everyone knows he is a millionaire.

I try to persuade Forbes to write an autobiography. He has doubts as to whether such a book would find enough readers. I say: "Anyone who has had an interesting life can also write an interesting autobiography and should do so." What's more, he knows so many people personally and can certainly tell a lot of stories about them. At the end, Forbes gives me his personal email address and we agree to stay in touch. He also promises to come to the press meeting that Deroy Murdock is organizing two days later. Since our meeting, Forbes has repeatedly helped with introductions.

From New York I travel to Boston, where I am invited by the Intercollegiate Studies Institute to give two lectures, one at Northeastern University and one at Boston College. The Intercollegiate Studies Institute was founded in 1953 and organizes roughly 100 to 150 lectures a year at universities with guest lecturers from the libertarian and conservative scenes. When I ask whether these events are often disrupted by left-wingers, Thomas Sarrouf, who invited me, says that this is particularly the case when it comes to lectures on subjects such as "transgender" issues. The group at Boston College belongs to the Young Republicans, a Republican youth organization. Most of them are Trump supporters, a few are also DeSantis supporters. Of course, these students have a hard time at their universities because they are such a small minority. You can only admire them for their steadfastness, even if you don't always share their opinions, because they are in enemy territory at their universities. It's only small groups of students that I speak to in Boston.

During my conversations with Trump supporters and right-wing conservatives in the U.S., I keep noticing that many harbor strong resentment against the rich and "big business." Thomas Sarrouf says that most billionaires today support the Democrats and that many companies share the "woke" ideology. In the radio interviews I conduct on a daily basis, this bias is often evident: capitalism yes, big business no.

In Boston, I have a meeting with Phil Gramm. He is 80 years old, but very active and highly alert. Gramm has just given a lecture on his book, *The Myth of American Inequality*, which I have already mentioned. In the book, he shows that official statistics on inequality in the United States are a methodological disaster and do not even come close to reflecting reality. He wants to encourage an initiative on this topic in Congress – let's see if the Republican Party understands the importance of the issue.

Gramm began his political career as a Democrat, but switched to the Republicans in 1983. He ran against future candidate Bob Dole in the 1996 Republican Party presidential primaries. As a senator, he frequently called for tax cuts. He applied his "Dickey Flatt Test" ("Is it worth taking money out of Dickey's pocket?") to determine whether federal programs deserve to be funded. Richard "Dickey" Flatt owned a family printing business founded by his father and mother in Mexia, Texas. In Gramm's eyes, Flatt epitomized the pressures faced by a typical independent small business owner.

Gramm is one of the most vehement advocates of tax cuts and deregulation in the U.S. The left-wing economist and Nobel Prize winner Paul Krugman called him "the high priest of deregulation,"[172] and so I greet him with the

---

172   MSNBC interview of Paul Krugman by David Gregory, 22 September 2008, https://www.youtube.com/watch?v=YwqcLbZJ4HA.

words: "It is an honor for me to meet the man that left-wing economist Paul Krugman called the high priest of deregulation. I think you should be proud of that and use it as the title of your autobiography."

On the evening of April 5, Deroy Murdock – the well-known libertarian-conservative political commentator and think-tank scholar who I had recently met in New York – hosts a dinner to present my book, *In Defence of Capitalism*. Twenty high-ranking representatives of conservative and libertarian media have joined us, including James Taranto, who is in charge of the *Wall Street Journal's* op-ed pages, Steve Forbes from *Forbes* magazine, Liz Peek from *Fox News*, John Fund from *National Review*, James T. C. Moore, the Vice President of the media company, *Newsmax*, Kelly Torrance from the *New York Post* and Guy Benson from *townhall.com*. I present my book and then we discuss it for two hours. Opportunities like this are invaluable for making important contacts. One by one, I get to know the leading protagonists of the libertarian and conservative media scene in the United States.

John Fund introduces me to Roger Kimball, the editor of *The New Criterion* and publisher of Encounter Books. I have always wanted to publish a book with Encounter because I really enjoyed books like *Becoming Europe* by Samuel Gregg and *Please Stop Helping Us* by Jason Riley. I meet with Kimball, who is both a very political person and an art expert. For me, he embodies the type of conservative-libertarian intellectual, of which there aren't all that many. I also find something in my conversations with him that I encounter again and again in the United States: a harsh criticism of large corporations in the U.S., which are perceived as enemies because they provide billions of dollars of support for groups like "Black Lives Matter" and other left-wing organizations. He gives me a pile books, including *The Dictatorship of Woke Capital. How Political Correctness Captured Big Business* by Stephen R. Soukup, which I read immediately.

Soukup quotes Salesforce founder Marc Benioff, whose fortune is estimated at 7.6 billion US dollars: "Yet, as a capitalist, I believe it's time to say out loud what we all know to be true: Capitalism, as we know it, is dead ... Capitalism as it has been practiced in recent decades – with its obsession on maximizing profits for shareholders – has also led to horrifying inequality."[173] Ray Dalio, one of the richest hedge fund managers in the U.S. with a net worth of around 15 billion US dollars, wrote that capitalism is at an end, that "it must be reformed to provide many more equal opportunities and to be more productive."[174]

The mainstream media likes to quote statements attacking capitalism from hedge fund manager George Soros and other rich Americans calling for higher taxes. But aren't these the exceptions? Probably yes, because the public pressure *against* pro-capitalist and *for* left-wing viewpoints is so strong that even billionaires are affected – and often prefer to remain silent. While the voices of anti-capitalists such as Benioff, Soros, and Tom Steyer can be heard loud and clear, pro-capitalists rarely speak out in public. In their book, *Democracy in America?*, the American political scientists Benjamin Page and Martin Gilens refer to the "public silence of most billionaires." David Koch, who died in 2019 having funded libertarian initiatives and think tanks, only spoke publicly about tax policy once in a ten-year period; his brother Charles Koch never said anything about these issues.

"The public silence of most billionaires," Page and Gilens write, "contrasts markedly with the willingness of a small, unusual group of billionaires – including Michael Bloomberg, Warren Buffett, and Bill Gates – to speak out about specific public policies ... All three have favored a substantial social safety net, progressive taxes, and moderate regulation of the economy. An ordinary American who tried to judge what U.S. billionaires think and do about politics by listening to Bloomberg, Buffett, or Gates would be badly misled."[175]

Until now, I have considered statements such as those quoted above from Benioff and Dalio, or from the powerful Blackrock founder Larry Fink, to be outsider positions. But Stephen R. Soukup's book gives me food for thought. "Activists" in the U.S., Soukup explains, are no longer limited to shouting

---

173 Quoted in Soukup, 119.
174 Quoted in Soukup, 104.
175 Page / Gilens, 106.

down free speech at universities (Cancel Culture), but have long since arrived in the financial sector. Political activism at annual shareholder meetings almost always comes from groups of left-of-center shareholders – the number of shareholders who actively oppose this kind of corporate activism can be counted on one hand.[176]

And the politicization of business is becoming an ever-greater problem in the U.S, and not just there. Even someone like Warren Buffett, who is himself moderately left-wing, warned back in 2019 about the politicization of business and the financial industry. "It was wrong," he said in an interview with *The Times*, "for companies to impose their views of 'doing good' on society. What made them think, they knew better?" He added: "This is the shareholders' money. Many corporate managers deplore government allocation of the taxpayer's dollar, but embrace enthusiastically their own allocation of the shareholder's dollar."[177]

ESG (Environmental, Social and Governance) has long been more than just a buzzword. It has become a slogan used by so-called activists, as well as fund managers and company leaders, to push through certain notions of "sustainability," "diversity," etc. These buzzwords are used by left-wing ideologues who smell "racism" or "sexism" everywhere, and many companies have now capitulated. Presumably, the managers first conformed outwardly, and then internally. In psychology, this is known as "cognitive dissonance": people experience mental discomfort when their words and actions do not line up with their true beliefs. First, they adopt left-wing slogans out of opportunism and convenience, then, over time, they adapt their inner attitude to match the outward one.

Billionaires such as Jeff Bezos and Apple CEO Tim Cook have donated millions to social justice organizations such as Black Lives Matter – often from their companies' shareholders' money! Many managers and entrepreneurs hope to buy their way out of being targeted by left-wing "activists" by donating millions to left-wing organizations or publicly criticizing capitalism

---

176 Soukup, 145.
177 Buffett, quoted in Soukup, 143–144.

and speaking out in favor of higher taxes on the rich. But the strategy doesn't always work. Those who give in to blackmailers once will be asked for ever larger sums in the future.

Even sections of the advertising industry are now bowing to the left-wing "woke" ideology. Advertising to increase sales and profits – in an age when profit is considered immoral – is a goal people in the advertising industry widely reject. Apparently, advertising is no longer about promoting a product's benefits in order to increase sales. No, advertising must proclaim political messages and re-educate people.

A few years ago, Gillette prompted a backlash with its campaign against "toxic masculinity." It is because of the traditional toxic image of masculinity, Gillette claimed, that children bully each other, men sexually harass women, and male employees do not let their female colleagues have a say. While the ads generated a lot of attention, they certainly didn't help sell more products.

The Calvin Klein brand, which previously ran adverts featuring attractive women and men with great figures, also joined the woke trend and instead ran a campaign featuring an overweight man and an overweight woman – the man has a beard and is wearing a bra. Responses to the photoshoot were predominantly negative. The tweet: "Calvin Klein wants to go bankrupt" by the doctor Anastasia Maria Loupis was viewed seven million times. She was referring to the ad, which features a trans man living in The Netherlands – Bappie Kortram – alongside the plus-size model Jamilla Grannetia. Both are wearing the brand's sports bras. The campaign sparked predominantly negative comments: "Which women should this appeal to?" was asked thousands of times on social media.

The American beer brand Bud Light also caused its own advertising disaster when it launched a politically correct and woke advertising campaign, prompting sales and the company's share price to plummet. The company achieved its goal of generating a lot of attention, but attention in itself is of no value if you alienate the actual target group that your product is intended to appeal to.

On the last day of my trip to the U.S., I am invited by a libertarian group within the Young Republicans. The Young Republicans were founded in New York in 1912, but until a few years ago they were an insignificant, largely inactive group of just fifty (in New York), most of whom were no longer all that young. They have since been joined by more than 1,200 young New Yorkers – about half of whom are likely to be supporters of Trump and Florida Governor Ron DeSantis. The libertarian faction within the Young Republicans is fighting against anti-capitalism within the Republican Party, which is also becoming increasingly strong on the political right, as Frank Filocomo, who invited me, explains to me.

April 2023
Bucharest, Romania

The Piteşti experiment was a re-education program devised by the Romanian secret service Securitate (then officially Direcţia Generală a Poliţiei de Siguranţă, DGPS) between 1949 and 1952, in which attempts were made to turn political prisoners into communists through brainwashing and torture: "The most vile tortures imaginable were practiced in Piteşti. Prisoners' whole bodies were burned with cigarettes: their buttocks would begin to rot, and their skin fell off as though they suffered from leprosy. Others were forced to swallow spoonfuls of excrement, and when they threw it back up, they were forced to eat their own vomit." Christian seminarians, who refused to renounce their faith, were "baptized" as follows: "Some had their heads repeatedly plunged into a bucket of urine and fecal matter while the guards intoned a parody of the baptismal rite."[178] Prisoners had to "re-educate" their best friends, torturing them with their own hands and becoming executioners themselves.[179]

This was the beginning of the communist reign of terror in Romania. Even though these extreme torture methods were later abandoned, the Securitate remained one of the most feared secret police forces in the world until the fall of communism. At the end of communist rule, the Securitate employed 14,259 full-time staff, and the number of informants is estimated at between 400,000 and 800,000.[180] From March 1984 onward, every privately-owned typewriter was registered with the police along with a sample of the typeface. And anyone who did not report a conversation with a foreigner within 24 hours was liable for prosecution.[181]

---

178 Bartosek, 420–421.
179 Bartosek, 421.
180 Kunze, 323.
181 Kunze, 326.

The Securitate liked to recruit its personnel at an early age from orphanages. "Orphans were trained like animals and knew no 'father' other than the officer training them and, of course, 'Father Ceauşescu,' for whom they themselves learned to kill."[182]

Professor Johannes Kneifel asked students in Romania to write down what their parents and grandparents said about their experiences of the socialist era. The reports are all similar, with one saying: "Electricity and heating were only available for a few hours a day; huge queues outside the stores to buy food, which was rationed; people had money, but couldn't buy anything with it. The TV schedule included a lecture from the dictator on all of Romania's achievements, news, folk music, and a short Russian cartoon for children."[183]

A typical television broadcast schedule was as follows: 8 p.m. news; 8.20 p.m. *We Praise our Country's Leader* (poems, an honorary anthology, in color); 8.40 pm *The Radiant Theorist and Founder of Communism* (documentary, dedicated to the theoretical work of Comrade Ceauşescu, in color); 9 p.m. *Glory to the Supreme Commander* (television play, produced with assistance of the army's artistic ensemble); 9.30 p.m. news; then, end of broadcast.[184]

Another report states: "Romanians were constantly asked to save electricity. Pupils and students had to study and do homework in the evening in the light of kerosene lamps ... The use of refrigerators and washing machines was also limited because electricity was scarce. In winter, food was kept cold on balconies or in courtyards ... Hot water was only available for a few hours a day."[185]

The most difficult time for Romanians was in the 1980s, because Ceauşescu launched an austerity program after announcing that his government was aiming to repay its vast foreign debts ahead of schedule. The drastic fall in living standards followed an official decision to reduce the general supply of food, a reduction Ceauşescu claimed was based on the latest nutritional science. In view of the supply crisis, Ceauşescu asked his personal physician

182 Kunze, 325.
183 Quoted in Kneifel, 170.
184 Kunze, 317.
185 Quoted in Kneifel, 157–158.

to draw up a "Rational Eating Program." Touted as being based on "scientific research," Ceauşescu had food rations set for every Romanian beginning in 1982, and steadily lowered their annual calorie allowances every year.[186]

The energy crisis in Romania worsened from 1984 onwards. "Soon Romanians were not only starving, they were also freezing. Electricity and gas cuts were the order of the day. Street lighting was no longer switched on at night, with a few exceptions in Bucharest. From 1986, the temperature in Romanian prefabricated buildings was not allowed to exceed 12 degrees Celsius in winter."[187]

Up until 1989, there was a partial ban on driving on Sundays. On one Sunday, cars with license plates with even numbers were allowed to drive, followed by odd-numbered vehicles the next Sunday. East German Trabants, Trabis for short, were particularly popular because they had engines that could run on cheap white spirit. "Local public transport was almost non-existent. Anyone who didn't live close to where they worked could often only get to work by hitchhiking."[188]

Only 5 percent of Romanians actually owned a car. Incidentally, only 7.6 percent had a vacuum cleaner, 19.1 percent a television set, 14.7 percent a washing machine, and 17.6 percent a refrigerator. Nevertheless, Ceauşescu still claimed in 1989: "We can and must assert most powerfully that only socialism could make such grandiose and wonderful achievements of our nation possible and eliminate backwardness and poverty, laying the foundations of true socio-economic independence, prosperity and happiness."[189]

The communists destroyed countless villages in order to better monitor the population in communal housing. 90 percent of villages were collectives, but more food was produced on the remaining, privately farmed, 10 percent.[190] In 1988, a program was launched to destroy around half of the remaining 13,123 villages and relocate the inhabitants to agro-industrial centers. "The

---

186 Kunze, 312.
187 Kunze, 312.
188 Kunze, 312.
189 Quoted in Kunze, 314.
190 Kneifel, 78.

apartments consisted of two rooms and a four-square-meter kitchen with no water supply, which had to be shared by at least six people ... There was no bathroom. The only toilet in the block of flats was in the courtyard. The Securitate officer lived on the first floor. His job was to wake up the residents in the morning, hand out spades, scythes and pitchforks, and drive them to work. In the evening, he locked the door behind them."[191]

Nicolae Ceauşescu ruled until the end of 1989. He and his wife Elena (who had only attended school for four years, but was appointed "President of the Supreme Council for Science and Education")[192] lived in a luxury villa, and they had around 80 villas and hunting lodges in the country at their disposal.[193]

The balance sheet of socialism in Romania: around two million innocent prisoners were arbitrarily detained in 100 prisons and around 100,000 Romanians were murdered. Around 90,000 prisoners starved to death or died during the construction of the Black Sea Canal.[194]

Ceauşescu constantly traveled abroad, but never understood the cultures of other countries. On a state visit to the U.S. in 1978, there was no escaping the demonstrations against him. A displeased Ceauşescu called on U.S. President Jimmy Carter to have the demonstrators arrested on the spot. Carter tried to explain to Ceauşescu that people were free to demonstrate in the United States and that there were also demonstrations against Carter himself. The Romanian dictator left in disgust and had 800,000 Romanians bussed to the airport in his home country to greet him enthusiastically.[195]

Ceauşescu officially gave himself the title *Conducător*. The fascist dictator Ion Antonescu had already claimed this title for himself during the Second World War. Ceauşescu was praised as "the chosen one, our earthly god, and the genius of the Carpathians." The famous poet Adrian Păunescu wrote: "I dare not mention your name. For fear of diminishing your greatness if I

---

191 Kneifel, 79.
192 Kneifel, 87.
193 Kneifel, 94.
194 Kneifel, 10.
195 Kneifel, 74.

speak of you. But history demands it of me. We should all love you: You who embody victory in the battle for the people."[196] Other poets described him as the "supreme embodiment of good," the "guarantor of Romania's wealth," and it was said that Alexandrina, Ceaușescu's mother, had given birth to a son who could free the world from misery.[197] Ceaușescu, it was claimed, was the "most profound social thinker of all time" and the "Titan of Titans."[198]

In late December 1989, as revolution spread, Ceaușescu was overthrown; many of the revolutionaries were workers. Ceaușescu and his wife fled from the party headquarters in Bucharest by helicopter, but were arrested in Târgoviște, over 62 miles away, and shot after a short "trial" before a military tribunal. In the moments leading up to his execution, the dictator intoned the communist battle song, "The Internationale."

After the revolution, the elites remained essentially the same, as the new president was an ex-communist, Ion Iliescu, and the communists rebranded themselves as social democrats. With more than half a million members, the social democratic PSD is still the largest party in the country, followed by the National Liberal Party, which has around half as many members.

But in the 2000s, free-market policies prevailed. Romania's progressive income tax system was abolished and replaced by a flat tax. The personal income tax rate in Romania today is only 10 percent and the corporate tax rate is 16 percent. As a result, Romania scores almost maximum points for tax policy in the Heritage Foundation's *2023 Index of Economic Freedom* (94.4 out of a possible 100). Romania also does well in the property rights category with 81 points. In contrast, the country received poor ratings for fiscal health (14.7 points) and government integrity (47.2 points). Overall, Romania ranked 53rd in the world in 2023.[199]

This places Romania lower than Poland (in 40th), but higher than, for example, France or Italy. But more important than the absolute rank is the number of points gained since 1995, when the index was first collated. At

---

196 Quoted in Kneifel, 91.
197 Kneifel, 92.
198 Oancea, 48.
199 Heritage Foundation, *2023 Index of Economic Freedom*, 298–299.

that time, Romania scored 42.9. By 2021, Romania's score reached a high of 69.5.[200] Such an increase – of 26.6 points – is sensational and even surpasses Poland and Vietnam!

In his 2016 book, *Ruling Ideas. How Global Neoliberalism Goes Local*, Cornel Ban argues that Romania has a weaker welfare state, a less regulated labor market,[201] and lower taxes than many other countries. In 2007, Spain spent 20 percent of GDP on public social expenditure, while Romania recorded "the lowest rate of social protection expenditure per inhabitant (PPP) in the EU" at just 13 percent.[202] Ban criticizes this development and says that Romanian politicians enacted radical "neoliberal" tax and labor market reform policies.[203]

It is not often that politicians charge the director of the IMF with being a left-wing ideologue with a fondness for "state capitalism" that can be traced back to his communist youth – but that is exactly what happened in Romania in 2010.[204]

But the free-market reforms have paid off. From 1991 to 2021, the gross domestic product per capita (in constant dollars) in Romania almost tripled.[205] GDP increased by 2.1 percent per year in real terms between 2008 and 2018. Only Poland and Slovakia had higher growth rates among eastern EU countries during this period.[206]

In Romania, Ipsos MORI surveyed a representative sample of 1,000 people from June 17 to 21, 2022 to find out what they think of capitalism. Our survey of 35 countries shows there are 22 countries that have more anti-capitalist tendencies than Romania and twelve countries that have a more positive attitude towards capitalism. So, while Romanians do not view capitalism as

200 Heritage Foundation, *2023 Index of Economic Freedom*, 401.
201 Ban, 220.
202 Ban, 67.
203 Ban, 89–90.
204 Ban, 210.
205 The Global Economy, https://www.theglobaleconomy.com/Romania/GDP_per_capita_constant_dollars/#:~:text=For percent20that percent20indicator percent2C percent20we percent20provide,2021 percent20is percent2011541.78 percent20U.S. percent20dollars.
206 Müller-Heinze, https://www.bpb.de/themen/europa/suedosteuropa/322454/rumaenien/.

positively as Poles or Czechs, they do view it more positively than people in seven other Eastern European countries where the survey was conducted.

At the beginning of April, I give two lectures in Bucharest and present the results of the surveys. After my lecture at Bucharest University of Economics, I speak to several economists about the situation in Romania. I ask Tudor Smirna what further free-market reforms were urgently needed in Romania.

Tudor Smirna is president and co-founder of the Ludwig von Mises Institute Romania and assistant professor at the Faculty of International Economic Relations at the Academy of Economic Studies. His answer:

"Property: The protection and assurance of private property is the basis of society. Allow for parallel, competitive legal services. Allow for a free market of private protection agencies to compete with traditional police in defending people and property.

Money: Inflation and crises are crucial in undermining prosperity and trust in the capitalist system. Allow for legal tender in any currency, cryptocurrencies included. This would create a strong incentive for the central bank and the banking system to keep money as sound as possible.

Education: The education system is in very bad shape in Romania, with declining performance each year. Allow for a true free market in education by permitting families freedom of education and defund the public education budget for each pupil that deregisters from public education. Thus, you will have less deficit spending and more demand for private, capitalist educational offers.

Labor: Abolish minimum wage laws that keep low skilled labor unemployed or on the black market and keep or turn investment away from the Romanian market. Simplify the very complicated legislation on labor. Greatly diminish the power of labor inspection agencies. Allow for part-time contracts and diminish labor-related taxation if you want less corruption and less black-market employment. Abolish the withholding of wage taxes and allow for employees to receive the complete, full wage before having to pay taxes individually. Zero taxes for minimum wage employees, as it is discussed in Romania, is not as good as abolishing the minimum wage decree, but it is a

217

good step toward more labor freedom and it has the advantage that it is more acceptable for the people short term.

Health: Health taxes are 10 percent of wages. Deregulate and allow for private health services. Allow taxpayers to use their taxes to pay for these services if they choose them instead of public services.

Pensions: Contributions amount to 25 percent of wages. The pay-as-you-go pension system is underperforming and forecasts are pointing toward a future deficit. Allow for more liberty in private pension services. Ultimately allow for freedom for each individual to save and invest as much as they want for retirement."

So much for the thoughts of Tudor Smirna.

You sometimes find libertarians in the last place you would expect them. In Bucharest, Cristian Popa, board member of the National Bank of Romania, the country's central bank, suggests a meeting. He and his colleague are both big fans of Friedrich August von Hayek and Milton Friedman; and they have seen every episode of the *Free to Choose* series. They give me a tour of the building, which also houses a museum with historical coins and gold bars, and is home to valuable, historical paintings.

The bank's website proudly states: "The Old Palace of the National Bank, considered 'the most beautiful building in Bucharest' by architect Ion Mincu, impresses through its monumentality, regularity, distinction and size. The contrasting interior, with an 'ample and spectacular configuration that is very well contained' (architect Nicolae Lascu), is suited to the aesthetic and functional needs of a central bank at the end of the 19th century. It is the first important bank building in Bucharest, the most imposing building of a financial institution, which can be compared with other great constructions of the time in European capitals." And it's true: it's one of the most beautiful buildings I've ever seen.

Another impressive building is the "House of the People," where another presentation of my book takes place on April 26. The host is Claudiu Năsui from the USR party. The USR received 15 percent of the vote in the parliamentary elections in 2020, while Năsui himself received 30 percent in the capital Bucharest. The party describes itself as "progressive," but some MPs like Năsui (he is the party's vice president) are trying to turn it into a libertarian party. The likeable 37-year-old, who studied in Paris, used to be left-wing himself – today he is a follower of Mises, Hayek and Friedman.

I deliberately suggested the "House of the People" as the venue. It is the second largest government building in the world after the Pentagon. The largest hall in the "House of the People" measures 16 meters in height and covers an area of 2,200 square meters, with a total floor area of 336,000 square meters. The building is 86 meters high and extends 92 meters underground, where there is a gigantic tunnel system. It is 275 meters long and 235 meters wide.

It is one of the most magnificent palaces I have seen in my life. But its history is characteristic of socialism. Ceaușescu had the magnificent building constructed in the 1980s, at the same time as his people were living in abject poverty. The construction costs consumed around 40 percent of Romania's annual gross national product. To make room for the building, 40,000 apartments, a dozen churches and three synagogues were demolished. Today it is used by the Romanian parliament and political parties.

April 2023
Tbilisi, Georgia (meeting with Russian exiles)

In April, I am invited to give the opening speech at the Kakha Bendukidze Forum in Tbilisi. Kachaber "Kakha" Bendukidze was a Georgian-Russian entrepreneur and politician who was instrumental in reforming the Georgian economy from 2004 to 2007, simplifying the tax system, and dismantling a host of regulations. The conference, a meeting place for Russian exiles in Georgia, is named after him.

At the beginning of my lecture, I ask how many of the 250 or so participants are Georgian and how many are Russian. There is not a single Georgian present. After the Russian war against Georgia in 2008, and in some cases even before, about half of the Libertarian Party's supporters fled Russia, many of them to Georgia. Some of the participants have traveled from Russia, including the chairman of the Hayek Foundation in St. Petersburg, who also regularly publishes my articles and promotes my books in Russia.

I had been corresponding with the former chairman of the Libertarian Party, Sergei Boyko, who in turn put me in touch with my Russian publisher Alexander Kouryaev, who has since published four of my books in Russia and will be publishing more. Boyko had been denied entry to the country. According to participants at the event, Georgia often refuses entry to prominent opposition figures because the government is afraid that Russia will submit extradition requests to have them arrested. If the Georgian government complies with these requests, it causes resentment in Georgia; if they do not comply, it means trouble with Russia. The Georgian government has therefore chosen to take the "easy" route and not even allow high-profile opposition figures to enter the country.

I talk to many exiled Russians on the sidelines of the event. Artem, a young Russian who emigrated a few days before the mobilization, tells me how he walked eight miles over the mountains to reach the border. Many Russians have fled to Georgia: officially there are 112,000 in April 2023 but, in reality, there are perhaps twice as many. They are not always welcome, even if they are members of the anti-Putin opposition. After all, you can't tell by looking at them what they think, but you can hear them speaking Russian on the street. It is important not to forget that Russia has waged war against Georgia several times and still occupies 20 percent of the country.

Some migrants from Russia earn very good salaries because they work for American companies. They are welcome in Georgia and have made a major contribution to the country's economic upswing. I meet Maxim, a software developer who has been working for an American company for ten years, first in Russia and now in Tbilisi. He earns around 4,000 to 5,000 US dollars a month, which is about ten times the average salary in Georgia. But, as Ute Kochlowski-Kadjaia from the Friedrich Naumann Foundation tells me, there can also be envy and bad blood when some Russians show off their wealth – and rents for apartments in Tbilisi skyrocket at the same time. The German foundation, which used to be based in Moscow, was closed from one day to the next in April 2022, a month and a half after the Russian invasion of Ukraine – like all local offices run by German political party foundations. It now supports libertarian Russians from its base in Tbilisi, including the Kakha Bendukidze Forum.

A libertarian Russian, Fima, tells me that he organized demonstrations against Putin in Russia for ten years. He went into exile because he became frustrated: "70 to 80 percent of Russians support Putin. After hundreds of discussions, I eventually gave up trying to argue with them." He did not leave Russia because of Putin, but because he believes that the majority of his compatriots cannot be swayed and he was tired after all the years of unsuccessful opposition.

Fima hasn't managed to find a well-paid job yet. Does he have a wife and family? No, he lives alone. He tells me that many migrant relationships break up. "As a migrant, you are lonesome," he says. Of course, he would also like a wife or girlfriend, but almost all exiles from Russia are men. And finding a Georgian partner is difficult – because of the language barrier, because the women's parents in Georgia are against it, and because they have nothing to offer financially. A sad story. I find his words repeatedly going through my mind afterwards: "As a migrant, you are lonesome."

Another Russian, Ivan, says that many of his compatriots are living in the past, especially the older ones. They are frustrated that the great, military superpower of the Soviet Union no longer exists, he explains. Getting "revenge" for their country's defeat in the Cold War is more important to them than the economy. In some respects, things are different among younger people: "They see how people live in the West on the internet." Ivan is a devotee of Mikhail Svetov, a successful 38-year-old blogger who held a conference with the libertarian anarchist Hans-Hermann Hoppe in Moscow in 2019 – with an audience of 1,500 in attendance.

Most of the people I speak to are members of the Libertarian Party in Russia. The first time I speak to Sergei Boyko on a Zoom call, I ask him whether he has any problems in Russia. The conversation takes place before the war. "Problems?" he responds, "Well, I was in prison a few months ago." Opposition members tell me that the Russian state does not usually take formal action against them on political grounds, but uses allegations of financial offenses as a pretext, charging them with embezzlement or tax evasion, for example.

Dmitry is also a member of the Libertarian Party. He is very frustrated about the lack of support from the global libertarian movement. In the United States, he says, a number of so-called libertarians openly oppose Ukraine and some even sympathize with Putin. "How can you be pro-freedom and pro-Putin? How can you be pro-freedom and not be pro-Ukraine?" In addition, he complains, opposition Russians in exile are supported by other NGOs, for example with employment contracts, but there is no support from the libertarian movement.

In my speech, I explain how widespread anti-capitalist thinking is in Russia. Our survey in Russia was completed exactly one day before the outbreak of war, after which it would probably have been impossible. The result: of the 35 surveyed countries, Russian respondents had the most negative attitudes toward the market economy – Poland registered the highest levels of approval. A comparison of the survey's findings in these two countries reveals major differences: in Poland, people are in favor of economic freedom, in Russia they are in favor of state regulation.

Russia provides a very good illustration of the connection between economic freedom and political freedom. The starting points for the abolition of all freedoms in Russia were two attacks on private property, in 1917 and 2003. The first time, the Bolsheviks abolished private property after seizing power and, step by step, all other freedoms followed.

After the collapse of the Soviet Union, private property rights were reintroduced. Putin, who came to power in the early 2000s, appeared to many at the time as a politician who advocated both reform and law and order. In fact, his rule began with a positive development. The Swedish economist Anders Åslund, one of the leading experts on Russian economic developments, writes in his book, *Russia's Crony Capitalism. The Path from Market Economy to Kleptocracy*: "The period 2000–2003 represented the height of Russia's market economy. This was a time of macroeconomic balance and competitive markets. The private sector thrived as never before or after. State subsidies were minimized, and the result was a high growth rate averaging 7 percent a year from 1999 to 2008. Russia had never grown faster."[207]

However, this market economy phase did not last long. Economic historians identify Putin's crackdown on Mikhail Khodorkovsky, the richest man in Russia at the time, as a turning point. Putin decided to act against this powerful critic in order to demonstrate to potential challengers that no matter how rich and seemingly powerful you may be, you can still lose everything if you criticize Putin. Khodorkovsky was arrested in 2003 and spent ten years in prison. His company Yukos was expropriated and most of his assets were transferred to the state-owned company Rosneft at knockdown prices in closed auctions. This action by the state sent an important signal. It marked

---

207 Åslund, 73.

the beginning of the second phase of the abolition of private property in Russian history.

Unlike in the October Revolution, however, private property was not abolished by official decree, but formally remained in place. In his book, *Property Rights in Post-Soviet Russia*, Jordan Gans-Morse, professor at Berkeley and one of the foremost experts on the Russian economy, writes: "...after the Khodorkovsky incident, bureaucrats and law enforcement officials of all ranks increased their pressure on firms. These threats included the seizure of a firm's assets, facilitation of illegal corporate raiding, extortion, illicit fines, and unlawful arrests of businesspeople."[208]

More and more companies were taken under state control – especially banks and companies in the energy industry. Joshua Kurlantzick from the Council on Foreign Relations (CFR) wrote in his 2016 book, *State Capitalism. How the Return of Statism is Transforming the World*: "... in Russia, state companies throttle any potential private-sector competitors. Under Putin, the Kremlin has allowed just one or two state firms to dominate nearly every leading industry, with each company staffed by Putin loyalists. Companies that have resisted state takeover have been sacked with enormous tax bills until they sell out. Many of the most promising young entrepreneurs in Russia simply have fled the country."[209]

I agree, but the terms "state capitalism" and "crony capitalism" are misleading. There is no such thing as "state capitalism," just like there is no such thing as a square circle. Capitalism is based on private property, and the destruction of private property means the destruction of capitalism.

What happened in Russia is more reminiscent of the economic system of National Socialism, where private property remained formally intact, but was increasingly eroded until only the formal legal title remained. Ludwig von Mises described the phenomenon very clearly:

"The German pattern of socialism (*Zwangswirtschaft*) ['compulsory economy'] is characterized by the fact that it maintains, although only

---

208 Gans-Morse, 191.
209 Kurlantzick, quoted in Åslund, 99.

nominally, some institutions of capitalism. Labor is, of course, no longer a 'commodity'; the labor market has been solemnly abolished; the government fixes wage rates and assigns every worker the place where he must work. Private ownership has been nominally untouched. In fact, however, the former entrepreneurs have been reduced to the status of shop managers (*Betriebsführer*). The government tells them what and how to produce, at what prices and from whom to buy, at what prices and to whom to sell. Business may remonstrate against inconvenient injunctions, but the final decision rests with the authorities."[210]

---

210 Gordon, https://mises.org/wire/it-wasnt-capitalism-mises-explains-nazi-economics.

May 2023
Rome and Milan, Italy

In recent years, I have visited Milan and Rome on several occasions, each time at the invitation of the libertarian think tank *Istituto Bruno Leoni* (IBL), which is named after the notable Italian legal philosopher. I still fondly remember an invitation in May 2022 to the home of the institute's president, Franco Debenedetti, who was born in 1933. He was a former entrepreneur and member of the Senato della Republica.

The most eminent and impressive figure in the Italian libertarian movement is Professor Alberto Mingardi. Alberto has headed the prestigious *Istituto Bruno Leoni* since it was founded 20 years ago. He says of his political background:

"An old friend, an economics professor, used to joke that in Italy he knew only two people that were never Marxists: himself, because he was too old; and me, because I was too young. At 42, I'm not young any more."

Alberto developed an interest in politics very early on, which is something we both have in common. "As a young boy, aged 8 or 10, I read the newspaper, *Il Giornale*, that my parents bought every day (a lost habit for anybody now, my parents included). *Il Giornale* was edited by Indro Montanelli and was to the right of all other available options, though we would better describe it as 'moderate' or 'centrist.'"

One of the newspaper's most prominent columnists was the economist Sergio Ricossa. He was, together with Antonio Martino, who would later go into politics with Berlusconi, the most important classical liberal in Italy. Ricossa was also a school friend of Alberto's grandparents. "They were buddies from age 5 to age 19, then they lost track of each other. But my grandpa always remembered that friend of his who reached relative notoriety. My grandpa was not well off at all, but he remembered that Sergio was really a poor kid, so poor that he took notes in class because his family couldn't afford textbooks and not to kill time, as most students do. That inoculated me right from the beginning against the idea that the free market was something which benefited the right. To the contrary, a freer market creates opportunities for those whose parents lack resources."

At the age of 14 – when I was devouring the works of Marx, Lenin and Mao – Alberto read Milton Friedman. At 15, he read the books of Milton Friedman's son, David. That's how he became a libertarian. "We were at the dawn of the internet, which allowed me to meet the handful of Italian libertarians. Some of them are still my dearest friends. With two of them, Carlo Lottieri and Carlo Stagnaro, I founded *Istituto Bruno Leoni* in 2003. I had been an intern at the Heritage Foundation in Washington and dreamt of founding something similar in Italy. We never became as opulent as U.S. think tanks but survived 20 years, published hundreds of papers and books, some of our former fellows ended up in politics, some became recognized authorities in their respective fields. Public opinion and top newspapers are certainly more open to classical libertarian ideas now than when we started, but the country (and Europe) are far less libertarian now. I'm not an economist by background. After establishing IBL, I graduated in political philosophy and later got a PhD in political science. I'm now a full professor in history of political thought."

Alberto invited me to Milan several times to present the Italian editions of my books, *The Power of Capitalism* and *The Rich in Public Opinion*. In May 2023, I have been invited to present the Italian edition of *In Defence of Capitalism* in Milan and Rome. My Italian publishers have frequently come up with especially attractive book covers, including the one for *In Defence of Capitalism*, which they have called *Elogio del Capitalismo*. It's a cheerful and colorful cover emblazoned with a piece of chocolate and a rainbow. Alberto's institute has a good relationship with all of the most important media outlets in Italy – my books have always been positively reviewed in the highest-circulation Italian daily newspaper *Corriere della Sera*, and I was allowed to write a whole page about *Elogio del Capitalismo* in this prestigious publication.

A few words about Italy's recent history: Fascism in Italy had left-wing roots. Before founding his fascist party, Benito Mussolini was editor-in-chief of *Avanti!*, the central organ of the *Partito Socialista Italiano* (PSI). Many of his supporters also came from the left-wing camp.

For many years after the Second World War, the Italian political landscape was shaped by communists. The *Partito dei Comunisti Italiani* (PCI) drew its legitimacy primarily from its earlier resistance against fascism. Even when the Christian Democrats (DC) held power, it was the communists who dominated the public discourse. "The DC was content with power, the cultural leadership went to the left," is the concise assessment of Rudolf Lill and Wolfgang Altgeld.[211]

For many years, the PCI won around a third of the vote and was by far the strongest communist party in any Western country. In addition to the communists, there were numerous Maoist and anarchist groups, some of whom were terrorists, such as the *Brigate Rosse*, which carried out 73 assassinations and a host of bank robberies and kidnappings from the early 1970s to the end of the 1980s. Their common goal: the abolition of the capitalism they so detested.

In 1978, far-left terrorists murdered former Italian Prime Minister Aldo Moro after kidnapping him and holding him captive for two months. His murder also ended the cooperation between the two strongest parties in Italy at the time, the Christian Democrats, who were drifting to the left, and the Communists.

Corruption, which infected large swathes of the political class in Italy, the growing power and influence of the mafia, constant government crises, and the ever-widening gap between the productive north and the unproductive south led to the destabilization of Italy. Compounding all this, Italy experienced escalating national debt and, in recent years, ever-increasing illegal immigration. Today, the left and communists no longer play a major role in Italy. From 1994 to 2011, the billionaire and media entrepreneur Silvio Berlusconi held the office of prime minister four times with his right-wing

---

211 Lill / Altgeld, 501.

alliance, and in October 2022, Giorgia Meloni from the right-wing *Fratelli d'Italia* party was sworn in as head of government.

Public opinion polls in Italy constantly confirm the long-lasting influence of left-wing thinking on the country's older generation. And this was particularly clear in my survey on perceptions of the rich. In the United States, young people are far more critical of the rich than their older compatriots – in Italy, the opposite is true. The Ipsos MORI survey I commissioned revealed that younger Italians have a significantly more positive attitude towards the rich than older Italians.

Based on their answers to the survey questions, we divided respondents into two groups: social enviers, who primarily harbor envy towards the rich, and non-enviers, for whom this is not the case. The difference between the generations in Italy are striking: a majority of young Italians (52 percent) are non-enviers, while only 16 percent of respondents under the age of 30 are enviers. And the proportion of "hard core" enviers among young Italians is a paltry 1 percent. In contrast, only a third (34 percent) of respondents over the age of 60 are non-enviers, while almost half (45 percent) are enviers.

As a result, the social envy coefficient SEC (which we use to measure levels of social envy against the rich) also differs for younger and older respondents: For the Italian population as a whole, the social envy coefficient is 0.62, which is lower than for the German and French populations as a whole, but higher than for the populations of the UK, the U.S., and Poland. For younger Italians, the SEC is 0.31, which is roughly on par with the countries with the lowest levels of social envy (Poland, Japan, and South Korea). For older Italians, the social envy coefficient is 1.32, which is higher than the highest social envy coefficient for the entire population of any country in international comparison (France has the highest SEC of any suveyed country at 1.26).

When we analyze levels of agreement with positive and negative statements about the rich, we see that younger Italians generally agree more with positive statements and less with negative statements. The opposite is true for older respondents. Of nine positive statements about the rich, younger Italians more often agree with seven than do older people; both groups agree equally with two statements. Older Italians do not agree with any of the positive statements more than younger people.

Younger and older Italians also have very different opinions of the personality traits of the rich. Our respondents were presented with a list of 14 personality traits, some of which were positive and some negative. They were asked which of these were most likely to apply to the rich. Of the younger Italians, 29 percent described the rich as greedy, compared to 44 percent of older respondents; 9 percent of younger Italians believe that the rich are cold-hearted, compared to more than twice as many older Italians (19 percent); 20 percent of Italians under the age of 30 say that the rich are industrious, while only 11 percent of older people share this view; and 30 percent of younger Italians think that rich people are bold and daring, compared with only 17 percent of older people. On the other hand, there are significantly fewer personality traits for which older Italians give a more positive assessment than their younger compatriots – 36 percent of Italians under the age of 30 describe rich people as arrogant, whereas only 32 percent of Italians over the age of 60 say the same.

In our second survey, on the image of capitalism, however, we did not see the same differences between younger and older Italians. Overall, this survey revealed a skeptical attitude towards capitalism in Italy. Without exception, the six most frequently selected statements were all negative: "Capitalism leads to growing inequality" was selected by 43 percent of respondents; 42 percent say "Capitalism is dominated by the rich, they set the political agenda"; 36 percent claim that "Capitalism leads to monopolies where individual companies control the entire market"; 35 percent believe that "Capitalism promotes selfishness and greed"; 34 percent fear that "Capitalism entices people to buy products they don't need"; and 29 percent blame capitalism for environmental destruction and climate change. The findings are thus very clear: In Italy, anti-capitalism dominates.

In the 1990s, when capitalist reforms were implemented almost everywhere in the world, there was also a period of reform in Italy, which Alberto describes as follows: "Italy had a phase of fiscal probity. In 1994, after a whole ruling class had been wiped away by the Clean Hands investigations in Milan, the country was weak and perceived as an economic basket case ... Italy did its homework. In the course of six years, the government enacted 14 'budgetary corrections' and two substantial reforms of the social security system (in 1992 and 1995). The country also put together a wide program of privatizations, ranging from the state telephone company to highways to banks and insurance companies."[212]

But that was all a very long time ago. Today, Italy is one of the least economically free countries in Europe. In the *2023 Index of Economic Freedom*, Italy ranks 36th out of 44 countries in Europe and 69th worldwide. Even France is slightly better off than Italy (33rd in Europe, 57th worldwide). Italy receives its lowest scores in the categories Government Spending, Fiscal Health and Tax Burden.[213] The national debt is more than 140 percent, and of all European countries only Greece is worse. Italy also traditionally ranks poorly in Transparency International's *Corruption Perceptions Index*.[214]

I meet with several journalists in Milan, including Stefano Magni, who interviews me for the Catholic newspaper *La Nuova Bussola Quotidiana*. Magni sees a source of anti-capitalism in Italy in "CathoCommunism," a mixture of Catholicism and communism, as was also popular in Latin America in the 1960s and 1970s. The extreme version of this is demonstrated by the founder of *Brigate Rosse*, Renato Curcio, who came from a Catholic background. This is of course an extreme manifestation, but the combination of Catholicism and anti-capitalism plays a major role in Italy. I also asked Magni what he thinks of today's parties in Italy in terms of their positions on the market economy. Giorgia Meloni's party is predominantly anti-free-market, although the same cannot be said of her personally. In any case, her thinking is more free-market oriented than her supporters and she is strongly influenced by her connections in the United States.

The opposite is true of Matteo Salvini's *Lega Nord*: he himself is anti-free-

---

212 Mingardi, 608.
213 Heritage Foundation, *2023 Index of Economic Freedom*, 188–189.
214 Transparency International, "CPI 2022: Tabellarische Rangliste," https://www.transparency.de/cpi/cpi-2022/cpi-2022-tabellarische-rangliste

market, but there are certainly elements within his party that are in favor of the market economy. *Forza Italia*, founded by Berlusconi, and the newly founded *Azione*, are also moderately pro-free-market. However, there has not been a truly libertarian, free-market party in Italy since 2018. The most anti-capitalist party is the Five Star Movement with its leader Giuseppe Conte, who was prime minister from 2018 to 2021.

My first stop in Rome is the parliament building, which is very beautiful from the outside and the inside. Following so quickly on the heels of my recent visit to Romania, however, I'm not all that impressed. I meet Giulia Postorella, who invites me to lunch. She sits in parliament for the *Azione* party. It's rare to find Italians who speak such perfect English, but no wonder, she studied at Oxford and was named by *Forbes* magazine in 2017 as one of the 30 most influential people under 30 in Europe in the field of law and politics.

In the 2022 parliamentary elections, she ran on the *Azione - Italia Viva* alliance ticket in the Lombardy constituency of the Chamber of Deputies (informally known as *Milano Centro*) and secured 23 percent of the vote, while the alliance landed at just under 8 percent nationwide. What I find interesting is that, like me, her party is clearly in favor of nuclear power, which is particularly appealing to young Italians.

Why are the forces in favor of a market economy so weak in Italy? I talk about this in Rome with journalist Giorgio Rutelli from the magazine *Formiche*. The 40-year-old is the son of the former mayor of Rome and knows the history of the libertarian movement in Italy from personal experience.

Rutelli explains that in the 1990s, Silvio Berlusconi (who died a month after I was in Italy) rallied the supporters of the market economy, including some excellent economists such as Antonio Martino, who studied under Milton Friedman. Later, however, Berlusconi increasingly adopted a more populist position. In any case, no free-market reforms were implemented during Berlusconi's time in office.

There was another attempt to initiate a libertarian movement in 2012 when Oscar Giannino founded *FARE Fare per fermare il declino* (Act to Stop the Decline) and announced that he would run for prime minister in the

2013 Italian elections. He got off to a promising start and gathered a team of excellent economists to his cause. However, everything collapsed after it was discovered that Giannino had falsified his CV and, for example, invented his law degree.

Another beacon of hope was Matteo Renzi, leader of *Partito Democratico* from 2013 to 2018 and President of the Council of Ministers of the Italian Republic from February 2014 to December 2016. During his time in office, Renzi pushed through a labor market reform that provided for a relaxation of safeguards against redundancy and tax breaks for companies that create new, full-time jobs. However, he sought a constitutional reform in a referendum on December 4, 2016 and failed, with 41 percent voting in favor compared to 59 percent voting against, whereupon he resigned. In 2019, he founded his own party, *Italia Viva*.

So, there have been some attempts to reform Italy's system and implement a more free-market-oriented economy but, so far, they have all failed to achieve lasting success.

And the economic balance sheet after the first year of Meloni's government? Unlike the last coalition, in which the right-wing populist *Lega* was involved, Meloni as head of government has largely blocked the implementation of expensive election pledges such as lowering the retirement age. On the positive side, *Reddito di Cittadinaza*, which cost eight billion euros in 2022, was largely scrapped. Secondly, Meloni's coalition severely restricted the "110 percent super bonus" renovation incentive, which allowed 110 percent write-offs for energy efficiency measures. However, this bonus nevertheless proved to be an unjustifiably bottomless pit, especially given the war in Ukraine and soaring inflation, and cost the state almost 80 billion euros by October 2023 alone.[215]

"The first year of the Meloni government was a quiet year by Italian standards in terms of fiscal policy, which went better than expected," says

---

215   Kirst, https://www.welt.de/wirtschaft/plus247987938/Italien-Die-ueberraschend-gute-oekonomische-Zwischenbilanz-des-Landes.html?source=puerto-reco-2_ABC-V32.7.B_test and Schwarz,
https://swz.it/superbonus-am-weg-zum-110-milliarden-bonus/

Lorenzo Castellani, a political scientist at LUISS University in Rome. The reason for this was the strong growth following the Covid pandemic. "But now we are facing much bigger problems with high interest rates, lower growth, and high public debt."[216]

After my lectures and talks in Milan and Rome, I treat myself to a few days in Capri with Jenna – a place I really like. I particularly appreciate the small, exclusive hotels where you are greeted personally and where service is a top priority – this time I stay at JK Capri.

---

216 Kirst, https://www.welt.de/wirtschaft/plus247987938/Italien-Die-ueberraschend-gute-oekonomische-Zwischenbilanz-des-Landes.html?source=puerto-reco-2_ABC-V32.7.B_test.

May 2023
Seoul and Gangwon, South Korea

South Korea – at least its capital, Seoul – is more European than I had been expecting before my first visit in 2019. I am struck by the sprawling, ultra-modern, shopping centers, some of which look far more advanced than any I have seen in Germany. My hotel, the Fairmont Ambassador, is located next to the largest shopping center, and as soon as I enter the center, a robot comes driving towards me, communicating with young people. It drives back and forth all the time, presumably replacing some of the security staff.

One thing I especially like is that Koreans brush their teeth far more frequently than Germans. I always brush my teeth after I eat, even when I'm not at home, and sometimes get strange looks from people in Germany when they see me in a public restroom brushing away. If you are in an office in Korea and go to the restroom, you will often find toothbrushes and dental floss left at the sinks by employees, and every now and then you will meet someone brushing their teeth.

When I'm abroad, I sometimes like to go to normal, inexpensive restaurants, not just the ones in the hotel. As I can't eat with chopsticks, I ask for a knife and fork. The first time I was handed a pair of giant scissors instead of a knife, I thought it was a linguistic misunderstanding. The second time, I understood that some restaurants don't actually have knives, so if you want to chop something up, you have to do so with the giant scissors.

What is also striking in South Korea is that the proportion of beautiful women is significantly higher than in Germany, let alone the United States and the UK. Korean women take great pride in their appearance, and cosmetic surgery became a mass phenomenon as early as the 1980s. There are said to be more than 500 clinics in Seoul alone. But I suspect that even without all these operations, there would still be a lot of beautiful women in South Korea.

In May 2023, I am traveling to Seoul for the second time; the first time was in May 2019 at the invitation of one of my publishers in South Korea. This time I have been invited by the publisher of the Korean edition of *In Defence of Capitalism*. However, the publisher does not speak English, and I am grateful that Professor Sooyoun Hwang, who translated the book into Korean, accompanies me the whole time. Sooyoun has made a major contribution to spreading free-market ideas in South Korea and has translated a total of 56 books to date, including works by Gordon Tullock, Randall Holcombe, and Eamonn Butler.

Sooyoun is 72 years old and used to teach Public Choice and Austrian Economics at Kyungsung University in Busan. He was particularly inspired by the public choice theorist Gordon Tullock, whom he met as an exchange scholar. "Gordon was influenced by Ludwig von Mises' *Human Action*, so I started reading Mises and the Austrian School of Economics." He later became president of the Korean Hayek Society and was the first recipient of the Market Economy Education Award from the Center for Free Enterprise (CFE) think tank. This think tank was founded in 1997 by Choi Jong-hyun, who was at the time the president of the Korean Confederation of Industry. Since then, the CFE has been a leading institution in disseminating free-market ideas to the South Korean public.

The CFE has helped dozens of universities to organize annual lectures on the market economy. The think tank's program allowed each university to invite about ten external lecturers from the fund provided by the CFE to speak on entrepreneurship, economic regulation, and other related topics. All lectures had to include at least one practicing entrepreneur. The CFE also provides the Fraser Institute with data from South Korea and helps them compile the Economic Freedom of the World Index. I was particularly pleased that the CFE made it possible for me, as the first foreign academic, to regularly publish my articles in a separate section of their website – and it is Sooyoun who translates these articles for me.

South Korea is a particularly impressive example of what capitalism can achieve. In the 1960s, the two Koreas, which were separated in 1948, were still extremely poor countries. As poor as the poorest African countries are today. North Korea took the path of a centrally-planned economy, while South Korea opted for the capitalist path. In North Korea, people still go hungry today when harvests fail. A situation report published by the UN children's aid organization UNICEF from the end of 2020 states that more than ten million people in North Korea are considered food-insecure and 2.67 million children needed humanitarian assistance. Shortly before my trip to South Korea, there are renewed reports of famine in North Korea.

The starting position for South Korea after the Second World War was even more difficult than in the North: the country initially received no financial aid whatsoever from the U.S., while North Korea received considerable support from the Soviet Union and China. South Korea was an agricultural country without any significant mineral deposits, while almost all of the peninsula's natural resources, which include iron ore, gold, copper, lead, zinc, graphite, molybdenum, limestone and marble, are located in the North.[217] South Korea's population grew very quickly – from 16 million to 21 million between 1945 and 1947 alone – due to the influx of refugees from the communist North. Many people lived at or below subsistence level.[218]

In July 1961, the Japanese government listed seven reasons why economic independence would be impossible for South Korea: overpopulation, lack of resources, lack of industrialization, massive military obligations, lack of political skills, lack of capital, and lack of administrative skills.[219] South Korea's failure to achieve any meaningful economic progress in the 1950s, immediately after the Korean War, initially appeared to confirm this view. At 79 US dollars, South Korea had one of the lowest per capita incomes in the world.

The country's prospects finally started to improve with Park Chung-hee's rise to power in 1961. By the time the autocratic ruler was assassinated by the director of the Korean Central Intelligence Agency in 1979, he had become the founding father of South Korea's economic miracle. Park initially favored

---

217 Schneidewind, 109.
218 Köllner, 51.
219 Schneidewind, 45.

a centralized state-controlled economic system but was persuaded otherwise by Samsung founder Lee Byung-chul, who is reported to have advised him "that only a relatively liberal market economy would be able to release the entrepreneurial initiative and creative thinking required to compete in the global market and ensure the availability of state-of-the-art products."[220]

South Korea is now one of the leading export nations (6th place after Japan), and brands such as LG and Samsung are household names for consumers all over the world. According to the *2023 Index of Economic Freedom*, South Korea ranks 15th on the list of the world's most economically free countries, far ahead of the United Kingdom (28th) and the United States (25th). In comparison: North Korea ranks 176th, last place in the ranking. South Korea scored particularly well in the categories Fiscal Health, Property Rights and Business Freedom, while there is a need for reforms in the area of Labor Freedom given the excessive regulation of the labor market.

Perceptions of capitalism in South Korea are very positive. In our survey of 35 countries, the only countries in which capitalism enjoyed a better image are Poland and the United States (South Korea has a pro/anti-capitalism coefficient of 1.23).

A positive attitude toward capitalism dominates across all age groups, although approval for capitalism among respondents over the age of 45 (or even over the age of 60) was higher than among younger respondents. Even among people who described themselves as being on the left of the political spectrum, our survey did not identify a strong anti-capitalist bias – among those on the right, support for capitalism was very strong.

Social envy is also significantly lower in South Korea than in other countries. At 0.33, South Korea's social envy coefficient SEC was extremely low among the 13 countries we surveyed – only Poland and Japan had lower SECs.

In South Korea, a country where capitalism enjoys a comparatively positive image and social envy is rather low, I notice that the people I speak to are somehow reluctant to believe the survey's findings. Frequently, they admit that they consider their fellow citizens to be extremely envious and

---

220 Schneidewind, 138.

anti-capitalist. In countries such as Turkey, where anti-capitalism is rampant, no-one doubts the findings of the survey. In countries such as Poland, on the other hand, where the concentration of anti-capitalists is low, the people I speak to remain skeptical and are not entirely convinced by the results.

However, the surveys were conducted in almost all countries by the same institute (Ipsos MORI) using the same methods and the same questionnaire. I think the reason why the people I meet in countries such as South Korea and Poland have doubts is that they are usually enthusiastic supporters of capitalism who measure their own opinions against those of their fellow citizens. Moreover, they often confuse public opinion (as measured by polls) with published opinion (i.e. the tenor of the media).

When I traveled to South Korea in 2019, it was ruled by a rather left-wing government under President Moon Jae-in. Since 2022, in contrast, Yoon Suk-yeol has been in power, a politician who often invokes Milton Friedman and Ludwig von Mises.[221] However, the people I speak to in South Korea are disappointed that Yoon has done little to reform the economy. His free-market rhetoric has not been followed by action, despite the fact that a liberalization of the labor market is urgently needed. The strict employment protection regulations, for example, put a block on new hires. But Yoon does not have a majority in parliament, which limits his room for maneuver. In South Korea, there is essentially a two-party system, similar to the United States, with a conservative party that supports Yoon and a left-wing Democratic Party. The parties occasionally merge with other lists on their respective spectrums or rename themselves. What is missing, however, is a libertarian party.

Unfortunately, the libertarian movement in South Korea is still weak. Apparently, during the leftist Moon administration, the government put pressure on big companies (*chaebols*) to stop financially supporting a number of libertarian think tanks, which made things difficult. However, there are some news outlets and academics who are very active in promoting capitalism in South Korea. In Seoul, I meet Professor Byungtae Lee from KAIST Business College and Professor John Junggun Oh, who founded

221 Yim Hyun-su, http://www.koreaherald.com/view.php?ud=20211105000646.

Citizens Action for True Media (CATM). Both are passionate advocates of capitalism in South Korea and have also helped me to promote my book, *In Defence of Capitalism*.

The organization Citizens Action for True Media has set itself the task of uncovering and correcting fake news and ideologically distorted reports in the media – especially on the subject of capitalism. South Korea's YouTubers are particularly remarkable, as I had already noticed during my first visit in May 2019. Back then, I was a guest on *Pen and Mike*, a YouTube channel that is set up like a professional TV show and has 800,000 subscribers in South Korea. This time, Byungtae Lee conducts a 90-minute interview with me for this channel.

My schedule on these trips is sometimes quite exhausting. On one of my days in South Korea, I am up and about for 18 hours: a lecture at the renowned Korea University in the morning, followed by a two-hour drive to Gangwon Province, where I give a lecture to scholars at the Gangwon Institute, then another lecture at the National Gangwon University in front of an audience of students.

My talks focus on the fallacious arguments propagated by anti-capitalists and the "Seven Laws of Financial Success." I particularly enjoy the second lecture, which I have also given frequently in China and Vietnam: telling young people how important it is to set big, ambitious goals (and to write them down). Unfortunately, English is sometimes a problem. At the top university, Korea University, the students' English was good, but at other universities, I need an interpreter.

Fortunately, I can sleep any time and anywhere – and if that's not possible, I do autogenic training, for example on the car journey, or I ask for a quiet room to be made available for me, which I use as a private retreat between lectures. It's exhausting to answer dozens of emails and give written or telephone interviews in between and then to conduct other interviews in the evening, at night, or early in the morning, for example with media outlets in the United States and Germany. I find myself having to deal with three different time zones: New York is, depending on summer or winter time,

13 or 14 hours behind South Korea, which means that if an interview is scheduled for 7 p.m. New York time, it is already 8 a.m. the next morning in South Korea.

When I speak at the Buddhist Dongguk University in Seoul, I notice that the chairs are firmly attached to the tables. I find this very restrictive because I like to move around with the chair and sometimes rock back and forth. I feel really cramped and wonder how you can think freely if you can't even rock freely with your chair. At many of my lectures, they show my film *Life Behind the Berlin Wall*, which is interesting for South Koreans, who also live in a divided country. There are now subtitles for the film in 17 languages (you can watch the film for free on YouTube), and I made sure that Korean subtitles were added before my trip to South Korea. However, Professor John Junggun Oh tells me that there is a big difference to Germany: many young Koreans are skeptical of the idea of reunification, he says, as they fear it would entail a massive economic burden on their country.

The next day, I meet Taekyu Lee from the Korea Economic Research Institute, a market-oriented research institute that provides policy advice. He explains to me that what people think about North Korea sometimes depends on how they feel about the United States. As in Europe, there are pro- and anti-Americans. And just like in Europe, when it comes to North Korea, the anti-Americans in South Korea also operate according to the motto: "The enemy of my enemy is my friend." He explains that there are even people in South Korea who admire Kim Jong-Un and North Korea. Hard to believe, really. But it's the same reflex that turns anti-Americans in Europe into friends of Putin. Of course, this is a small minority in South Korea, but they are by no means without influence in the powerful trade unions and other organizations. Since, as I have already mentioned, I not only answer journalists' questions in the numerous interviews, but also ask questions of my own, on the last day of my trip to South Korea I want to know from the editor-in-chief of *Asia Today* whether there really are people who see North Korea as a role model. He answers in the affirmative. Although this is of course a minority, he says, it is particularly strong in the Korean Teachers' Union.

May/June 2023
Ulaanbaatar, Mongolia

I'm particularly curious about Mongolia. I don't know much about the country, although I did have a girlfriend from Mongolia for a while. Mongolia, which is located between Russia and China, is almost five times the size of Germany. But with a population of just 3.3 million, it has fewer inhabitants than the German capital, Berlin. You would think there would be enough space for everyone, but on the drive from Genghis Khan airport to my hotel, I find myself in a traffic jam the likes of which I have never experienced – even in Manhattan. Almost half of Mongolia's population lives in the capital, Ulaanbaatar. Since there is no subway or streetcar, all the traffic is jammed onto the streets. According to a study, the only place in the world with worse traffic conditions is Mumbai.[222]

Everyone I meet complains about the endless traffic jams, which are getting worse all the time and exert a heavy toll, both in terms of time and nerves. Some of the people I talk to blame the constant gridlock on extremely low-priced cars from Japan and incredibly low gasoline prices, which mean that everyone can afford to drive a car. You have to make driving more expensive, like in Singapore, they say. I am not convinced.

On the second day of my visit, I am invited to a book fair, where three of my books are presented in Mongolian. It's a huge fair, but it takes place outdoors, in countless tents in the center of the city, where publishers exhibit their books. My publishing house, Nepko, is the largest in Mongolia. I think Mongolians must be real bookworms. Just imagine if a U.S. publishing house were to sell its books exclusively in a city with 3 million inhabitants! How many publishers would survive?

My publisher, Boldbaatar Batamgalan, adds: "Actually, the target group is

---

222 Mongolei-Blog, http://mongolei-blog.de/2019/12/24/ulaanbaatar-und-der-verkehr/.

even smaller, because half of the population lives far away, some 1,200 miles, in rural areas. We sell over 90 percent of our books in the capital."

The book fair in Ulaanbaatar has stands from 200 publishers, printers, bookshops, etc. Several hundred authors are present and Boldbaatar estimates that there are between 100,000 and 200,000 visitors.

According to the fair, 95 percent of visitors buy a book. The book fair's motto is "Let's all read more!" Although my publisher has only recently published three of my books so far (*Dare to Be Different and Grow Rich*, *The Power of Capitalism*, and *In Defence of Capitalism*), he has now acquired licenses for three more of my books.

Books by Friedrich August von Hayek, Ludwig von Mises, Ayn Rand, and Milton Friedman can be found at one of the stands – all translated into Mongolian. This time, however, the fair is focusing on children's books. The head of a publishing house shows me his most successful children's book, which uses pictures and short texts to explain to children how digestion and bowel movements work. The cover features a drawing of a child doing its business. There is another children's book, also very successful, which explains to children that there is nothing embarrassing about passing wind and that it is unhealthy to suppress a fart.

The three-day fair takes place outside the parliament building, which looks just like a palace. In front of the building there are three huge monuments to Genghis Khan – one statue shows him sitting down, the other two on horseback. Genghis Khan is omnipresent in Mongolia. Around 30 miles from the capital, the largest equestrian statue in the world was erected in 2008 in honor of Genghis Khan, in a place where, according to legend, he found a golden whip.

On the fourth day of my stay, I visit this memorial site, which is also home to a museum. We take photos for a newspaper with my books and the equestrian statue in the background. A certificate hangs at the museum's entrance: "The world's tallest equestrian statue recorded in year 2016 Guinness World Records, Chinggis Khaan Statue Complex. It is 40 m tall … completed in the year 2006."

It takes us almost three hours to drive the 30 or so miles back because of traffic. I can't imagine that it will be easy for Mongolia to attract international investors if they are in a state of constant, traffic-jam-induced frustration. Unlike in Hanoi or other Asian cities, there are hardly any motorcycles, mopeds or bicycles, and only a few ancient buses. This is because it is freezing cold in winter, when the temperature can drop to -40°F. In winter, I was told, the city also experiences heavy smog as all households heat their homes with coal stoves. There are no streetcars in the city either. You have to get around by car or on foot. A business traveler I met at the airport said that one of his colleagues got out of the car about a mile before his destination and walked the rest of the way, where he then had to wait 45 minutes for the rest of his party to arrive.

But back to Genghis Khan, whose name has not only been given to the airport, but also to hotels and countless other places. A large museum that has only recently opened is called the Genghis Khan Museum. I visit the museum, thinking beforehand that it is dedicated exclusively to the Mongolian ruler. Of course, he plays a major role, but it is a general museum about the history of the country and is simply named after Genghis Khan.

The founder of Mongolia, whose real name was Temüjin, conquered the Mongol and Turkic peoples who had settled on the Mongolian plateau in just 20 years between 1184 and 1204. He then occupied the territories of other neighboring clans. In 1206, he had an army numbering 95,000 troops. By 1227, the year of his death, he had captured a huge swath of land stretching from China to Europe. His forces also continued to expand, reaching an estimated 123,000 men by 1227.

One of Genghis Khan's most notable strategies was the use of psychological warfare. Reports of his terrible cruelty and the bloodshed inflicted on cities that resisted him served to persuade the populations of other nearby settlements to surrender without a fight, avoiding the need for time-consuming sieges.

Fast-forward 700 years and the Mongolian People's Republic was founded in November 1924. After the Soviet Union, which had been proclaimed two years earlier, Mongolia was the second country to adopt Marxism-Leninism as its state ideology. The communists renamed the capital Ulaanbaatar (Red Hero). As in the Soviet Union, the communists abolished private property. Forced collectivization was as much a catastrophe as in other countries. The livestock population fell rapidly from 24 million in 1930 to just 16.2 million in 1932. There were popular uprisings against collectivization, often led by monks but bloodily suppressed.[223]

In other ways too, the communists followed the example of their idol Stalin, who appointed Marshal Choibalsan as governor. "In 1937, Choibalsan founded a commission based on the Soviet model to pass judgement on 'counter-revolutionaries' in summary trials. In the years of the 'Great Purge' between 1937 and 1939, tens of thousands fell victim to state terror. During this period, Choibalsan also purged his own party of so-called 'class enemies' and counter-revolutionaries. Almost the entire new Mongol elite was wiped out."[224] Of the more than 700 monasteries and temples, almost all were destroyed and over 20,000 monks were murdered.[225]

The communists ruled until 1990. The first counter-demonstrations took place at the end of December 1989, leading to democratic elections in July 1990. I speak with Ganbold Davaadorj, at that time one of the key leaders of the anti-communist opposition movement that also gave rise to the Mongolian Democratic Party. From 1990 to 1992 Davaadorj was deputy prime minister and responsible for economic reforms. "The focus back then was on privatization," he explains. "But there wasn't even a word for it in our language, we had to invent one." Today he is skeptical about the situation: "After the privatizations, perhaps 30 percent of the companies were in state hands and 70 percent were private. Today it is the other way around. The state has created lots of new state-owned enterprises. And our current president and former prime minister Ukhnaagiin Khürelsükh declared his opposition to the market economy years ago."

---

223 Kollmar-Paulenz, 106–107.
224 Kollmar-Paulenz, 106.
225 Kollmar-Paulenz, 106.

In Mongolia today, there is effectively a two-party system. The former communist party MRPP, which renamed itself MPP (Mongolian People's Party) in 2011, has spent most of the time in power. The MPP has a social democratic or socialist agenda. The opposition party is the Democratic Party (DP), which governed from 1996 to 2000 and again (in coalition with smaller parties) from 2012 to 2016. There is no libertarian party, but there are libertarian groups in Mongolia, too.

I meet Amartuvshin Dorj, who founded the Mises Institute in 2017 and has published several books by Mises and Murray Rothbard in Mongolian. Dorj has almost 120,000 followers on Facebook and a successful YouTube channel. What would he change in Mongolia? "We have too many large state-owned enterprises, especially in mining, where the largest coal and copper companies are still in state hands. But there is now a public debate underway in Mongolia about their privatization."

He has created something positive, namely a libertarian café, Liberty Hub, where libertarians from Ulaanbaatar can come together. The walls are adorned with pictures of Hayek, Mises, Rothbard and the slogan "Laissez faire." When I post a tweet about this on Twitter (now X), someone arrogantly asks whether there are more than three libertarians in Ulaanbaatar. Well, my little talk in the café was attended by about fifty.

On the third day, I meet a small group of entrepreneurs from different sectors, including banking and real estate. What needs to change, I ask. Foreign banks must be allowed to operate in Mongolia, says one. Another criticizes the country's completely inadequate rule of law. And everyone complains about excessive regulation, but I hear this complaint all over the world – and rightly so!

The *2023 Index of Economic Freedom* states: "Mongolia's economic freedom score is 61.7, making its economy the 73rd freest in the 2023 Index ... Mongolia is ranked 15th out of 39 countries in the Asia–Pacific region, and its overall score is above the world and regional averages. Economic reforms have supported economic expansion and reductions in poverty. The entrepreneurial sector benefits from an open trade regime, but corruption and the weak rule of law discourage economic development. Judicial reforms and a more streamlined public administration would help to sustain economic growth and broaden the improvement of living standards."[226]

When a journalist from a Mongolian daily newspaper asks me what I would recommend to her country, I reply: You urgently need to reduce your dependence on coal and copper. Every country needs a vision. Especially for a small (in terms of population) country like Mongolia, it could be a vision to catch up with the most economically free countries in the world. Of course, it would be a long journey to get there, because Mongolia is still in a bad state in many regards. Nevertheless, of the seven most economically free countries in the world, four have only five million inhabitants or fewer: Singapore, Ireland, Luxembourg and Estonia. Why don't the Mongols take a country like Singapore as a role model?

By the way, my poll on the image of the market economy and capitalism was also conducted in Mongolia, which wasn't so easy because Ipsos MORI doesn't organize surveys there. However, we finally identified an institute to conduct the survey and found that Mongolians (regardless of whether one uses the word capitalism or not) have a rather neutral view of the market economy and capitalism, i.e. neither particularly positive nor negative (with an overall coefficient of 0.91).

Before my meeting with a small group of entrepreneurs, I gave lecture at a university, in this case the University of Finance & Economics. My lectures to students often focus on the topics of "success" and "financial freedom." While I am on stage, I quickly gain a sense of which students will go on to be successful later in life. They usually sit in the front row, speak good English, and when I ask if they write down their goals, they are among the few who say they do. In addition, if someone has experience in sales or is involved in competitive sports, then my feeling is that they are more likely to make it than someone who hides in the back row, who barely understands English, and has never done anything ambitious outside of school or university. When I feel

---

226 Heritage Foundation, *2023 Index of Economic Freedom*, 252.

that someone will be able to succeed in life, I tell them so – and that usually motivates them a lot.

My days are packed with lectures to representatives of the political opposition (Democratic Party), entrepreneurs and students, as well as interviews with daily newspapers and television. *The Daily News* even reports on my visit on its front page. I give several television interviews, including one with *Bloomberg TV Mongolia*. The news director who interviews me, Ankhbayar Enkh-Amar, tells me that he is currently working on a book about successful people around the world and asks me if he can send me some questions for his book.

Jargalsaikhan Dambadarjaa, whose name is difficult to remember and who therefore simply calls himself Jargal Defacto, interviews me for the television station *NTV Mongolia*. He is the host of the TV show *Interview DeFacto* and of the radio show *Defacto*. Almost everyone in Mongolia knows him, and he also hooked me up with my publisher. We hit it off right away and one of the first things Dambadarjaa talks to me about is bodybuilding because he used to be a bodybuilder and competed in championships. He is a year younger than me and has similar political views. I actually wanted to meet him at the conference of the Mont Pelerin Society in Oslo in 2022, but Covid put a stop to my plans at that time.

An impressive entrepreneur I meet is Tsenguun Purevjav, who owns numerous companies, chiefly in the food industry. He became a staunch supporter of capitalism in Prague in the 1990s, where he lived for 15 years and met reformers such as Václav Klaus, who greatly impressed him. He has had several libertarian books translated into Mongolian and most recently funded a film project about the history of Mongolia, which is intended to educate people – particularly young people – about the communist period. The world would certainly be a better place if more entrepreneurs were as strongly committed to capitalism.

Getting home is difficult because my flight is canceled at short notice. There is initially no information about a replacement flight. However, in a small country like Mongolia, distances are short and everyone knows everyone. My publisher Batamgalan says: "No problem, I'll call the transport minister." Half an hour later I have confirmation of my flight the next day.

During this trip I also find myself living in three time zones because of my interviews with journalists in both the United States and Europe. This massively reduces my night-time rest. But, luckily, I can sleep at any time. I start autogenic training and fall asleep in two or three minutes. And if I can't get enough sleep at night, I sleep two or sometimes even three times during the day for an hour each time, which means I'm always well rested.

I make friends in many countries, including Mongolia, where I met Tsenguun, a smart and beautiful woman in her mid-20s who lived in Vienna for a while and speaks German. She has a fiancé in Vienna and I ask her why she returned to Mongolia: she works in the family's successful business here, but also wants to make a difference politically, campaigning for more democracy and more capitalism. A year later, she tells me that she has started to get involved in politics and is now active in the opposition Democratic Party and putting an election program together. She has since become a member of parliament, as the Mongolian Minister of Economy told me when I met him in Hamburg in October 2024.

June 2023
Madrid, Spain

I've been to Madrid several times before, but this time I'm surprised by the progress the city has made over the past few years. The airport, which is something of a calling card for any city, looks modern and clean. Madrid is different from many other Spanish cities, a fact reflected in the following figures: the gross domestic product per inhabitant in the Madrid region is 35,876 euros, in the city of Madrid 46,715 euros, and in Spain as a whole just 26,438 euros.

Madrid is also a sunny city. While Berlin gets 1,730 hours of sunshine a year and Rome 2,615, Madrid has 3,220. However, I was unlucky this time – after a beautiful sunny day with temperatures of over 80 °F, it rained almost non-stop on the other days.

Spanish people are known to be particularly hospitable, and this certainly applies to my friend Diego Sánchez de la Cruz, who invited me to Madrid. Diego has already translated five of my books into Spanish and made valuable contacts for me – not just in Spain, but all over the world. For example, it was Diego who introduced me to the CEO of the Atlas Network, Brad Lips.

The likeable Spaniard is not so tall in stature, but all the greater in his diligence and commitment to capitalism. At just 35 years of age, Diego is already one of the most influential economic commentators in Spain. He has made a name for himself by translating 30 pro-free-market books into Spanish. Diego teaches at various universities and business schools, works in the research departments of three libertarian think tanks in Spain, and advises a number of national and international companies.

When I ask him how he was drawn to the libertarian movement, he explains: "My father emerged from poverty and made it through life thanks to his entrepreneurial spirit. I remember his example inspiring me to delve into the roots and causes of poverty and wealth. This led me to renowned Spanish liberal thinkers such as Pedro Schwartz and Carlos Rodríguez Braun. I gained invaluable insights from their conferences and seminars. Through the years, I also connected with significant figures in global economic libertarianism, such as Mario Vargas Llosa, Arthur Laffer, Johan Norberg ... Their influence was pivotal."

While he was still at university, Diego founded his own consulting firm. At the same time, he began writing about the financial crisis of 2008 and criticized the mistakes in monetary policy and financial regulation that triggered the collapse of the banking system. He rejects the anti-capitalist myth that "market failure" and "deregulation" caused the crisis. "My generation entered the labor market amidst an unemployment rate exceeding 25 percent, and youth unemployment close to 50 percent," says Diego. "I sought answers – and found them by developing an understanding of economics and deepening my engagement with libertarian thought."

As I always do before any of my visits, I had taken the time to look into the history of the country beforehand. Here are a few facts:

In 1936, Francisco Franco staged a coup against the left-wing Popular Front government, triggering the Spanish Civil War. Franco was supported by fascist Italy and National Socialist Germany, while the leftists were supported by the socialist Soviet Union. Franco was to remain in power until his death in 1975. After seizing power, he introduced a planned economy in order to achieve the goal of self-sufficiency. As the historian Walther Bernecker explains, "The result of this policy of economic control was a decline in the general standard of living, a constant increase in (officially non-existent) unemployment, large-scale botched investments, deficiencies in the quality of industrial products, stagnation in research and development, an inadequate level of production and productivity, and – as a result of black markets, favoritism and speculation – the undermining of economic morale. Until the end of the 1950s, Spain remained an agricultural country with an industrial sector that was uncompetitive on the international stage."[227]

227 Bernecker, *Spaniens Geschichte*, 90.

In May 1950, an eyewitness vividly described the impact of the state-run planned economy in the *Neue Zürcher Zeitung*: "I have never forgotten how I felt when I saw the offices of a large company in which the department responsible for calculating and paying payroll taxes took up almost as much space as the rest of the accounting department put together ... Even worse is the totality of paralysis, delays, business failures and mistakes that this bureaucratic economic system left in its wake, the individual cases of which, however, defy enumeration." One example was the state-imposed ban on layoffs, which the eyewitness said discouraged new hires and thus "became a prime example of a social measure that inverts good intentions because it actually increased unemployment."[228]

However, a turning point occurred during the Franco era, when the Catholic Opus Dei, founded in 1928, came to play a decisive role in defining Spanish economic policy. Opus Dei combined the Catholic faith with a commitment to the market economy, ended the policy of autarky, and launched a series of market economy reforms. The move towards a more market-oriented economy began with the Stabilization Plan of 1959. As is so often the case, the reforms led to a temporary economic downturn because, for example, previously hidden unemployment now came to light. But after just two to three years, the reforms began to pay off. According to Walther Bernecker, "The measures in the foreign trade sector eliminated autarky and led to Spain's integration into the international capitalist system ... The Spanish 'economic miracle,' which lasted a decade, had begun."[229]

The growth rate in the years 1961 to 1974 averaged 7 percent. Only Japan achieved an even higher rate in the same period. Within 15 years, Spain transformed itself from a developing to an industrialized country. Steel production increased fivefold, while car production soared from 40,000 vehicles in 1960 to 700,000 in 1974.[230]

This impressive phase ended in the mid-1970s and global economic

---

228 *Neue Zürcher Zeitung*, 14 May 1950, quoted in Bernecker, *Spaniens Geschichte*, 92–93.
229 Bernecker, *Spaniens Geschichte*, 122.
230 Bernecker, *Spaniens Geschichte*, 128–129.

problems were exacerbated by interventionist economic policies. However, in the early 1980s, Spain returned to more market-oriented policies and pushed forward with labor market deregulation and privatizations. Remarkably, these policies were implemented by the social democratic PSOE party. In the 1990s, the social democrat Felipe González also pursued a policy agenda based on partial market liberalization in line with the global zeitgeist at the time.

Under the conservative José María Aznar (1996 to 2004), free-market reforms were accelerated and there were further privatizations and greater liberalization of the labor market. In just a few years, Spain's *Index of Economic Freedom* score rose from 59.6 (1996) to 68.9 (2004).

However, despite various reforms, the level of economic freedom in Spain today is disappointing. From 1995 to 2023, the country's *Index of Economic Freedom* score fluctuated between 58.6 (1997) and 70.1 (2009) and, at 65 points in 2023, was only marginally higher than in 1995.[231] In 51st place, Spain is well ahead of Italy (69th) and France (57), but still well behind countries such as Poland (40), Portugal (30), and Sweden (10).

The 2023 index states: "Spain's economic freedom score is 65.0, making its economy the 51st freest in the 2023 Index .... Spain is ranked 29th out of 44 countries in the Europe region, and its overall score is above the world and regional averages. Spain's progress toward greater economic freedom has been limited and uneven. Regulatory efficiency and the rule of law have been relatively well maintained, but long-term gains have been modest. Fiscal freedom, government spending, and financial freedom challenges are significant. Fiscal deficits and high public debt reflect a need to reform financial management."[232]

The Spanish population is also strongly anti-capitalist. With a pro-/anti-capitalism coefficient of 0.70, Spain is one of the seven most anti-capitalist countries in our survey – on a similar level to France. In 28 countries, our survey reveals attitudes towards capitalism that are more positive or at least less negative. Spaniards associate capitalism above all with increasing

231 Heritage Foundation, *2023 Index of Economic Freedom*, 401.
232 Heritage Foundation, *2023 Index of Economic Freedom*, 335.

inequality, selfishness and greed, and believe that capitalism means being ruled by the rich.

Differences between political camps are even more pronounced in Spain than in other countries: Those on the moderate right of the political spectrum in Spain are clearly pro-capitalist (coefficient of 1.38), and those on the far right are extremely pro-capitalist (coefficient of 2.05). On the far left, 67 percent complain that capitalism leads to rising inequality, compared to only 25 percent and 23 percent of those on the moderate and far right, respectively. One in two Spaniards on the far left of the political spectrum blames capitalism for environmental destruction and climate change, while only one in ten of those on the far right do the same.

In Spain, too, there are also several think tanks committed to promoting capitalism. The oldest of these is the Institute of Economic Studies (IEE), headed by the economist Gregorio Izquierdo. It was founded in the early 1980s and is financed by the business confederation CEOE. The most effective reforms carried out by José María Aznar and Mariano Rajoy bear the IEE's signature.

The primary home of libertarians is the Juan de Mariana Institute (IJM), which has produced studies on issues such as decarbonization that have been debated and presented before the U.S. Congress. IJM hosts numerous conferences and runs a very successful summer school that attracts participants from all over the country and even from Latin America, where the IJM also exerts significant influence.

The conservative political party *Partido Popular* (PP) set up the FAES think tank, which now operates independently of the party. For decades, former President José María Aznar used the think tank as a platform to promote the spread of libertarian ideas. Other think tanks making an active contribution to Spain's intellectual landscape include Fundalib, which scrutinizes the tax burden in various regions of the country, and the Diego de Covarrubias Center, an organization with a libertarian-conservative outlook.

The right-wing Vox party, which was founded in 2013 by former members of *Partido Popular*, originally combined an anti-migration and anti-feminist stance with a pro-capitalist agenda. I speak to Manuel Llamas Fraga and Juan Manuel López Zafra from the *Partido Popular* in Madrid, who say that Vox has followed a similar path to many other right-wing parties in Europe: it started out with a clear free-market position but, over time, anti-capitalists gained greater influence and saw that they could win over former left-wing voters (from *Podemos*). Nevertheless, both politicians see an alliance with Vox as the only way to advance their positions. This would not be possible under any circumstances in coalition with the Socialists, they tell me.

Daniel Lacalle, a well-known Spanish economist, says that Vox is a party that both advocates tax cuts but also "opposes globalization," which means it is against free trade and in favor of protectionism. In this respect, the party's policies are similar to those of politicians such as Donald Trump.

I ask the well-known journalist Maite Rico (formerly of *El Pais*, now writing for *El Mundo*) for her assessment. She says that Vox is home to a mixture of very different political viewpoints, but she shares the view that the pro-free-market faction has lost a great deal of influence compared to the party's early days.

I also meet Eduardo Fernández Luiña, who is Head of Studies at the Disenso think tank at the time of my interview. Disenso has close links with the Vox party. Shortly after our interview, he left the think tank, another indicator of the party's shift away from supporting the market economy. Luiña has been Professor of Political Science at the Universidad Francisco Marroquín for ten years.

Back to *Partido Popular*, which, with its economic experts Manuel Llamas Fraga and Juan Manuel López Zafra, wants to turn Greater Madrid into a kind of special capitalist zone in Spain. They have completely abolished the wealth tax, inheritance tax, and gift tax in the region, and the initial tax rate of 8.5 percent is the lowest in Spain. The maximum tax rate is still high at 45 percent, but in other Spanish regions it can be as high as 54 percent. Special taxes, which exist in many other regions of Spain for anything and everything, have been completely abolished, and the property transfer tax on real estate has been reduced.

Manuel Llamas Fraga calculates that inhabitants of the Madrid region have saved more than 74 billion euros since 2004 thanks to various tax breaks. Since the pro-capitalist Isabel Díaz Ayuso has been President of the Autonomous Regional Government of Madrid – Diego admires her and repeatedly emphasizes all that she has achieved for the Madrid region – the residents there have paid 24 billion euros less in taxes. And the tax cuts have brought about growth: "Between 2004, when the Community of Madrid began its policy of lowering taxes, and 2021, regional GDP growth has been 29 percent, 16 percentage points above the national average (13 percent)," says Llamas Fraga. The lower tax rates have also helped to reduce the shadow economy, a major problem in Spain, which is now far more pronounced in the kingdom's other regions.

Madrid has once again confirmed that tax cuts lead to significantly higher tax revenues – something the left will never understand. Every reduction in income tax rates has led to higher tax receipts. Arthur Laffer can be pleased that his theory has once again proved itself to be true.

Madrid is not only pursuing a more market-based policy with regard to taxes, it has also been deregulating many other areas of the economy. For example, fast-track investment processes have been introduced, allowing projects to be approved far more quickly and cutting the time required for administrative procedures by a third. Another important step: Madrid is the first region in Spain where companies from all over the country can start operating without having to apply for permits or licenses that they already have in their home regions.

I have an interesting talk with José Luis Moreno, an economic consultant who is working on a number of projects, including "Madrid Nuevo Norte." This is a gigantic real estate development project with a volume of 25 billion euros on an area of 2.36 million square meters. The plans envisage twenty skyscrapers – one of which will be even taller than London's 310-meter-high Shard. But it's not just about the real estate project. Moreno describes how the investors want to turn Spain into the "new Miami" and in particular attract entrepreneurs from Mexico, Peru, Colombia, and other Latin American countries. Madrid will become even more attractive, he explains, with low taxes and more personal freedom. Moreno points out that Madrid pursued less restrictive policies during the Covid pandemic than many other Spanish and European cities.

Although Spain's regions have a certain degree of autonomy, fundamental changes can only take place if there is a change of government. But that is not about to happen any time soon. One month after my visit to Spain, elections are held. The conservative PP wins 33 percent of the vote (2019: 21 percent), followed by the PSOE in second place on 28 percent (2019: 28 percent). Vox, led by Santiago Abascal Conde, land in third place on 12 percent. Contrary to some people's expectations, Vox failed to improve its position and actually lost ground compared to the 2019 elections, when it achieved 15 percent. This may in part be due to the fact that the PP has adopted some of Vox's policies. The radical left-wing alliance Sumar came fourth (12 percent). The conservatives narrowly missed out on winning a majority in the 350-seat parliament – by just four seats.

Pedro Sánchez was re-elected as Spain's head of government in November 2023. In the vote in the Chamber of Deputies, the socialist received 179 votes, three more than the absolute majority of 176 votes he needed in the first round of voting. A total of 171 MPs voted against him. In the run-up to the election, there were demonstrations in many parts of Spain because Sánchez had allied himself with left-wing extremists and separatist parties from Catalonia: he promised amnesty to hundreds of separatists who are being prosecuted by the judiciary in connection with Catalonia's failed attempt to secede. These include the separatist leader Carles Puigdemont, who wanted to secede Catalonia from the rest of Spain in 2017.

June 2023
Adam Smith's birthday

In April 2023, Ralph Benko, whom I met in Washington, reminded me that Adam Smith would have celebrated his 300th birthday in June 2023. He suggests that I use the date of Smith's baptism, June 16, 1723 (no-one knows his exact birthday), not only to commemorate Adam Smith, but also as an opportunity to demonstrate the superiority of capitalism.

The first thing I do after this conversation is order more than a dozen biographies and studies on Adam Smith and re-read his two main works from cover to cover. Then I develop a plan to draw global attention to this significant day. I realize that some commentators try to portray Adam Smith as a left-winger and that they are also sure to voice their opinions – so write an article called "Was the King of Free Market Economics Left-Wing?"

I write several more articles and call on my worldwide contacts, asking ten leading economists from nine countries for their thoughts on Adam Smith's legacy. Professor Leszek Balcerowicz from Poland and the President of the Adam Smith Institute in London, Eamonn Butler, are among those who reply. The Chinese economist Zhang Weiying from Peking University writes me: "Adam Smith's most important contribution to economic thought: self-interested strangers in a large-scale society can cooperate, benefit one another, and be in harmony through a division-of-labor-based market system. Individuals can benefit only by serving others first in the market. Seeking of self-interests in the market is not immoral. For Adam Smith, the market is a spontaneously evolving order, not a designed order. China's rapid economic development over the past four decades is a victory of Adam Smith's idea of the market. China needs Adam Smith, not John M. Keynes."

Alberto Mingardi, Associate Professor for History of Political Thought at IULM University in Milan, also answers: "I think it is hard to overstate the importance of Smith. True enough, other people wrote about economic matters before him and indeed you have many substantial contributions in the earlier eighteenth century: from Richard Cantillon to the Fisiocrats. Certainly, Hume's essays planted the seeds of classical economics too and you got brilliant insights on commerce in authors such as Montesquieu. But economics was lacking the sort of ponderous treatise which can truly be seen as a foundational text. Smith supplied it, writing a book which is unique in being many different things at once, but all brilliantly. It is a theoretical work, it lays down the foundations of a science, but is also a work of history and something of a reportage. It is written by a man whose passion was to understand and explain, but it could persuade: and, in fact, it did persuade many, opening their eyes to the virtues of free exchange and the limits of the mercantile system."

Most of these experts emphasize Smith's virtues, but there is also one decidedly negative assessment – from Professor Jesús Huerta de Soto, Professor of Political Economy at King Juan Carlos University Madrid: "Adam Smith's importance is overstated and he cannot be considered the founder of Economics at all but Richard Cantillon and the Spanish Scholastics. Every one of his correct contributions was not his but co-opted from his predecessors. Those he did originate were wrong: his support of the navigation acts, his tax ideas and above all his long-term equilibrium analysis based on the cost of production (labor). Smith's analysis is the foundation of Marxism (labor theory of value) and interventionism. With friends like Adam Smith, free-market libertarians do not need any enemies (with Adam Smith it is enough!)"

Indeed, Smith was mistaken about many things. His labor theory of value, which Marx later expanded upon, was wrong. And, as Murray N. Rothbard has shown, in some respects he even fell short of the insights provided by economists such as Richard Cantillon, who had a much better understanding of the economic function of the entrepreneur than Smith[233]. Nevertheless, it would be wrong to call Adam Smith a left-winger. Above all, his deep distrust of

---

233 Rothbard, Murray N., *Economic Thought Before Adam Smith. An Austrian Perspective on the History of Economic Thought, Volume 1*, Ludwig von Mises Institute, Auburn, Alabama 2006, S. 433–474

government intervention in the economy is the main argument against labeling him so. When the economy is ruined, it is, according to Smith, never by entrepreneurs and merchants, but always by the state: "Great nations are never impoverished by private, though they sometimes are by public prodigality and misconduct," he wrote in his magnum opus, *The Wealth of Nations*.[234]

And he added optimistically: "The uniform, constant, and uninterrupted effort of every man to better his condition, the principle from which public and national, as well as private opulence is originally derived, is frequently powerful enough to maintain the natural progress of things toward improvement, in spite both of the extravagance of government and of the greatest errors of administration. Like the unknown principle of animal life, it frequently restores health and vigour to the constitution, in spite, not only of the disease, but of the absurd prescriptions of the doctor."[235]

This metaphor says a great deal: private economic actors represent healthy, positive development, while politicians obstruct the economy with their nonsensical regulations. Adam Smith would have been very skeptical today if he could see governments in Europe and the United States increasingly intervening in the economy and politicians who believe they are smarter than the market. "Every individual," Smith writes, "is continually exerting himself to find out the most advantageous employment for whatever capital he can command. It is his own advantage, indeed, and not that of the society, which he has in view. But the study of his own advantage naturally, or rather necessarily, leads him to prefer that employment which is most advantageous to the society."[236] Legislators, Adam Smith believed, should have more confidence in the fact that "every individual, it is evident, can, in his local situation, judge much better than any statesman or lawgiver can do for him."[237]

Perhaps the interpretation of Smith as a left-winger is also due to the fact that he repeatedly used his work to advocate improved conditions for workers. However, according to Smith, improving the situation of ordinary

234 Smith, *The Wealth of Nations*, 305.
235 Smith, *The Wealth of Nations*, 306.
236 Smith, *The Wealth of Nations*, 397.
237 Smith, *The Wealth of Nations*, 399.

people would not come about through redistribution and excessive state intervention, it would be the natural result of economic growth, which in turn needed one thing above all: economic freedom. To the extent that economic freedom prevails and markets expand, people's standard of living will also rise. Three hundred years after Smith's birth and some 250 years after the publication of *The Wealth of Nations*, we know that the moral philosopher and economist was right.

I spend two months preparing for June 16, 2023. I contact two members of the German Bundestag, Oliver Luksic from the FDP and Christian von Stetten from the CDU, and propose a memorial event in the German Bundestag at which I would give a commemorative speech in Smith's honor. The event takes place on June 12. I write an article for the *Wall Street Journal*, which is published on June 16 and attracts a lot of attention. *Fox News* broadcasts a summary and invites me to give an interview about Adam Smith a few days later. The British daily newspaper *City A.M.* even publishes three full-page articles by me on this day – "Was the King of Free Market Economics Left-Wing?," an interview with the President of the Adam Smith Institute, and the collected quotes from my survey of economists in nine countries. A total of 34 of my articles on Adam Smith also appear in 14 other countries on the same day, including China, South Korea, Vietnam, France, Germany, Italy, Spain, Portugal, Poland, and Sweden.

My favorite quote from Adam Smith comes from a lecture he gave in 1755, two decades before the publication of *The Wealth of Nations*, in which he said:

"Man is generally considered by statesmen and projectors as the materials of a sort of political mechanics. Projectors disturb nature in the course of her operations in human affairs; and it requires no more than to let her alone, and give her fair play in the pursuit of her ends, that she may establish her own designs ... All governments which thwart this natural course, which force things into another channel, or which endeavour to arrest the progress of society at a particular point, are unnatural, and to support themselves are obliged to be oppressive and tyrannical."[238]

---

238 Smith, *Essays on Philosophical Subjects*, 322.

These were indeed prophetic words. The biggest mistake planners have always made was clinging to the illusion that it is possible to plan an economic order on paper. They believe that an author, sitting at a desk, can fashion an ideal economic order and that all that remains is to convince enough politicians to implement this new economic order in practice.

July 2023
Memphis, United States

I submitted the film *Poland. From Socialism to Prosperity* to the Anthem Film Festival, which took place as part of Freedom Fest 2023 in Memphis. Unfortunately, my efforts were in vain. Through a personal contact, I tried to get an invitation to speak at Freedom Fest, but this was also unsuccessful.

So, I was all the more delighted when Mark Skousen wrote to me personally at the end of June to invite me to speak at Freedom Fest. Steve Forbes had recommended me as a speaker. Now I will have an opportunity to meet Skousen in person. When the economist and initiator of Freedom Fest invites me, the program is already set, but he spontaneously offers: "I'll open the event and give you half of my time. You can speak right after me." Wow!

Skousen is an impressive individual and has achieved a huge amount. He studied economics because it combined his main interests – politics, finance, and mathematics. "Fortunately, my university had just hired a new PhD graduate from the University of Chicago, Larry Wimmer, who disagreed with Paul Samuelson's Keynesian economic theory and became my mentor. He encouraged me to read Milton Friedman's book, *Capitalism and Freedom*, which I devoured. Although I thought Friedman's economics was going in the right direction, I was not entirely satisfied with the Chicago School."

In the early 1970s, when Skousen was working as an economic analyst at the CIA, his first job out of college, he discovered the writings of Murray Rothbard, in particular his books *America's Great Depression* and *Man, Economy, and State*. "I found Rothbard's writings far more coherent and understandable than those of Mises or Hayek." His doctoral thesis at George Washington University was on the 100 percent gold standard and was heavily influenced by Rothbard's thinking.

In 1980, he started his own monthly investment newsletter, *Forecasts &*

Strategies, which he expanded in the 1990s with the addition of a telephone hotline. The election of Ronald Reagan was a turning point for Skousen and his newsletter. He predicted: "Reaganomics will work! Sell all your gold and silver and buy stocks and bonds." His forecasts proved accurate, but it did not endear him to the gold standard movement.

In 2007, Skousen founded FreedomFest, Inc. as a for-profit organization. "The idea behind Freedom Fest," explains Skousen, "is that I have felt that we have been losing the battle for freedom for some time. Slowly but surely, over time and as a result of various crises, more and more of everything is either mandated or prohibited. So, I came up with the idea of creating a national gathering of freedom lovers where once a year we meet to learn from each other, network and socialize, and celebrate liberty (or what's left of it). We all live busy lives, but if we can come together once a year, we might turn the tide."

He quickly established the event as "the world's largest gathering of free minds," an independent organization with no political party affiliations. Freedom Fest takes place annually in Las Vegas or another city (in 2023, Memphis). You can find out all about past events and upcoming conferences at http://www.freedomfest.com. The speakers are authors, professors, historians, economists, and political thinkers. Around 2,000 to 3,000 participants attend each year. Adding to the festival's appeal is that it is organized in conjunction with several other events – the Global Financial Summit (an investor conference), the Anthem Film Festival (the largest libertarian film festival in the world), and the Punching Up Comedy Festival.

Every year there is a celebrity speaker. In the past, these have included the actor William Shatner (*Star Trek's* Captain James T. Kirk), boxing legend George Foreman, entrepreneur Kevin O'Leary (Mr. Wonderful from *Shark Tank*), and comedian and actor John Cleese. In 2023, the honor goes to Mike Rowe from the TV series *Dirty Jobs*. Freedom Fest's ambassadors include Steve Forbes, John Mackey (co-founder of Whole Foods Market) and Lisa Kennedy (from *Fox News*).

I like the fact that Freedom Fest was not launched as a non-profit organization, as is often the case in the libertarian scene. There may be good reasons for "non-profit" organizations, but I find it paradoxical when supporters of capitalism, who emphasize the importance of private profit as the engine of the economy, set up non-profit organizations.

A few days before Freedom Fest in Memphis, my father dies after a brief illness at the age of 94. As his passing is a highly personal matter, I won't say any more than that. But I'm sure you can imagine what it must have been like to travel to Freedom Fest to speak between my father's death and his funeral. I spend the day before I leave with my mother and call her several times a day during my trip.

The flight is a disaster: I originally plan to fly to Memphis via Frankfurt and Denver, but my flight is canceled at short notice, so I fly from Frankfurt to Munich and then on to Chicago. That flight is delayed, and in Chicago there are seemingly endless queues at immigration, so I miss my connecting flight to Memphis and am put on a waiting list. I only manage to get a flight to Memphis the next morning thanks to my Senator status with Star Alliance.

I am by no means the only one this is happening to – everyone who travels to the United States on a regular basis this year has tales to tell of the ongoing chaos with canceled or severely delayed flights. When something goes according to plan, it's a surprise.

Memphis is not a city I would like to live in. What I saw was run down. There are police cars on every corner, and with good reason: there are 1,750 crimes per 100,000 inhabitants; only three American cities have higher crime rates.[239] There are poor people on the streets almost everywhere you look.

This was a state of affairs that football coach Bill Courtney touched on in his indictment of the American justice system. Although the U.S. sends more people to prison than any other country, crime is constantly on the rise. The problem, he says, is the 70 percent recidivism rate. He showcases a number of private initiatives aimed at getting ex-prisoners into jobs, which have reduced the recidivism rate as low as 8 percent. Sometimes it starts with simple things, such as an initiative to get homeless people to take jogging classes: "At the

---

239 Kukksi USA, https://www.kukksi.de/das-sind-die-sieben-gefaehrlichsten-staedte-in-den-usa

beginning, only a few took part, later there were hundreds. Just learning the discipline of getting up at six every morning made a difference." His message: "Don't wait for the government. It will not solve the problems. Let's start ourselves." He is proud of the fact that his projects succeed without any government support: "Not one government dollar was involved."

Courtney has made a name for himself in Memphis as a volunteer football coach for the Manassas Tigers and as a successful businessman. Now he wants to reach a much wider audience with a new podcast called *An Army of Normal Folks*. Courtney's message to a high school football team in North Memphis became the subject of the Oscar-winning documentary *Undefeated*. He is also the author of the book, *Against the Grain: A Coach's Wisdom on Character, Faith, Family, and Love*.

How can libertarians reach more people and grow their movement? Which of their strengths should they focus on? These are among the questions addressed by T.K. Coleman from the Foundation for Economic Education (FEE) and co-host of the *The Minimalists Podcast*. With more than 100 million downloads, *The Minimalists Podcast* is one of the most popular podcasts in the world, despite its name. "If you want to know what our strengths are, just look at what the enemies of freedom and totalitarian states fear the most: humor, creativity, music, movies ... Rational arguments are important, but our opponents have arguments, too. But what do the representatives of the woke ideology attack? When someone makes a politically incorrect joke, for example. They want to control and censor what you can and can't laugh about."

"Wokeism" is the subject of numerous speeches, including one from Vivek Ramaswamy. The 38-year-old was the youngest candidate for the 2024 Republican Party presidential primaries (until his withdrawal in mid-January 2024). Born in Cincinnati to a family of Indian immigrants, he initially worked as an investment partner at a hedge fund before founding the biopharmaceutical company Roivant Sciences in 2014.

Above all, Ramaswamy has made a name for himself as a critic of "wokeism," and *The New York Times* called him an anti-woke candidate. The problem, he says, is that more and more Americans define themselves as "victims." He also opposes ESG guidelines (ideological guidelines on the environment, "social issues" and corporate governance), which he believes are leading to the politicization of the economy and ultimately amount to the abolishment of the free market economy, because entrepreneurs and consumers will no longer decide what to produce and where to invest. "Capitalism is the best system!" he exclaims – a conviction that, for all their differences, unites all libertarians at Freedom Fest.

Gloria Álvarez is another presidential candidate, having recently run for president in Guatemala, where she was ultimately defeated by two other candidates. Like Ramaswamy, she is 38 years old and established herself as a libertarian radio and TV commentator. In 2014, the good-looking libertarian became famous overnight thanks to a YouTube video in which she denounced populist regimes. Within three days, it had clocked up more than 20 million views.

Socialists now rule in most Latin American countries – recently winning in Brazil, Colombia, Peru and even Chile. According to Álvarez, the real reason for the socialist candidates' success across Latin America is the failure of conservative governments, which have often been corrupt and only concerned with defending entrenched privileges. "Privatization," she explains, has usually meant "selling" former state-owned enterprises on the cheap to friends.

Tax receipts, Álvarez complains, are misused, largely funding inflated bureaucracies and trade unions – only 2 percent of government spending, she points out, is invested in the important area of internal security. The rule of law, she says, must be massively strengthened and the share of spending on security should be increased to 50 percent of government spending. At the same time, she advocates the legalization of marijuana and prostitution, because it is only organized crime that benefits from bans – and the police and courts cannot focus on really important tasks.

By advocating the right to abortion and the legalization of drugs, libertarians such as Álvarez distinguish themselves from traditional conservatives, but in the field of economic policy, she advocates a flat tax, a considerable reduction in the role of the state, and more capitalism. Her thesis: the state is too strong where it should be weak – especially in the economy – and too weak where it should be strong, i.e. in the area of internal security. Less state interference in the economy, and more money for police and justice, are her solutions.

Steve Forbes takes to the stage to criticize the U.S. and Europe for increasingly turning to "modern socialism." By this he means that in the past, socialists nationalized private property; today, the same goal is being pursued through ever more state mandates and regulation. This, he explains, undermines private property until only an empty shell remains. Increasingly, it is politicians and civil servants – and not companies and consumers – who decide what is produced. Central banks, he continues, are acting more and more like planning authorities in socialist countries. As Forbes sees it, we need to return to the gold standard.

The transformation of the economy today is primarily taking place under the banner of the fight against climate change, which is the topic of Michael Schellenberger's speech. Unlike many Trump supporters, he does not deny climate change, but believes that its effects have been exaggerated by falsified statistics and unsubstantiated worst-case scenarios. He also points to the contradictions of many governments' policies: in Germany, for example, the government has decided to phase out nuclear power plants, leaving the country dependent on imports of electricity generated from burning coal in other countries. In fact, the madness goes even further: decommissioned coal-fired power plants have been reconnected to the grid in Germany, the supposed model state for the green energy transition, while the last three nuclear power plants have been rendered unusable in order to ensure that the nuclear phase-out cannot be reversed.

The topic of another session is whether or not to raise taxes on the rich in the United States. Economist Lanny Ebenstein argues that taxes on the rich should be increased to 50 percent. His argument: even when the tax rate was 70 percent or higher, the U.S. economy experienced impressive growth, while in times of low taxes, it has tended to stagnate. The economist Arthur

Laffer, who became famous as an advisor to Ronald Reagan and whose name became associated with the "Laffer Curve," which states that lower taxes lead to higher tax revenues and more growth, vehemently disagrees.

Ebenstein's mistake: He confuses marginal tax rates with taxes actually paid. In the periods of very high tax rates, there were so many tax saving schemes that hardly anyone paid the high tax rates he uses as an argument. For example, the top rate of income tax in 1962 was 91 percent. After deductions and credits, only 447 tax filers out of 71 million paid any taxes at the top rate. Even when the top tax rate was lowered to 70 percent, not much changed. Only 3,626 out of 75 million taxpayers actually paid taxes up to 70 percent.

There was a heated discussion about the new nationalism in the U.S. and whether it is a danger or not. Bryan Caplan, a libertarian who advocates Open Borders, believes nationalism is a major threat. All around the world, nationalism is a danger, whether in Russia, China or the USA, he claims. Rich Lowry, opposing Caplan's position, argues that at a time when the left is trying to divide society through "woke" identity politics, there is one loyalty that holds the country together, and that is the commitment to the nation.

The beauty of Freedom Fest is that there are so many different opinions, some reasonable, some less so. Daniel Miller of the Texas Nationalist Movement, for instance, argues that Texas should break away from the United States and form its own nation. Today this sounds unrealistic, but those interested in history may know that Texas fought a successful war of independence against Mexico in 1835 and proclaimed the Republic of Texas the following year. In the event, independence lasted nine years before Texas became a U.S. state.

In my opinion, the discussion on "war and peace" and the conflict in Ukraine is far too one-sided. In the United States, Scott Horten from the Libertarian Institute sees an anti-war movement forming on the right that is even stronger than the left-wing movement that opposed the Vietnam War in the 1960s. By "anti-war" he means isolationism and unilateral criticism of the United States: "The enemy is always our own government, no-one else," he says, sharpening this position and comparing the supposed "demonization" of

Saddam Hussein with the supposed "demonization" of Putin. Doug Bandow from the Cato Institute also blames NATO's expansion into Eastern Europe for the war in Ukraine. To be fair, it has to be said that many libertarians have adopted a very different position – including the Atlas Network, for example – which is clearly on the side of Ukraine.

Libertarians are, however, united in their commitment to capitalism and entrepreneurship. One of the event's highlights is the launch of a new video series: *Steve Forbes on Achievement* by Steve Forbes and izzit.org. *Heroes of Capitalism* might be a better title, as Forbes profiles ten entrepreneurs (www.izzit.org/forbes) and highlights what we can learn about the market economy from their lives.

I have an incredible time at Freedom Fest. I consider it a great honor to speak directly after Mark Skousen's opening speech. I also give a second lecture on Poland and Vietnam – and show excerpts from the film that was not accepted by the Anthem Film Festival. And I get to meet authors and economists I have long admired, such as George Gilder, whose book, *Wealth and Poverty,* was one of Ronald Reagan's favorites. I also meet the legendary Arthur Laffer. I've stayed in touch with both of them since Freedom Fest, and both are writing forewords to books of mine: Laffer for the new edition of my book, *The Power of Capitalism,* and Gilder for the English edition of my book on Poland and Vietnam, *How Nations Escape Poverty.* And last but not least, I have the opportunity to see Alica again, who is in New York at the time and is coming down to Freedom Fest, which we previously attended together in 2022.

As there are usually fewer events in the summer, I don't have all that many book launches and lectures in my diary in July and August. That suits me fine because I want to take a few days off to relax anyway. I'll be spending a few days in Mallorca with a girlfriend and two weeks later another few days with Jenna in the south of France, right on the border with Monaco. I'm not really a fan of French hotels because I've had bad experiences with their poor service and English language skills in the past. This time I am pleasantly surprised. However, the hotels (Hotel Maybourne Riviera and Hotel Cap Estel) cost more than 2,000 euros a night, so you should be able to expect first-class service.

I am struck by something of a paradox. Nowhere is social envy as pronounced as in France, as my international survey of 13 countries has shown. The social envy coefficient for France is even higher than it is for Germany. And France, as my survey on the image of capitalism has also revealed, is one of the most anti-capitalist countries in the world. That's why I am only traveling to France on vacation. Although my books have been translated into over 30 languages, not a single one is available in French.

At the same time, hardly any other country celebrates luxury to the same extent as France. Dinner for my girlfriend and me at the Hotel Cap Estel costs 600 euros, even though I only drink carrot juice and don't eat any meat. I'm by no means a gourmet – I like Greek yogurt with strawberries and nuts just as much as a menu in a Michelin-starred restaurant. But I'm happy if I can make a girlfriend happy, and she certainly enjoys it.

Of course, my summer does not pass entirely without lectures. At the end of July, I give a speech at the Academy of Freedom of the Friedrich August von Hayek Society in Potsdam. The Academy of Freedom is aimed at young people and most of the participants are probably between 20 and 25 years of age. The fee is only 200 euros as the Friedrich August von Hayek Society covers the additional costs of around 900 euros per person for successful applicants.

At the beginning of August, I give a talk at a castle in Nordhausen (Thuringia) to Liberty Rising, a group of young men and women I have never met before. About 100 young people attend, mostly young men. Liberty Rising is inspired by the Russian-American philosopher Ayn Rand. Young people love to be provocative – it's something the youth organizations of left-wing and right-wing political parties are famous for. However, being provocative is different at Liberty Rising: A huge poster hangs in the event room: "*Leistung statt Hängertum. Sozialstaat abschaffen*," which roughly translates as "High-achievers not hipsters. Abolish the welfare state." The banner comes from a campaign that the group carried out in five German cities.

Every year, the group organizes events such as "Soul of Liberty," to which I am invited as a guest speaker to give a talk on "The Fallacies of the Anti-Capitalists." The festival features a series of lectures and workshops on topics such as capitalism and philosophy of life, but also on Bitcoin, modern architecture, and how to become a high-achiever.

The group's co-founders, Stefan Griese and Max Remke, have known each other for a long time: they both started out in the far-left scene and used to be active members of the Left Party's youth organization. "What got us thinking at the time was the contradiction between theory and practice," recalls Max Remke. "The left promised prosperity and delivered scarcity of goods and poverty. They promised freedom and established totalitarian dictatorships wherever they came to power." Griese and Remke set out in search of thinkers who were better suited to their goals. They started with the Austrian-American philosopher Karl Popper and ended up with Ayn Rand.

As of August 2023, Liberty Rising has organized around 70 lectures and training events, but also uses direct action to draw attention to itself. For example, members held up a banner with the slogan "Commuters not climate activists – industry & capitalism not environmental diktats" in front of the HQ of the environmental doomsday cult, "Last Generation." Members of

Last Generation had been gluing themselves to roads in Germany and other countries for months in protest against climate change, annoying commuters trying to get to work.

Liberty Rising also unveiled four large banners emblazoned with the words "Communism Kills" in front of the Marx-Engels monument in Berlin. The banners contained explanatory texts, a list of the people shot while trying to escape from East to West Germany, and a list of the victims of communism. On the anniversary of the proclamation of the socialist soviet republic in Germany on November 9, 1918 by the communist Karl Liebknecht, the group organized an event in front of the historic palace portal in Berlin under the motto "Minimal state now!"

"Originally, we joined the protests against the government's Corona virus policies," says Griese, "but we disassociated ourselves from that movement because it increasingly attracted conspiracy theorists and people with questionable ideologies – including anti-Americanism."

It was important to them to occupy the pre-political arena. "I learned that from the left," Griese explains. The group deals with individual philosophies of life and strategies for developing self-confidence. It runs a music project called Capitalist Squad and the online store Capitalist Aesthetics. "We want a guiding culture of individualism and achievement and our long-term goal is a libertarian minimalist state and a society that values freedom and personal responsibility," says Griese. He and his friends are equally opposed to left- and right-wing collectivists and anti-capitalists. They describe themselves as "radical capitalists."

"In the beginning, we were much closer to the libertarian scene. But large sections of the libertarian scene in Germany have become increasingly conservative, conspiracy theorist, and Russia-friendly in recent years, so we distanced ourselves in 2022," explains Griese. Liberty Rising clearly supports Ukraine and also joined demonstrations for more arms deliveries. Their motto: "Freedom and capitalism will not fight for themselves." To commemorate the popular uprising in East Germany on June 17, 1953, in which workers rebelled against socialism, Liberty Rising campaigned against the Soviet victory memorials in Berlin and Stendal under the motto "70 years of popular uprising – no more taxpayer's money for totalitarian monuments."

Immigration policy is a subject of heated debate in many countries today. While left-wing politicians in many countries call for open borders and a welfare state, Liberty Rising believe that the two cannot co-exist. They are in favor of abolishing the welfare state – and they believe that doing so would remove the false financial incentives for immigration. "Anyone who earns a living through their own efforts, is not a criminal, and does not subscribe to an ideology that is hostile to freedom and the rule of law, should have the right to come here. But they should not expect any state welfare payments," says Griese. Incidentally, he wrote his master's thesis on libertarian immigration policies and interviewed activists from the libertarian movement in the United States.

In a day and age when more and more young people are aligning themselves with either the radical left or radical right, it is heartening to know that there are also young people who are willing to fight for freedom and capitalism.

August 2023
Stockholm, Sweden

For decades, the production and sale of alcohol was heavily regulated by the state in Sweden. When it came to beer, for example, the state prescribed a maximum limit of around 3 percent alcohol by volume – anyone who wanted to drink stronger beer had to buy it on prescription from a pharmacy and, even then, the beer's strength was limited by the state. These regulations were only abolished when Sweden joined the EU on January 1, 1995. In 2010, a now well-known brewery, Omnipollo, was founded, and it has gone on to become famous for its imaginative beercan designs, among other things. This story was related by Mattias Svensson from the renowned newspaper *Svenska Dagbladet* at the launch of the Swedish edition of my book, *In Defence of Capitalism*.

I have been invited to Stockholm by my friend Anders Ydstedt. Anders is an entrepreneur and investor and, together with his wife Susanne, owns or co-owns several companies in industries as diverse as online services, cleantech investments, and public restrooms in train stations. He is also a board member of Godsinlösen Nordic, a listed company on Nasdaq First North in Stockholm.

In addition, Anders advises large Swedish industrial companies and business organizations on behalf of the consulting firm Scantech Strategy Advisors. And there is something else Anders is rightly proud of: he worked for the Confederation of Swedish Enterprise on its campaigns to abolish the country's inheritance and wealth taxes. These campaigns were successful and, in 2004, every party in the Swedish parliament, from communists to conservatives, voted in favor of abolishing inheritance tax. After these reforms, successful entrepreneurs no longer felt the need to leave Sweden. They stayed in the country, continued to develop their companies, and invested in start-ups. This gave rise to several Swedish unicorns, such as Spotify and Klarna.

Anders is an enthusiastic champion of capitalism, private property, and low taxes. He has even published several books on these topics. In 2012, he bought the magazine and publishing house *Svensk Tidskrift* and developed it into a think tank that is now part of the Atlas Network. Anders is also a member of the Mont Pelerin Society.

He published my book, *The Rich in Public Opinion,* in Swedish, and this book has, as he says, influenced the tax debate in Sweden. There are forces in Sweden – as in other countries – that want to further increase what are already high taxes on the "rich." In the book, however, I show, based on a survey conducted in several countries, that social envy in Sweden and support for higher taxes are significantly lower than in Germany and France, for example.

My survey on the image of the market economy and capitalism, conducted by the opinion research institute Ipsos MORI, also confirmed that Sweden is among the countries with the most pronounced pro-market attitudes. In only six out of a total of 35 countries is support for the market economy stronger (the pro/anti-market economy coefficient for Sweden is 1.21). In questions that explicitly used the term capitalism, approval drops. But, even then, there are only nine countries that have a more positive attitude toward capitalism than Sweden, compared with 25 in which attitudes are more negative (Sweden's pro/anti-capitalism coefficient is 0.97).

If Sweden was once a socialist country, that was several decades ago. But just as people find it difficult to shrug off an established image long after it no longer holds true, so too do nations. We are generally very slow to adjust our familiar image of a nation.

To be clear: Sweden is not a socialist country today. In the Heritage Foundation's annual ranking of the world's most economically free countries, Sweden is one of the ten most market-oriented economies.[240] In tenth place in the *2023 Index of Economic Freedom*, Sweden is well ahead of the United States (25th place). The extent of its progress in the rankings is particularly

---

240 Heritage Foundation, *2023 Index of Economic Freedom*, 342–343.

remarkable: Sweden has gained 16 points over the past 28 years – from 61.4 points in 1995 to 77.5 points in 2023.[241] Only a small handful of countries, including Vietnam and Poland, have seen a slightly greater increase in economic freedom. By comparison, the United States lost six points in the same period and is now well behind Sweden, on 70.6 points.

Nonetheless, anyone who looks for features of socialism in Sweden will find them. Swedish government spending is still high, amounting to 49.6 percent of gross domestic product in the years 2020 to 2022. And while the tax burden in Sweden is nowhere near as high as it once was, it is still almost the highest in the world at 42.6 percent of domestic income. The top tax rate for individuals is still high at 57 percent and the top tax rate for businesses is 20.6 percent. On the other hand, what many people don't know is that – unlike most countries – Sweden no longer has inheritance, gift, or wealth taxes, all of which have been abolished. However, the labor market is still far more heavily regulated than in a vast majority of other countries.[242]

So, there are still remnants of socialism in Sweden today, even though capitalist features have come to dominate. The socialist image of Sweden and other Scandinavian countries stems from the 1970s and 80s. The public sector absorbed all of Sweden's labor force growth between 1970 and 1984, with new jobs primarily in the social services sector.[243] As late as 1960, for every 100 Swedes who earned most of their income in the private sector, there were 38 who received their money from the state. Thirty years later, in 1990, that number had risen to 151.[244] During the same period, the number of people working in the private sector decreased from three million to 2.6 million, while the number of people receiving most of their money from the state grew from 1.1 million to 3.9 million.[245]

These radical socialist policies alienated even those who were sympathetic to the Swedish Social Democratic Party's project. Astrid Lindgren, the world-

241 Heritage Foundation, *2022 Index of Economic Freedom*, 402.
242 All figures taken from Heritage Foundation, *2022 Index of Economic Freedom*, 393.
243 Mehrtens, 91.
244 Lindbeck, *Experiment*, 1279.
245 Lindbeck, *Experiment*, 1279.

famous author of a raft of children's classics including the *Pippi Longstocking* series, is just one example. By the 1930s, she had become a supporter of the Social Democrats. But Lindgren was also hit by the high tax rates and vented her indignation by publishing a "tax fairy tale" in a leading Swedish daily newspaper, where she calculated that her earnings in 1976 had been subject to a 102 percent (!) marginal tax rate. And, contrary to what the title suggested, this was in real life, not just a fairy tale.

Pushback against socialist ideas increasingly gained momentum, and by the 1990s there was a comprehensive counter-movement that, without fundamentally questioning the Swedish model of high taxes and comprehensive welfare benefits, nevertheless eliminated many of its excesses. A tax reform in 1990/91 slashed taxes in all areas and later abolished inheritance, gift and wealth taxes. The number of billionaires in Sweden has risen sharply ever since. In his book, *It's Okay To Be Angry About Capitalism,* the left-wing US politician Bernie Sanders, who has mistakenly cited Sweden as a model for his flavor of "socialism," says there should not be a single billionaire in the United States.[246] He probably doesn't know that the number of billionaires in Sweden today – relative to population size – is significantly higher than in the United States.

The socialist period in Sweden did not last very long, roughly from 1970 to 1990. The period before that, from 1870 to 1970, was characterized by "decentralization and limited government," and during these years Sweden had one of the least regulated economies in Europe, as the Swedish economist Assar Lindbeck has shown.[247]

Adam Smith's book, *The Wealth of Nations*, published in 1776, has become famous all over the world. But eleven years earlier (1765), the Finnish-Swedish economist Anders Chydenius published a booklet, *Den nationella vinsten* (in English: *The National Gain*), which presented very similar thoughts to those contained in Smith's work. The Swedish book was very thin (36 pages) and not comparable to Smith's monumental text, but the central theses were identical. Chydenius explains that politicians lack the knowledge to recognize which

---

246 Sanders, 96–121.
247 Lindbeck, "Swedish Lessons for Post-Socialist Countries," 1.

businesses have the greatest chances of success. When government decisions favor a particular business, he argues, people are drawn to it who would otherwise engage in more productive activities elsewhere in the economy. He points out that parts of Sweden that had more free-market economic policies were also more successful economically at the time. Like Smith, Anders Chydenius advocated free trade and opposed excessive government regulation.

In a paper on "The evolution of the Swedish market model" published in 2023 in *Economic Affairs*,[248] the economists Nima Sanandaji, Victor Ström, Mouna Esmaeilzadeh and Saeid Esmaeilzadeh show that "Sweden historically pioneered many aspects of a modern market economy."[249] For example, Sweden hosted the world's first public company, which financed the Falun copper mine, which in turn supplied two-thirds of the world's copper production in the seventeenth century. The first known share in the Falun mine was awarded in 1288. Stock corporations are a cornerstone of modern capitalism, "and it is relevant in an account of the evolution of the Swedish market model to point out that the oldest known company with shares in the world has roots in the country," the four authors explain.[250]

Sweden was also the first country to allow women to pursue professions and own businesses. And both the first bank to issue credit notes and the first central bank were also established in Sweden. "This is again an example of how the Swedish market model has influenced the development of global economics."[251]

What are conditions like for entrepreneurs in Sweden today? I talk about this very subject with Staffan Salén, CEO of Salénia AB. He is on the list of the 100 richest Swedes and is particularly involved in the real estate sector (logistics and light industrial properties). He also regularly writes a pro-free-market column for the Swedish business newspaper, *Affärsvärlden*. Taxes for entrepreneurs are not as big a problem as one might think, he explains,

248 Sanandaji et al., 170.
249 Sanandaji et al., 170.
250 Sanandaji et al., 173.
251 Sanandaji et al., 174.

as corporate taxes are lower in Sweden than in most European countries, and the same applies to taxes on profit distributions. There are also many tax optimization options for companies to reduce their tax burdens. High income taxes are more burdensome. But the biggest problems, according to Salén, are the extremely long planning approval processes and excessive red tape. In Sweden, the green ideology has meant that obtaining planning and construction permits is becoming more and more time-consuming all the time. Sometimes, Salén says, a construction project can grind to a halt because a single protected species of bird has been found.

However, Salén believes that the influence of green ideologists in Sweden is now on the wane. Young people in particular are increasingly voting for conservative parties. My friend Anders Ydstedt confirms that hardly anyone in Sweden is interested in climate crusader Greta Thunberg any more. She was more popular in Germany, at least until she morphed from a climate activist into an anti-Israel activist.

The declining influence of the Greens and other left-wing ideologues in Sweden is, at least in part, due to the impact of the country's immigration policies. Sweden was once known as a peaceful country, but mass illegal immigration has caused significant problems. In September 2023 alone, the month after I was in Sweden, twelve people are killed in gang shootings.

Mustafa Panshiri was born in Afghanistan and came to Sweden at the age of eleven. He is a trained police officer and works as an integration coach in the country's problem neighborhoods. In an interview, he explains how children in the suburbs were now becoming killers: "As early as 2018, there were bombings and gang shootings in various parts of Sweden. It's always about the same things: territory, drugs, and money. But what is happening now is a new level of violence. Basically, there is an all-out war between two gangs. They are literally hunting each other's relatives down and murdering innocent family members in revenge killings. Boys between the ages of 10 and 13 are increasingly being recruited to carry out murders in Sweden – by puppet masters abroad."

Sweden's Prime Minister Ulf Kristersson blames "irresponsible immigration policies and failed integration" for the increasing violence. Panshiri agrees: "You just have to look at the list of perpetrators and victims; they are all immigrants. Sweden has welcomed two million people in the past twenty years, more per capita than almost any other country in Europe. We have had a problem with criminal gangs for a long time. Speaking openly about this has so far been very difficult. It has long been an off-limits subject. But this is how it is. And it's now clear to everyone."[252]

After my trip to Stockholm, I fly directly to Zurich with my girlfriend Jenna, who is accompanying me, as I am invited to speak at an event organized jointly by the Universities of Trier and Zurich, the "Culture in Economics and Finance Conference." I talk about the findings of my research into perceptions of the rich in 13 countries. This results in a collaboration with Professor Marc Oliver Rieger. He will help to analyze the results of my surveys on the image of capitalism in 35 countries and the image of the rich in 13 countries in more detail than I would have been able to on my own.

---

252 Fürsen, https://www.welt.de/politik/ausland/plus248145832/Schweden-Am-besten-waere-es-die-Einwanderung-komplett-zu-stoppen.html.

September 2023
Amsterdam, the Netherlands

In September 2023, I travel to Amsterdam for a few days to present the Dutch edition of my book, *In Defence of Capitalism*. It is supposed to be the middle-leg of a ten-day tour that begins in Berlin with a lecture at the Friedrich Naumann Foundation. The day after that, I give a lecture at the Saar Liberal Foundation in Saarbrücken. Then, the day after my return from Amsterdam, a lecture at the Global Ethic Institute in Tübingen is planned. I have spoken at both institutes several times in the past, and this time my film, *Poland: From Socialism to Prosperity*, will be shown.

My trip to the Netherlands does not get off to a good start. Even though I'm staying in one of the most expensive hotels in the city, I'm annoyed as soon as I check in. First, they give me a room that is way too noisy, then one that is cold because the heating doesn't work. And even after ordering my beloved milk four times, they don't bring me any and I have to go to the supermarket to buy it myself.

But this is just the beginning of a fruitless journey; things would soon get much worse. Contact with the publisher who released my book in the Netherlands is made through the Mises Institute in Amsterdam. I didn't know the publisher, but I trusted the institute. This turns out to be a mistake. Because, when I arrive in Amsterdam, I find that the foreword has been co-authored by Thierry Baudet, head of the far-right "Forum for Democracy" party in Amsterdam.

When I find out, I cancel my appearance at the book launch, especially as I am informed that Baudet is also due to be speaking there. I tell the publisher that I will return to Berlin immediately and blame my withdrawal on painful tendonitis in my shoulder, which is true. But I add: "Even regardless of that, I would not have appeared with Thierry Baudet today. I am a center-right libertarian and if I lived in the Netherlands, I would be a member of the VVD. Baudet is much further to the right than I am and in Germany, or any other country for that matter, I would never share a stage with someone who is so far to the right. I also disagree with his stance on the war in Ukraine – I think every libertarian has a duty to support the Ukraine ... In future editions, you should include a foreword written by Willem Cornax without any involvement from Baudet, as was originally agreed. Also, I do not want the interviews we did yesterday to be published."

I had given several interviews leading up to the book launch, but the media outlets agree to my request that they should not be published. The publisher also agrees that all subsequent editions of my book will be published without a foreword by Baudet. My books have appeared in more than 30 languages, but this is the first time anything like this has ever happened to me.

The Netherlands has lurched to the right. And this – as in other countries – is largely the result of a completely misguided immigration policy. Two months after my trip, this was confirmed by the results of new parliamentary elections, in which anti-Islam politician Geert Wilders's "Party for Freedom" (PVV) doubled its share of the vote compared to the last election and became the strongest party.

Although I did not complete my travel itinerary as planned, I still want to write something about the Netherlands in this chapter because – as always – I prepared intensively for the trip, looked into the country's history and economy, and had surveys conducted in the Netherlands.

In 2023, the renowned academic publisher Princeton University Press published a book entitled *Pioneers of Capitalism*, which makes it possible for the first time to understand how crucial a role the Netherlands played in the historical development of capitalism. It is a book about the history of the country, and the authors Maarten Prak and Jan Luiten van Zanden write: "The Netherlands was one of the forerunners in the emergence of capitalism."[253]

The Netherlands was one of the earliest and strongest capitalist countries. Its economic progressiveness was one reason why this small country (with a population of just two million at the time) rose to become the world's leading

253 Prak / Zanden, 2.

power and trading nation. In the seventeenth century, the Netherlands was "the leading economy in the world. During this period, Dutch ships dominated the world's seas and Dutch merchants spun an intercontinental commercial network in which grain, wine, spices, sugar, tobacco, porcelain, and humans were bought and sold. They developed new ways of doing business, the best known of which is the financing of commercial enterprises through the issuing of shares."[254]

The driving force behind the Netherlands' global expansion was not the state, but the first two joint stock companies in history, the Dutch East India Company (VOC), founded in 1602, and the Dutch West India Company (WIC).

The Netherlands has been one of the most economically free countries in the world ever since. In the *2023 Index of Economic Freedom*, which rates economic freedom in 176 countries, the Netherlands is in 8th place – far ahead of the U.S. (25th) and the UK (28th), which are often referred to as the birthplaces of capitalism. The Heritage Foundation, which compiles the *Index of Economic Freedom*, praises above all the strong "Rule of Law" in the Netherlands and the healthy state of "Government Finances." However, it awards negative ratings for "Government Spending" and the Netherlands' excessive "Tax Burden."[255]

From 2010 to late 2023, the Netherlands was ruled by Mark Rutte of the center-right VVD. It was Rutte who formulated the following classic liberal commitment: "The state must be small and strong, not a happiness-making machine that takes responsibility for people's entire lives out of their hands. People need to be able to be dynamic and be given the space to make something extraordinary out of their lives. The VVD fights for the elevation of the underclass; via good education and by not making people dependent on government, by helping them to stand on their own two feet. Happiness is found in people, not the state."[256]

254 Prak / Zanden, 200.
255 Heritage Foundation, *2023 Index of Economic Freedom*, 264–265.
256 Rutte, interview with Joost Oranje, *NRC Handelsblad*, 28 August 2008 https://web.archive.
org/web/20100106125843/http://www.nrc.nl/binnenland/article1965113.ece/Nederland_moet_
af_van_terreur_van_de_middelmaat.

From the perspective of libertarians in the Netherlands, however, Rutte is more of a social democrat. And it has to be said that the libertarian movement in the narrower sense is extremely weak in the Netherlands. There is one small party that advocates a negative income tax and the further liberalization of drug policy. In Amsterdam, I meet the party's leading candidate, Tom van Lamoen, who is also a member of parliament and parliamentary group leader of the *Amersfoort voor Vrijheid* party in the city of Amersfoort. He is above all a Bitcoin enthusiast, like many libertarians. On the topic of immigration, which is hotly debated in the Netherlands, he says that although he is, in principle, in favor of open borders, as long as the welfare state exists, this is not possible. I decide to keep in touch with him in the future.

Although the *Index of Economic Freedom* ranks the Netherlands as one of the most economically free countries in the world, capitalism and the market economy have a poorer image here than in almost any other country in the world. The survey on popular perceptions of the market economy and capitalism I commissioned Ipsos MORI to conduct in 35 countries showed that there are only seven countries in which capitalism is more firmly rejected than in the Netherlands.

And this is by no means only due to the word "capitalism" itself, which is anathema in the Netherlands. The survey also included several questions that deliberately avoided using the word capitalism and instead described a free-market system – without actually using the inflammatory word. The results were no better. On the contrary: in only two of the 35 countries, Russia and Bosnia-Herzegovina, were attitudes toward the market economy even worse than in the Netherlands!

According to the survey, higher earners and those who place themselves on the right of the political spectrum are quite indifferent toward the market economy and capitalism. In many other countries, high earners and those on the right are usually among the staunchest advocates of capitalism. All data from the Netherlands point in the same direction: the Dutch reject the market economy and capitalism. The statements that received the greatest support in the Netherlands were "Capitalism promotes selfishness and greed"

285

(44 percent) and "Capitalism leads to growing inequality" (41 percent). In contrast, the statement "Capitalism is an especially efficient economic system" received the least support (9 percent).

At the same time, the Netherlands has long been extraordinarily economically successful. At 73,000 euros, its GDP per capita in 2022 was higher than in Germany, Great Britain, France, Spain, Italy, and most other European countries. And in 2022, the Netherlands was the fourth strongest exporting nation in the world, ahead of Japan and South Korea![257] This is remarkable, especially considering that the Netherlands has only 17.5 million inhabitants – Germany, as the third largest exporting country, has five times more inhabitants, No. 1 China has 84 times more inhabitants, and the United States, at No. 2, has 20 times more inhabitants than the Netherlands.

From this example, it is clear just how long-lasting the impact of historical and economic traditions can be. Even though the Netherlands has long since ceased to be the world's leading economic power, there is no country of comparable size that exports as many goods all around the world – which is why it is also so appropriate that Europe's largest port is located here, in Rotterdam.

---

257 Urmersbach, "Die 20 größten Exportländer weltweit im Jahr 2022," https://de.statista.com/statistik/daten/studie/37013/umfrage/ranking-der-top-20-exportlaender-weltweit/

October 2023
Sofia, Bulgaria

A few days before I am due to leave for Bulgaria, Professor Oliver Pott invites me to a "mastermind" seminar at Weissensee Castle, where I meet a young German entrepreneur who has just moved from Berlin to Sofia. When I ask him why, the first thing he mentioned is taxes. In Bulgaria, companies and individuals pay 10 percent tax, regardless of how much they earn.

At the airport, I exchange euros for levs. For 100 euros you get around 200 levs. After numerous national bankruptcies in the twentieth century, the lev was pegged to the German mark at a ratio of 1:1 in 1999; today it is pegged to the euro. In the next few years, Bulgaria is expected to join the eurozone, but many Bulgarians are against the currency union because they are worried it will lead to price increases.

I have been invited to Bulgaria at the beginning of October by Krassen Stanchev. He is two years older than me and is a Professor of Public Choice and Macroeconomic Analysis at Sofia University, where he also teaches economic history. He is also CEO of the consulting firm KC 2 Ltd. and Chairman and Founder of IME, Bulgaria's first independent, free-market think tank. In 1990 and 1991, Stanchev was a member and committee chairman of the Bulgarian Constituent Assembly and one of the initiators of the reforms that led Bulgaria from a planned economy to a market economy.

His personal journey toward a libertarian worldview was shaped by various drastic experiences in the late 1960s and mid-1980s: "My classical liberal views of the world and, later on, my political involvement in promoting libertarian values in my country of Bulgaria and elsewhere, came first from life rather than from reading or education. I witnessed the invasion of Czechoslovakia in August 1968 first-hand and saw the suffocation of the longing for freedom through the Warsaw Pact and at the time, as a thirteen-year-old fan of international companies and rock music, I was shocked."

But the decisive experience for him was the Chernobyl reactor disaster in April 1986 and the way the communist system reacted: "It proved to the majority that no further evidence of the regime's antihuman nature was needed. I learned about the accident when lecturing at the Economic University (then called the Karl Marx Economic Institute) on resource scarcity and using examples from the energy sector. A student remonstrated and told the class I was talking 'complete bullshit'; the BBC had reported on a terrifying accident at a Soviet nuclear plant. I ended the lecture and rushed to check the news by changing the radio-waves from East to West. Everywhere except for Bulgaria and the Soviet Union the public was getting sufficient information on what had happened and how to avoid the risks of radiation exposure. My wife was pregnant at the time. I took the government's deliberate misinformation as a personal insult and decided to do everything I could to dismantle this antihuman system."

After the collapse of socialism, Stanchev became involved in environmental issues: "As one of the few activists with knowledge of comparative environment law, I was invited to take part in the first post-Communist constitutional elections in June of 1990, to chair the environmental protection committee. I won in the largest electoral district, drafted the environmental law, and took part in legislating taxation, privatization, restitution of expropriated rights, and the liberalization of markets."

And yes, environmental standards improved significantly in Bulgaria after the end of socialism. That's why Stanchev doesn't understand the EU's "Green New Deal," which he sees as yet another attempt to solve problems using a planned economy – something that has always failed everywhere it has ever been tried.

Older Bulgarian intellectuals like Stanchev are often anti-communist and pro-capitalist. But their younger compatriots learn little about the history of socialism in school. I conduct several interviews in Sofia, including with Ludmilla Dimova, a well-known journalist. She is my age and says: "When you are older, like us, you have been cured of Marxism. But young Bulgarians who have studied in Europe or the United States are coming back and enthusiastically writing papers on Marxist theory here."

There has been no real coming to terms with Bulgaria's communist past. Here are some facts: on September 9, 1944, the Bulgarian Communist Party overthrew the government in a military coup. The day before, the Soviet army had invaded Bulgaria. The new, communist government began to exercise its power with total terror. "In the first few days and weeks, around 30,000 people were murdered by so-called 'troikas' (execution squads) made up of Communist Party activists and amnestied criminals, without any 'legal formalities' such as charges or court verdicts."[258]

A "People's Tribunal" issued a total of 9,550 judgments in 135 trials: 2,730 people were condemned to death and 305 were sentenced to life imprisonment. Around 200 of those facing death sentences were killed before their cases even reached trial. More than 200 businesses were expropriated, as were a large number of properties and possessions, and 4,325 families of relatives of convicts were displaced, totaling almost 12,000 people.[259]

Shortly after they seized power, the communists set up a network of prison camps modeled on the Soviet Gulag system. Between 1945 and 1962, there were dozens of forced labor camps (TWOs) and forced labor "work groups."[260] Tens of thousands of Bulgarians were forced to labor under the most difficult conditions for decades. Many died or suffered throughout their lives as a result of torture, starvation, and forced labor.[261]

The new government ordered the abolition of private property and immediately began to nationalize industry, commerce and banking, and to collectivize agriculture. Just a few years later, the communists proudly

---

258 Raichevsky, 13.
259 Memory 1944–1989, https://pametbg.com/index.php/de/ and https://pametbg.com/index.php/en/.
260 Raichevsky, 261.
261 Raichevsky, 256.

declared that not a single private enterprise now existed in industry, crafts, finance, trade or services.[262]

First, the government introduced a "one-off tax on real estate and other assets," which amounted to one third of the value of the property. In a second phase, the properties were expropriated under a new Bill for Large Urban Properties. "The reprisals against the owners did not end with the expropriation of their property. Forced relocations followed, some owners were interned in labor camps, and their descendants had to write in their official biographies that their parents had been subjected to 'measures of the people's rule.'"[263]

Preparations for the process of nationalization were conducted in absolute secrecy. On the day of the expropriations, representatives of the Communist Party gathered in the early hours. All across the nation, groups of these representatives suddenly appeared on businesses' doorsteps at 10:30 a.m. to tell the owners of each business that their company had been expropriated. The communists seized the keys to the business's safe and locked the account books away. The owner was then forced to hand over the keys to the company's cash register and to his office, and made to sign a general statement confirming that he had submitted his business to the "people's government" before being allowed to pick up his coat and walk out. Once this had all happened, the factory loudspeakers announced that the decision of the communist party and the government to expropriate this particular business had been carried through.

Not only were owners removed from their companies, they also lost their working capital, bank deposits, and financial investments, as well as most of their personal property, houses, jewelry, cars and other belongings. The communists declared the owners of villas to be "enemies of the people" and seized their properties. These were then given to Communist Party officials or their representatives and employees.[264]

---

262 Raichevsky, 15.
263 Raichevsky, 201.
264 Raichevsky, 211.

In this way, 6,100 companies were nationalized in Bulgaria in a matter of hours.[265] As the historian Stoyan Raichevsky explains in his book on Bulgaria under communist rule: "Most of them were well-established small, medium and large-sized enterprises, textile, chemical, leather, canning factories, etc. They had survived the war and were successfully exporting their products on the world market. Once they had been nationalized, they no longer had a future."[266]

Having removed all of the directors and engineers from these businesses, the communists now replaced them with "progressive" technicians who were unqualified for such tasks but loyal to the communist regime. Anyone with the right disposition, but lacking in higher education, was legally treated on an equal footing with people who had gained a higher education.[267]

The new regime was by no means the paradise the workers had been promised – quite the opposite. Wages were the lowest in Europe. Technology and production processes became increasingly outdated and, after the end of socialism, it was clear that they were in no way competitive. Thus, after the system change, production fell massively and many people became unemployed. Decades of socialism had ruined Bulgaria.

As socialism collapsed in the Soviet Union and the other socialist states, there was also a change in Bulgaria. The Communist Party, which had renamed itself "Socialists," won the 1990 elections. The political and economic elite initially remained almost unchanged. Members of the former state security service took over large sections of the economy. They often joined up with organized criminals. Between 1996 and 2008, around 300 members of the Bulgarian mafia – including a number of politicians – killed each other.[268]

Simeon Djankov, deputy prime minister and finance minister from 2009 to 2013, writes: "The biggest mistake in Bulgaria's transition process was the failure to adopt a lustration law for members of the former secret police in

265 Raichevsky, 206–207.
266 Raichevsky, 207–208.
267 Raichevsky, 213.
268 Djankov, 137.

the first years of the transition."[269] Lustration laws were introduced in other Eastern European countries, but in Bulgaria the members of the former secret police were able to take over large parts of the political apparatus and the economy.

There has been very little discussion of the communist past and young people's knowledge of this period is scant, to say the least, as a survey conducted in 2014 showed: "Done by Alpha Research, arguably the most reliable polling agency in the country, the survey – done among 1,200 Bulgarians aged over 16 – found that the collective memory of Bulgaria under communism had gradually faded away and knowledge of the period was disappearing.

The survey found that 94 percent of people aged 16-30 knew extremely little about this time, and 40 percent could not identify whether the end of communism was marked by the fall of the Berlin Wall or walls in Moscow, Sofia, or China; 92 percent knew neither the effective, nor the metaphorical borders of the former communist bloc …

It would be an overstatement to say that Bulgaria wholly neglects its recent past, although it also would be true to say that a Bulgarian school pupil in the first decades of the 21st century would likely know more about the 7th to 11th century First Bulgarian Kingdom or the 1876 failed April Uprising against the Ottoman Empire than about the realities of the 20th century lives of his parents or grandparents."[270]

The first decades after the end of socialism saw continuous changes of governments, which often did not stay in power for more than a year. Paradoxically, this also had a positive side, because corrupt structures entrenched over years or even decades are even worse than instability.[271] Governments that implemented economic reforms were replaced by others that partially reversed these reforms, only to be replaced by yet others that restarted reform efforts.[272]

---

269 Djankov, 144.
270 Leviev-Sawyer, 135.
271 Åslund, *How Capitalism was Built*, 272–273.
272 Djankov, 136-146.

Despite all this, the bottom line is that some very positive reforms have been implemented. As mentioned, Bulgaria has a flat tax of only 10 percent, so it has a dream score of 93.7 out of 100 points in the *2023 Index of Economic Freedom's* "Tax Burden" category. The ratings for "Property Rights" and "Fiscal Health" are also positive, although there are significant deficits in the area of "Government Integrity." Overall, Bulgaria now ranks 32nd in the *Index of Economic Freedom* – having gained 19.3 points between 1995 and 2023.[273]

Although Bulgaria has experienced economic growth over the past 20 years, many Bulgarians have left their homeland and emigrated to Germany, Spain and Italy, where the standard of living is higher. The population has shrunk from almost nine million to just 6.5 million, but the decline has now slowed.

Overall, it is fair to say that developments in Bulgaria place the country somewhere in the middle between successful former socialist countries – Poland and the Czech Republic – and catastrophic Russia and the former Yugoslavia. The same can be said of Bulgarians' attitudes to economic freedom and capitalism. With a pro-anti-capitalism coefficient of 0.84, Bulgaria occupies the middle ground between the group of very pro-capitalist countries (Poland and the Czech Republic, for example) and the group of staunchly anti-capitalist countries (Russia and the successor states of Yugoslavia). In my study of the image of capitalism, 16 countries are more pro-capitalist than Bulgaria, as opposed to 18 countries that have more negative attitudes.

But pro- or anti-capitalism is not the topic that most concerned the Bulgarians I meet in Sofia. They are far more concerned about attitudes towards Russia, which are really dividing the country. Bulgaria's leader is President Rumen Radev, who is strongly pro-Russian. His critics say he has been bought by the Russians. The socialists and the right-wing extremist *Vasrashdane* party are also pro-Russian. However, Prime Minister Nikolai Denkov, a physics professor who was elected in 2023, is resolutely anti-Russian and pro-Ukraine. This issue is currently dividing Bulgarian society.

On a personal level, my trip to Bulgaria is a success: I have many interviews

273 Heritage Foundation, *2023 Index of Economic Freedom*, 74–75 and 398.

with media and television channels, plus lectures at the NBU New Bulgaria University and the Saint Clement of Ohrid University. I am really impressed by a sweeping, very peaceful, and well-kept park near my hotel. Hundreds of people go there to relax, and there are plenty of children's playgrounds, none of which have any traces of vandalism. The contrast to my hometown of Berlin, where many parks have become drug dealing hotspots, is striking. Apparently, even a country that only taxes its citizens 10 percent can afford to maintain attractive public amenities.

October 2023
Tirana, Albania

Albania is an increasingly popular tourist destination. In 2022, 7.5 million holidaymakers visited the small country, which is home to just 2.8 million people, and the numbers continue to rise. The Mediterranean weather and low prices make the southern European coastal state extremely attractive. In mid-October 2023, I am visiting Albania for the second time, this time to promote the Albanian edition of my book, *In Defence of Capitalism*. As the rain falls in Germany and the temperature in Berlin hovers between 52 to 58°F, Tirana is a sunny 77°F.

I want to launch the book in the former house of the dictator Enver Hoxha, but it is currently being renovated. So the presentation takes place in a museum that documents the atrocities of the communist security service, the Museum of Secret Surveillance. One wall is covered from top to bottom with names in small print – the names of all the political prisoners who were killed because they opposed Hoxha's dictatorship.

I am filmed for some scenes that will appear on Albanian television and conduct an interview about my book in front of a building that looks like a pyramid. In the years immediately after Hoxha's death, it served as a museum in honor of the dictator. Today it is an IT hub.

As I sign copies of my book, one reader spells out: "Please sign it to Marenglen." Marenglen is short for Marx-Engels-Lenin, a popular first name in Albania during the socialist era. When I post this on Facebook, some people ask whether I am joking. No, if you Google Marenglen, you'll see just how common a name it is in Albania.

Adri Nurellari, whom I met during my previous visit to Tirana, picks my girlfriend Trang and me up at the airport. In the short time since I was last in Albania, things look very different. A lot of high-rise buildings have been built, some as office complexes, others for a range of different purposes. Many of them were probably financed with the profits from the drug trade, Adri notes. There are currently around 40,000 vacant apartments in Albania – most of which are used to launder money from the criminal drug trade (one of the most important "economic sectors" in the country).

David Hudhri, my publisher in Albania, says that recently cameras were installed all over the city, and most people thought they were state surveillance cameras or set up by the police. In fact, they belonged to drug lords, who used them to monitor what the police were doing across the city.

The Marriott Hotel that Trang has chosen didn't even exist when I was in Tirana a year earlier. It's much better than the old-fashioned Xheko Imperial Hotel I stayed in last time. And at a sensationally low price. We pay 600 euros for a spacious suite on the nineteenth floor for four days. There's a soccer match right outside our hotel, Albania versus the Czech Republic – we can see the European Championship qualifier in the huge stadium from our window. Unfortunately, I'm not a soccer fan, otherwise I would have enjoyed watching the match live and free of charge from my hotel suite. Albania wins 3:0 and there is great joy everywhere.

The streets are decorated with flags of the European Union and the United States. A high-level meeting of the "Berlin Process" is due to take place a few days from now. The Berlin Process was launched in 2014 as a platform for cooperation between high-ranking representatives of the Western Balkan states, nine EU countries (Austria, Bulgaria, Croatia, France, Germany, Greece, Italy, Slovenia, and Poland), and the UK. This year, high-ranking representatives from Spain, Hungary, Romania and the Netherlands, will be attending. EU institutions, international financial institutions, and companies from the region are also involved in the process. Albania is aiming to become a member of the EU, and in none of the potential accession countries is approval of the EU as high as in Albania.

Adri invites us to a vegetarian restaurant as soon as we arrive. Albania is famous for its excellent food, which is also available at sensationally low prices. As pizza is a popular "currency," I often compare the price of a pizza in different countries: in Albania, a pizza costs three dollars.

Over dinner, Adri explains that without the EU, there is no prospect of progress toward democracy, rule of law, and a market economy in Albania. He says this even though he is aware of the EU's many failings. But especially in a country like Albania, where there are hardly any traditions of democracy, rule of law, or a market economy, it is hardly possible to move in this direction without outside help. The power of the elites, who have essentially remained the same for decades, is too strong. Corruption and nepotism are so widespread that Adri believes the best way to make progress is through massive pressure from the EU. However, the examples of Bulgaria and Romania have shown that even EU membership will by no means automatically solve these problems, he concedes. After its experiences with Bulgaria and Romania, the EU has again raised the hurdles for admission.

The population of Albania is strongly pro-Western. "We compete with the Poles for the title of the most pro-American country in Europe," says Adri. I think people in Albania are even more pro-American than the people of the United States itself. Adri is also staunchly pro-American. Before our trip, I was worried whether he would be able to find time for me at all, because Serbia had amassed large numbers of troops on the border with Kosovo and the outbreak of a new war seemed imminent. Adri, who is Albanian but has been politically active in Kosovo for years, believes that the Russians and Serbs wanted to test whether the West was really prepared to defend Kosovo. The EU had – as always – reacted hesitantly and weakly, but the United States had sent a strong and clear signal to Belgrade that no aggression would be tolerated.

According to Adri, the Americans have also been instrumental in reforming the judicial system in Albania in recent years. What gives hope to most Albanians, however, is perceived as a threat by the elites, as they worry about losing some of their power if Albania opens up to the outside world and an independent judiciary emerges. Because of the population's strong support for EU membership, the Albanian government is also in favor of accession, but in fact, in Adri's opinion, it is hindering the process of rapprochement with the European Union.

In Tirana, I meet Sali Berisha, two days before his 79th birthday. He is Albania's highest-profile politician and was the founder and long-time leader of the Democratic Party of Albania (PD). He was Prime Minister of Albania between 2005 and 2013, but was defeated by the former mayor of Tirana, Edi Rama, in 2013.

Berisha, who comes from a simple farming family, studied medicine in Paris and later became a renowned cardiologist. He proudly tells me about his research, which has even been reported in respected medical journals in France and the UK. As a doctor during the dictatorship, he had seen that most people in Albania were severely malnourished because they lacked essential amino acids as a result of inadequate food and protein intake. "In 1989, a television crew even came to me to do an interview on this topic, but later everything critical was cut out and only a few seconds of me being very nervous were shown."

People were so poor back then that many kept a pig in their cramped apartments to at least have something to eat. As this was forbidden, they invented "operations" so that the pig could no longer grunt and alert neighbors to the illegal roommate next door. "Back then, almost everyone in Albania was starving."

After the death of dictator Enver Hoxha, Ramiz Alia stepped in as his political heir and took over the leadership of the party in 1985. "That was the same year that Gorbachev took over the leadership of the party in the Soviet Union, and some initially hoped that Alia could become an Albanian Gorbachev," explains Berisha. "But on the first anniversary of Hoxha's death, on April 11, 1986, I saw Alia kissing Hoxha's gravestone – and that was a clear signal to me that he would not become an Albanian Gorbachev."

Berisha takes a critical view of the situation in Albania today. "Albania is a drug state. The government is closely intertwined with international organized crime, all the way to drug cartels in Mexico. I call the system today a 'mobocracy,' rule by the mob and criminal gangs." When the codes of encrypted cell phones owned by criminals were recently broken by the French, it turned out that the second most common language used to communicate was Albanian.

Berisha's critics accuse him of being equally corrupt. And just three months after I met him, Berisha is indeed arrested for corruption and placed under house arrest.

For many, Albania is a country firmly in the grip of organized crime, and it doesn't seem to make much difference which of the two parties is in power.

Again and again, Adri and I discuss the best ways to free a country from the clutches of organized criminals. In Albania, I often hear that the country is ruled by mobs of gangsters. I meet Ismail Kadare, by far the most famous Albanian writer. He is one of the most influential European authors and intellectuals of the twentieth century and a major literary voice against totalitarianism. When I ask him what he would change in Albania, he replies that he would first throw a number of government officials into prison.

The 87-year-old lived in Paris for three decades and I want to know what he thinks of the intellectuals there. He says he was an outsider because of his pro-American stance. Many French intellectuals admired Stalin and Mao, such as Jean-Paul Sartre, who once refused to attend a meeting because Kadare was also going to be there. The conversation with Kadare is difficult, probably because of his age and because he has just conducted a long and exhausting interview with a French daily newspaper.

I also had the survey on the image of capitalism conducted in Albania. It is among the group of countries in which capitalism has a negative image, with similar responses to Serbia, Greece, France and Spain. The image of capitalism is poor across all social and age groups, although among younger Albanians and higher earners, the image is not quite as negative as among older respondents and those on low incomes.

And this negativity is not only due to the word "capitalism" itself. Even when the word was not used, support for anti-market statements (for example, that the state should set prices for rent and food) is higher than for pro-market statements. The terms that Albanians most often associate with capitalism are "greed" and "corruption" (tied on 83 percent each) and indeed corruption is very high in Albania – it ranks 101st out of 180 in Transparency International's Corruption Perceptions Index.

Albanians also associate the term "capitalism" with inequality, hunger and poverty. In contrast, not even one in ten Albanians (9 percent) agree with the statement: "Capitalism is irreplaceable; past attempts to replace capitalism have always resulted in dictatorships and suffering." And only one in ten (11 percent) say: "Capitalism may not be ideal, but it is still better than all other economic systems." This is astonishing for a country that was the poorest in Europe under the Stalinist dictatorship of Enver Hoxha.

November 2023
Bogotá and Medellín, Colombia

Christopher Columbus, after whom Colombia is named, never actually set foot in the country. It was discovered in 1499 by Alonso De Ojeda and Amerigo Vespucci.

In November 2023, I visit the country for the first time. With 51 million inhabitants, Colombia is the fourth largest economy in Latin America. Colombia borders Venezuela, Brazil, Peru, and Ecuador. Over 80 percent of the people live in cities. My first ports of call are the capital Bogotá, which has almost eight million inhabitants, and the second largest city Medellín (2.6 million inhabitants), which has gained questionable notoriety due to the drug cartel named after it.

I don't know all that much about the country – except that it has been suffering from drug-related crime and left-wing terror for decades. Before my trip, I heard a lot about how dangerous it can be in Colombia and that you can even be "kidnapped" for a short time and robbed of your credit card in normal airport cabs – or that you can be drugged with knockout drops.

Colombians have not gotten used to the high crime rate either. When I ask Ana Milena, a beautiful 25-year-old woman who works for a member of parliament in Bogotá and is active in the libertarian movement, what she sees as the biggest problem in the country, she doesn't mention – the way libertarians in other countries do – excessive high taxes or overbearing government regulation, but the high crime rate.

Omnipresent crime leads to omnipresent mistrust, even in very small ways. In Bogotá, for the first time in my life, when I ask the hotel to lend me an umbrella, they say they will only do so if I leave my passport as a deposit. The reason: so many umbrellas are stolen. At the hotel in Medellín, you can only get a massage if you show your ID (reason: otherwise they can't really know if I'm who I say I am) and you have to sign several documents before and after the massage. Even in such an upscale hotel, hairdryers are only available on request, apparently for fear of theft.

But, of course, there is another Colombia that you don't hear much about. On the first day, I have interviews with the leading business newspaper *La República*, as well as with *Forbes Colombia*, and both journalists are very well read and extremely well-prepared business experts. On the third day, we drive to the Universidad de la Sabana, a private university founded by Opus Dei. It's an impressive university campus with lots of greenery and tasteful architecture, and no graffiti or vandalism of the kind you often see at German universities.

There are also libertarian initiatives in Colombia, such as *El Bastiòn*, a regional newspaper that I have written for before through Joanna Gabriela Guerra (who is also accompanying me on my Latin America tour this time). In the early evening of the first day, I have a book presentation at *Escuela Libertad*, a libertarian think tank that focuses on teaching young people about the market economy. The event's participants are mostly around 20 years of age, and although English is not normally a good language to use in Latin America, I am surprised that no-one seems to need my words to be translated into Spanish here. In contrast, even in my hotel, Tequendama (supposedly one of the best in Bogotá, but I doubt it), the staff have considerable problems with English.

In the evening, I am invited to dinner at the home of Eduardo Salazar Yusti. An impressive villa that looks more like an art gallery. Here, too, you are reminded of the omnipresent dangers, as the villa is surrounded by a wall and protected by security guards. Eduardo made his money with a strategic management consultancy firm. He recently set up a private equity fund that invests in the United States. That evening, I get to know the proverbial hospitality of the South Americans, Eduardo has invited a musician, and there is a vegetarian meal especially for me. And politically, the guests he has invited are on the same wavelength: Latin America also needs more capitalism.

I would like to add: Above all, Colombia also needs a different drugs policy. Nowhere is it clearer than here that the fight against drugs has failed. In no other country has the United States tried so hard to fight the drug cartels – but to no avail. Bloomberg reported in 2023 that cocaine was set to overtake oil and become Colombia's main export. According to the report, production of the narcotic has continued to expand, while oil exports have recently declined. In 2022, the country is said to have exported drugs worth the equivalent of around 18.2 billion dollars, while oil exports at the time amounted to around 19.1 billion dollars.[274]

For decades, since President Richard Nixon was in office, the U.S. tried to stop the production of cocaine in the country between the Caribbean and the Andes. The Americans spent billions of dollars on military operations, small farmers were sent to prison, and the herbicide glyphosate was sprayed from airplanes onto fields in the rainforest. But all these efforts have failed. A large proportion of the cocaine sold around the world today comes from Colombia.[275]

There have always been proposals in favor of legalizing drugs in Colombia. César Gaviria was president of the country from 1990 to 1994. After his term of office, Gaviria became one of the leading advocates of global drug policy reforms. He called for some drugs to be regulated and decriminalized in order to solve the problems associated with the drug trade. Alejandro Gaviria was Minister of Health and Social Protection in Colombia between 2012 and 2015. In the early 2000s, he campaigned for the decriminalization of drugs. Sergio Fajardo was Mayor of Medellín from 2004 to 2007 and then Governor of Antioquia from 2012 to 2015. In 2022, his government's plans included the legalization of drugs. Juan Manuel Santos was President of Colombia from 2010 to 2018. During his presidency, Santos made considerable efforts to combat the drug problem. Although he did not explicitly support the full legalization of drugs, Santos did advocate more pragmatic approaches.

However, none of these initiatives were successful, and it was not these

---

274 Medina, https://www.bloomberg.com/news/articles/2023-09-14/cocaine-is-set-to-overtake-oil-to-become-colombia-s-main-export.
275 Buschschlüter, https://www.bbc.com/news/world-latin-america-66784678.

initiatives that gained notoriety, but the drug lords who lived off the trade's illegality, like the well-known drug lord Pablo Escobar, also known as "el patrón." Escobar started out as a petty criminal in Medellín, Colombia's second largest city. At the height of his power, he had an entire cocaine processing factory with 1,000 employees built, which he called *Transquilandia*. The result was a network of criminal enterprises that went down in history as the "Medellín Cartel." It fought a war with the "Cali Cartel" for supremacy in the drugs business, a war that was fought with firearms and car bombs on the streets of Colombia's cities.

Escobar tried to portray himself as a modern-day Robin Hood who redistributed the money of the rich – including many clients from the United States. For many years, his office as a member of Congress protected him from prosecution.[276] After an assassination attempt on Justice Minister Rodrigo Lara Bonilla in 1984, Escobar – suspected of being the mastermind – was stripped of his mandate as a member of parliament and fled to Nicaragua, which was ruled by the socialist Sandinistas. He then returned to Colombia and began a veritable war against the state, in which he is said to have been supported by the extreme left-wing terrorist group M-19.[277]

The situation became increasingly absurd, as Escobar negotiated with the government on the terms of his "surrender." He was allowed to build his own "prison" on a hill above Medellín. It was essentially a luxury palace for him and other drug lords, complete with a soccer pitch, sauna, swimming pool, and disco. He ran the drug business from his lofty perch.[278] The story ended with Escobar shot dead in December 1993 while fleeing across a rooftop. The Medellín Cartel was thus considered to have been broken up. The Cali Cartel was also put out of business. Although no such dominant centralized criminal organizations emerged after that, a large number of criminal and terrorist gangs continued to dominate the drug trade, including the Marxist terrorist organization FARC and its no

---

276 Specht, 81.
277 Specht, 82.
278 Specht, 82–83.

less violent offshoots. Forbes reported in 2015 that FARC had an estimated annual turnover of 600 million dollars.[279]

Founded in the mid-1960s, the Fuerzas Armadas Revolucionarias de Colombia – Ejército del Pueblo (FARC-EP or FARC) is a Marxist–Leninist guerrilla group. It was founded as the armed wing of the Partido Communista de Colombia (PCC).[280] FARC finances itself through kidnappings and ransoms, illegal mining, extortion, and the production and distribution of illegal drugs.

In 2000, FARC's "Law 002" stipulated that every Colombian with assets of more than one million dollars would have to pay a "revolutionary tax" of between 10 and 30 percent on their assets to avoid being kidnapped – the tax percentage depended on the actual (estimated) assets. Kidnappings were used to exert pressure and force people to pay this "tax." In the summer of 2008, FARC rebels held between 700 and 1,000 hostages and demanded high ransoms for their captives. The hostage aid organization *País Libre* (Free Country), founded by Colombia's Vice President Francisco Santos, estimated that 472 people had been kidnapped.[281]

Colombia has suffered under the terror of left-wing extremist guerrilla groups for more than 50 years. Over 450,000 people have died in the fighting between left-wing and right-wing extremist groups and government forces, and more than eight million have been displaced.[282] In 2016, the government agreed a peace treaty with FARC that would grant extensive amnesties to the terrorists and set up expensive reintegration programs. In particular, the fact that the guerrilla leaders would not be sent to prison for their crimes and would be allowed to move into politics, for example as members of Congress, met with massive criticism.[283]

---

279 Carafano, https://www.forbes.com/pictures/gkll45fk/3-farc-annual-turnover-6/?sh=65944f65413c.
280 Graaf, 18.
281 Alsema, https://colombiareports.com/farc-has-472-hostages-pais-libre/.
282 Auswärtiges Amt, https://www.auswaertiges-amt.de/de/service/laender/kolumbien-node/politisches-portraet/212762#:~:text=Nach percent20starkem percent20Wachstum percent20stagnierte percent20die,Land percent20allerdings percent20vor percent20gro percentC3 percent9Fe percent20Herausforderungen.
283 Graaf, 26.

In a referendum, a narrow majority of Colombians rejected the agreement, which was subsequently renegotiated and then signed without a referendum. The Marxist terrorist group never had a majority of the population on its side. On the contrary, there were repeated protests against FARC, such as in February 2008, when 1.5 million Colombians took part in demonstrations against the Marxist terrorists in Bogotá alone. People also took to the streets against FARC in 45 other cities all across Colombia. The fact that the left-wing Fuerza Alternativa Revolucionaria party, which emerged from FARC after the peace treaty was signed, only won 0.2 and 0.3 percent of the vote in the 2018 and 2022 parliamentary elections for the Senate and Chamber of Deputies shows just how little support FARC enjoyed among the population as a whole. The only reasons FARC still has five deputies in each of the country's two chambers of government are the provisions of the peace treaty.[284] In addition to FARC, another left-wing extremist group, ELN, has played and continues to play an important role.

Terror continues even after the peace agreement. For example, on January 17, 2019, at least 21 people were killed in an attack attributed to ELN at the General Santander police academy in the south of the capital Bogotá when a car loaded with explosives was driven onto the school grounds. Not for the first time, President Iván Duque was left with little choice but to break off all talks with ELN.

In February 2024, the Colombian government began new peace talks with renegade FARC fighters. An eleven-point document signed by both sides announced the start of talks aimed at concluding a peace agreement between the Colombian government and the armed rebel organization Segunda Marquetalia, a group of former FARC members led by the guerrilla's former number two in command, Iván Márquez.[285]

As far as Colombia's economy is concerned, the *Index of Economic Freedom* ranks Colombia 62nd in the world in terms of economic freedom,

284 FAZ, "Kolumbien," https://www.faz.net/aktuell/politik/ausland/kolumbien-wahldebakel-fuer-partei-der-frueheren-farc-guerilla-15489505.html.
285 Junge Welt, https://www.jungewelt.de/artikel/469651.lateinamerika-kolumbien-verhandelt-mit-farc-guerilla.html.

well behind Chile (22nd) and Uruguay (27th), but ahead of Argentina (144th) and Venezuela (174th). In 2022, Gustavo Petro from the left-wing electoral alliance Pacto Histórico was the first left-wing president to be elected in the country's history. This put Colombia in line with the trend in Latin America, as many other countries, including Brazil, Chile, Peru and of course Venezuela, are governed by socialists.

In Medellín, I meet the journalist Christian Del Toro, who interviews me for the media outlets *El Bastión*, *Al Poniente*, and *Revista Alternativa*. I ask him for examples of Petro's socialist agenda. Del Toro first mentions tax policy. Petro has increased taxes for "high earners" who earn more than ten million pesos (around 2,150 dollars) per month. Profits from sales and inheritances are no longer taxed at 10 percent, but at 15 percent. And anyone who has assets of more than three billion pesos (around 660,000 dollars) has to pay a wealth tax of 0.5 percent. From five billion pesos (approx. 1.1 million dollars) the tax rate increases to 1 percent and from ten billion (approx. 2.2 million dollars) it rises to 1.5 percent. The tax on corporate dividends has also been increased to between 15 and 20 percent.[286]

But that's not all. A punitive tax has also been introduced on certain foods that are classified as fattening or otherwise harmful to health. The country that supplies the world with cocaine is now cracking down on sweetened drinks and foods that are high in salt and fat. The tax on such products is being progressively hiked from 10 percent (2023) to 15 percent (2024) and again to 20 percent (2025).

The socialists are celebrating the appointment of the black activist Francia Márquez, who is vice president and heads a new Ministry of Equality and Equity.[287] The ministry has been established with the aim of reducing Colombia's Gini coefficient and is committed to equality for women and any and all conceivable minorities. The LGBTIQ+ population, members of Afro-Colombian and indigenous communities, Roma, people with disabilities,

---

286 Weber, https://amerika21.de/2022/11/261102/kolumbien-reiche-staerker-besteuert.
287 Ministerio del Interior, https://www.mininterior.gov.co/micrositios/english-site/the-national-government-has-instituted-a-bill-to-establish-the-ministry-of-equality-and-equity/.

homeless people and migrants, etc. are all now under the protection of the newly created institution.

Petro committed himself to "anti-patriarchal" policies during the election campaign. He gave the Ministry of Mines to the environmental activist Irene Vélez, who promptly announced a halt on any new concessions for oil and mining projects.[288]

Petro's *Pacto Histórico* electoral alliance, which comprises twenty small parties, represents less than a quarter of the representatives in the two chambers of Congress, and shortly after taking office he lost important alliance partners who did not want to follow his radical left-wing agenda. After corruption allegations against people close to Petro, his party suffered significant losses in local elections in October 2023. Why a country that is dominated by crime and in which the only thing that really thrives is the drug trade, is primarily concerned with the realization of utopian ideals of equality, remains a mystery only the socialists will ever understand.

Colombians are very dissatisfied with Petro's policies, as was shown in local elections held across the country at the end of October 2023: the alliance of left-wing President Gustavo Petro did not win a majority in any of the country's largest cities. Pacto Histórico only has governors in two of 32 regions. It did not win majorities in either regional parliaments or city councils. Even in the capital Bogotá, which was considered more left-wing, Petro's preferred left-wing candidate and party comrade Gustavo Bolivar only came third.

288 Zelik, https://www.rosalux.de/news/id/50936/kolumbien-an-der-regierung-aber-nicht-an-der-macht.

November 2023
Buenos Aires, Argentina

Since I first visited Argentina in May 2022, the economic crisis and inflation have worsened. The poverty rate rose to 40 percent in the first half of 2023, according to the national statistics authority INDEC. In the first half of 2022, the poverty rate was 36.5 percent.[289] INDEC also states that the inflation rate was 94.8 percent in 2022, compared to 50.9 percent in 2021. In November 2023, the inflation rate then jumped to 161 percent compared to the same month of the previous year.[290] Thus, the inflation rate is at its highest level since the end of the 1980s – and is one of the highest inflation rates in the world in recent times.

The government reacted to the situation as helplessly and irrationally as governments in most countries react to currency devaluations: In December 2022, the government, led by President Alberto Fernández, launched a "Fair Prices" plan. Under this agreement with producers of food and hygiene products, the prices of around 2,000 basic products were frozen until March 2023. In return, manufacturers were given the opportunity to offer around 30,000 other items at 4 percent higher prices every month.

At the end of 2017, a 1,000-peso bill was introduced as the largest banknote, and 2,000-peso bills were printed for the first time in 2023. According to the official exchange rate, 1,000 pesos was equivalent to around 4.25 US dollars; on the black market, 1,000 pesos only cost 2.00 US dollars.

The central bank kept the money printing presses running at full speed, but could not produce bank notes fast enough to meet demand. It therefore

289 Reuters, https://www.reuters.com/world/americas/argentina-poverty-rate-rises-401-first-half-2023-2023-09-27/#:~:text=BUENOS percent20AIRES percent2C percent20Sept percent2027 percent20(Reuters,reported percent20a percent20rate percent20of percent2036.5 percent25.
290 Muschter, "Argentinien: Inflationsrate," https://de.statista.com/statistik/daten/studie/988114/umfrage/monatliche-inflationsrate-in-argentinien/.

placed printing orders with France and Malta. The national currency, the peso, continued to depreciate against the dollar and the mountain of debt kept growing.[291]

Argentina is one of the most economically unfree countries in the world. In the 2023 *Index of Economic Freedom*, it ranks 144th out of 177 countries – and even in Latin America, only very few countries (above all Venezuela) are more economically unfree. In comparison, let's look at Chile: although the situation in Chile has deteriorated since the socialist Gabriel Boric came to power in March 2022, Chile is the 22nd most economically free country in the world and Uruguay is in 27th place (the United States is in 25th place, with the UK just behind in 28th).[292]

When I arrive in Latin America on November 19, 2023, I find two WhatsApp messages on my phone. "We won," a representative of Javier Milei's party writes to me. I had been talking about Milei a lot for about a year and a half and thought he had a good chance of becoming president. The second WhatsApp message comes from José Fucs, editor-at-large of the leading Brazilian newspaper *O Estado de S. Paulo*: "You were the first one to tell me he had huge support in Argentina, mainly among younger people, and could win the election."

Milei won a clear majority of 55.7 percent in the run-off election, while the left-wing candidate Sergio Massa received 44.3 percent. Milei won in 21 of the country's 24 provinces. It was only in the Peronist stronghold of Buenos Aires that government-backed Massa came out on top. "Now the reconstruction of Argentina begins," said Milei to his cheering supporters after the election victory. He announced "drastic reforms."

In the first round of the presidential election in Argentina, which was held on October 22, 2023, the left-wing Peronist Sergio Massa received the most votes, ending up on 36.8 percent. Massa was Minister of the Economy and stood for the left-wing governing alliance UP. He dug deep into the state

---

291 Deutsche Börse, https://www.boerse-frankfurt.de/nachrichten/Hohe-Inflation-Argentinien-fuehrt-2000-Pesos-Schein-ein-24bb86d0-9817-4c58-9b33-42883cd3b619.

292 Heritage Foundation, *2023 Index of Economic Freedom*, https://www.heritage.org/index/

coffers to keep voters happy, ordered mass recruitment in the public sector, approved higher income tax allowances, and granted one-off payments to employees and pensioners.[293] Milei received 30 percent of the vote in the first round, Patricia Bullrich from the conservative JxC won 23.8 percent, but declared shortly after the election that she would support Milei.

The results of a survey conducted by the opinion research institute RDT from October 20 to October 23 show that around half of female voters and almost two thirds of male voters under the age of 30 voted for Milei in the first round. In contrast, the results among voters over the age of 50 were below average for Milei. Massa and especially Bullrich, on the other hand, were able to win over voters over the age of 50.[294]

The polling institute AtlasIntel conducted a survey of 6,897 Argentinians shortly before the run-off election – from November 15 to November 17, 2023 – which showed that Milei had strong support among young voters.[295] In the 16-to-24 age group, support for Milei was twice as high as for the left-wing Peronist Massa. In contrast, Massa received more support from the over-60s. Among male voters, Milei enjoyed a 15 percent lead over female voters. The differences between income groups were smaller than for gender or age. Among higher income groups, Massa and Milei elicited the same level of approval, while Milei was slightly ahead among low-income voters.

The most important issues according to the AtlasIntel survey were the fights against inflation (77.5 percent) and corruption (46.5 percent), and for increased domestic security (38 percent). Milei performed significantly better than Massa when respondents were asked who was more competent to win the fight against corruption (17 percentage points more than Massa), against inflation (10 percentage points more than Massa), and against violence and insecurity (9 percentage points more than Massa).

---

293 Spiegel Ausland, https://www.spiegel.de/ausland/argentinien-regierungskandidat-massa-gewinnt-erste-wahlrunde-gegen-populist-milei-a-9327b316-69e5-475f-adc4-0d92fa1bf9aa.
294 Presentation by the opinion research institute RDT on a survey conducted from October 20 to 23, 2023.
295 Presentation by the opinion research institute AtlasIntel on a survey of 6,897 people conducted from November 15 to 17, 2023.

But Milei won't have it easy. On November 24, just a few days after the election, I meet Nicolás Emma, the leader of the Buenos Aires office of Milei's libertarian party, at the party's headquarters in the country's capital. Several other party organizers are also present, including Gustavo Federico and Facundo Ozan Carranza. In the evening, I am invited to a private party with around 100 people to celebrate Nicolás taking over Milei's previous parliamentary seat. During my conversations with these and other leading figures from Milei's party, representatives of think tanks, and Argentinian journalists (including Sergio Serrichio from *Infobae*), tell me time and time again that Milei faces a truly Herculean task:

Milei's party has only 35 out of 257 deputies in Argentina's Chamber of Deputies (*Cámara de Diputados*). His fiercest opponents, the left-wing Peronists and other leftists, hold 105. In the Senate (*Senado*), Milei's party has only eight out of 72 members. That surprised me at first, but it is because only half the seats in the lower house were up for election this time around. It will be another two years before the other seats are contested. In the Senate, only a third of members were newly elected. Milei can issue presidential decrees to force through some policy changes, but any tax reforms will need to be approved by both the Chamber of Deputies and the Senate. Milei can also use referendums to mobilize popular opinion, but referendums can only be held on certain issues and are not binding.

During my discussions, representatives of Milei's party repeatedly single out Argentina's trade unions as their main adversaries. The trade unions are extremely strong in Argentina, very political, and firmly in the hands of the Peronists. Milei's people expect particularly strong opposition in response to his plans to privatize his country's main public broadcaster. And they are right: in the first few months after Milei's election victory, there were violent protests, strikes, and demonstrations throughout the country, led by the trade unions, who have rallied their members against his reform plans.

One pivotal question, and one that I ask again and again, is whether the people of Argentina will have enough patience for Milei's reforms, especially if the situation initially deteriorates? The answer from Milei's people: He has already repeatedly pointed out that it would take at least three terms to push through his reforms and make Argentina successful again.

The main issue for Argentines, as all polls show, is the fight against inflation. Agustín Etchebarne from the *Libertad y Progreso* think tank believes that Milei's promised dollarization of the currency will not take place for at least the first two years, especially as the banks are mounting strong resistance and the economy minister and head of the central bank are appointed by Macri supporters. All that remains is the radical reduction of subsidies in order to stabilize the budget.

Just how loyal will supporters of Mauricio Macri, with whom Milei formed an alliance to win the run-off election, prove to be in the longer run? And how much influence do right-wing nationalists exert within the ranks of Milei's libertarian party?

Milei's people say that there are hundreds of thousands of "employees" in the civil service who literally do nothing but draw their pay checks and stand up for the Peronists day in, day out. As soon as their jobs come under threat, there will be massive resistance.

In addition, Milei must first establish a proper, nation-wide political base. There are currently various independent branches of the party in the country's individual regions. The people I meet in Buenos Aires are working on creating the legal conditions to merge them into one party.

I made these notes a few days after Milei's election. In a nutshell: It is by no means certain that Milei will be able to implement his planned reforms given his lack of a majority in Parliament and the Senate. If he can implement them, the next challenge will arise. Experience from other countries (the UK in the 1980s, Poland in the 1990s) has shown that capitalist reforms initially lead to a temporary worsening of the situation as subsidies are cut and hidden unemployment becomes open unemployment. It is only after a lean period, which in the best case can last two years, that things improve. So even if Milei succeeds in implementing his reforms despite lacking a majority in parliament and the senate (the first hurdle), everything will depend on whether the Argentinians have enough patience to endure the lean period required for these reforms (the second hurdle) to take effect.

What's more, will Miliei's personality, which helped him so much in the election, get in the way of governing? His style is often somewhat reminiscent of Donald Trump or the former President of Brazil Jair Bolsonaro. However, these comparisons are misleading because Milei has more substance and he is not a traditional conservative, but a libertarian. There is a lot about Milei that appears contradictory: he is a professor of economics with very sensible views and profound knowledge, and at the same time he is a man who lives with five dogs, which he has named after well-known, free-market economists such as Milton Friedman. His main advisor during the election campaign was his sister, who is said to believe in astrology.

Milei went into the election campaign with the libertarian demand to abolish the central bank and allow free competition between currencies, which would probably lead to the US dollar becoming the most popular means of payment. He announced that he would first propose such reforms to Congress and, if it rejected them, hold a referendum.[296]

He also called for the privatization of state-owned companies, the abolition of numerous subsidies, the reduction or abolition of 90 percent of taxes,[297] and the liberalization of the labor market. He promised to reduce the number of ministries to eight: Economy, Foreign Relations, Public Works, Human Capital (which includes Childhood, Health, Education, and Labor), Defense, Security, Justice, and Interior. On his very first day in office, he signed a decree to implement this promise.

In the education sector, Milei called for funding to be switched to a voucher system.[298] Milton Friedman was an early advocate of this kind of system, in which tax money no longer flows directly to schools. It is the pupils themselves (or their parents) who receive education vouchers that they can

---

296 Galligani, https://www.infobae.com/politica/2023/04/29/las-10-propuestas-de-javier-milei-si-llega-a-ser-presidente-dolarizacion-recortes-y-que-hara-con-las-empresas-publicas/.
297 Colini, https://www.lanacion.com.ar/economia/punto-por-punto-el-plan-de-gobierno-que-presento-javier-milei-nid02082023/.
298 Galligani, https://www.infobae.com/politica/2023/04/29/las-10-propuestas-de-javier-milei-si-llega-a-ser-presidente-dolarizacion-recortes-y-que-hara-con-las-empresas-publicas/

redeem at private or state schools. Schools then submit these vouchers to the state treasury in exchange for money, which they can use to pay for staff, premises, and other materials as they manage their own budgets. This is intended to promote competition between different educational institutions.

I have several interviews with newspapers (including, for example, *Fortune* and *Infobae*) and radio stations in Buenos Aires, and the journalists all want to know whether it is right to compare Milei with Orbán, Trump, or Bolsonaro. My answer: "We don't know yet. We'll know in a few years' time. I hope he will be compared to Thatcher or Balcerowicz. But that remains to be seen." Journalists also ask me what advice I would give to Milei. I recommend including Leszek Balcerowicz from Poland in his team of advisors. Unfortunately, I can't get through to Milei himself these days, as he is understandably busy with a thousand things and everyone wants something from him.

As I emphasize in the interviews, Milei has an opportunity given the change in sentiment that I identified in my survey in Argentina. Many Argentinians have had enough of left-wing Peronism and are turning away from the statism that has shaped their country for decades. In the survey I commissioned for my book, *In Defence of Capitalism*, Argentina was among the countries in which people were most supportive of the market economy. From April 12 to 20, 2022, Ipsos MORI surveyed a representative sample of 1,000 people in Argentina about their attitudes toward the market economy and capitalism.

First, we wanted to find out what Argentinians think of the market economy. We presented respondents in Argentina with six pro-state and pro-market statements in which the word capitalism was not used. When we combine responses to the pro-state and pro-market statements, we see that statements in favor of stronger government interference in the economy found approval among 19 percent of respondents and pro-market statements among 24 percent. When we divide the average of the positive statements by the average of the negative statements, the result is a coefficient of 1.24. This means that opinions in favor of a market economy clearly dominate in Argentina.

The statement that elicited the highest level of approval in Argentina (28 percent) was: "In a good economic system, I think the state should only own property in certain areas; the lion's share of property should be privately owned." And the lowest level of approval (13 percent) was for the statement: "Social justice is more important in an economic system than economic freedom."

We conducted the same survey in 34 other countries, but in only five countries (Poland, the United States, Czech Republic, South Korea, and Japan) were attitudes to the market economy more positive than in Argentina, and in 29 countries they were more negative.

In addition, all respondents were presented with ten terms, both positive and negative, and asked which of them they associated with the word "capitalism." The result: negative terms such as "greed," "coldness," and "corruption" were selected by an average of 64 percent of respondents. In contrast, positive terms such as "prosperity," "progress," and "freedom" were selected by 67 percent. Argentines therefore associate positive and negative terms with "capitalism" in roughly equal measure. It can be seen that approval is no longer as high as in the first set of questions on the market economy, in which the term "capitalism" was not used. But even when the word "capitalism" is mentioned, the image of capitalism is only more positive in seven out of 35 countries than is the case in Argentina!

Libertarian think tanks in Argentina have made a key contribution to this shift in opinion. In Buenos Aires, I meet Agustín Etchebarne, founder of *Libertad y Progreso*, probably the country's most influential libertarian think tank. He used to be a fund manager, but sold his company (along with his farm) in 2007 because he wanted to set up a think tank.

In 2011, Etchebarne completed a course for think tank founders at the Atlas Network and later merged three small think tanks to form *Libertad y Progreso*. That same year, he applied the knowledge he had acquired and, together with a libertarian network, organized a campaign against tax increases for farmers (Regulation 125), which was ultimately successful and was able to prevent the tax increases. A year later, he organized a campaign against government plans to expropriate citizens with savings in a pension fund (AFJP), from whom the state wanted to sequester 30 billion dollars. "This campaign, unlike the first one, was unfortunately not successful; only 10,000 demonstrators turned up," he reports.

His think tanks were more like "action tanks," he says, because they focused on initiating large-scale campaigns. On November 8, 2013, they succeeded in getting one million people to take to the streets throughout Argentina to protest against the planned expropriation of the country's largest media group. Etchebarne and his fellow campaigners have learned a lot from the political left. Above all, they have understood the importance of generating striking images for the media – something organizations such as Greenpeace are very successful at. At the million-strong demonstration, several giant balloons were launched into the sky with words such as "*Libertad*" written on them in massive letters.

Libertad y Progreso also founded an organization that trained 50,000 election observers – this helped to ensure that the 2015 elections were conducted correctly and that Mauricio Macri's victory was not stolen by electoral manipulation.

Research by the *Libertad y Progreso* think tank found that only seven million Argentines work in the private sector (not including the six million who are employed illegally). In contrast, 22 million Argentines live off the state in some form or other. Etchebarne and his colleagues succeeded in publicizing the results of such studies very effectively, with major daily newspapers reporting on their findings in front-page stories.

The small group of just 18 employees has succeeded in attracting a great deal of attention, particularly through social media. Videos against populism, which they produced together with the libertarian Gloria Álvarez from Guatemala, have been watched by many millions of people. I remain in close contact with Etchebarne even after my visit to Argentina. He has a direct line to Milei, who also tells him that he greatly appreciates my books. Agustin also put me in touch with the economist Manuel Adorni, who is President Milei's spokesman and wrote the foreword for the Argentinian edition of my book, *How Nations Escape Poverty*.

It was good to be in Argentina just a week after Milei's election. At best, Buenos Aires could become for libertarians what Moscow was for communists from all over the world. But only if Milei succeeds in tackling the gigantic challenges. And if the Argentinians have the necessary patience.

Milei gave a remarkable speech at the World Economic Forum in Davos on January 17, 2024, which quickly went viral on YouTube. As it clearly outlines his thinking, I had a transcription made immediately afterwards and summarized the most important passages in five theses supplemented with my explanatory comments. Below is my article, which was published in English, German, Spanish, Italian, French, Portuguese, and Polish:

Thesis 1: Capitalism is the best and only recipe against poverty

Milei begins with a historical review and makes it clear that it was only capitalism, which emerged around 200 years ago, that has given a large proportion of the world's population an opportunity to escape poverty.

Milei: "… when you look at per capita GDP since the year 1800 and until today, what you will see is that after the Industrial Revolution, global per capita GDP multiplied by over 15 times. Which meant a boom in growth that lifted 90 percent of the global population out of poverty. We should remember that by the year 1800, about 95 percent of the world's population lived in extreme poverty and that figure dropped to 5 percent by the year 2020, prior to the pandemic. The conclusion is obvious. Far from being the cause of our problems, free trade capitalism as an economic system is the only instrument we have to end hunger, poverty and extreme poverty across our planet."

Milei is right: Before capitalism, 90 percent of the global population lived in extreme poverty. Today, according to World Bank figures, it is only 8.5 percent. And the biggest decline has occurred in the past few decades!

Thesis 2: Against "social justice" and the zero-sum mindset

Milei makes it clear that redistribution is not the way to solve society's problems and that it only creates new problems. Anti-capitalists think in zero-sum terms – they believe that a predefined economic pie needs to be distributed, when in fact the point is to increase the size of the pie.

Milei: "The problem is that social justice is not just – and it doesn't contribute either to – the general well-being ... Those who promote social justice, the advocates, start with the idea that the whole economy is a pie that can be shared differently, but that pie is not a given. It's wealth that is generated in what Israel Kirzner, for instance, calls a market discovery process. If the goods or services offered by a business are not wanted, the business will fail, unless it adapts to what the market is demanding. If they make a good quality product at an attractive price, they will do well and produce more. So the market is a discovery process in which the capitalists will find the right path as they move forward."

Thesis 3: Socialism has never improved people's lives – it has 100 million dead on its conscience

So many variations of socialism have been tried in so many countries – in the Soviet Union it was different to the version in Yugoslavia, in the GDR it was different to the version in Poland, in China and Albania it was different to the version in Romania, and in Venezuela it was different to the version in North Korea – but nowhere has socialism improved people's lives. Over 100 million people died as a result of socialist experiments, 45 million in China alone between 1958 and 1962 in the largest socialist experiment in human history, Mao's "Great Leap Forward."

Milei: "It should never be forgotten that socialism is always and everywhere an impoverishing phenomenon that has failed in all countries, where it's been tried out. It's been a failure economically, socially, culturally and it also murdered over 100 million human beings."

Thesis 4: The West is threatened by modern socialism

The most important thesis is the fourth: The West is under threat from socialism. Milei addresses the objection that today, as with classical socialism, the issue is not the nationalization of the means of production. This is no longer necessary today: the free market is being increasingly stifled by government intervention, over-reaching regulation, taxation, and the policies of central banks. The means of production or real estate may remain private property on paper, but it is only the formal legal title of ownership that remains, because the supposed owner increasingly loses control over their asset as the state tells them what to do (and what not to do) with it.

Milei: "The West has unfortunately already started to go along this path. I know that to many it may sound ridiculous to suggest that the West has turned to socialism, but it's only ridiculous if you limit yourself to the traditional economic definition of socialism, which says that it's an economic system, where the state owns the means of production. This definition, in my view, should be updated, in the light of current circumstances. Today, states don't need to directly control the means of production to control every aspect of the lives of individuals. With tools such as printing money, debt, subsidies, controlling the interest rate, price controls and regulations to correct so-called market failures, they can control the lives and fates of millions of individuals."

Thesis 5: Entrepreneurs should start to defend themselves

Milei ends with an appeal to entrepreneurs, who too often bend opportunistically to the zeitgeist and to the politically powerful. They should no longer allow themselves to be intimidated by politicians, they should be proud and start to fight back. And one of his last sentences is: The state is not the solution, the state is the problem. I would like to put it this way: Capitalism is not the problem, it is the solution.

Milei: *"Therefore, in concluding, I would like to leave a message for all business people here and for those, who are not here in person, but are following from around the world. Do not be intimidated either by the political caste or by parasites, who live off the state. Do not surrender to a political class that only wants to stay in power and retain its privileges. You are social benefactors, you're heroes, you're the creators of the most extraordinary period of prosperity we've ever seen. Let no-one tell you that your ambition is immoral. If you make money, it's because you offer a better product at a better price, thereby contributing to general well-being. Do not surrender to the advance of the state. The state is not the solution. The state is the problem itself."*

November 2023
Asunción, Paraguay

I fly from Buenos Aires to Paraguay at the end of November. Last year, when we crossed the border it was by car. I have again been invited by the German entrepreneur Carsten Pfau. He brought my first book on capitalism to Paraguay (and, incidentally, gave a copy to Javier Milei at the time) and is now helping me to launch *In Defence of Capitalism* here, which I am due to present to leading business people over lunch.

Pfau has been living in Paraguay for 25 years. There is certainly a lot for entrepreneurs to do here. Pfau is currently gearing up to start construction on the largest luxury hotel in the country, a J.W. Marriott with 145 rooms. He is also planning to build a 3,900-acre gated community with 5,000 houses. However, it is not just designed to appeal to the rich; most of these homes are being built for the middle-class – a house will cost between 200,000 and 250,000 US dollars. The development is less than 20 miles from the capital, with at least 20 tennis courts, a shopping mall, and restaurants.

Pfau owns numerous companies, greenhouses, and plantations, primarily growing strawberries and tomatoes. He is now also active in the United States. He raises around half of the capital for his investments in the U.S. and the other half in Germany. Politically, he is a libertarian and for a while he made and broadcast the show *Libres para elegir* (*Free to Choose*) on his own TV station together with Javier Milei, with whom he has a close relationship: "Milei is highly intelligent, even if, like many successful people, he is not always an easy guy." Of course, he sincerely wishes Milei every success, but Pfau believes that it will be difficult for the new president of Argentina because both the Peronists and Macri's supporters want him to fail so that they can return to power.

But back to Paraguay. In terms of size, the country is as large as Germany and Switzerland combined, but with fewer inhabitants than Switzerland alone

(6.7 million). Paraguay is the world's leading producer of hydroelectricity, a quarter of which is generated by the state-run Itaipú dam. The Itaipú dam is jointly owned by Paraguay and Brazil, and a renegotiation of the financial terms is crucial for Paraguay's budget finances.

Paraguay is one of the few countries in Latin America that is not governed by a socialist; its President is Santiago Peña from the center-right Colorado party. In the elections in April 2023, he won a resounding victory against his left-wing opponent. "The people here are very conservative, always have been," says Carsten Pfau. "Family, church, and agriculture are the values that count here. Some might say that the country and its people are a bit backward. But we like it, even if there are many people here who are more conservative than I am." This explains why there were such huge protests when it was announced that the EU was linking aid money for the education system amounting to 38 million euros to the inclusion of gender issues in the school curriculum. "There were huge protests, and parliament was finally forced to declare that the money would only be accepted if no such strings were attached. Many even said the money shouldn't be accepted at all."

The Index of Economic Freedom has the following to say: "Paraguay's economic freedom score is 61.0, making its economy the 76th freest in the 2023 Index … Paraguay is ranked 16th out of 32 countries in the Americas region, and its overall score is above the world and regional averages. The economy underperforms in many critical areas. The absence of an independent judiciary weakens the rule of law and undermines long-term economic development. Reform measures have been pursued and have encountered entrenched resistance. A lack of deeper commitment to enhanced regulatory efficiency impedes the emergence of a more vibrant private sector."[299]

Paraguay is exemplary in terms of taxes and receives almost the maximum number of points (96 out of 100) from the Heritage Foundation in this category. The income tax rate is just 10 percent. However, as everywhere in Latin America, corruption is widespread, and the rule of law is weak.

---

299 Heritage Foundation, *2023 Index of Economic Freedom,* https://www.heritage.org/index/country/paraguay.

From the capital Asunción, where he lives, Pfau views things in Germany with great skepticism: "The conservatives and liberals have no guts and are letting themselves be pushed around by the Greens. I certainly haven't regretted emigrating. Yes, of course there is envy here in Paraguay, too, just like everywhere else. But the rich are not hated here, they are admired. When I drive an expensive car here, people greet me with a friendly smile, which is very different to Germany."

Santiago de Chile, Chile

I land in Chile on November 29. The journey was a little stressful because there are no direct flights from Paraguay and I have to fly back from Asunción to Buenos Aires at 2.50 a.m., wait almost three hours, and then fly on to Santiago de Chile. But this hassle is soon forgotten once I arrive: after you've been to countries like Colombia, Argentina, and Paraguay, you feel like you're on a different continent in Chile. The difference between the dirty and outdated airports in Argentina and the airport in Santiago de Chile couldn't be greater. I feel like I'm back in Europe.

In general, I am very positively surprised by the flights in Latin America. I've taken numerous flights between different countries in Latin America over the past two weeks, none of which were late, and I never had to wait longer than ten minutes at security or immigration. U.S. Americans won't like to hear this, but the flights I took in Latin America were far more reliable and punctual than in the United States. Even in Europe, and in Germany in particular, we are unfortunately no longer spared frequent delays and cancellations. And entering a Latin American country is not only quicker, the officials are also much friendlier than those in the U.S., where you are often viewed with suspicion and a smile is the exception rather than the rule.

Once I arrive in Chile, I enjoy the warm sun by the pool and relax a little before attending several appointments and a lecture at the *Libertad y Desarrollo* think tank in the evening. I've forgotten a cap and sunscreen, but Joanna knows what to do: "No problem, there's an app here that lets you order anything you want and you can have it delivered within 20 to 30 minutes." In Germany, the only app I know of that does that is a pizza app. Capitalism is great! No socialist government has ever invented an app like this.

The last time I was in Chile, discussions about a new constitution took center stage. It's the same again this time. The first – very left-wing – draft constitution was rejected by 62 percent of the population. In search of an acceptable constitution, the government set a new process in motion. Bettina Horst, who has invited me to give a lecture to present my book, explains why the first constitution so clearly failed and what followed. Horst is General Director of the *Libertad y Desarrollo* think tank and also President of RELIAL (the Latin America libertarian network). Above all, however, she is one of the 24 members of the Experts' Committee working on the second draft constitution.

The first draft constitution failed because left-wingers held such a large majority in the Constitutional Council and were able to push through their radical socialist ideas. But their proposals did not even appeal to a majority of the indigenous groups, whose rights were very generously interpreted in the draft constitution. "Chileans want freedom of choice, for example in the school system, between private and state education. Today, 55 percent of educational institutions are private, financed by a voucher system. Many Chileans feared that this freedom of choice would be curtailed under the new constitution," says Horst.

Many also feared that private property would no longer be given the same level of protection as it was under the old constitution. In addition, the new constitution could be interpreted in such a way that abortion would be generally permitted, even after the first three months. "Whether by lower- or upper-income groups, young or old, or by members of indigenous minorities – the left-wingers' draft was rejected by all population groups," explains Horst.

With voters having overwhelmingly rejected the new constitution in the first referendum, a new three-stage process was established:

1. Twelve general constitutional principles were laid down and enforced by the Experts' Committee tasked with preparing the second draft. These included both left-wing and right-wing principles.
2. The Experts' Committee of 24 people, including Horst, was convened to prepare a new draft between March and June 2023.

3. A new Constitutional Council was elected in May 2023, this time with left-wing representatives making up only around a third of the council. A majority of councilors came from the center or right of the political spectrum.

The committee elaborated a new draft constitution, which has been rejected by the left in Chile because they are disappointed that their project for a radical socialist constitution has failed. They describe the new draft as "neoliberal." But a minority of right-wingers has also rejected the new proposal because they consider the original constitution to be better and see no need for change. Axel Kaiser tells me that he is neither for nor against the new draft constitution: the draft is worse than the original constitution, but this has already been amended and made worse several times. Background: changes to the original constitution used to require a two-thirds majority; however, that hurdle was lowered to four-sevenths. A vote on the new draft constitution was finally held on December 17, with only 44.2 percent of voters supporting it and 55.7 percent rejecting it.

Chile was long regarded as a model capitalist country in South America. In the *2022 Human Development Index*, Chile ranks first among all Latin American countries.[300] And in the Heritage Foundation's *2022 Index of Economic Freedom*, Chile is in 20th place globally, ahead of the United States and the UK (it fell slightly to 22nd place in the 2023 index).[301] Thus, Chile is the most economically free country in Latin America. Despite these successes, there were massive demonstrations and outbreaks of violence in October 2019, which led to the election of socialist President Gabriel Boric in 2021. Boric, who has promised to bury "neoliberalism,"[302] currently governs the country in a coalition with the Communist Party.

In order to understand why Chileans voted for the socialist Boric, the

300 Data available at United Nations Development Programme, https://hdr.undp.org/data-center/country-insights#/ranks.
301 Heritage Foundation, *2022 / 2023 Index of Economic Freedom*.
302 The Economist, https://www.economist.com/the-americas/2021/12/20/chiles-new-president-promises-to-bury-neoliberalism.

answer is not to be found in objective economic data, because these data confirm the success of capitalism in Chile. The answer lies in a change in public opinion. Ultimately, Chile is a striking example of a phenomenon we also see in other countries today: after a certain period of time, nations "forget" why they have become economically successful. The economic elites focus on their businesses, but leave the arena of public opinion to their opponents, who dominate the universities and the media. There, "the rich" are increasingly denounced as scapegoats for negative developments in society and, as a result, an anti-capitalist interpretation of reality increasingly comes to dominate the public discourse.

In Santiago de Chile on November 30, I take great pleasure in being able to present a book I co-authored with my friend Axel Kaiser: *El Odio A Los Ricos* (*Hatred of the Rich*). The interest in the book is greater than I expected and we have sold around 7,000 copies in Chile even before its official launch. The leading daily newspaper *Mercurio* features an in-depth interview with Axel Kaiser and myself and shortly after publication the book reaches the top of the non-fiction bestseller list in Chile.

Our book is presented by Gonzalo Sanhueza, Professor of Economics at the Catholic University, who has worked as a consultant for the International Monetary Fund (IMF) and the World Bank, and Gerardo Victorino Varela Alfonso, Chile's Minister of Education under President Sebastián Piñera. I contributed the results of a survey on perceptions of the rich in Chile to the book. Here are some of the results of this survey:

From August 19 to 30, 2022, Ipsos MORI conducted a large-scale representative survey of 1,000 Chileans to find out in more detail what they think of the rich. This survey was part of the long-standing "The Rich in Public Opinion" project, which saw Ipsos MORI ask the same questions in the United States, United Kingdom, Germany, France, Italy, Spain, Sweden, China, Japan, Poland, South Korea, and Vietnam. This survey has, for the first time, made it possible to compare attitudes towards the rich in so many different countries.

The overwhelmingly negative image of the rich in Chile can be ascertained from the list of traits that respondents most frequently said apply to rich people.

We presented respondents with a list of seven positive and seven negative personality traits that could be attributed to the rich. Without exception, the five most frequently selected traits in Chile are negative: 58 percent say the rich are "materialistic"; 56 percent say they are "arrogant"; 55 percent consider them to be "greedy"; 52 percent say "self-centered"; and 39 percent say "superficial." It is only outside the top five that positive traits such as "visionary and farsighted" (36 percent), "intelligent" (36 percent), "bold, daring" (31 percent), and "industrious" (28 percent) appear. The trait least often associated with the rich is "honest," which is cited by only 4 percent of respondents.

It is worth noting for comparison that the five most frequently selected personality traits in Vietnam were all positive: the rich are seen there as "visionary and farsighted" (74 percent), "intelligent" (69 percent), "bold, daring" (67 percent), "industrious" (63 percent), "imaginative" (62 percent). And only 12 percent of Vietnamese think that rich people are "self-centered" and "ruthless."

In this overall assessment, it is noticeable that in three countries – France, Spain, and Germany – overall attitudes towards the rich are somewhat more negative than in Chile, while attitudes are more positive in seven countries: Sweden, the United States, the UK, South Korea, Japan, Vietnam, and Poland, where people have a far more upbeat view of the rich than is the case in Chile.

So much for the results of the surveys, which I present in much greater detail in the book, *El Odio A Los Ricos*. In his part of our joint book, Axel Kaiser explains why attitudes toward the rich are so crucial. As the book has only been published in Spanish, I have asked him to briefly summarize his findings. Here is a longer passage from Axel Kaiser:

"Without a doubt, Chile is one of those countries where the anti-rich rhetoric ruined progress. In fact, the numbers show a clear difference between the rates of progress Chileans experienced in each of the past two decades. After 2014, Chilean politics and economy took a populist turn that slowed those glimpses of progress. Between 2014 and 2023, annual GDP growth was 1.9 percent, equating to just 0.6 percent in per capita terms.[303]

---

303 Claro / Sanhueza, 24.

The anti-business reforms from Bachelet's second government (2014-2018) led to decreases in investment and job creation while real wages stagnated.

While the analysis of the economic slowdown is clear, the causes of it are more complex: an ideology motivated by a vengeance against Chile's rich. In her second term, the Bachelet administration put a lot of effort into promoting the message that the rich did not pay their fair share of taxes; therefore, a tax reform was due. Obsessed with reducing inequality, that government would go as far as to say the 1 percent should pay for almost all of new tax revenue, which would ensure public education of greater quality and free of charge, better public healthcare and more hospitals, better access to culture, sports, a cleaner environment, and better pensions for the retired. In other words, as far as the government was concerned, the greedy rich that did not want to pay more of their income in taxes was the only reason Chileans did not have a better quality of life.[304]

Bachelet's tax reform was far from successful because it destroyed incentives for investment and it pushed an anti-wealth narrative that disregarded its impact on the economy and the general population. In fact, Bachelet's former finance minister (2006-2010), Andrés Velasco, warned at the time that the analysis on the tax reform's implications on savings, investment and growth was non-existent.[305] Moreover, the tax reform also failed to deliver as much revenue as the government had initially planned for that year and the ones to follow. Economists Gonzalo Sanhueza and Arturo Claro explain that if Chile's economy had grown at 3.8 percent in real terms since 2013, government tax revenue in 2023 would have been 26 percent higher.[306]

Even though most economists agree that economic growth is the source of social progress, employment, creation of opportunities and government revenue, the Chilean left insists on creating punitive tax measures that the middle class and the poor end up paying for with less opportunities. The

---

304   Gobierno de Chile, https://www.youtube.com/watch?v=YaYKtVkfdk8&t=128s.
305   https://www.emol.com/noticias/economia/2014/05/27/662226/andres-velasco-reforma-tributaria-ha-sido-mal-tramitada-y-tiene-un-problema-de-origen.html.
306   Claro / Sanhueza, 2023.

tax system, then, as the left understands it, is a weapon – wielded in the name of inequality – used to aid the class struggle against the rich. That is the reason Chile's current president, Gabriel Boric, and his current finance minister, Mario Marcel, led another tax reform in 2022 that would put even more of a strain on investment. This reform would decrease the tax credit business owners can deduct from their personal income taxes, increasing their marginal tax burden. In addition, this reform considered a wealth tax of 1 percent or 1.8 percent, depending on the size of the wealth, which completely ignores the tendency of OECD countries that once adopted this tax but have now gotten rid of it because of its inefficiency. Eventually the tax reform was rejected by congress. Nevertheless, Chilean leftist politicians continue to use a logic that wants to raise taxes not because they need more resources to help those in need, but because they just want to punish those who are rich. Besides, the Chilean public spending is far from efficient. Compared to developed economies, Chile's public spending is wasted – in greater proportion – in bureaucracy and does not have any significant effect on reducing the Gini index.[307]

The 2019 social crisis was largely the result of the collapse of Chileans' capacity to create prosperity due to the reforms of Bachelet. However, instead of showing any signs of self-critique, Chilean politicians chose to blame the deteriorated state of the economy on the international context.

A clear example of a line of thought that prioritizes the distribution of wealth over the creation of wealth was the book, *El otro modelo*, which served as the ideological guide for Bachelet's second term and it reflects the dominant philosophy of the Boric administration. The book argues for a state-controlled approach in various sectors, advocating for the exclusion of individual choice in favor of a standardized provision of services.[308] The authors of the book lean heavily on the notion that the rich are inherently neglectful of the concerns of others. According to them, the market ideal is inhumane, fostering individualistic cruelty and leaving the vulnerable to fend for themselves. This

---

307 Cifuentes, unnumbered.
308 Atria et al.

dogmatic approach, fueled by envy, has led Chile to undermine institutions that could foster progress, sacrificing overall prosperity in the pursuit of enforced equality.

However, and contrary to popular belief, a closer analysis of income inequality, particularly through professor Claudio Sapelli's study, reveals a substantial improvement in recent decades.[309] His research, spanning different generations of Chileans, demonstrates a trend toward lesser income inequality among younger cohorts. Sapelli stresses that the focus should not be on equalizing outcomes, but rather on addressing poverty and creating opportunities for the most disadvantaged. Along similar lines, renowned Chilean economists Velasco and Huneeus, have argued that the key to reducing inequality is in addressing the lack of jobs in the economy.[310] In their view, without constant job opportunities being created, especially for poorer Chileans, inequality will not go away.

Even though it is only capitalism that can create the new opportunities referred to by Velasco and Huneeus, in a July 2023 interview with *BBC News*, President Boric acknowledged a desire to 'overthrow capitalism'.[311] Minister and government spokesperson Camila Vallejo displayed similar economic ignorance by supporting Boric's claims, emphasizing that the capitalist model is not the sole solution to Chile's social issues, advocating for the advancement towards a welfare state."[312]

That was Axel Kaiser's analysis.

I learned a lot about Chile from my co-author. How did a socialist manage to get elected in the most successful capitalist country in Latin America? Between 1975 and 2015, the income of Chileans increased more than in any other country in Latin America. Life expectancy rose from 69 to 79 years. And social mobility, i.e. the opportunity for people to move up the social

---

309 Sapelli, 59-84.

310 Velasco / Huneeus.

311 Toro / Mellado, https://www.emol.com/noticias/Nacional/2023/07/24/1101888/reacciones-boric-derrocar-capitalismo.html.

312 Calderara, https://www.t13.cl/noticia/politica/reafirma-convicciones-vallejo-defiende-dichos-boric-sobre-derrocar-capitalismo-24-7-2023.

ladder, was greater than in any other Latin American country, as an OECD report confirmed in 2017.[313]

Despite all of these successes, a survey from the summer of 2021 shows how strong anti-capitalism was in Chile:

From July 30 to August 9, 2021, Ipsos MORI surveyed 1,000 representatively selected people in Chile. Combining responses to the survey's pro-state and pro-market statements, we find that statements in favor of a stronger role for the state meet with 23 percent approval and statements in favor of economic freedom elicit 19 percent approval. Dividing the average of statements for and against economic freedom yields a coefficient of 0.80.

Among Chileans under the age of 30, pro-market statements gained approval from 19 percent of respondents and pro-state statements from 26 percent. Among those over the age of 60, the relationship between support for the market economy (22 percent) and for a stronger role for the state (19 percent) is reversed. For example, 33 percent of Chileans under the age of 30 agree that "The state should set the prices for rent and food and should set minimum and maximum wages; otherwise, the system becomes socially unfair." Of those over the age of 60, only 16 percent support this opinion. Older Chileans may be more likely to remember what socialism – under Allende in the early 1970s – meant to the economy, and that a freer market improved their lives in the decades that followed.

Respondents were also presented with a total of 18 statements about capitalism, ten of which were negative and eight of which were positive. Agreement with negative statements (averaging 28 percent) clearly outweighs agreement with positive statements (averaging 20 percent).

The six most frequently selected statements were, without exception, all negative. "Capitalism is determined by the rich, they set the political agenda" was selected by 44 percent of respondents; 37 percent agree that "Capitalism leads to growing inequality"; 36 percent affirm that "Capitalism leads to monopolies where individual companies (e.g. Google or Amazon) control the entire market"; 35 percent agree that "Capitalism promotes selfishness and greed"; 32 percent believe that "Capitalism is responsible for environmental

313 Kaiser, *The Fall of Chile*, 687–688.

destruction and climate change"; and 30 percent concur that "Capitalism entices people to buy products they don't need."

I suspect, however, that conducting the same survey again today could result in different findings, because there are many indications that sentiment in Chile has shifted again towards a more market-oriented economy.

December 2023
Kathmandu, Nepal

On December 11, I land in Kathmandu, the capital of Nepal. My flight takes me via Doha, an airport I have never seen before and where I have a three-hour layover. Great architecture, great service, absolute cleanliness, and lots of greenery. If you want to sleep a little, the airport even has personal sleeping rooms at no extra cost, with a fridge and drinks. And there are spacious, modern shower cubicles to freshen up. The service in Qatar Airways' Business/First Class lounges is also much better than I had experienced in Latin America, where I was just a week before.

Nepal lies between China and India and has a population of around 30 million. The capital Kathmandu is officially home to 1.4 million people, but there are really many more people living here. Kathmandu is located in a valley in the middle of the Himalayas with the highest mountain on earth, Mount Everest at 29,030 feet.

About six weeks before I arrive, there was an earthquake in Nepal in which around 150 people died. Earthquakes are a frequent occurrence in Nepal. Numerous historic buildings around Durbar Square, including the famous royal palace Hanuman Dhoka, were destroyed or extensively damaged by an earthquake in 2015 and had to be partially rebuilt.

The first thing I do after I arrive is visit this impressive square, which is a World Heritage Site. It is a sprawling complex of buildings and includes the royal palace of the Malla kings and the Shah dynasty, which covers an area of around twelve acres. The Hanuman Dhoka Palace owes its name to the standing stone statue of Hanuman (the monkey god), which has been located on the east side of the main entrance since 1672. "Dhoka" means "door" or "gate" in Nepali. There are also large markets on the grounds, where traders sell everything from bananas to swords.

Beyond that, you see bitter misery everywhere you look in the city: run-down stores, crumbling houses, poverty, and a tangle of electrical cables, all of which seem to be laid above ground.

I am accompanied by Basanta Adhikari, who picks me up from the airport together with the founder of my publisher WeRead, Rajeev Dhar Joshi. I had already worked with Basanta as he and his people translated my book, *In Defence of Capitalism,* into Nepali and introduced me to a publishing house in Nepal, which also published my book, *Dare to Be Different and Grow Rich,* which is called *Set Yourself Bigger Goals* in Nepal.

Basanta almost didn't make it to the airport because his flight was canceled due to heavy fog. He doesn't live in the capital, he lives in Biratnagar, yet he still manages to arrive on time after a 16-hour bus ride. I'm actually supposed to give lectures in Biratnagar, too, but the risk would have been too great that I wouldn't have been able to fly back to Kathmandu.

Before I report more about Nepal, I want to write something about China, because I originally wanted to combine a trip to China with my visit to Nepal. I had already booked the flights to Beijing and applied for a visa for China when I received the following message from my publisher in China, SSAP: "According to a newly released government regulation notice, SSAP needs special approval for promotional events with authors from regions outside China ... Many things have changed in the last three years and possibly very few newspapers or other media outlets would like/dare to handle such kind of interview/topic."

I have the impression that things are becoming increasingly difficult in China. I can't publish my books on the subject of capitalism anyway because of censorship, but several of my books on the subject of "wealth" had been published in China a few years ago and sell very well there.

Before I focus on Nepal, let me summarize some impressions of my travels to China, even though China was unfortunately not part of my tour this time, contrary to my plans.

In August 2018, I traveled to five cities – Beijing, Guangzhou, Nanjing, Shanghai, and Shenzhen, held talks in each city and gave dozens of interviews. The dimensions in China are very different than those in Europe.

A video interview I gave about my book was viewed 850,000 times in one week. The Chinese are incredibly curious and, above all, hungry for success. Young Chinese people are full of optimism and ambition. After my lecture in Beijing, a ten-year-old student came up to me. He spoke good English and wanted my advice on when he should start working alongside school, perhaps setting up his own business to become rich.

The Chinese believe in economic progress – not only for themselves, but also for their country. At the lecture in Shanghai, I asked how many of those present were better off than their parents. They all responded by raising their hands.

And that shows exactly what has happened in China. According to World Bank figures, 88 percent of Chinese people were still trapped in "extreme poverty" as recently as 1981; today the figure is less than 1 percent. Hundreds of millions of people have risen from poverty to the middle class. It all began in the 1980s with Deng Xiaoping's slogan: "Let some people get rich first!" Today, millions are emulating these "some people."

I spoke to Professor Zhang Weiying, one of China's most renowned economists. I had previously read and learned a lot from his book, *The Logic of the Market*. I met him in Beijing and we discussed the latest developments. We both agreed that China's successes in recent decades were not based on some unique "third way" between capitalism and socialism, but solely on the fact that the power of the state in the economy had been successively reduced – in favor of more marketization and private ownership. But Zhang Weiying became increasingly skeptical over the next few years, during which we remained in contact, and criticized – as far as anyone can criticize such things in China – the move back to more state.

In December 2019, shortly before the outbreak of the Covid pandemic, I was in China again. During my lectures, I repeatedly saw just how interested Chinese people are in the topics of wealth and success. In Shenzhen, I spoke at a small university, Peking University HSBC Business School: out of 1,000 students, over 800 came to hear my talk and the lecture hall was so crowded that some of the students had to stand or sit on the window sills.

But, as I have said above, a lot has changed in recent years. Censorship and controls have tightened. China, which was so successful for decades because it moved towards more market freedom, has shifted into reverse gear and increased the scope of state control. I noticed that it was becoming increasingly difficult and time-consuming to publish my books in China. The publication of my book, *The Rich in Public Opinion,* was postponed over and over again for years.

After canceling the planned book presentation in China, I don't want to disappoint Basanta in Nepal, who invited me and also translated my book, so I decide to travel to Nepal anyway. And above all, of course, I am very curious about the country, which is also known as the "roof of the world" because of its high mountains.

Agreeing on a schedule is not easy, as I learn that Nepal celebrates long and hard. Several of my suggestions aren't possible, as Basanta writes to me: "Actually, the festivals run from October 15 until November 19, but there will be a gap of 15 days in-between and we were planning our program in the gap between the two holidays. But people will still be in a holiday mood on those days." When I go to the Embassy of Nepal in Berlin to apply for my visa, I'm initially faced with closed doors. A sign says that they are closed for two days due to public holidays in Nepal. Officially, there are 35 non-working holidays in Nepal, more than anywhere else in the world, but the people I speak to say there are actually over 50.[314]

I take the liberty of saying that it is difficult for a country to be economically successful if you celebrate festivals for five weeks. Basanta agrees: "I totally agree with you, we have very long holidays, and our work culture is not so good, that is also why we are far behind the developed nations."

Basanta Adhikari is the founder of the Bikalpa-an Alternative, an aspiring public policy think tank. This man with a long beard – even longer than Karl

314 Bam, https://myrepublica.nagariknetwork.com/news/nepal-tops-global-list-for-public-holidays/#:~:text=World percent20Statistics percent20has percent20taken percent20data,BS percent20on percent20March percent2015 percent2C percent202023.

Marx's – is now an ardent freedom activist, even naming his daughter Liberty and his son Freedom. He talks about his life and his political journey:

"After completing my Master's degree at Sonk Konghoe University in South Korea in 2011, I returned to Nepal with the aim of doing something meaningful with my life. At that time, Nepal was on the verge of finalizing a new constitution – again, because we are world champions in drafting new constitutions. But the country was in a catastrophic state and on the verge of anarchy. I started working in eastern Nepal for the 'Gari KhanaDeu' campaign launched by the Samriddhi Foundation. The campaign focuses on three fundamental values: 'security of life and property,' 'rule of law,' and 'freedom of enterprise.' I realized that these values are crucial for the survival and economic prosperity of the country.

Before I got involved in the campaign, I too was sympathetic toward leftist ideologies. I saw Mao and Stalin as role models. In 2012/13, Robin Sitoula, the executive director of the Samriddhi Foundation, encouraged me to participate in the Atlas Network/CPPR Summer School research program. In the same year, I attended the Asia Liberty Forum in Delhi, where I had the opportunity to learn about and experience the global libertarian freedom movement. In July 2013, I left Biratnagar to do an internship at the Samriddhi Foundation in Kathmandu. I stayed there for about six months and founded an organization named Bikalpa-an Alternative to promote the values of freedom and entrepreneurship in Biratnagar.

There were many organizations working on various issues, but hardly any of them were working on reducing poverty through an entrepreneurial approach. After returning to Biratnagar in February 2014, I opened a one-room office with very little money, and today there are nine dedicated full-time employees working in the think tank. Every year, we train more than 1,000 young people and teach them the values of freedom and entrepreneurship. In May 2022, Bikalpa's advocacy work helped facilitate the issuing of motorcycle driving licenses in Biratnagar. This was a practical example of how we improved people's lives and livelihood, as previously it often took over a year to get a motorcycle license due to bureaucratic hassles and red tape, and many people in Nepal were driving without a license as a result. After the reform, which we initiated together with others, it now only takes two weeks. This was particularly important for the common people, who need motorcycle licenses to earn their living."

In Kathmandu, this acceleration of what is actually a simple administrative process still doesn't seem to have arrived. As a journalist who interviews me the next day confirms: he shows me the receipt for the driving test he passed a year and a half ago, but he still doesn't have the document in his hands.

The gross national product per capita in Nepal is just 1,331 US dollars.[315] With an average annual income of 315 US dollars per capita, Nepal is the second poorest country in Asia after Afghanistan and one of the ten poorest countries in the world.[316] On the current *Human Development Index*, Nepal ranks 143rd out of 191 countries evaluated.[317] Poverty is clearly visible in the streets, both in the capital and beyond, and the stores and houses are run-down. Of all the countries I have been to, this is the worst poverty I have seen.

Nepal is also very unstable politically. I wonder if there is another country in the world that has had seven different constitutions in 80 years?[318] Nepal was a Hindu kingdom for 240 years. After a ten-year civil war with the Maoists – more on this in a moment – a democratic federal republic was proclaimed in 2008. Since then, there have been eleven governments in Nepal, and most prime ministers do not even stay in office for a full year.[319] This instability has long been typical of Nepal: in the second half of the twentieth century, there was a new prime minister nearly every year on average.[320] However, it has to be said that this also happens in developed countries – Italy is the first that springs to mind.

---

315 Muschter, "Asien: Ranking der 10 Länder," https://de.statista.com/statistik/daten/studie/1070438/umfrage/die-laender-asiens-mit-dem-niedrigsten-bruttoinlandsprodukt-bip-pro-kopf/.

316 Alles über Nepal, https://www.allesuebernepal.com/info/wirtschaft/.

317 BMZ, https://www.bmz.de/de/laender/nepal.

318 Bhatta, https://www.orfonline.org/expert-speak/nepals-political-and-economic-transition/

319 Pfeifer, https://www.sueddeutsche.de/politik/nepal-pushpa-kamal-dahal-indien-china-1.5729675.

320 Michaels, 221.

In 2023, the Maoist rebel leader Pushpa Kamal Dahal (who is also known as Prachanda, or "the fierce one") was appointed prime minister for the third time. In the 2008 Constituent Assembly elections, the Maoists won half of the 240 seats.[321] Prachanda was elected Prime Minister for the first time in August 2008, eight years later in August 2016 for the second time, and again a good six years later, in December 2022, for the third time.

The party system in Nepal is very confusing and constantly in flux. There are several Marxist-Leninist and Maoist parties that are constantly splintering and reuniting. The Maoists alone have split into at least six different parties since the 2006 peace process. The United Marxist-Leninists have also shared this fate since the 1990s. Of the 119 parties registered with the Nepal Election Commission, at least 86 are either socialist, communist, Maoist, Marxist-Leninist, or otherwise left-leaning.[322] As I drive back to Kathmandu airport, I see red flags with hammers and sickles everywhere outside an event venue. When I ask Rajeev what's going on, he replies: "Oh, the Maoists are holding a big conference there."

Basanta explains: "Most political parties in Nepal believe in leftist ideologies. After India gained independence in 1947, the country pursued socialist policies. China introduced communism after its revolution in 1949. Nepal is in between these two countries, and they have a great influence on us. Our political leaders look up to Mao and Nehru as their role models, they very much take inspiration from them. In addition, Nepal received a lot of development aid from Russia in the 1970s. When I was young, there were countless Russian books that had been translated into Nepali. That's one reason why so many people in Nepal, and most political parties, sympathize with left-wing ideas."

The chairman of one of the Maoist parties is the already mentioned Pushpa Kamal Dahal. He was the leader of the Maoist rebel uprising that began in 1996. The armed struggle initially broke out in western midland regions and

---

321 Pettigrew, vii.
322 Election Commission Nepal, https://election.gov.np/en/page/registered-political-parties-updated-list.

districts such as Rukum, Rolpa, Salyan, Jajarkot, and Dailekh. The uprising began with isolated attacks on police stations, at first with homemade guns and hand grenades. "The police and army maintained a presence only at a few strategically important places, and the poverty-stricken peasants, who were concerned mostly with managing their food supplies and shelter, were, at least at the start, openly inclined sympathetic toward the Maoists fighting for them."[323] The army did not intervene in the conflict in the early years – the army, like the Maoists, did not trust the parliamentary system.[324]

The civil war claimed 17,000 lives and eventually led to the Maoists controlling around 80 percent of the country. In 2006, the uprising ended with a compromise that also led to the abolition of the monarchy.

It is surprising that Maoism was so strong in Nepal in the 1990s. At that time – after the collapse of the Soviet Union and the socialist regimes of Eastern Europe – communism was in decline all around the world. China still officially honored Mao but, in reality, Deng Xiaoping was busy implementing a policy that was the opposite of Maoism. And it was precisely at this time that Maoism experienced a major resurgence in China's neighboring country.

Interestingly, however, Maoism did not come to Nepal from China, but from India. It was in India, not China, that the left-wing rebels received their training – the border between Nepal and India was completely open for Nepali citizens, so Maoists came from India into the neighboring kingdom.[325]

I ask Basanta why the Maoist movement in Nepal became so strong and active in the 1990s, at a time when people in China had stopped believing in Mao and communism seemed to have lost its appeal globally. "Maoist ideology can assert itself wherever society is poor. Nepal is one of the poorest countries in the world and was therefore a fertile breeding ground for Maoism. Nepal's landscape is very varied with mountains and jungle and the state cannot make its presence felt everywhere. The Maoists were therefore able to move freely and spread their ideas in the remote areas where the state

---

323 Michaels, 224–225.
324 Michaels, 226.
325 Pettigrew, viii.

barely existed. Left-wing ideologies propagate that the rich are rich because they live at the expense of the poor. They say it is the rich man's fault that you are poor. If we take away their property and redistribute it among the poor, the poor will be better off.

The system oppressed the poor for so long. Then the Maoists came and promised them heaven on earth if they could overthrow the government and the system. Many oppressed people saw the Maoists as liberators who would give them a dignified life. Many were even prepared to die for their party. But some also joined the party for completely different reasons, not for ideological reasons, but simply to exercise power and assert their own personal interests."

Arpita Nepal (no mistake, she really does share her name with her country) from the Samriddhi Foundation has another explanation for the success of the Maoists: "In the 1960s, Nepal was a hippie paradise, many people came here because Nepal was the leading country for marijuana. Cannabis was legal in Nepal until the 1970s and there were legal hashish stores everywhere. But 1973 was the last year that people in Nepal could legally smoke cannabis. Cultivation was banned and many people lost their livelihoods. especially in places where the Maoists proliferated (Rukum, Rolpa, and Jajarkot). This pushed people into poverty and provided additional incentive to join the Maoists."

The success of the "Maobadis" ("Heralds (of the teachings) of Mao"), as Prachanda's followers are known, was in part based on the fact that they skillfully appropriated traditional and religious symbols for their own purposes. "They organized their entry into villages as 'ritual processions' (*jātrā*) and their gatherings as 'ritual festivals' (*melā*). The red colors of their flags were the colors used on religious holidays, when women dress in their best saris and when temples are decorated ... The broad red spot of vermilion on the forehead that one traditionally receives from the priest upon visiting a temple adorned many rebels in their camouflage suits, announcing a 'pious' fighter."[326]

Fortunately, that era is now over. But I wonder why the people in Nepal

---

326 Michaels, 241.

can't see that so many other countries in Asia have become successful through free market reforms, while they are still living in misery. Whether it's Taiwan, Singapore, South Korea, Vietnam, or China, more market and less state have led to greater prosperity everywhere.

Nepal, on the other hand, only ranks 142nd out of 177 countries in the *Index of Economic Freedom*: "The government's statist approach to the economy seriously weakens economic freedom and development in Nepal. Corruption, a lack of transparency, and a burdensome business approval process impede much-needed expansion of private investment and production. Property rights are poorly protected by the inefficient judicial system, which is subject to substantial political influence."[327] Nepal also scores very poorly in Transparency International's *Corruption Perceptions Index*, where it is 110th out of 180.[328]

I meet Manish Jha, a member of parliament in Nepal for the Rastriya Swatantra Party (which translates as National Independent Party NIP). NIP was in a coalition with the Prachanda-led government from December 26, 2022 to February 5, 2023, but then fell out with the other parties. NIP is currently the fourth largest national party in Nepal, and Jha says it is the only party that clearly advocates a market economy. "The biggest problems in our country are the lack of rule of law, corruption, and too much state intervention in the economy." New political constitutions have been discussed repeatedly for years, Jha explains, but there is too little awareness that the key to improving living standards lies in economic reforms. Jha himself is an entrepreneur and says that no other party has as many entrepreneurs among its MPs as NIP.

On the second day of my visit, Jha presents my book. The room is well filled and the publisher has organized the event more perfectly than I have ever experienced at any of my many book presentations. The presenter is from LOLA (Ladies for Liberty), some of whose members I had met just two weeks ago on the other side of the world in Chile.

---

327 Heritage Foundation, *2023 Index of Economic Freedom*, 262.
328 Transparency International, "Nepal," https://www.transparency.org/en/cpi/2022/index/npl

The head of the most influential think tank in Nepal, the Samriddhi Foundation, Arpita Nepal, takes to the stage and makes the connection between my book and her country's problems: "The chapter on the financial crisis is particularly relevant for Nepal at the moment. Our central bank keeps pointing to the balance of payments to prove that the economy is doing well. At the same time, the banks are sitting on excess liquidity and the market is facing a credit crunch. You only need to look at the guidelines issued by the central bank to understand this situation, rather than blaming big bankers for sitting on cash. The chapter on anti-capitalist criticism of consumerism is also interesting for Nepal. Nepal has a list of so-called 'luxury goods' (determined by bureaucrats). Unfortunately, the bureaucrats and politicians who have decided that motorcycles and cars are 'luxury goods' and tax them at 114 to 117 percent (motorcycles) and up to 205 percent (cars) continue to drive expensive cars they bought with taxpayers' money, while taxpayers have to ride on shoddy public transport or spend a large portion of their savings on private vehicles. So, this book helps us all to understand that many of the problems we face in Nepal are not market failures but due to government intervention."

I meet with the entrepreneur, Niranjan Shrestha from the Laxmi Group, one of the largest companies in Nepal. He has a number of business interests, including in the car import segment, and says that the figures Arpita quotes are an understatement: "A BMW X5 costs the equivalent of around 400,000 euros in Nepal due to the high taxes. On this specific model, the luxury tax amounts to as much as 328 percent." The import of used cars is prohibited, just as many other things are prohibited in Nepal. Shrestha: "In the mid-90s, we experienced something of a new beginning in Nepal with a number of free market reforms. Taxes were reduced and deregulated, which, among other things, led to the shadow economy falling from around 90 to 30 percent. The ratio of taxes to GDP was only 10 percent. Then came the civil war with the Maoists, and the political unrest, and the reforms were not continued, they were reversed. Today, the ratio of taxes to GDP is 25 percent, and the shadow economy has bounced back to 75 percent," says the entrepreneur. Incidentally, he visits me in Berlin two months after my trip and I put him in touch with an entrepreneur friend of mine. Maybe they'll do some business together.

I meet up with around a dozen employees of the Samriddhi Foundation for a lengthy discussion. The foundation was established in 2006 by Robin Sitoula and was the first libertarian think tank in Nepal; today there are seven. During our conversation, I realize that Nepal really is a socialist country. No-one is allowed to make a profit of more than 20 percent on any goods they sell. My publisher, for example, is not allowed to sell a book for more than 20 percent above cost. If you make a bigger profit, you either have to bribe the tax inspectors or pay a fine, and in the worst case you could lose your company. Originally, the law provided for a prison sentence of five years, which has since been reduced to one year. As the term "goods" is not defined in the law, district administrative authorities can interpret it at their own discretion.

The ridiculous regulations have been around for a long time and, as Arpita explains to me, they go back to the Black Marketing and Other Social Offences Act of 1975: "This is a remnant of a time when the Nepalese economy was closed, and the system of governance was a party-less panchayat system. Trade negotiations with India had not begun at this time and all imports were either through informal channels or through diplomatic channels to make provisions for the monarch. Nepal's Fourth Periodic Plan (1970–1975) laid the basis for the adoption of a policy that limits the scope of profiteering. The fourth periodic plan assumes the government's role in commercial activities to provide 'adequate quantity at fair prices.' This vision of planned development and the state as a benevolent provider is the guiding factor in the adoption of the Black Marketing and Other Social Offences Act. Amongst other things, the legislation places a cap on profiteering."

I also approach the entrepreneur Niranjan Shrestha about this 20 percent profit limit. Shouldn't there be a campaign against it? "The problem," he says, "is that not only politicians, but most people in Nepal think that profit is theft, that profit is a bad thing. Envy of the successful is the source of this evil."

There are many other government restrictions on economic life, for example long lists of areas of the economy in which foreigners are not allowed to invest. Foreign investment is largely unwelcome – in part because there is a fear that India would gain too much influence.

The country's rating in the *2024 Index of Economic Freedom* is particularly poor in the "Investment Freedom" category, where Nepal scores only 10 out of a possible 100 points (the same as Cuba). Only five out of 176 countries in the world have a worse score in this category, including three socialist countries and one Islamic dictatorship (North Korea, Eritrea, Venezuela, Zimbabwe, and Iran). India, which is in 126th place in the overall ranking, scores 40 points in the "Investment Freedom" category, while China, which is in 151st place, has 20 points in this category.[329]

On a personal level, I had a great week in Nepal. I met impressive people, e.g. my publisher Rajeev Dhar Joshi, who organized many, many interviews with the media and lectures in colleges, including arranging a half-page interview with by far the largest newspaper in Nepal, *Kantipur Daily* (circulation around 450,000 copies a day). The newspaper headlined the interview: "It is wrong to demonize capitalism."

I learned a lot from Rajeev about the realities of people's lives in Nepal. I was amazed to learn that, according to him, in well over 90 percent of marriages, the parents still choose the spouse. "Love marriages are an exception. They are increasing in Kathmandu, but the rule is still that the parents propose a spouse." You can reject their suggestions, even several times. "That happened to me. I was rejected seven times by women because they didn't find my job attractive. So, I changed jobs and then found the right woman."

I enjoyed the lectures in Kathmandu: I spoke to groups of 50 to 100 students, including at King's College and APEX College. This time I didn't talk about *In Defence of Capitalism*, but about my book, *Dare to Be Different and Grow Rich*, which is called *Set Yourself Bigger Goals* in Nepal. It's great to meet young, motivated people who want to learn more about success and

329 Heritage Foundation, *2024 Index of Economic Freedom*, 7–8.

financial freedom – about ways in which not only their country but they themselves can escape from poverty.

Scores of ambitious people are leaving Nepal today – hundreds of thousands of highly qualified Nepali's have already emigrated to the United States and countries in Asia. It's what happens in all socialist countries that don't lock everyone up, whether East Germany, Cuba, or Venezuela: the best and the brightest leave the country. I hope that one day there will be a move towards more capitalism in Nepal, so that these people can come back to their country with what they have learned elsewhere and help to build a prosperous society in their home country, too.

December 2023
Monaco

Monaco was not actually on my travel list. I've been there several times, most recently in August 2023 with Jenna – not as a stop on my "Liberty World Tour," but because I was on vacation in the south of France and our hotel was right on the border with Monaco.

However, I am visiting the small principality with fewer than 40,000 inhabitants again because, at the end of December, I am meeting Titus Gebel there, the initiator of the "Free Private Cities" project. In 2006, he co-founded Deutsche Rohstoff AG, which he headed until 2014. He became wealthy thanks to the company and, a year after selling it, Gebel, who is ten years my junior, moved to Monaco. He believes the Principality "can be exemplary for Free Private Cities in many respects,"[330] although it does differ from his concept in many respects.

Monaco is widely regarded as the home of the rich and about a third of its inhabitants are said to have liquid assets of more than one million US dollars.[331] One reason for its reputation is that Monaco is widely regarded as a tax haven because it does not levy income, inheritance, or capital gains taxes. About half of the state budget is funded by value-added tax.[332]

Politically, the country is a constitutional monarchy. The Principality is extremely safe and there is hardly any crime.[333] Convicted Non-Monégasques must leave the Principality, possibly after serving a prison sentence.[334] In his book, Gebel relates an example: Having been found guilty of shoplifting 100 euros, someone was not only imprisoned for seven days, but was also

---

330 Gebel, *Free Private Cities*, 141.
331 FAZ, "Wo die Millionäre wohnen," https://www.faz.net/aktuell/wirtschaft/wirtschaftspolitik/reichtum-wo-die-millionaere-wohnen-staedte-ranking-13060176.html.
332 Gebel, *Free Private Cities*, 142.
333 Wikipedia, "Öffentliche Sicherheit in Monaco," https://de.wikipedia.org/wiki/ percentC3 percent96ffentliche_Sicherheit_in_Monaco.
334 Gebel, *Free Private Cities*, 143.

deported from Monaco. And this can happen very quickly if you are not a citizen. Monaco operates a zero-tolerance policy toward all crime.

Gebel picks Jenna and me up at the Hôtel de Paris and shows us the city. We see stunningly beautiful Art Nouveau houses, Belle Époque villas next to the kind of ugly 1970s buildings you would also find in a problem district in Germany. I ask why they don't demolish some of them and put up nicer houses: "That happens fairly often, but the problem is that many apartments are condominiums. So, the buildings are divided up and owned by different people, which makes it extremely difficult to get consent from everyone." At the same time, he says, this also shows how much property rights are respected in the Principality. There is a saying: Monaco is the only city where millionaires live in social housing. The price per square foot starts at around 1,800 euros and can go up to over 10,000 euros, says Gebel. The average price is over 4,500 euros, but the median is around 2,700 euros.

What I didn't know is that round 15 percent of Monaco's 0.8 square miles was created artificially, i.e. heaped up in the sea – a very expensive process, but the demand for housing is high and the population density, at more than 63,000 people per square mile, is higher than in any other country in the world. In Singapore, for example, there are around 22,250 people per square mile. There is simply no space in Monaco. This has stimulated the imagination of planners, and now even streets are being roofed over in order to build apartments on the newly created areas. And a lot happens underground: the train station, for example, is underground.

And this is where Titus Gebel, who developed the concept of Free Private Cities, lives. Before I visit him, I read his book, *Free Private Cities: Making Governments Compete For You*. I oscillate between sympathy for some of his ideas and equally great skepticism because I am generally suspicious of all idealized social systems constructed by humans. But I am always open to new ideas, and first of all I would like to briefly outline what is meant by a Free Private City.

In a Free Private City, there is no such thing as politics. As a citizen, you sign a contract with a private, for-profit service provider, who provides all of the services you would normally get from a government. Any citizen can terminate their contract at any time, but the operator can only terminate the contract for good cause and cannot unilaterally change it at a later date.

I share Gebel's opinion that private service providers could deliver most of the services that states now provide much more cost effectively. The difference can be seen very clearly in private space travel, which is many times cheaper than state-run space travel. And if this is true for such a complex service, one that even involves rockets, then it is even more so for others. I also share his opinion that free private cities would act as beacons and encourage people to initiate further such projects.

Since there is hardly any "no man's land" in the world that does not belong to a state, the initiators of a Free Private City need to conclude a contract with a "host nation" that grants the operating company the right to establish a Free Private City on a defined territory. Gebel admits that convincing existing states to give up part of their sovereignty is certainly not an easy task. Nevertheless, in Gebel's opinion, this path seems easier than changing existing systems "from within" towards more freedom, legal security and self-responsibility.[335]

But why should existing states agree to relinquish some of their power over a specific territory? Gebel's answer: because they expect to benefit from it, for example in the form of foreign investment and a share of the profits generated by the operator. The existence of a large number of special economic zones worldwide demonstrates states' general willingness to take this path.[336]

Special economic zones are defined territories within an existing state that offer more attractive conditions for investors than the rest of the country. One example of this is Shenzhen, today a vibrant metropolis in China that began as a special economic zone. I visited the city twice, in 2018 and 2019, and spoke to entrepreneurs there.

During Mao's time, the district of Shenzhen in Guangdong province was the main conduit for illegal emigration to the British crown colony of Hong Kong. Much like in Germany, where an increasing number of people fled

335 Gebel, *Free Private Cities*, 96.
336 Gebel, *Free Private Cities*, 176.

from the East to the West prior to the construction of the Berlin Wall, many Chinese tried to leave the People's Republic for Hong Kong. Year after year, thousands of people risked their lives attempting to cross the heavily guarded border from socialist China into capitalist Hong Kong. The majority either were captured by border patrols or drowned making their attempt to swim across the maritime border. The internment camp close to the border, where those captured by the Chinese were held, was hopelessly overcrowded.

The reformer Deng Xiaoping was smart enough to realize that military intervention and stricter border controls would not solve the underlying issue. When the party leadership in Guangdong province investigated the situation in more detail, it found refugees from mainland China living in a village they had set up on the opposite side of the Shenzhen River on Hong Kong territory, where they were earning 100 times as much money as their erstwhile compatriots on the socialist side.[337]

Deng's response was to argue that China needed to increase living standards in order to stem the flow.[338] Shenzhen, then a district with a population of fewer than 30,000, became the site of China's first free-market experiment in this special economic zone, enabled by party cadres who had been to Hong Kong and Singapore and seen at first hand that capitalism works far better than socialism.

From being a place where many put their lives at risk to leave the country, this former fishing village has today become a thriving metropolis with a population of almost 13 million and a higher per-capita income than any other Chinese city except for Hong Kong and Macau and has left Shanghai, long the economic flagship city of the People's Republic, behind. The electronics and communications industries are the mainstays of the local economy. Only a few years into the capitalist experiment, the Shenzhen city council had to build a barbed-wire fence around the Special Economic Zone in order to cope with the influx of migrants from other parts of China.[339]

337 Coase / Wang, 60.
338 Lee, 188–189.
339 Lee, 191.

Soon, other regions followed suit and tried the Special Economic Zone model. Low taxes, low land lease prices and low bureaucratic requirements made these Special Economic Zones extremely attractive to foreign investors.[340]

However, Gebel's Free Private Cities are more than special economic zones, because they are almost completely autonomous, and not just in economic terms. Gebel says they can be described as "special economic zones plus." Nations, he believes, would more easily understand the modification of an existing concept than something completely new.

Since I am always very suspicious of theoretical concepts constructed in authors' minds, the chapters in Gebel's book I found most convincing are those in which he depicts network states and charter cities, which, in his view, are precursors to free private cities. He mentions, for example, the former British crown colony of Hong Kong, which implemented a very successful capitalist concept for decades and was always at the top of the *Index of Economic Freedom* together with Singapore (today it is no longer listed as a separate entity in the index). Of course, as is well known, in recent years China has increasingly undermined the original promise, which was described as "one country, two systems." This shows the threats to such projects from powerful states that tend to seek to expand their power whenever they can.

Singapore is another example of a successful capitalist experiment. It now ranks at the top of the *Index of Economic Freedom*, making it the most capitalist of 177 countries ranked by the Heritage Foundation in 2023. I met legendary investor Jim Rogers in Singapore. From 1990 to 1992, he spent two years riding a motorcycle around the world with his girlfriend. He covered 100,000 miles, traveled to six continents, and his journey was listed in the *Guinness Book of Records*. From January 1, 1999 to January 5, 2002, he went on another trip around the world with his wife – this time he drove more than 152,000 miles in a custom-made Mercedes and visited 116 countries. So, he really has seen the whole world and can make a judgment call: for him,

---

340 ten Brink, 177.

Singapore is the best country in the world, with the best healthcare system, the best education, and the best security. Accordingly, at the end of 2007, he sold his home in New York City for about 16 million US dollars and moved to Singapore, where he lives today.

Another example Gebel cites is Dubai, which was only a small city-state of regional significance when Great Britain granted it independence in 1971. Today, Dubai attracts investors and entrepreneurs from all over the world, in part thanks to its promise of extensive tax exemptions. Dubai does not levy income taxes, and corporations are taxed only 9 percent of their profits.

The advantage of the models applied in Liechtenstein, Monaco, Dubai, or Singapore? They work in practice. Of course, they are not identical to the far more comprehensive concept of free private cities that Gebel favors.

Established nations such as the United States or countries in Europe will not be won over to Free Private Cities' projects in the foreseeable future. Countries in Latin America and Africa are more likely candidates, but they are often politically unstable. There is, therefore, a risk that a change of government will lead the next rulers to comprehensively review the free private city project.

One example of this can be found in Honduras. A private city was founded on the territory of this Central American country (between Guatemala and Nicaragua). The model was called ZEDE – the Spanish acronym for "zones for economic development and employment." In 2013, the Parliament of Honduras passed a law establishing such "zones" and even changed the country's constitution to accommodate them.

Gebel reports: "In collaboration with the government, we were able to launch a special zone in Honduras five years ago, called Próspera, which uses an open source legal package. We have succeeded in building a judicial center with the best judges from all over the world in a country that otherwise has major problems with the independence of its own judiciary.

A significant number of companies have settled in Próspera over the past few years and the first apartments are currently being built and sold. The fee charged by the operator is only 260 US dollars per year for Hondurans, making it affordable even for lower income groups. Incidentally, the minimum wage in Próspera is higher than anywhere else in Honduras.

In addition to Próspera, Honduras has also created the Morazan special zone. Here, Honduran workers from the nearby big city can rent an air-conditioned apartment for 120 US dollars a month. A local security service protects the 25 families in a region that otherwise has one of the highest murder rates in the world. Residents only pay 5 percent taxes.

Both zones are growing and thriving, most of the residents are Hondurans, and demand remains high. And this despite the fact that the new socialist government wants to abolish the special zones. However, the Special Zones Act stipulates that even after they are abolished, the existing zones will continue to exist for 50 years. The new government must also adhere to this."[341]

Gebel says he has now spoken to almost a dozen governments about implementing similar projects, primarily in Latin America, the Caribbean, and Africa. Anyone who believes in the idea can also invest in it – the vehicle is called Tipolis. Tipolis Pte. Ltd is a Singapore-based public company that aims to establish a global network of "International Cities." "International Cities are the next evolution of Special Economic Zones," says the company's website. "Tipolis is committed to becoming the creator, owner, and operator of a global portfolio of International Cities characterized by a high degree of autonomy."

I come to Gebel with a few questions that I want to discuss with him. Do we really need such concepts in their purest, "idealized" form, a form that doesn't exist anywhere, only in theory? As difficult as it is to reform existing systems, is it really easier to persuade states to give up some of their sovereignty? Gebel does not believe that there is any hope of lasting reform in larger nation states: "As soon as they become prosperous, people will once again turn to politicians who promise them 'free' services, which are actually financed on credit – and with their tax money, of course."

But don't concepts for a "perfect world" also attract large numbers of weirdos, utopians, and ideologues who destroy the inherently pragmatic approach? Gebel admits that could happen. There is even a risk that organized criminals could infiltrate such cities and use them as safe havens. But the operator can of course choose who comes into the city and expel people who have provided false information when they were admitted or who have violated their contract with the operator.

And doesn't his idea retain some of the constructivism that Hayek and others rightly criticized so harshly? Gebel resists calling his concept a "utopia," but isn't that what it is in the end? He disagrees and points, for example, to the extremely successful International Financial Centers in Dubai and Abu Dhabi, which are not identical to his concept of Free Private Cities but do have some of the same elements.

Dubai generates 14 percent of its GDP on the 0.4 square miles of its International Financial Center. Such projects lead to imitators and, above all, to further developments. For example, there is now also an International Financial Center in Kazakhstan. Gebel also mentions the NEOM project on the Red Sea in northwestern Saudi Arabia, which will not only provide a home for companies, but also for ordinary residents. Saudi Arabia at least promises to put the principle of "one country, two systems" into practice.

Back to Monaco: I spend New Year's Eve at the turn of the year 2023/24 with Jenna at a party at the Yacht Club de Monaco. The Mediterranean Principality is famous as a harbor for the luxury yachts of the super-rich. In the Marina Port Hercule, a berth for a 200-foot luxury yacht costs around 1,200 euros per night. During the annual Formula 1 race, yacht owners pay up to 90,000 euros for a long weekend. In contrast, the ticket price for the New Year's Eve party in the exclusive Yacht Club was affordable at 350 euros per person. Since I don't drink alcohol and don't eat meat or fish, and the vegetarian options were very limited, I am sure I must have been the cheapest guest to cater for because I only ate two slices of wholemeal bread with cheese and drank two glasses of water. I don't see much to confirm the stereotype of Monaco as a place for the rich and famous. Apart from Jenna, I only saw three beautiful women at the party.

My capitalist world tour, which has taken me to very poor and very rich countries – and to many that are neither very poor nor very rich – began in Zurich and ends in Monaco, two cities with the highest densities of millionaires in the world; two cities that, along with Singapore, are among the safest and cleanest in the world, and where the poor are faring much better than in economically unfree, non-capitalist countries.

It is not easy to summarize all the impressions I have gathered over these 20 months. In the last four weeks in particular, the contrasts have been immense. In countries where wealth is seen in a positive light – whether in Poland, South Korea, or Vietnam – the economy is growing and average citizens and the poor are doing better as a result. However, in countries where governments are imposing more and more restrictions on the economy and politicians are constantly coming up with new laws that they claim will increase "social justice," but which in fact only make life more difficult for entrepreneurs, the only things that are increasing are substantial declines in wealth and sizeable increases in abject poverty.

The journey continues...

July 2024
Fairlee, and Las Vegas, USA

Even though I completed my 30-country tour with my visit to Monaco, my journey is far from over. Over the next few years, I want to return to many of the countries I've already visited. Mainly because I want to produce more films. For example, I'm planning a film about Vietnam. I am in the process of seeking financial support for these upcoming projects, as the costs involved are beyond what I can cover independently in the long run.

In July 2024, I return to the United States. I start by meeting with representatives of the Free to Choose network at Capitaf, Milton Friedman's summer residence, and then accept an invitation from the renowned Dartmouth College to give a lecture. Afterwards, I fly to FreedomFest, which is back in Las Vegas again. Mark Skousen has invited me to take part in the World Economic Summit and another panel and to give a lecture. The motto of this year's Freedom Fest is: "Are We Entering a Brave New World?"

"Although written in the early 1930s, the storyline of Aldous Huxley's book, *Brave New World*, fits the modern-day world in many ways", says the economist and initiator of FreedomFest Mark Skousen. "There is constant pressure to conform, to achieve stability and security at the expense of freedom and independence. Everyone must be happy or else! In the novel, the people of the world have become fully indoctrinated from birth, regimented and sedated with the drug soma. Those who oppose this 'Brave New World' are shipped off to Iceland or another far away outpost." Huxley described it as "a place where you meet the most interesting set of men and women to be found anywhere in the world. All the people, who for one reason or another, have got too self-consciously individual to fit into community life. All the people who aren't satisfied with orthodoxy, who've got independent ideas of their own. Everyone, in a word, who's anyone." Skousen: "Where is this bastion of intellectuals and free thinkers today? At FreedomFest!"

The central theme of the world's largest libertarian event, which brings together over 2,000 participants, is the erosion of economic and intellectual freedoms. At 120 degrees Fahrenheit, the outside temperature is unbearable even for a heat lover like me, prompting one speaker to remind us what we would be without air conditioning – the event couldn't have taken place at all.

There are many distinguished speakers, including Steve Forbes, editor-in-chief of Forbes magazine, and Harvard scientist Steven Pinker, who spoke on "Human Rationality and Academic Freedom." I have been corresponding with Pinker for several years and had interviewed him for *Forbes*, but this was the first time I had met him in person.

Academic freedom is under threat due to massive politicization, said Pinker, even more so than in the McCarthy era. The following attacks on academic freedom were registered between 2014 and 2022:

- 877 attempts to punish scholars for constitutionally protected speech
- 114 incidents of censorship
- 156 firings (44 of them tenured professors)

The number of unreported cases is likely significantly higher. The politicization of science has resulted in a notable shift towards the left, as demonstrated by Pinker through the example of his own university. The political orientation of the Harvard Faculty 2022:

- 37.43 percent identified as "very liberal" (where "liberal" is synonymous with left-wing in the United States)
- 45.03 percent identified as "liberal"
- 16.08 percent identified as "moderate"
- 1.46 percent identified as "conservative" or "very conservative"

Pinker reminded us of the foundations of academic freedom, namely the principles: "No-one is infallible or omniscient. Intellectual progress is driven by conjecture and refutation: Some people propose ideas, others probe whether they are sound: In the long run, the better ideas prevail." Any institution that disables this cycle is doomed to error, explained Pinker. Moreover, this undermines public trust in science: "Why should I trust the consensus, when it comes from a clique that allows no dissent?"

Justin Amash then made the point that fundamental rules necessary for the proper functioning of institutions are being increasingly violated in the United States. Amash served as the U.S. representative for Michigan's 3rd congressional district from 2011 to 2021, left the GOP and became an independent on July 4, 2019. In April 2020, he joined the Libertarian Party, leaving Congress in January 2021 as the only Libertarian to serve in Congress. He garnered national attention when he became the first Republican congressman to call for the impeachment of Donald Trump, a position he maintained after leaving the party.

Amash criticized the lack of respect for Congress: "We sometimes received bills with up to 5,000 pages and were supposed to read them in one day. I refused to vote on any bill if I couldn't read it before the vote. In extreme cases, we were only given a few hours." Voters, Amash stressed, should not only consider a candidate's policies, they should also weigh up whether they are committed to upholding the fundamental processes outlined in the constitution.

It is not only academic and political freedom, but above all economic freedom in the United States is under threat from ever greater state interference in the economy, rampant bureaucracy, and an almost insane orgy of debt. Steve Forbes spoke of "modern socialism," which differs from classic socialism in that companies are no longer formally nationalized, but the state increasingly determines what is produced, leading to a hollowing out of private property rights.

Whole Foods founder John Mackey presented his new book, *The Whole Story: Adventures in Love, Life, and Capitalism*. "It is all fun and games until bureaucrats get involved," is how he characterizes his entrepreneurial experiences.

August 2024
Buenos Aires, Cordoba, and Mendoza, Argentina

In August 2024, I travel to Argentina for the launch of the Spanish edition of my book, *How Nations Escape Poverty*. I reach out to Javier Milei to inquire about writing the foreword. Although he expresses his admiration for my work, he directs me to his government spokesperson, economist Manuel Adorni, who agreed to write the foreword: "For this distinguished advocate of liberty to invite me to introduce his latest essay is an immense honor that will undoubtedly become unforgettable for me. 'How Nations Escape Poverty' is a magnificent book in which Zitelmann explains in a sublime manner why freedom is the path to escape from poverty. This is a lesson that politicians need to learn but, above all, Zitelmann's insights must be taken into account by the citizens of those countries that have been devastated by populism, such as Argentina today."

Why is the publication of this book in Argentina so important to me? Javier Milei has embarked on a mission to combat poverty in Argentina. The success of Poland, which was transformed from one of the poorest countries in Europe into the continent's growth champion by the capitalist shock therapy of Leszek Balcerowicz, serves as a shining example that what Milei has set out to do in Argentina is possible and can lead Argentina to a bright future.

The situation was similar when Leszek Balcerowicz initiated a series of free-market reforms in Poland. Poland's debt burden to Western creditors had grown larger and larger and, by 1984, Poland was the third largest debtor in the world. Poland's gross foreign debt ballooned from USD 1.1 billion in 1971 to USD 40 billion in 1989, more than in any other socialist country. In 1989, annualized inflation was 640 percent in Poland.

Like Milei, Balcerowicz was an economist who adhered to the principles of the Austrian School of economics, drawing inspiration from the works of Ludwig von Mises and Friedrich August von Hayek. And, like Milei in Argentina, he implemented "shock therapy" in Poland.

The case of Poland shows that capitalist reforms and shock therapy work! But Poland also offers a second lesson that is at least as important for Argentinians today: before things got better, Poland endured a period of hardship lasting two years.

A predictable negative consequence of economic reforms was that GDP slumped for a few years before returning to growth. In Poland, the decline was 11.6 percent in 1990 and 7.6 percent in 1991.

The example of Poland thus highlights two key lessons:

1. Capitalist shock therapy works. Milei is following the same economic doctrines and principles as Balcerowicz. Both were confronted with the same problems: extreme national debt, extreme inflation, poverty and a state that was strangling the economy.
2. Before things get better, many things will have to get worse. It is totally unrealistic to expect decades of damage to be fixed in a year.

Having visited Argentina in 2022 and 2023, I have returned in August 2024 to assess the current mood and see how people's lives have changed. Recent surveys indicate that Milei is still supported by a majority of Argentines, with 55.4 percent holding a favorable opinion of him and 44.3 percent expressing a negative view.

During my visit to Córdoba, the second largest city in Argentina, I have the opportunity to engage in a lengthy discussion with Mayor Alfredo Cornejo. As a member of the Radical Party, Mayor Cornejo initially harbored doubts about Milei. However, he expressed to me that his skepticism has since transformed into confidence: Argentina is heading in the right direction.

In Buenos Aires, I also meet up again with Agustín Etchebarne, General Director of the libertarian think tank *Libertad y Progreso*. He says: "Young people and the poor continue to stand by Milei. Most of them voted for him and they remain steadfast in their support." If they criticize him at all, says Etchebarne, it is at most because they think he is not being radical enough. They want him to take even tougher action against the despised "Casta" that brought such ruin upon the country.

But Milei cannot implement his program the way he wants because he only commands the support of seven out of 72 senators and 38 out of 257 members of Parliament. He proposed a new law called "Ley Bases" of which 600 articles would have been passed into law. But he withdrew the law when he realized that he would not get a majority in Congress. Afterwards he presented a shorter law, with less reforms and only 200 articles. That was accepted with minimal changes.

However, the elections in October 2025 could potentially shift the balance of power, with a third of the Senate and half of Parliament up for re-election and Milei's party is likely to gain a significantly larger number of seats in Parliament.

What has changed for the better, what has changed for the worse? On a positive note, skyrocketing inflation, which Argentinians identified as the primary issue during the election, has decreased significantly. Monthly inflation in Argentina was 12.8 percent in November 2023, and 25.5 percent in December 2023, the month Milei started his government. In July 2024, inflation was only in single digits and stood at 4 percent.

What is also very important: Minister Federico Sturzenegger, recently appointed as Minister of State Reform and Modernization, has been instrumental in advancing a comprehensive deregulation agenda, which will be crucial for Argentina's economic recovery. One initial success is the liberalization of rental legislation. Despite extremely high inflation rates, it was forbidden to adjust rents accordingly before Milei. Many landlords stopped renting out apartments and the supply continued to fall. Shortly after Milei liberalized the rental law, the supply of apartments increased by almost 40 percent.

But at the same time, there has been a decline in economic output, which is having a direct impact on people's lives. The poverty rate has risen from 40 to around 55 percent. The middle class has been particularly hard hit. This is because the poorest Argentines can still rely on state welfare payments under Milei. What Milei has changed, however, is to allocate funds directly to those in need, bypassing the intermediaries, the left-leaning political organizations, that claimed to support the poor but siphoned off most of the money for themselves. "Milei," says Etchebarne, "now gives the money directly to the poor, while the left-wing organizations are left empty-handed. That is the big difference to the conservative Macri, who inadvertently bolstered his left-wing political adversaries with massive cash payments during his time in office. By cutting out the intermediaries, the poorest Argentines now receive twice as much assistance as they used to get. The problem is that only the poorest benefit from these measures; it is difficult for the middle class, some of whom are slipping into poverty themselves."

Do the Peronists pose a threat to Milei? Not at the moment. As one scandal after another is uncovered, the full extent of their corruption is being revealed. One such revelation is that 80 percent of state film funding did not go to film producers, it went to state bureaucrats. And the situation was similar in many areas.

Milei's alliance with Mauricio Macri's conservative party is a difficult one. In the run-off elections, Milei prevailed against the conservative candidate Patricia Bullrich. Bullrich then endorsed Milei in the run-off elections and is now Minister of Security. She was even planning to merge her party with Milei's, but failed to overcome opposition from Macri. Enrique Duhau, President of *Libertad y Progreso*, explains: "The main problem is that there are two parties on the right, Macri's and Milei's, which means the libertarians and conservatives will always find it hard to win a majority against the left-wing Peronists."

Duhau and Etchebarne praise Bullrich, the Minister with responsibility for homeland security. First of all, she has stopped the streets from being blocked by left-wing demonstrators on a daily basis. Demonstrations are still allowed, but the protesters are now required to gather on sidewalks or in parks – in places where they cannot block the flow of traffic.

In my opinion, Milei's success will depend above all on whether Argentines have the patience required to give Milei's reforms the time they will need to succeed. Milei has the potential to achieve the same level of success as Leszek Balcerowicz in Poland and Maggie Thatcher in the UK. However, in both cases, things started off by getting worse (e.g. economic output fell) before getting much better. This is always the case with market economy reforms, and I hope Milei's supporters will understand this and not lose patience. After all, as I wrote earlier, decades of damage cannot be fixed in a year.

Argentina now stands at a crossroads: either they understand the above and have the necessary patience to weather the storm and get through two difficult years – or they don't have the patience and succumb to the allure of quick fixes promised by the Peronists, who want to return to power. If they have patience, Argentina will have a prosperous future. If not, Argentina will sink back into a maelstrom of debt, inflation, and poverty. I shared this message in numerous interviews in Argentina, including one with the daily newspaper *Infobae*, which has a very wide circulation in Argentina. Coverage of my interview was given an extra boost when Milei shared it on X.

If Milei succeeds, it will spark a capitalist revolution in South America, particularly in countries like Bolivia and Brazil. Argentina has the potential to become a counter-model for Venezuela, where almost eight million people have now fled. In July, the opposition in Venezuela achieved a significant victory, garnering around 70 percent of the vote. However, the dictator Maduro rigged the election and is clinging to power. During my time in Buenos Aires, I meet Adriana Flores Márquez, a young woman who fled Venezuela and now represents the leader of the democratic opposition in Argentina, María Corina Machado. I had previously met Daniel Di Martino, a well-known libertarian activist who fled the socialist country years ago, at the Free to Choose meeting at Milton Friedman's summer residence. It is impressive to hear the stories of these people. Both shared a poignant warning that resonates deeply with me: "Venezuela has gone from being the richest country in Latin America to being the poorest – because of the socialists. Venezuela was a democracy, now we live in a dictatorship. If it can happen here, it can happen anywhere in the world."

About the Author

Rainer Zitelmann was born in Frankfurt am Main, Germany in 1957. He studied history and political science from 1978 to 1983 in Darmstadt and graduated with distinction. In 1986, he was awarded the title Dr. Phil for his thesis Hitler. *Selbstverständnis eines Revolutionärs* (English: *Hitler's National Socialism*) under the mentorship of Professor Freiherr von Aretin. The study, which was awarded the grade "summa cum laude," received worldwide attention and recognition.

From 1987 to 1992, Zitelmann worked at the Central Institute for Social Science Research at the Free University of Berlin. He then became editor-in-chief of Ullstein-Propyläen publishing house, at that time Germany's third-largest book-publishing group and headed various departments of the leading German daily newspaper *Die Welt*. In 2000, he set up his own business, Dr. ZitelmannPB. GmbH, which has since become the market leader for positioning consulting for real estate companies in Germany. He sold the business in 2016.

In 2016, Zitelmann was awarded his second doctorate, this time in sociology, with his thesis on the psychology of the super-rich under the mentorship of Professor Wolfgang Lauterbach at the University of Potsdam. His second doctoral dissertation was published in English as *The Wealth Elite* as well as in China, Russia, South Korea, and Vietnam, and deals with the psychology of the super-rich.

Zitelmann has written a total of 29 books, which have enjoyed substantial success in more than 30 languages around the world. He is a much sought-after guest speaker in Asia, the United States, Latin America, and Europe. Over the last few years, he has written articles and given interviews to many of the world's leading media outlets, including *Wall Street Journal*, *Newsweek*, *Forbes*, *The Daily Telegraph*, *The Times*, *Corriere della Sera*, *Frankfurter Allgemeine Zeitung*, and numerous media in Asia and Latin America. Readers of this book are especially recommended to read his books *The Power of Capitalism* and *In Defence of Capitalism*. Detailed information about the life of Rainer Zitelmann can be found at https://www.rainer-zitelmann.com/.

Bibliography

Ahrens, Sandra, "Exportmenge von Reis weltweit in den Jahren 2000/2001 bis 2023/24," 03 January 2024. https://de.statista. com/statistik/daten/studie/456376/umfrage/exportmenge-von-reis-weltweit/#:~:text=F%C3%BCr%20das%20Erntejahr%20 2023%2F24,rund%2055%2C8%20Millionen%20Tonnen (accessed 06 March 2024).

Alles über Nepal, "Wirtschaft," undated. https://www.allesuebernepal.com/ info/wirtschaft/ (accessed 05 March 2024).

Alsema, Adriaan, "FARC has 472 hostages: País Libre," *Colombia Reports*, 30 March 2009. https://colombiareports.com/farc-has-472-hostages-pais-libre/ (accessed 05 March 2024).

Ambos, Kai, "Drogenwirtschaft und Drogenhandel," in Fischer, Thomas, Susanne Klengel, Eduardo Pastrana Buelvas (eds.), *Kolumbien. Politik, Wirtschaft, Kultur heute*, Vervuert Verlag, Frankfurt am Main, 2017, 381–398.

Åslund, Anders, *How Capitalism Was Built. The Transformation of Central and Eastern Europe, Russia, The Caucasus, and Central Asia*, Second Edition, Cambridge University Press, New York, NY, 2013.

Åslund, Anders, *Russia's Crony Capitalism. The Path from Market Economy to Kleptocracy*, Yale University Press, New Haven and London, 2019.

Åslund, Anders, Simeon Djankov (eds.), *The Great Rebirth. Lessons from the Victory of Capitalism over Communism*, Peterson Institute for International Economics, Washington, DC, 2014.

Aswestopoulos, Wassilis, *Griechenland – eine europäische Tragödie*, Ambition Verlag, Berlin, 2011.

Atria, Fernando, et al., *El otro modelo. Del orden neoliberal al régimen de lo público*. Random House Mondadori, Santiago de Chile, Chile, 2013.

Auswärtiges Amt, "Kolumbien: Politisches Porträt," last updated 05 March 2024. https://www.auswaertiges-amt.de/de/service/laender/kolumbien-node/politisches-portraet/212762#:~:text=Nach%20starkem%20 Wachstum%20stagnierte%20die,Land%20allerdings%20vor%20 gro%C3%9Fe%20Herausforderungen (accessed 05 March 2024).

Balcerowicz, Leszek, *Socialism, Capitalism, Transformation*, Central European University Press, Budapest, London, and New York, NY, 1995.

Balcerowicz, Leszek, "Stabilization and Reform under Extraordinary and Normal Politics," in Åslund, Anders, Simeon Djankov (eds.), *The Great Rebirth. Lessons from the Victory of Capitalism over Communism*, Peterson Institute for International Economics, Washington, DC, 2014, 17–38.

Bam, Arun, "Nepal tops global list for public holidays," *My República*, 4 October 2023. https://myrepublica.nagariknetwork.com/news/nepal-tops-global-list-for-public-holidays/#:~:text=World%20Statistics%20has%20taken%20data,BS%20on%20March%2015%2C%202023 (accessed 05 March 2024).

Ban, Cornel, *Ruling Ideas. How Global Neoliberalism Goes Local*, Oxford University Press, Oxford, 2016.

Bartosek, Karel, "Central and Southeastern Europe," in Courtois, Stéphane, Nicolas Werth, Jean-Louis Panné, Andrzej Paczkowski, Karel Bartosek, Jean-Louis Margolin, *The Black Book of Communism. Crimes, Terror, Repression*, Harvard University Press, Cambridge, MA, and London, 1999, 394–456.

Bazydło, Cezary, "Petr Pavel: Wer ist der neue tschechische Präsident?," *mdr. de*, 09 Mach 2023. https://www.mdr.de/nachrichten/welt/osteuropa/politik/petr-pavel-praesident-tschechien-100.html (accessed 05 March 2024).

Bello, Omar, Adriana Bermúdez, "The Incidence of Labor Market Reforms on Employment in the Venezuelan Manufacturing Sector, 1995-2001," in Hausmann, Ricardo, Francisco Rodríguez, (eds.), *Venezuela Before Chávez. Anatomy of an Economic Collapse*, University Park, Pennsylvania, 2014, 115–155.

Benko, Ralph, "To Understand Capitalism, We Must Debunk Its Myths," Newsmax, 12 April 2023. https://www.newsmax.com/ralphbenko/capitalism-myths-debunk/2023/04/12/id/1115921/ (accessed 05 March 2024)

Bernecker, Walther, *Spaniens Geschichte seit dem Bürgerkrieg*, 6. Auflage, C.H. Beck Verlag, Munich, 2018.

Bernecker, Walther, Horst Pietschmann, *Geschichte Portugals*, C.H. Beck Verlag, Munich, 2008.

Bhatta, Chandra D., "Nepal's political and economic transition," *Observer Research Foundation*, 15 July 2022. https://www.orfonline.org/expert-speak/nepals-political-and-economic-transition/ (accessed 12 February 2024).

BMZ – Bundesministerium für wirtschaftliche Zusammenarbeit und Entwicklung, "Nepal: Große Herausforderungen, grundlegender Wandel, anspruchsvolle Ziele," undated. https://www.bmz.de/de/laender/nepal (accessed 05 March 2024).

Boothroyd, Peter, Pham Xuan Nam (eds.), *Socioeconomic Renovation in Viet Nam. The Origin, Evolution, and Impact of Doi Moi*, International Development Research

Centre Ottawa etc. and Institute of Southeast Asian Studies, Singapore and Ottawa, 2000.

Brink, Tobias ten, *China's Capitalism: A Paradoxical Route to Economic Prosperity*, translated by Carla Welch, University of Pennsylvania Press, Philadelphia, PA, 2019.

Buschschlüter, Vanessa, "Colombia cocaine: Coca cultivation reaches record high," BBC News, 12 September 2023, https://www.bbc.com/news/world-latin-america-66784678 (accessed 19 February 2024).

Calderara, Camilo, "'Reafirma sus convicciones': Vallejo defiende dichos de Boric sobre 'derrocar el capitalismo,'" *T13*, 24 July 2023. https://www.t13.cl/noticia/politica/reafirma-convicciones-vallejo-defiende-dichos-boric-sobre-derrocar-capitalismo-24-7-2023 (accessed 05 March 2024).

Calic, Marie-Janine, *A History of Yugoslavia*, Purdue University Press, West Lafayette, IN, 2018.

Carafano, James, "The World's 10 Richest Terrorist Organizations," *Forbes*, 22 July 2015. https://www.forbes.com/pictures/gkll45fk/3-farc-annual-turnover-6/?sh=1fca3139413c (accessed 05 March 2024).

Chiou, Pauline, "Nguyen Thi Phuong Thao takes VietJet from 'bikini flights' to IPO in 5 years," *CNBC*, 24 May 2016. https://www.cnbc.com/2016/05/24/nguyen-thi-phuong-thao-takes-vietjet-from-bikini-flights-to-ipo-in-5-years.html (accessed 04 March 2024).

Chun, Nuguyen Trong; Nguyen Minh Luan; Le Huu Tang – with Peter Boothroyd and Sharon Manson Singer, "Social Policy," in Boothroyd, Peter, Pham Xuan Nam (eds.), *Socioeconomic Renovation in Viet Nam. The Origin, Evolution, and Impact of Doi Moi*, International Development Research Centre Ottawa etc. and Institute of Southeast Asian Studies, Singapore and Ottawa, 2000, 141–172.

Cifuentes, C., "Política fiscal: ¿gastar más o gastar mejor?" *CEF Análisis, n°62*, ESE Business School, Universidad de los Andes, Bogotá, Colombia, 2022. https://www.ese.cl/ese/site/artic/20221116/asocfile/20221116093039/informe_cef_n__62_noviembre.pdf (accessed 14 November 2023).

Claro, A, and G. Sanhueza, "Una década Perdida," in *Mirada FEN – Revista de Economía y Administración, 2023, n° 184*, 22–31.

Coase, Ronald and Ning Wang, *How China Became Capitalist*, Palgrave Macmillan, New York, NY, 2012.

Colini, Gonzalo, "Punto por punto: el plan de gobierno que presentó Javier Milei," *La Nacion*, 02 August 2023. https://www.lanacion.com.ar/economia/punto-por-punto-el-plan-de-gobierno-que-presento-javier-milei-nid02082023/ (accessed 06 March 2024).

Courtois, Stéphane, Nicolas Werth, Jean-Louis Panné, Andrzej Paczkowski, Karel Bartosek, Jean-Louis Margolin, *The Black Book of Communism. Crimes, Terror, Repression*, Harvard University Press, Cambridge, MA, and London, 1999.

Destatis, "Frauen in Führungspositionen in der EU," *Statistisches Bundesamt (Destatis)*, 25 September 2023. https://www.destatis.de/Europa/DE/Thema/Bevoelkerung-Arbeit-Soziales/Arbeitsmarkt/Qualitaet-der-Arbeit/_dimension-1/08_frauen-fuehrungspositionen.html#:~:text=Lettland%20war%20mit%20einem%20Frauenanteil,mit%20lediglich%2021%2C3%20%25 (accessed 04 March 2024).

Deutsche Börse, "Hohe Inflation: Argentinien führt 2000-Pesos-Schein ein," Börse Frankfurt, 22 May 2023. https://www.boerse-frankfurt.de/nachrichten/Hohe-Inflation-Argentinien-fuehrt-2000-Pesos-Schein-ein-24bb86d0-9817-4c58-9b33-42883cd3b619 (accessed 05 March 2024).

Devlin, Kat, "40 years after fall of Saigon, Vietnamese see U.S. as key ally," *Pew Research Center*, 30 April 2015. https://www.pewresearch.org/short-reads/2015/04/30/vietnamese-see-u-s-as-key-ally/ (accessed 04 March 2024).

Dikötter, Frank, *Mao's Great Famine: The History of China's Most Devastating Catastrophe, 1958–1962*, Bloomsbury, London and New York, NY, 2010.

Dikötter, Frank, *The Cultural Revolution. A People's History. 1962–1976*, Bloomsbury Press, London, Oxford, New Delhi and Sydney, 2017.

Djankov, Simeon, "Bulgaria. The Greatest Vacillations," in Åslund, Anders and Simeon Djankov, *The Great Rebirth. Lessons from the Victory of Capitalism over Communism*, Petersen Institute for International Economics, Washington, DC, 2014, 135–148.

Edwards, Chris, "Margaret Thatcher's Privatization Legacy," *Cato Journal 37, no. 1 (Winter 2017)*, 89–101. https://www.cato.org/sites/cato.org/files/serials/files/cato-journal/2017/2/cj-v37n1-7.pdf (accessed 05 March 2024).

Election Commission Nepal, "Registered Political Parties (Updated List)," undated. https://election.gov.np/en/page/registered-political-parties-updated-list (accessed 05 March 2024).

Elits, Walter, "The Key to Higher Living Standards," *CPS Policy Study No. 148*, London, 1996.

FAZ, "Kolumbien: Wahldebakel für frühere Farc-Guerilleros," *Frankfurter Allgemeine Zeitung*, last updated 15 March 2018. https://www.faz.net/aktuell/politik/ausland/kolumbien-wahldebakel-fuer-partei-der-frueheren-farc-guerilla-15489505.html (accessed 04 March 2024).

FAZ, "Wo die Millionäre wohnen," *Frankfurter Allgemeine Zeitung*, last updated 23 July 2014. https://www.faz.net/aktuell/wirtschaft/wirtschaftspolitik/reichtum-wo-die-millionaere-wohnen-staedte-ranking-13060176.html (accessed 05 March 2024).

Fevziu, Blendi, *Enver Hoxha. The Iron Fist of Albania*, I.B. Tauris, London and New York, NY, 2016.

Fischer, Thomas, Susanne Klengel, Eduardo Pastrana Buelvas (eds.), *Kolumbien. Politik, Wirtschaft, Kultur heute*, Vervuert Verlag, Frankfurt am Main, 2017.

Forbes.com, "Thi Phuong Thao Nguyen, Real Time Net Worth," *Forbes.com*. https://www.forbes.com/profile/thi-phuong-thao-nguyen/?sh=201a6941a222 (accessed 04 March 2024).

Francovich, Eli, "In Ukraine, an informal web of Libertarians becomes a 'resistance network,'" *Spokesman Review*, 3 April 2023. https://www.spokesman.com/stories/2022/apr/03/in-ukraine-an-informal-web-of-libertarians-becomes/ (accessed 06 March 2024).

Friedman, Milton, *Capitalism and Freedom*, The University of Chicago Press, Chicago, IL, 1962.

Fürsen, Rixa, "Schweden: Am besten wäre es, die Einwanderung komplett zu stoppen," *Die Welt*, 30 October 2023. https://www.welt.de/politik/ausland/plus248145832/Schweden-Am-besten-waere-es-die-Einwanderung-komplett-zu-stoppen.html (accessed 06 March 2024).

Galligani, Federico, "Las 10 propuestas de Javier Milei si llega a ser presidente: dolarización, recortes y qué hará con las empresas públicas," *Infobae*, 28 April 2023. https://www.infobae.com/politica/2023/04/29/las-10-propuestas-de-javier-milei-si-llega-a-ser-presidente-dolarizacion-recortes-y-que-hara-con-las-empresas-publicas/ (accessed 05 March 2024).

Gans-Morse, Jordan, *Property Rights in Post-Soviet Russia, Violence, Corruption, and the Demand for Law*, Cambridge University Press, New York, NY, 2017.

Gebel, Titus, "Die ARD enthüllt eine Millionärs-Verschwörung," *Achgut*, 11 June 2023. https://www.achgut.com/artikel/die_ard_enthuellt_eine_millionaers_verschwoerung (accessed 06 March 2024).

Gebel, Titus, *Free Private Cities: Making Governments Compete For You*, 3rd updated and expanded edition, Free Cities Foundation, Liechtenstein, 2023.

Geiger, Raphael, "Neuwahl in Griechenland: Der neue Premier ist der alte," *Süddeutsche Zeitung*, 25 June 2023. https://www.sueddeutsche.de/politik/griechenland-wahl-mitostakis-wahlsieg-wahlrecht-1.5968221 (accessed 05 March 2024).

Gobierno de Chile, "La Reforma Tributaria no la pagará la clase media," 28 April 2014. https://www.youtube.com/watch?v=YaYKtVkfdk8&t=128s (accessed 05 March 2024).

Gomułka, Stanisław, "Poland's Economic Growth in the Global and Long-Term Perspective. Until 2015, The Last Two Years, Forecast," in *Perspectives for Poland. The Polish Economy from 2015-2017. Against the Background of the Previous Years and Future Forecasts (Summary in English)*, Civil Development Forum, Brussels. https://www.politico.eu/wp-content/uploads/2017/11/Report-Perspectives-for-Poland.-The-Polish-Economy-from-2015%E2%80%932017-Against-the-Background-of-the-Previous-Years-and-Future-Forecasts.pdf (accessed 12 February 2024).

Gonda, Peter, "Summary of the Publication: 'Socialism. Reality instead of Myth,'" Bratislava, 2020 https://tearingdownmyths.com/socialism-reality-instead-of-myths/ (accessed 12 February 2024).

Gordon, David, "It Wasn't Capitalism: Mises Explains Nazi Economics," 04 February 2022, https://mises.org/wire/it-wasnt-capitalism-mises-explains-nazi-economics (accessed 12 February 2024).

Graaff, David, "Frieden und Postkonflikt," in Fischer, Thomas, Susanne Klengel, Eduardo Pastrana Buelvas (eds.), *Kolumbien. Politik, Wirtschaft, Kultur heute*, Vervuert Verlag, Frankfurt am Main, 2017, 17–38.

Gramm, Phil, Robert Ekelund, John Early, *The Myth of American Inequality. How Government Biases Policy Debate*, Rowman & Littlefield, Lanham, Maryland, 2022.

Haße, David, "Das ist der Übernahmekandidat Tap Air Portugal," *airliners.de*, 17 July 2023. https://www.airliners.de/hintergrund-uebernahmekandidat-tap-air-portugal/69772 (accessed 04 March 2024).

Hausmann, Ricardo, Francisco Rodríguez, (eds.), *Venezuela Before Chávez. Anatomy of an Economic Collapse*, University Park, Pennsylvania, 2014.

Hayek, Friedrich August von, *The Road to Serfdom*, University of Chicago Press, Chicago, IL, 1944.

Helliwell, John F., et al., "World Happiness Report 2022," Sustainable Development Solutions Network, https://worldhappiness.report/ed/2022/happiness-benevolence-and-trust-during-covid-19-and-beyond/#ranking-of-happiness-2019-2021 (accessed 12 February 2024).

Helliwell, John F., et al., "World Happiness Report 2023," Sustainable Development Solutions Network, https://happiness-report.s3.amazonaws.com/2023/WHR+23.pdf (accessed 12 February 2024).

Heritage Foundation, *2022 Index of Economic Freedom* and *2023 Index of Economic Freedom 2023*. https://www.heritage.org/index/ (accessed 04 March 2024).

Honigmann, Daniea, "Staatsschulden Tschechiens steigen auf Rekordwert von knapp drei Billionen Kronen," *Radio Prague International*, 01 Mach 2023. https://deutsch.radio.cz/staatsschulden-tschechiens-steigen-auf-rekordwert-von-knapp-drei-billionen-8776405 (accessed 05 March 2024).

Jandieri, Gia, "Brief Economic History of Georgia. A Lesson Has to be Remembered," Rondeli Foundation, 2014. https://gfsis.org.ge/publications/view-opinion-paper/22 (accessed 12 February 2024).

Jandieri, Gia, "Tax Reforms in Georgia 2004-2012," *Tax Foundation, Fiscal Fact, Nr. 665*, July 2019. https://taxfoundation.org/research/all/global/tax-reforms-in-georgia-2004-2012/ (accessed 12 February 2024).

Jaroszewicz, Marta, "Polen als Land der politischen Immigration aus Belarus," Zentrum für Migrationsforschung, Warsaw, 07 June 2022. https://laender-analysen.de/polen-analysen/294/polen-als-land-der-politischen-immigration-aus-belarus-zwischen-schwieriger-geschichte-technokratischer-einstellung-und-grosser/ (accessed 04 March 2024).

Jorge, Pedro Almeida, "Cycle analysis of the Portuguese economy of the last two decades," *Master en Economia OMMA/UFM, 12. edición*, Prof. Juan Ramón Rallo.

Junge Welt, "Kolumbien verhandelt mit FARC-Guerilla," *Junge Welt*, last updated 09 February 2024. https://www.jungewelt.de/artikel/469651.lateinamerika-kolumbien-verhandelt-mit-farc-guerilla.html (accessed 05 March 2024).

Kachlíková, Markéta, "Löhne in Tschechien bei 43 Prozent des EU-Durchschnitts," *Radio Prague International*, 04 June 2020. https://deutsch.radio.cz/loehne-tschechien-bei-43-prozent-des-eu-durchschnitts-8682554 (accessed 05 March 2024).

Kaiser, Axel, Rainer Zitelmann, *El Odio a los Ricos, Igualitarismo, Decandencia Económica y Percepión Pública*, Ediciones El Mercurio, Santioago de Chile, 2023.

Kaiser, Axel, "The Fall of Chile," in *Cato Journal, Vol. 40, No. 3* (Fall 2020), 685–700.

Kaiser, Axel, "The Roar of the Argentinian Lion," *Discourse Magazine*, 21 November 2023. https://www.discoursemagazine.com/p/the-roar-of-the-argentinian-lion (accessed 04 March 2024).

Kapur, Roshni, "Vietnam's Lethal Traffic," *The Diplomat*, 20 May 2016. https://thediplomat.com/2016/05/vietnams-lethal-traffic/ (accessed 04 March 2024).

Kirst, Virginia, "Italiens überraschend gute ökonomische Zwischenbilanz," *Die Welt*, 18 October 2023. https://www.welt.de/wirtschaft/plus247987938/Italien-Die-ueberraschend-gute-oekonomische-Zwischenbilanz-des-Landes.html?source=puerto-reco-2_ABC-V32.7.B_test (accessed 05 March 2024).

Klaus, Václav, "Czechoslovakia and the Czech Republic: The Spirit and Main Contours of the Postcommunist Transformation," in Åslund, Anders, Simeon Djankov, (eds.), *The Great Rebirth. Lessons from the Victory of Capitalism over Communism*, Peterson Institute for International Economics, Washington, DC, 2014, 53–72.

Kneifel, Johannes, *Rumäniens steiniger Weg. Von der Ceauşescu-Diktatur bis zur fragilen Demokratie*, Engelsdorfer Verlag, Leipzig, 2022.

Koehler, Benedikt, *Early Islam and the Birth of Capitalism*, Lexington Books, London, 2014.

Köllner, Patrick, "Südkoreas politisches System," in Kern, Thomas, Patrick Köllner, (eds.), *Südkorea und Nordkorea. Einführung in Geschichte, Politik, Wirtschaft und Gesellschaft*, Campus Verlag, Frankfurt and New York, NY, 2005, 50–70.

Kollmar-Paulenz, Karénina, *Die Mongolen. Von Dschingis Khan bis heute*, Verlag C.H. Beck, Munich, 2011.

Kote, Kristo, "SMI Accuses Premier of Creating 'Europe's Colombia,'" *Albanian Daily News*, 4 May 2022. https://albaniandailynews.com/news/smi-accuses-pm-of-creating-colombia-of-europe-after-zdf-s-report-1-1 (accessed 04 March 2024).

Kukksi, "Das sind die 7 gefährlichsten Städte in den USA," *Kukksi. de*, 27 May 2023. https://www.kukksi.de/das-sind-die-sieben-gefaehrlichsten-staedte-in-den-usa/ (accessed 05 March 2024).

Kunze, Thomas, *Nicolae Ceauşescu. Eine Biografie*, Ch. Links Verlag, Berlin, 2000.

Lee, Felix, *Macht und Moderne. Chinas großer Reformer Deng Xiaoping. Die Biographie*, Rotbuch-Verlag, Berlin, 2014.

Leviev-Sawyer, Clive, *Bulgaria: Politics and Protests in the 21st Century*, Riva Publishers, Sofia, 2015.

Lill, Rudolf, Wolfgang Altgeld, "Italien als demokratische Republik," in Altgeld, Wolfgang et al., *Geschichte Italiens*, Philipp Reclam jun. Verlag, Ditzingen, 2021, 500–605.

Lindbeck, Assar, "Swedish Lessons for Post-Socialist Countries," Seminar Papers 640, Stockholm University, Institute for International Economic Studies, 1998. https://ideas.repec.org/p/hhs/iiessp/0640.html (accessed 12 February 2024).

Lindbeck, Assar, "The Swedish Experiment," *Journal of Economic Literature* Vol. 35, No. 3 (Sep., 1997), 1273-1319.

Lithuania Free Market Institute, "2020 Employment Flexibility Index, EU and OECD countries," 2019. https://www.llri.lt/wp-content/uploads/2019/12/Employment-flexibility-index2020.pdf (accessed 05 March 2024).

LPB – Landeszentrale für politische Bildung Baden-Württemberg, "Wirtschaft in der Slowakei," undated. https://osteuropa.lpb-bw.de/wirtschaft-slowakei (accessed 05 March 2024).

Markaris, Petros, "Griechenland. Wo alles 'sozialistisch' ist," in *WOZ Die Wochenzeitung, Nr. 21*, 27 May 2012, https://www.woz.ch/1021/griechenland/wo-alles-sozialistisch-ist (accessed 12 February 2024).

Marques, A. H. de Oliveira, *Geschichte Portugals und des portugiesischen Weltreichs*, Kröner Verlag, Stuttgart, 2001.

McGurn, William, "The Man Who Made Milton Friedman a Star," *Wall Street Journal*, 30 October 2020. https://www.wsj.com/articles/the-man-who-made-milton-friedman-a-star-11604073953 (accessed 04 March 2024).

Medina, Oscar, "Cocaine Is Set to Overtake Oil to Become Colombia's Main Export," *Bloomberg*, 14 September 2023, https://www.bloomberg.com/news/articles/2023-09-14/cocaine-is-set-to-overtake-oil-to-become-colombia-s-main-export (accessed 19 February 2024).

Mehrtens, Philip, *Staatsschulden und Staatstätigkeit. Zur Transformation der politischen Ökonomie Schwedens*, Campus Verlag, Frankfurt and New York, NY, 2014.

Memory 1944–1989, *Pametbg.com*. https://pametbg.com/index.php/de/ and https://pametbg.com/index.php/en/ (accessed 05 March 2024).

Michaels, Axel, *Nepal: A History from the Earliest Times to the Present*, Oxford University Press Inc, New York, NY, 2024.

Mingardi, Alberto, "Why Italy's Season of Economic Liberalism Did Not Last," in *The Independent Review, Vol. 25, No. 4 (Spring 2021)*, 593–616 https://www.jstor.org/stable/48617838 (accessed 12 February 2024).

Ministerio del Interior, "The National Government has instituted a bill to establish the Ministry of Equality and Equity," 18 October 2022. https://www.mininterior.gov.co/micrositios/english-site/the-national-government-has-instituted-a-bill-to-establish-the-ministry-of-equality-and-equity/ (accessed 05 March 2024).

Mises, Ludwig von, *Socialism: An Economic and Sociological Analysis*, Liberty Fund, Indianapolis, IN, 1981.

Mitchell, Dan, "Argentina and the Grim Consequences of Democratic Socialism," *Center for Freedom and Prosperity*, 15 August 2019. https://freedomandprosperity.org/2019/blog/big-government/argentina-and-the-grim-consequences-of-democratic-socialism/ (accessed 04 March 2024).

Mongolei-Blog, "Ulaanbaatar und der Verkehr," 24 December 2019. http://mongolei-blog.de/2019/12/24/ulaanbaatar-und-der-verkehr/ (accessed 05 March 2024).

MSNBC interview of Paul Krugman by David Gregory, "Paul Krugman says "I'd blame Alan Greenspan and Phil Gramm," 22 September 2008. https://www.youtube.com/watch?v=YwqcLbZJ4HA (accessed 05 March 2024).

Müller-Heinze, Annett, "Rumänien," *Bundeszentrale für politische Bildung*, 14 January 2022. https://www.bpb.de/themen/europa/suedosteuropa/322454/rumaenien/ (accessed 05 March 2024).

Muschter, René, "Argentinien: Inflationsrate von Januar 2023 bis Januar 2024," *Statista*, 15 February 2024. https://de.statista.com/statistik/daten/studie/988114/umfrage/monatliche-inflationsrate-in-argentinien/ (accessed 05 March 2024).

Muschter, René, "Asien: Ranking der 10 Länder Asiens mit dem niedrigsten Bruttoinlandsprodukt pro Kopf in 2022," 02 January 2024. https://de.statista.com/statistik/daten/studie/1070438/umfrage/die-laender-asiens-mit-dem-niedrigsten-bruttoinlandsprodukt-bip-pro-kopf/ (accessed 05 March 2024).

Nguyen, Tam T.T., *Vietnam und sein Transformationsweg. Die Entwicklung seit der Reformpolitik 1986 und aktuelle Herausforderungen*, Diplomica Verlag, Hamburg, 2014.

Nguyen Trang Chuan, Nguyen Mink Luan, Le Huu Tang, "Social Policy," in Boothroyd, Peter, Pham Xuan Nam (eds.), *Socioeconomic Renovation in Viet Nam. The Origin, Evolution, and Impact of Doi Moi*, International Development Research

Centre Ottawa etc. and Institute of Southeast Asian Studies, Singapore and Ottawa, 2000, 139–171.

North, Michael, *Geschichte der Niederlande*, 4th edition, Verlag C.H. Beck, Munich, 2013.

Oancea, Georgeta Daniela, *Mythen und Vergangenheit – Rumänien nach der Wende*, dissertation, LMU Munich, Faculty of History and the Arts, July 2005.

Page, Benjamin I., Martin Gilens, *Democracy in America? What Has Gone Wrong and What We Can Do About It*, The University of Chicago Press, Chicago, IL, and London, 2017.

Pettigrew, Judith, *Maoists at the Hearth. Everyday Life in Nepal's Civil War*, University of Pennsylvania Press, Philadelphia, PA, 2013.

Pfeifer, David, "Nepal: Alle Macht dem 'Kämpferischen,'" *Süddeutsche Zeitung*, 11 January 2023. https://www.sueddeutsche.de/politik/nepal-pushpa-kamal-dahal-indien-china-1.5729675 (accessed 05 March 2024).

Piątkowski, Marcin, *Europe's Growth Champion. Insights from the Economic Rise of Poland*, Oxford University Press, Oxford, 2018.

Pirie, Madsen, "Review: The Power of Capitalism," *Adam Smith Institute*, 12 November 2018. https://www.adamsmith.org/blog/the-power-of-capitalism (accessed 05 March 2024).

Poller, Horst, *Mehr Freiheit statt mehr Sozialismus. Wie konservative Politik die Krisen bewältigt, die sozialistisches Wunschdenken schafft*, Olzog Verlag, Munich, 2010.

Prak, Maarten, Jan Luiten van Zanden, *Pioneers of Capitalism, The Netherlands 1000–1800*, Princeton University Press, Princeton, NJ, and Oxford, 2023.

Raichevsky, Stoyan, *Bulgarien unter dem kommunistischen Regime 1944–1989*, Osteuropa Zentrum Berlin-Verlag, Berlin, 2016.

Rentsch, Hans, *Wie viel Markt verträgt die Schweiz? Ökonomische Streifzüge durchs Demokratieparadies*, NZZ Libro, Zurich, 2017.

Reuters, "Argentina poverty rate rises to 40.1% in first half of 2023," 27 September 2023. https://www.reuters.com/world/americas/argentina-poverty-rate-rises-401-first-half-2023-2023-09-27/#:~:text=BUENOS%20AIRES%2C%20Sept%2027%20(Reuters,reported%20a%20rate%20of%2036.5%25 (accessed 05 March 2024).

Riekenberg, Michael, *Kleine Geschichte Argentiniens*, Verlag C.H. Beck, Munich, 2009.

Rist, Manfred, Phnom Penh, "Kriegsheldinnen, Männerersatz und viele Blumen – Vietnam hat gleich zwei Frauentage," *Neue Zürcher Zeitung*, 08 Mach 2021. https://www.nzz.ch/international/in-vietnam-spielen-frauen-eine-starke-gesellschaftliche-rolle-ld.1605284?reduced=true (accessed 04 March 2024).

Ritter, Johannes, "Die Schweizer sind dreimal so reich wie die Deutschen," *Frankfurter Allgemeine Zeitung*, 15 August 2023. https://www.faz.net/aktuell/finanzen/die-schweiz-hat-die-reichsten-menschen-der-welt-globales-vermoegen-19104655.html# (accessed 12 February 2024).

Rose, David, "So viel Geld floss nach Griechenland," *tagesschau.de*, 19 May 2021. https://www.tagesschau.de/wirtschaft/weltwirtschaft/rettungspakete-101.html (accessed 05 March 2024).

Rössler, Hans-Christian, "Ein Rücktritt, der nun voreilig wirkt," *Frankfurter Allgemeine Zeitung*, 05 December 2023. https://www.faz.net/aktuell/politik/ausland/portugal-mit-politischer-krise-ein-ruecktritt-der-nun-voreilig-wirkt-19368127.html (accessed 12 February 2024).

Rothbard, Murray N. *Economic Thought Before Adam Smith. An Austrian Perspective on the History of Economic Thought, Volume 1*. Ludwig von Mises Institute, Auburn, AL, 2006.

Rutte, Mark, "Nederland moet af van terreur van de middelmaat," interview with Joost Oranje, *NRC Handelsblad*, 28 August 2008. https://web.archive.org/web/20100106125843/http://www.nrc.nl/binnenland/article1965113.ece/Nederland_moet_af_van_terreur_van_de_middelmaat (accessed 05 March 2024).

Sanandaji, Nima, Viktor Ströhm, Mouna Esmaeilzadeh, Saeid Esmaeilzadeh, "The evolution of the Swedish market model," in *Economic Affairs, Volume 43, Number 2*, June 2023, 170–184. https://onlinelibrary.wiley.com/doi/full/10.1111/ecaf.12573 (accessed 05 March 2024).

Sanders, Bernie, *It's OK To Be Angry About Capitalism*, Penguin Books (Allen Lane), Dublin, 2023.

Sapelli, C., "Desigualdad, movilidad, pobreza: necesidad de una política social diferente," *Estudios Públicos*, 2014, *134*, 59–84. https://www.estudiospublicos.cl/index.php/cep/article/view/250 (accessed 08 December 2023).

Schmieding, Holger, "Vor Thatcher war Großbritannien ein Trümmerhaufen," *Die Welt*, 09 April 2013. https://www.welt.de/wirtschaft/article115147486/Vor-Thatcher-war-Grossbritannien-ein-Truemmerhaufen.html (accessed 05 March 2024).

Schneidewind, Dieter, *Wirtschaftswunderland Südkorea*, Springer Gabler Verlag, Wiesbaden, 2013.

Schwarz, Heinrich, "Superbonus am Weg zum 110-Milliarden-Bonus," *Südtiroler Wirtschaftszeitung*, 17 October 2023. https://swz.it/superbonus-am-weg-zum-110-milliarden-bonus/ (accessed 05 March 2024).

Sharma, Sudheer, *The Nepal Nexus. An Inside Account of the Maoists, the Durbar and New Dehli*, Penguin Viking, Haryana, India, 2019.

Silver, Laura, "How people in Asia-Pacific view China," Pew Research Center, 16 October 2017. https://pewresearch.org/short-reads/2017/10/16/how-people-in-asia-pacific-view-china/ (accessed 04 March 2024).

Smith, Adam, *The Wealth of Nations* (1776), David Campbell Publishers, London 1991.

Smith, Adam. *Essays on Philosophical Subjects*. Edited by W.P.D, Wightman and J.C. Bryce. Liberty Fund, 1990.

Soukup, Stephen R., *The Dictatorship of Woke Capital. How Political Correctness Captured Big Business*, Encounter Books, New York, NY, and London, 2021.

Specht, Martin, *Kolumbien. Ein Länderporträt*, Ch. Links Verlag, Berlin, 2018.

Spiegel Ausland, "Regierungskandidat Massa gewinnt erste Wahlrunde gegen Populist Milei," 23 October 2023. https://www.spiegel.de/ausland/argentinien-regierungskandidat-sergio-massa-gewinnt-erste-wahlrunde-gegen-populist-javier-milei-a-9327b316-69e5-475f-adc4-0d92fa1bf9aa (accessed 05 March 2024).

Statista Research Department, "Extreme poverty rate in Chile from 2006 to 2020," 26 July 2023. https://www.statista.com/statistics/1401306/extreme-poverty-rate-chile/ (accessed 04 March 2024).

Statista Research Department, "Percentage of households in poverty and extreme poverty in Venezuela from 2002 to 2021," 15 November 2023. https://www.statista.com/statistics/1235189/household-poverty-rate-venezuela/ (accessed 04 March 2024).

Statista Research Department, "Percentage of population living in extreme poverty in Venezuela in 2021, by state," 15 November 2023. https://www.statista.com/statistics/1243742/extreme-poverty-rate-venezuela-state/ (accessed 04 March 2024).

Statista Research Department, "Tschechien: Lebenserwartung bei der Geburt aufgeschlüsselt nach Geschlecht von 1950 bis 2022 und Prognosen bis 2050," 02 January 2024. https://de.statista.com/statistik/daten/studie/18645/umfrage/lebenserwartung-in-tschechien/ (accessed 05 March 2024).

Statista Research Department, "Verluste im Vietnamkrieg in den Jahren 1955 bis 1975," 02 January 2024, https://de.statista.com/statistik/daten/studie/1165881/umfrage/verluste-nach-kriegspartei-im-vietnamkrieg/#:~:text=Im%20Vietnamkrieg%20in%20den%20Jahren,und%20weitere%20300.000%20wurden%20verwundet (accessed 04 March 2024).

Tagesschau, "Deutsche Konzerne nicht mehr in Topliga," *Tagesschau*, 03 July 2022. https://www.tagesschau.de/wirtschaft/kurse/top-firmen-boerse-wert-101.html (accessed 04 March 2024).

Teichova, Alice, *Wirtschaftsgeschichte der Tschechoslowakei 1918–1980*, Böhlau Verlag, Vienna, Cologne and Graz, 1988.

Thatcher, Margaret, *The Downing Street Years*, Harper Collins, London, 1993.

The Economist, "Chile's new president promises to bury neoliberalism," *The Economist*, 20 December 2021. https://www.economist.com/the-americas/2021/12/20/chiles-new-president-promises-to-bury-neoliberalism (accessed 06 March 2024).

The Global Economy, "Romania: GDP per capita, constant dollars," *theglobaleconomy.com*, undated. https://www.theglobaleconomy.com/Romania/GDP_per_capita_constant_dollars/#:~:text=For%20that%20indicator%2C%20we%20provide,2021%20is%2011541.78%20U.S.%20dollars (accessed 05 March 2024).

The Global Economy, "Vietnam: GDP per capita, constant dollars," *theglobaleconomy.com*, undated. https://www.theglobaleconomy.com/Vietnam/GDP_per_capita_constant_dollars/ (accessed 06 March 2024).

The World Bank, "GDP per capita, PPP (current international \$) – Czechia." https://data.worldbank.org/indicator/NY.GDP.PCAP. PP.CD?locations=CZ (accessed 05 March 2024).

Toro, Daniela, Beatriz Mellado, "Una 'parte de mí' quiere derrocar el capitalismo: El debate que abrió el análisis del Presidente Boric," *Emol*, 24 July 2023. https://www.emol.com/noticias/Nacional/2023/07/24/1101888/ reacciones-boric-derrocar-capitalismo (accessed 05 March 2024).

TPN, "Immobilienblase in Portugal?," *The Portugal News*, 30 January 2022. https://www.theportugalnews.com/de/nachrichten/2022-01-30/ immobilienblase-in-portugal/64874 (accessed 04 March 2024).

Trading Economics, "Vietnam Exports of electrical, electronic equipment," undated. https://tradingeconomics.com/vietnam/exports/electrical-electronic-equipment (accessed 04 March 2024).

Tran, Thi Anh-Dao (ed.), *Rethinking Asian Capitalism. The Achievements and Challenges of Vietnam Under Doi Moi*, Palgrave Macmillan, Cham, 2022.

Transparency International, *Corruption Perceptions Index 2022*. https://www. transparency.org/en/cpi/2022 (accessed 12 February 2024).

Transparency International, "Corruption Perceptions Index 2022. Nepal," undated. https://www.transparency.org/en/cpi/2022/index/npl (accessed 05 March 2024).

Transparency International, "CPI 2022: Tabellarische Rangliste," undated. https://www.transparency.de/cpi/cpi-2022/cpi-2022-tabellarische-rangliste (accessed 05 March 2024).

Transparency International, "Our Work in Albania," undated. https://www transparency.org/en/countries/albania (accessed 05 March 2024).

Transparency International, "Our Work in Georgia," undated. https://www transparency.org/en/countries/georgia (accessed 05 March 2024).

Transparency International, "Our Work in Russia," undated. https://www transparency.org/en/countries/russia (accessed 05 March 2024).

Tschinderle, Franziska, *Albanien. Aus der Isolation in eine europäische Zukunft*, Czernin Verlag, Vienna, 2022.

UNHCR, "Venezuela Humanitarian Crisis," United Nation's High Commission for Refugees, undated. https://www.unrefugees.org. emergencies/venezuela/#:~:text=More%20than%207.3%20million%20 Venezuelans,(as%20of%20February%202023) (accessed 04 March 2024)

United Nations Development Programme, "Human Development Insights," undated. https://hdr.undp.org/data-center/country-insights#/ranks (accessed 05 March 2024).

Urmersbach, Bruno, "Bosnien und Herzegowina: Gesamtbevölkerung von 1950 bis 2022 und Prognosen bis 2050," *Statista*, July 2022. https://de.statista.com/statistik/daten/studie/383927/umfrage/gesamtbevoelkerung-von-bosnien-und-herzegowina/#:~:text=Die%20Gesamtbev%C3%B6lkerung%20von%20Bosnien%20und,ebenfalls%20 3%2C2%20Millionen%20prognostiziert (accessed 05 March 2024).

Urmersbach, Bruno, "Die 20 größten Exportländer weltweit im Jahr 2022," *Statista*, April 2023. https://de.statista.com/statistik/daten/studie/37013/umfrage/ranking-der-top-20-exportlaender-weltweit/ (accessed 05 March 2024).

Velasco, Andrés, Cristóbal Huneeus, *Contra la desigualdad: el empleo es la clave*, Editorial Debate, Santiago de Chile, Chile, 2012.

Voegeli, William, *Never Enough: America's Limitless Welfare State*, Encounter Books, New York, NY, 2010.

Weber, Hans, "Steuerreform in Kolumbien: Die Regierung besteuert Reiche und Ölmultis starker," *Amerika21*, 16 November 2022. https://amerika21.de/2022/11/261102/kolumbien-reiche-staerker-besteuert (accessed 04 March 2024).

WeltExporte, "Made in Vietnam – die meist exportierten Güter Vietnams," *www.weltexporte.de*, 30 October 2020. https://www.weltexporte.de/exportprodukte-vietnam/ (accessed 04 March 2024).

Wikipedia, "Liste der Länder nach historischer Entwicklung des Bruttoinlandsprodukts pro Kopf," undated. https://de.wikipedia.org/wiki/Liste_der_L%C3%A4nder_nach_historischer_Entwicklung_des_Bruttoinlandsprodukts_pro_Kopf (accessed 04 March 2024).

Wikipedia, "Öffentliche Sicherheit in Monaco," undated. https://de.wikipedia.org/wiki/%C3%96ffentliche_Sicherheit_in_Monaco (accessed 05 March 2024).

Wikipedia, "Parlamentswahl in Griechenland," undated. https://de.wikipedia.org/wiki/Parlamentswahl_in_Griechenland_September_2015#:~:text=Die%20Parlamentswahl%20in%20Griechenland%20im,Tsipras%20angef%C3%BChrte%20linksgerichtete%20Partei%20SYRIZA (accessed 05 March 2024).

Witzel, Martin Herrera, "Albanien ist weltweit siebtgrößter Cannabisproduzent," *Euractiv*, 29 June 2022. https://www.euractiv.de/section/eu-aussenpolitik/news/albanien-ist-weltweit-siebtgroesster-cannabisproduzent/ (accessed 04 March 2024).

World Bank Group, *From the Last Mile to the Next Mile, 2022 Vietnam Poverty and Equity Assessment*, Washington, DC, 2022. https://openknowledge.worldbank.org/handle/10986/37952 (accessed 12 February 2024).

Yim Hyun-su, "Where Yoon stands on jobs, taxes and real estate," *The Korea Herald*, 05 November 2021. http://www.koreaherald.com/view.php?ud=20211105000646http://www.koreaherald.com/view.php?ud=20211105000646 (accessed 05 March 2024).

Zedania, Giga, "Gleichzeitigkeit des Ungleichzeitigen, Paradoxien der Politik in Georgien," in *Osteuropa, 68. Jahrgang, Heft 7*, 2018, 106–116.

Zelepos, Ioannis, *Kleine Geschichte Griechenlands. Von der Staatsgründung bis heute*, 2nd edition, C.H. Beck, Munich, 2017.

Zelik, Raul, "Kolumbien: An der Regierung, aber nicht an der Macht," Rosa Luxemburg Stiftung, 23 August 2023. https://www.rosalux.de/news/id/50936/kolumbien-an-der-regierung-aber-nicht-an-der-macht (accessed 05 March 2024).

Zhang Weiying, *The Logic of the Market. An Insider's View of Chinese Economic Reform*, Cato Institute, Washington, DC, 2015.

Zitelmann, Rainer, "Attitudes towards the rich in China, Japan, South Korea, and Vietnam," *Economic Affairs, Vol. 42, Issue 2*, June 2022, 210–224. https://doi.org/10.1111/ecaf.12524 (accessed 12 February 2024).

Zitelmann, Rainer, "Attitudes towards capitalism in 34 countries on five continents," *Economic Affairs, Vol. 43, Issue 3*, October 2023, 353–371. https://onlinelibrary.wiley.com/doi/full/10.1111/ecaf.12591 (accessed 12 February 2024).

Zitelmann, Rainer, "Popular perceptions of the rich in 13 countries," *Economic Affairs, Vol. 44, Issue 2*, June 2024, 363–373. https://onlinelibrary.wiley.com/doi/10.1111/ecaf.12633 (accessed 8 November 2024).

Zitelmann, Rainer, *How Nations Escape Poverty: Vietnam, Poland, and the Origins of Prosperity*, Encounter Books, New York, NY, 2024.

Zitelmann, Rainer, *How People Become Famous: Geniuses of Self-Marketing from Albert Einstein to Kim Kardashian*, Management Books 2000, Oxford, 2021.

Zitelmann, Rainer, *In Defence of Capitalism. Debunking the Myths*, Management Books 2000, Oxford, 2023.

Zitelmann, Rainer, *The Power of Capitalism: Capitalism is not the problem, but the solution*, Management Books 2000, Oxford, 2024.

Zitelmann, Rainer, *The Rich in Public Opinion: What We Think About When We Think About Wealth*, Cato Institute, Washington, DC, 2020.

Zitelmann, Rainer, *The Wealth Elite: A Groundbreaking Study of the Psychology of the Super Rich*, LID Publishing, London, 2018.

Index of Persons

Note: Persons who are mentioned by their first names only in the text for reasons of confidentiality have not been included in this index.

www.ingramcontent.com/pod-product-compliance
Lightning Source LLC
LaVergne TN
LVHW021117050525
810407LV00008B/412